The Societies of t and North Africa

This new textbook explores the societies and populations of the Middle East and North Africa. Presenting original chapters written by the world's leading Middle East scholars, it analyzes the social fabric of the region's varied countries to uncover the organizing structures, human vulnerabilities, and dynamic forces that shape everyday lives. The volume can be used in conjunction with *The Government and Politics of the Middle East and North Africa* textbook for a comprehensive overview of the region.

Whether used as a companion text or a standalone volume, this work provides the historical and cultural context necessary for understanding the peoples inhabiting the Arab world, Israel, Turkey, and Iran since the early twentieth century. Linking past to present to future, it also ascertains the ongoing developmental trajectories of these societies, including their overall stability and prosperity. The chapters are clearly structured, and contain insightful case studies, illustrative photographs, and visualized data. They also end with discussion questions and annotated bibliographies to help spark further research. Among the rich topics covered are the following:

- Rural life
- Civil society and personal identities
- Economic challenges, oil legacies, environmental harm
- Religious movements, women and gender, and youth politics.

The Societies of the Middle East and North Africa is written in an accessible way, prioritizing social, cultural, and economic dimensions. As such this textbook provides a comprehensive introduction to the field and will be invaluable to students of Middle Eastern politics and society, as well as sociology, history, economics, and anthropology.

Sean Yom is Associate Professor of Political Science at Temple University and Senior Fellow at the Foreign Policy Research Institute. He is a widely published expert on regimes and development in the Middle East and North Africa, and regularly travels to the region for research.

The Societies of the Middle East and North Africa

Structures, Vulnerabilities, and Forces

Edited by Sean Yom

Routledge
Taylor & Francis Group
LONDON AND NEW YORK

First published 2019
by Routledge
2 Park Square, Milton Park, Abingdon, Oxon OX14 4RN

and by Routledge
52 Vanderbilt Avenue, New York, NY 10017

Routledge is an imprint of the Taylor & Francis Group, an informa business

© 2019 selection and editorial matter, Sean Yom; individual chapters, the contributors

The right of Sean Yom to be identified as the author of the editorial material, and of the authors for their individual chapters, has been asserted in accordance with sections 77 and 78 of the Copyright, Designs and Patents Act 1988.

All rights reserved. No part of this book may be reprinted or reproduced or utilised in any form or by any electronic, mechanical, or other means, now known or hereafter invented, including photocopying and recording, or in any information storage or retrieval system, without permission in writing from the publishers.

Trademark notice: Product or corporate names may be trademarks or registered trademarks, and are used only for identification and explanation without intent to infringe.

British Library Cataloguing-in-Publication Data
A catalogue record for this book is available from the British Library

Library of Congress Cataloging-in-Publication Data
A catalog record has been requested for this book

ISBN: 978-1-138-58048-0 (hbk)
ISBN: 978-1-138-58050-3 (pbk)
ISBN: 978-0-429-50731-1 (ebk)

Typeset in Sabon
by Apex CoVantage, LLC

Visit the companion website: www.routledge.com/cw/yom

Zeynep'im:

En güzel günlerimiz: henüz yaşamadıklarımız.

Our best days: what we have not lived yet.

CONTENTS

Preface viii
List of maps, figures, tables, boxes, and photos xi
List of contributors xiv

CHAPTER 1 Bringing society back in 1
    Sean Yom

PART I Societal structures 31
CHAPTER 2 Social life, from rural to urban 33
    Rachel Bahn, Tariq Tell, and Rami Zurayk

CHAPTER 3 Social mobilization and civil society 79
    Vincent Durac

CHAPTER 4 Identity, its power and pull 115
    P.R. Kumaraswamy

PART II Societal vulnerabilities 143
CHAPTER 5 Economic development: bread, jobs, and beyond 145
    Bessma Momani and Morgan MacInnes

CHAPTER 6 Social and cultural legacies of rentierism 177
    Hae Won Jeong

CHAPTER 7 Environmental change and human conflict 207
    Mohamed Behnassi

PART III Societal forces 235
CHAPTER 8 Religion and faith 237
    Ramazan Kılınç

CHAPTER 9 Women and gender 271
    Lindsay J. Benstead

CHAPTER 10 The youth generation: education and transition 307
    Sean Yom

Index 347

PREFACE

This edited volume explores the social life of the Middle East and North Africa (MENA). It is one of the rare regional primers that is concerned less with high politics and diplomatic machinations – the realm of states and governments – and instead the currents of *societies* and *populations*. Governments, politicians, kings, presidents: these are important actors, and still central ones in shaping the future of the region's nearly two dozen countries. But they are also well-studied actors, not least in the sister Routledge volume to this text, *The Government and Politics of the Middle East and North Africa*. This work instead is addressed to those interested non-specialists who may wonder about rules and elites, but also how ordinary people and communities go about their routines, struggles, and experiences. If *Government and Politics* drills historical and political knowledge through a systematic, sequential, and country-by-country framework, then this volume saunters as the more relaxed companion, immersing observers in the social and cultural terrain of the MENA through comparative analysis. Its chapters each apply a broad topic to a multitude of countries, emphasizing the distinctive patterns that emerge at the regional level. It takes an interdisciplinary approach, employing elements of not just political science but also economics, sociology, history, religion, environmental studies, food sciences, and other fields.

A few unique features of this text stand out. First, after the opening chapter, the book is organized thematically in three parts, which each have three chapters. These parts each analyze a different aspect of social life. The first is *societal structures*, which describe the human organization of social routines; the three topical chapters here entail rural versus urban life, social mobilization and civil society, and finally the power of identity. The second is *societal vulnerabilities*, which embody the material challenges that constrain and harm populations unless resolved; the three topical chapters here discuss economic underdevelopment, rentier energy dependency, and environmental insecurity. The third is *societal forces*, which refer to the actors and processes that are transforming the frontiers of social change; these three topical chapters are religion and faith, women and gender, and the youth generation. There are other structures, vulnerabilities, and forces that matter to MENA societies, and a far longer text could investigate them all.

For now, though, as either a stand-alone book or a sister volume to *Government and Politics*, this work is committed to furnishing the most important research-oriented insights regarding social life that every observer of the region should know.

Second, each chapter shares an identical set of tools to facilitate the absorption and understanding of knowledge. Each chapter begins with a rundown, breaking down the text into six concise themes – hummable tunes, in essence. While contributing authors have divided their analysis in different ways, the chapters all burst with useful data that are visualized in graphs, charts, and tables. Photographs usefully illustrate key points in ways that words cannot. Boxed case studies provide focal points of attention, applying the theoretical concepts and major ideas to specific countries and contexts. Discussion questions at the end of each chapter help direct reflections towards the principal arguments and controversies. A lengthy annotated bibliography likewise points the way to further research, with carefully cultivated descriptions and listings that detail the state-of-the-art in each field of inquiry. There is also a section for online sources; and while web links may change faster than book editions can be published, it is easy also to search directly for the organizations, blogs, databases, and portals cited. Discerning readers might note that printed URLs tend to become outdated rather quickly; thus, the most up-to-date links to Internet resources can be found not in these chapters, but in Routledge's online companion created to complement this volume.

Third, as an edited volume, this work draws upon a truly *global* congregation of scholars. Unlike most other books about the Middle East with a similar audience and purpose, this work was explicitly designed to draw upon the research acumen of MENA experts around the world. A glance at the contributor list reveals a roster of respected scholars based not just in Western academia but also the Middle East itself, and whose social diversity better reflects that of the worldwide community of scholars that write, teach, and publish on the region regularly. As a product of globalization – of the child of immigrants from an Eastern country, living and working in a Western country, and yet regularly traveling to and researching a third region that is neither East nor West – I take this imperative for cosmopolitanism seriously.

In sum, this work is an ambitious undertaking with the ultimate goal of making, for many readers, an unknown region seem *familiar*. It offers intellectual fruit during a worrying global moment, one defined by oft-vicious political and ideological polarization, renewed violence and conflict in the MENA, and the flailing promise of economic and social prosperity that roused previous generations. The project was conceived, like so many academic endeavors, in the margins of a conference some years ago with the gracious Ada Fung, and has been stewarded under the guiding hand of Joe Whiting and his editorial team at Routledge. It was birthed through the authorship and research of the contributors. And it is delivered, finally, now to readers.

MAPS, FIGURES, TABLES, BOXES, AND PHOTOS

MAPS
1.1 The Middle East   11
1.2 North Africa   12

FIGURES
2.1   MENA – proportion of rural population over time, 1960–2016   41
2.2   MENA – urban population, 1960–2016   43
2.3   MENA – urban population as share of total population, 1960–2016   44
2.4   Employment in agriculture, selected years, 1995–2017   52
2.5   Access to basic drinking water services in rural and urban areas, 2016   65
2.6   Access to improved sanitation facilities in rural and urban areas, 2016   66
3.1   Self-reported membership in civil society organizations before and after the Arab Spring from Arab Barometer, 2008 vs. 2017   109
3.2   Facebook usage and perceptions of civil society freedom from Arab Barometer, 2017   110
4.1   Revealed identity choices through Arab Barometer, 2017   119
5.1   MENA vs. global regions – GDP growth per worker (percent), 1960s–1990s   150
5.2   MENA countries – size of informal economic sectors, 2000–2007   165
5.3   GCC kingdoms – non-nationals in population and employment, 2010–2016   167
5.4   MENA vs. global regions – size of public sector by Government Wage Bill, 2016   170
5.5   Economic expectations from Arab Barometer, 2017   172
6.1   MENA countries – oil and gas as percent of all exported goods, 2014–2017 (latest available year)   180
6.2   Yemen, Sudan, Morocco, and Egypt – projected urbanization through 2050   190
6.3   Identification with country as citizen, 2017   194
6.4   GCC states – ratio of citizens vs. foreign residents, 2015–2017 (latest available year)   199
7.1   MENA vs. global regions: satisfaction with efforts for environmental preservation, 2017   226
8.1   Compatibility of Islam with democracy from Arab Barometer, 2017   248
8.2   Preference for democracy from Arab Barometer, 2017   249
8.3   Religious leaders vs. political authority from Arab Barometer, 2017   250
9.1   MENA vs. global regions in Global Gender Gap Index, 2017   273
9.2   Labor force participation rates by gender, 2017   292
9.3   Support for different areas of gender equality from Arab Barometer, 2008   295
10.1 MENA vs. global regions – proportion of regional population aged 0–14 years, 2017   309
10.2 MENA vs. global regions – youth literacy vs. adult literacy, 2017   313

10.3   Select global countries – scores for eighth grade TIMMS science achievement evaluation, 2015   314
10.4   Select global countries – scores for fourth grade PIRLS reading achievement evaluation, 2016   315
10.5   MENA vs. global regions – youth unemployment, 2017   319
10.6   Female vs. male youth unemployment rates, 2017   321
10.7   MENA countries vs. OECD – unemployment by educational level, 2017   323
10.8   Work preferences among Arab youth, 2010   327

TABLES

1.1   MENA countries – demographics and government, 2018   14
2.1   Rural population and growth rate, 1960–2016   42
2.2   Average annual urban population growth rate, 1960–2016   45
2.3   Population living in urban agglomerations and single largest city, 2016   46
2.4   Rural populations vs. income levels   48
2.5   Employment in the agricultural sector, selected years   51
2.6   Select MENA countries – distribution of farms and agricultural land, by farm size, 2016   54
2.7   Urban population living in slums, 2014   62
2.8   Rural and urban populations living in poverty, 2014–2017 (latest available year)   64
2.9   International migrants per host country, 2017   69
2.10 Refugees flows, 2016   71
2.11 Internal displacement due to conflict and disaster, 2016   73
5.1   Snapshot of economic vital data, 2017   166
6.1   Top recipients of Arab developmental assistance (foreign aid), 2011–2015   184
7.1   Major armed conflicts in MENA, 1945–2018   211
7.2   MENA vs. select global countries – total renewable water resources per capita, 2014   221
8.1   MENA – religious landscape, 2017   239
8.2   Five Muslim-majority MENA countries – frequency of religious service attendance, 2005–2009   246
8.3   Five Muslim-majority MENA countries – importance of religion to individuals, 2005–2009   247
9.1   Rates of enrollment for primary, secondary, and tertiary (college) education, 1970   284
9.2   Rates of enrollment for primary, secondary, and tertiary (college) education, 2005   285
9.3   Rates of enrollment for primary, secondary, and tertiary (college) education, 2011–2016   287
9.4   Female quotas in legislative bodies by type, 2018   289
9.5   Correlations between gender-related items from Arab Barometer, 2008   296
9.6   Theories of patriarchy in the MENA region   298
10.1 MENA vs. global regions – percent population using Internet, 2008–2017   338
10.2 MENA vs. global regions – mobile phone subscriptions (per 100 people), 2008–2017   339

BOXES

- 2.1 Case study – Cairene food insecurity 58
- 2.2 Case study – refugees in Jordan 72
- 3.1 Case study – anti-British resistance in colonial Egypt 87
- 3.2 Case study – the MEPI foreign aid program 105
- 4.1 Case study – dhimmi paradigm 125
- 4.2 Case study – Jordan and identity 136
- 5.1 Case study, part I – Egypt during the boom years 148
- 5.2 Case study, part II – Egypt during the bust years 154
- 6.1 Case study – rentier citizens or clients? 193
- 6.2 Case study – migrant workers in Qatar and Kuwait 200
- 7.1 Case study – natural resources and conflict 213
- 7.2 Case study – water scarcity in Yemen 223
- 8.1 Case study – Muslim Brotherhood of Egypt 251
- 9.1 Case study – Saudi Arabia and women's rights 282
- 9.2 Case study – North Africa and PSC 302
- 10.1 Case study – waithood and delayed transitions 328
- 10.2 Case study – hip-hop music 334

PHOTOS

- 1.1 *Bonaparte before the Sphinx* (1868), by Jean-Léon Gérôme 7
- 2.1 Camels and desert in Wadi Rum, Jordan, 2016 50
- 2.2 Bedouin herding small sheep flock, 2010 50
- 2.3 Small farm in Aswan, Egypt, 2012 55
- 2.4 Cairo slum, high view, 2014 62
- 3.1 Street march against Egyptian government, 2012 82
- 3.2 Human Rights Watch holding press conference, Egypt, 2008 103
- 3.3 Handicraft workshop for Egyptian youth, 2011 104
- 4.1 Kurdish flag as used in Kurdistan Region of Iraq 135
- 5.1 Bread carrier in downtown Cairo, 2007 162
- 6.1 Dubai skyline, 2016 189
- 6.2 Gulf traditional male garb in Kuwait, 2010 197
- 6.3 Gulf traditional female Garb in UAE, 2015 198
- 6.4 South Asian construction workers in Dubai, 2010 201
- 7.1 Power and desalination station in UAE, 2012 222
- 7.2 Qatar Climate Change March at UN Conference, 2012 227
- 7.3 Desertified and abandoned cultivation in Morocco, 2014 229
- 8.1 Ka'ba within sacred mosque in Mecca, Saudi Arabia, 2014 240
- 8.2 Beirut – St. Georges Maronite Cathedral next to Muhammad Al-Amin Mosque, 2009 243
- 8.3 Inside Al-Azhar University of Cairo, Egypt, 2014 259
- 9.1 Arab woman wearing abaya and niqab 275
- 9.2 Moroccan woman wearing loose scarf, 2016 276
- 9.3 Kuwaiti teenage girls with varying dress, 2011 277
- 10.1 Youth march to retake Tahrir Square, Egypt, 2011 330
- 10.2 Fans from the Kuwait Rock Army, 2011 334
- 10.3 Tunisian singer Emel Mathlouthi, 2014 341

CONTRIBUTORS

Rachel Bahn is the Coordinator of the Food Security Program and Instructor at the Faculty of Agricultural and Food Sciences at the American University of Beirut. Her current research interests include food security and food systems, and economic policies and programming in developing countries. Bahn co-edited *Crisis and Conflict in Agriculture* (2018). She was previously based in Washington, DC, and worked as an economist with the US Department of Treasury and the US Agency for International Development. She is a PhD candidate at Montpellier SupAgro (France).

Mohamed Behnassi is a Senior Research Professor at Ibn Zohr University of Agadir, Morocco, and the founding director of the Center for Environment, Human Security and Governance (CERES). His teaching and research areas cover environmental/climate change and human security politics. In addition to his expertise, Behnassi has organized many international conferences and has a substantial publication record in these areas. He has a PhD in International Environmental Law and Governance from Hassan II University of Casablanca.

Lindsay J. Benstead is an Associate Professor of Political Science in the Mark O. Hatfield School of Government and Director of the Middle East Studies Center (MESC) at Portland State University, USA. She is a Fellow at the Woodrow Wilson International Center for Scholars in Washington, DC, and an Affiliated Scholar in the Program on Governance and Local Development at the University of Gothenburg, Sweden. Benstead has conducted surveys in Morocco, Algeria, Tunisia, Libya, and Jordan, and her research on women and politics and public opinion surveys has appeared in *Perspectives on Politics*, *International Journal of Public Opinion Research*, *Governance*, and *Foreign Affairs*.

Vincent Durac is an Associate Professor in Middle East Politics in University College Dublin, Ireland, and a visiting professor at Bethlehem University. He is co-author (with Francesco Cavatorta) of *Politics and Governance in the Middle East* (2015) and *Civil Society and Democratization in the Arab World: The Dynamics of Activism* (2011). His most recent scholarly work has been published in *Mediterranean Politics*, *Democratization*, *British*

Journal of Middle Eastern Studies, *Journal of North African Studies*, and *Journal of Contemporary African Studies*.

Hae Won Jeong is an Assistant Professor of International Relations in Academic Programs for Military Colleges at Abu Dhabi University in the United Arab Emirates. Jeong holds a PhD in Politics and International Studies from the School of Oriental and African Studies (SOAS), University of London, UK. Her research interests include the political economy of rentier states, Gulf-Asian relations, energy security, and resource diplomacy.

Ramazan Kılınç is an Associate Professor of Political Science and Director of the Islamic Studies Program at the University of Nebraska in Omaha, USA. His most recent articles appeared in *Comparative Politics*, *Political Science Quarterly*, *Politics and Religion*, *Studies in Conflict and Terrorism*, and *Turkish Studies*. He is the author of *Alien Citizens: State and Religious Minorities in Turkey and France* (forthcoming) and co-author of *Generating Generosity in Catholicism and Islam: Beliefs, Institutions and Public Goods Provision* (2018).

P.R. Kumaraswamy is a Professor at the School of International Studies at Jawaharlal Nehru University in India. His works include *The Handbook of the Hashemite Kingdom of Jordan* (forthcoming), *India's Israel Policy* (2010), and *Historical Dictionary of the Arab-Israeli Conflict* (2015). In 2010 he created the Middle East Institute in New Delhi and continues to serve as its Honorary Director. He is also the editor of the ongoing series *Persian Gulf: India's Relations with the Region* and the journal *Contemporary Review of the Middle East*.

Morgan MacInnes earned his undergraduate degree in economics, political science, and philosophy from the University of Western Ontario, Canada, and his MA degree in Global Affairs from the University of Toronto's Munk School of Global Affairs. He subsequently joined the Centre for International Governance Innovation (CIGI) as a research associate, focusing on cybersecurity and electoral politics. His current research focuses on the global politics of artificial intelligence, and the long-term effects of automation technology on society and the economy.

Bessma Momani is a Professor of Political Science at the University of Waterloo and the Balsillie School of International Affairs in Canada. She is also a Senior Fellow at the Centre for International Governance and Innovation (CIGI),

Non-Resident Senior Fellow at the Stimson Center, previous Non-Resident Senior Fellow at the Brookings Institution in Washington, DC, and a visiting scholar at Georgetown University's Mortara Center. A widely published scholar with nine authored or co-edited volumes and several dozen journal articles, she is also a 2015 Fellow of the Pierre Elliott Trudeau Foundation and a Fulbright Scholar.

Tariq Tell is a political economist currently teaching in the Department of Political Science and Public Administration at the American University of Beirut, Lebanon. He earned his DPhil from Oxford University. He co-edited *Village, Steppe and State: The Social Origins of Modern Jordan* (1994) and edited *The Resilience of Hashemite Rule: Politics and the State in Jordan before 1967* (2001). He authored *The Social and Economic Origins of Monarchy in Jordan* (2013). His current research interests include the comparative history and politics of Arab monarchies, and the relationship between imperialism, development, and political ecology in the Middle East.

Sean Yom is an Associate Professor of Political Science at Temple University, USA, and Senior Fellow at the Foreign Policy Research Institute in Philadelphia. His research specializes in political regimes and economic development, especially in the Arab monarchies like Morocco and Jordan, as well as new dynamics of regional collaboration, transnational repression, and authoritarian order. He is author of *From Resilience to Revolution: How Foreign Interventions Destabilize the Middle East* (2016), as well as numerous articles in journals such as *Comparative Political Studies* and *Journal of Democracy*. He is also editor of *The Government and Politics of the Middle East and North Africa* (2019).

Rami Zurayk is a Professor at the Faculty of Agricultural and Food Sciences at the American University of Beirut, Lebanon. He earned his DPhil from Oxford University. He is a member of the steering committee of the High Level Panel of Experts of the World Committee on Food Security. He is active in Arab civil society and is a founding member of the Arab Food Sovereignty Network. He is also widely published on issues of farming, agrarian change, and food security. His latest books include *Food, Farming and Freedom: Sowing the Arab Spring* (2011) and the co-edited *Crisis and Conflict in Agriculture* (2018).

CHAPTER 1

Bringing society back in

Sean Yom

THE RUNDOWN: KEY TOPICS COVERED
- Social life
- Orientalism
- Regional geography
- Historical trends
- Political regimes
- Chapter summaries

INTRODUCTION

The Arab Spring was sparked by an unassuming young man – 26-year-old Mohamed Bouazizi, the Tunisian fruit vendor whose self-immolation in December 2010 instigated the Jasmine Revolution. Thereafter, a wave of popular uprisings would sweep across the Middle East and North Africa (MENA). Several years earlier, an obscure young Tunisian musician at about the same age, Emel Mathlouthi, sang "Kelmti Horra" (My Word Is Free) at a French musical festival. Nobody knew then that her enchanting melody's steely lyrics – *I am those who are free and never fear, I am the secrets that never die* – would later become Tunisia's revolutionary anthem after Bouazizi's death. During the Jasmine Revolution, "Kelmti Horra" was played, looped, and disseminated by legions of young protesters, activists, and students who led the unarmed insurrections that upended the dictatorship of President Zine 'Abidine Ben 'Ali. Mathlouthi would later perform the song to a global audience in December 2015 at Norway's annual Nobel Peace Prize concert, the ballad having become the haunting soundtrack to the entire regional upsurge of resistance and movement. By then, it had become clear that during the dramas and traumas of 2011–2012, "Kelmti Horra" embodied the anger and hope of many marginalized and alienated people who took to the streets demanding principles they felt had been denied to them – dignity, justice, freedom. And, like so many other expressions of the Arab Spring, both that song and memories of Bouazizi are easily found online now.

The Arab Spring was not the first moment of regional transformation, and it will not be the last. But it was an iconic moment nonetheless. In our reactions to this historic rupture, two narratives have predominated. One is about the brutality, rapaciousness, and power of dictators and regimes, alongside their international allies; the other is about the churning and burning of expressive energies by variegated societies whose individuals and groups sought to rewrite their own destiny. The former concerns political life; the latter animates social life. The latter impels this book, which begins with a song and proceeds with a premise. To fully comprehend the MENA, including spectacular and uncertain events like the Arab Spring, we must dismount the high throne of history and politics – at least temporarily – and instead engage the ideational and material currents swirling across the region and impacting entire populations with constraining *structures*, human *vulnerabilities*, and *forces* for change. We must interrogate not just states but societies as well. This is the mandate for this volume, which combines theoretical insights with curated data to investigate the social life of the region.

THREE VIGNETTES

Before systematically introducing the topics of this volume, consider three windows illuminating social life within very different communities in the contemporary MENA.

In September 2015, hundreds of Lebanese youths converged upon the Ministry of the Environment. Dozens occupied the offices inside, while the rest congregated outside demanding the resignation of its officials. The flashpoint culminated months of protests and remonstrations among those living in Beirut and Mount Lebanon, due to massive pile-ups of garbage and waste – the result of inadequate disposal facilities, overpaid collection contracts, and the lack of any regulatory framework. Led by the #YouStink campaign, and bolstered by other networks of activists, lawyers, and environmentalists, the new movement soon directed its energies upon the slew of new controversies that arose in reaction to the rubbish overflow, among them proposed incinerators trading ground rubbish for air pollution, moribund recycling projects, and endemic corruption. Yet, for outsiders, such an upswell of social mobilization seemed strangely out of place. In a country grappling with a million Syrian refugees, the painful legacy of civil war, and political paralysis between Hizbullah and other sectarian forces, why the concern over beach litter and landfills?

In September 2018, Qatar became the first Arabian Gulf kingdom to allow foreign workers to become permanent residents. As part of a wider reform package giving greater rights to the country's over two million expatriates, the move highlighted the social implications of the incredible demographic imbalance among the hydrocarbon-rich Arabian kingdoms. In all but Saudi Arabia, citizens had become a statistical minority, with migrant labor from across the world (but particularly Asia) performing most tasks in the economy. This relationship had grown taut; worsening human rights violations and employment abuses befell many foreign workers, with more than 1,200 perishing in Qatar while building the football stadiums required for the 2022 FIFA World Cup. In a place where the GDP per capita among citizens peaked at nearly $150,000 in 2011, it was controversial to suggest that migrants from poorer countries could integrate into a nation where every aspect of indigenous life – education, health care, employment, even diets – had been transformed by oil and gas wealth. What would such a patchwork society, where Qataris comprised just one in ten people, look like in a generation?

In November 2017, Turkish women's rights movements captured public attention by critiquing a new marriage law, which would allow Muslim clerics to conduct civil marital ceremonies. Some argued this would open the door for child marriages, polygamy, and other ills justified through outdated religious interpretations, while defenders noted that Turkey was joining other countries allowing religious communities to oversee marriages – including Israel, where legal marriages can only be performed by religious authorities and interfaith weddings are prohibited. The marital issue highlighted how women's bodies and gender equality had become a battleground. Ferocious debates centered upon whether the Muslim veil liberated or oppressed, the rising level of violence against women, and stubborn economic discrimination. Contestation spilled out over sexuality as well. LGBT orientation was never a crime, but in June 2018, authorities in Istanbul canceled the annual pride march (the largest in the Muslim world) for the fourth straight year. Such disruptions understandably generated fear: what were the moral boundaries of a country struggling to reconcile an Islamist renewal with its secular heritage?

The stories embodied in these vignettes are meaningful. Lebanese youths *did* become impassioned about pollution on their beachfront despite the geopolitical chaos unfolding around their country; for them, the environment and urban planning became a flashpoint of absurdity, desire, and struggle. Qataris *did* wonder about redrawing the boundaries of their nation, much like other citizens in the Arabian Gulf economies, because for them the cultural prospect of millions of foreigners – Pakistanis and Sudanese, Jordanians and Egyptians, Filipinos and Bangladeshis, Indians and Indonesians – actually constituting their nation was sobering. And Turkish women and LGBT groups *did* demand attention amidst the war on the Islamic State, refugee overflows, economic emergency, and fateful elections: for them, triumph and despair were measured by whether they subjectively felt free and safe over their own corporeal existence.

They, and thousands of other slices of social life that could be taken from random among the well over 500 million people living among the MENA's nearly two dozen countries, are authentic expressions of the region's public and private life. They are no less authentic to the Middle East than what usually crowds global headlines: a terrorist group declares a caliphate, politicians trade rockets over land, civil wars and military coups consume capitals, revolutionary leaders transform crowds into mobs, desperate refugees cross borders, oil price fluctuations mean pain at the pump, mullahs declare death to the West, and so forth. Women appear primarily as victims of subordination and oppression, or else as crusading heroines fighting against the establishment. Occasionally, human interest stories enter the news stream; global observers may hear about, for instance, the opulent decadence of kings and sultans, the pastel camels and dunes of a new touristic locale, or even the occasional Nobel Peace Prize winner with a message to share. But frustratingly, foreign audiences around the world are more likely to gaze upon the more morbid stories and geopolitical events with interest while ignoring the social undercurrents.

This is problematic for several reasons. The first is the distorted lens often given to curious readers who wish to explore and absorb the MENA. The problem is not that we should ignore terrible events or random curiosities; it is that they make us forget that there are *other* things happening in the lives of ordinary citizens in the region too, and those other things can be extraordinary – and thus worthy of engagement. Most people living in the region, after all, are not leaders, soldiers, militants, revolutionaries, or refugees. These are vital categories that tell us much about the rise and fall of governments and states, but they do not constitute the entire mosaic overlay of the region's communities and societies. These are filled not just with struggles and victories, but also the mundane actions that never enter into the worldwide media consciousness: the seasonal olive harvest for Jordan Valley farmers, the daily production benchmark at a Kuwaiti oil well, queuing for ticket releases for Morocco's music festivals, Algerian teachers fretting over whether Twitter leaked exam results early, the brainstorming sessions of an Egyptian civil society movement. Most people who care about global events never travel to the MENA; those that do seldom observe these snippets of unguided life, the quiet habituations that could be found anywhere else in the world, but here, in this region, happen to be inflected with the nuances of each country – its history and culture, its demography and organization, its social forces. If knowledge represents an iceberg, then outsiders typically only see the jagged tip protruding above the surface. Yet the jagged tip did not sink the Titanic; the unseen mass skulking underneath did. We risk ignoring knowledge of communities, societies, and populations at our own peril.

The second problem is that once observers do go beyond headlines and begin dissecting the unseen, the scholarship that greets them too often focuses disproportionately on *high politics*. In no small part because of news cycles and social media streams, researchers spend more time tracking the behavior of regimes and elites, tracing the relations between rulers and opposition, and debating foreign policy and geopolitics. The actions of the US and other global powers become magnified in importance, not least because Middle East affairs often force their way into political debates at home; thus, the fate of the entire region, and sometimes even grander notions like Islam itself, becomes subordinate to the decisions made in Washington, London, or Moscow. Virtually every handbook or primer introducing readers to the region devotes much, or sometimes all, of its energy upon this realm of high politics. Often, explosive topics like the Israeli-Palestinian conflict or US foreign policy become the guiding themes. In other cases, so much time is spent on regional history and its political movers and shakers, often in the hopes of drawing a majestic narrative arc connecting the dawn of Islam to the current day, that the voices of everyday people become merely background noise – the canvas to the political or historical paintbrush. There are exceptions, of course; anthropologists and ethnographers know well the dangers of emphasizing high politics to the detriment of everything else. That fewer students and scholars enroll in these disciplines over time, though, as compared to political science or history highlights the problem.

The challenge here is not that what kings and presidents say, or what regimes and institutions do, lack importance. Nor should we ignore the weight of nation-states and the mechanisms through which they shape, and reshape, the modern international system and global economy. Large-scale political structures and powerful elite figures are key determinants for significant policy questions. The proliferation of nuclear weaponry and Iran's place in the global order are important problems that are more likely to be adjudicated by diplomats and generals, not booksellers in the bazaars of Tehran (or, for that matter, readers in America). The paradigm that states "matter" is not disappearing. Rather, the challenge is to remain sensitive as well to issues and topics that happen *to not be* important policy questions, but still matter to legions of people whom we will never know and whose desires we will never feel, but who exist. If the goal is to fully understand the MENA region – to be able to give interesting answers to interested non-specialists who ask "What's the Middle East like?" – this task is vital. And, in a broader sense, it is intuitive. Intrepid explorers of the Middle East do not spend years learning Arabic, Hebrew, Persian, Turkish, and other languages merely to speak with a few parliamentarians, read the occasional newspaper, and then claim to know a society for decades after. There must be fluid understanding of what happens beneath and around the domain of politics, within the social and economic currents of public life.

THE UNCOMFORTABLE GAZE OF ORIENTALISM

There is another endemic problem afflicting how many people see and talk about the Middle East. This is the familiar beast of burden that, like Dr. Frankenstein's monster, continues to lumber onwards no matter how many times struck. That creature is Orientalism. By this, I mean the persistent tendency of many outsiders to see the MENA region, and all cultural and social aspects of it, through the lens of essentialism and darkness. It signifies not just the usual typecasts of Arabian life that flavor Western views – from snake charmers and magic carpets to bombastic dictators and snarling executioners – but the overall instinct to *imagine* this region as the exotic "Other" to the Western "Self." The result are vulgar categorical binaries that continue to drive public images and media representations. MENA authoritarianism opposes global democracy; Islamic dogma repulses secular reason; Arab traditions reject modern values; Middle Eastern violence contradicts European liberalism and peace. The inexorable results of such thinking are the worst expressions of Islamophobia. These are not difficult to find online today in terms of fear-mongering by alarmists regarding the existential threats to Western civilization posted by the great Islamic hordes, whether they take the form of terrorists or immigrants. It is the Battle of Vienna all over again.

Photo 1.1 depicts an archetypal example of this recurrent binarism in art. It depicts a famous 1868 painting, *Bonaparte before the Sphinx*, by French impressionist Jean-Léon Gérôme. The spacing captures well the leitmotifs of Orientalism: the Western conqueror Napoleon sitting astride the war stallion, facing off proudly against the decrepit face of an ancient civilization that can only watch as the shadowed French soldiers behind Napoleon march onwards, simultaneously occupying and liberating this bizarre land.

On a less extreme scale, by compartmentalizing the region's place in the collective mind, onlookers can ascribe a depressing sense of cultural fixity to Middle Eastern societies, such that any number of social and political problems can be said to stem from the innate timelessness of who these peoples inherently "are." Arabs, Turks, Persians, Kurds – it need not matter: according to this logic, we need only know from where they originate, and then we can predict their grim futures from their despotic selves. Repugnant phenomena like the Islamic State militant group are to be expected; the denigration of women's rights is par for course; the paucity of democratic politics is easily predictable. Such views are the cousin of the other great toxicity related to the MENA, anti-Semitism, which even after World War Two has periodically

PHOTO 1.1
Bonaparte before the Sphinx (1868), by Jean-Léon Gérôme.

Source: Public domain.
Online: https://commons.wikimedia.org/wiki/File:Jean-L%C3%A9on_G%C3%A9r%C3%B4me_003.jpg

reappeared in various guises, sometimes cloaked as innocuous nationalism and always claiming to "know" the future of Jews and Judaism.

How does one break free of this noxious ethnocentrism? It is not easy. The late anthropologist, Clifford Geertz, conjured this gauntlet less than two years after the 9/11 terrorist attacks in the US:

> We are, in this country right now, engaged in the process of constructing, rather hurriedly, as though we had better quickly get on with it after years of neglect, a standard, public-square image of "Islam." Until very recently, we had hardly more than the suggestions of such an image – vagrant notions of stallions, harems, deserts, palaces, and chants. A Peter Arno drawing in *The New Yorker* sixty-five years ago more or less summed the matter up. A stetson-hatted tourist leans out of his roadster to ask a turbaned man prostrate in prayer by the side of the road: "Hey, Jack, which way to Mecca?"[1]

The frustrating thing is not that this task requires an uncomfortable gaze into our cultural mirror. It is that we must do this *repeatedly*, over time, seemingly with every generation as some new crisis catapults the region onto smartphone newsfeeds and Twitter streams, into homepages and nightly broadcasts, which results in the fetishizing of difference.

Why does Orientalism linger? The obvious answer concerns its pervasiveness. Centuries of constructing monstrously outlandish caricatures of the Middle East are difficult to overturn through a few enlightened teachable moments in a classroom or seminar. Yet there are other reasons. One is intolerant tolerance. Often, even the harshest critics of ugly stereotyping prefer to refrain from sustained and honest discussion, and instead harangue violators in the name of pluralism. Think of a social network like Facebook, where the response to an obscene opinion might be to dislike the post and then unfriend the poster: out of sight, out of mind. But those offensive opinions still exist; no views have been changed, nor have ideas been provoked. Viral-video hunting and the shaming game only go so far until the cycle repeats. Another reason is the prickly fact that biases lurk everywhere, including among those who decry them – but rather than address complexity, simplistic worldviews are preferred. For instance, targets of Islamophobia may themselves espouse anti-Semitism; the targets of anti-Semitism may in turn generate ugly anti-Islamic imagery. At a wider level, those preaching open-mindedness may struggle with ideas, behaviors, and routines they encounter in the MENA region that they find distasteful or abhorrent, but fall back upon cultural relativism in hopes to remove themselves from the moral equation. How do we deal, for instance, with the complications that come from opposing patriarchy in its imperialistic version, manifest as foreign soldiers and imported administrators telling entire occupied societies what is best for family life, knowing well that their departure might open the door for practices of local oppression and violence that are no less smug and rapacious?

A final reason is the difficulty of extirpating the unconscious reproduction of bias among *ourselves* as scholars and specialists of the Middle East. What we say or think publicly is not always what we mutter or ruminate privately, but contradictions of behavior and discourse are treated as if they do not exist. For instance, American readers will be familiar with the idea that the frankest dialogues about race require pinching our conception of righteousness lest we, too, be exposed in hypocrisy. There are plenty of liberal voters who decry anyone operating under the faintest of racial stereotypes; and, when few are watching, they quicken their pace, walking alone at night, when they see African-American men approaching. There are progressive women who, as mothers, declare race to be dead in their color-blind society; but then quizzically ask why their Korean or Chinese friends' children struggle in math or science class. There are Americans who proudly chant their country must welcome all new immigrants, legal or otherwise, including the Spanish-speaking bystanders walking nearby – who, in fact, happen to be native-born citizens without the faintest clue why they have just been made to feel foreign. Let us return to the MENA: do these same jarring moments of realization hold for specialists of the Middle East (e.g., researchers, journalists, policymakers, teachers, activists) in that their public behavior, too, may sometimes commit the same unconscious bias? The answer is yes, and the reasoning hints at the power of civilizational tropes inherent to Orientalism. Combating it requires constant vigilance, even if this means spending as much energy problematizing private behavior and public mistakes as it does passionately debunking the nastiest assumptions echoing about Muslims and Jews, Arabs and Turks, Iran and the Qur'an.

This volume represents one modest effort to break free of these problems – distorted representations, the worship of high politics, the Orientalist legacy – by taking readers through a macroanalytic journey of MENA societies. Eschewing the terse study of states and governments, it instead delves into the social lives of populations to make the region seem less alien and more *familiar*. It consciously shies away from normative imposition in favor of describing and capturing, in the most empirically sophisticated way, the region's sense of place and its national contexts. Around its three organized themes of societal structures (namely the rural-urban cleavage, social mobilization, and identity), societal vulnerabilities (development, rentierism, and environment), and societal forces (religion, women, and youth), the arguments contained within take the form of *inductive, comparative analysis*. This means two things. First, the contributors draw upon existing theories and concepts but pay supreme attention to the facts on the ground. Through immersion in different streams of knowledge – quantitative data, qualitative case studies, and structured description – the chapters are implanted upon the middle ground between what our assumptions expect versus what research actually finds. Second, the emphasis falls upon not the minute details of a single country, but rather patterns across national cases. This mode of comparison enables the contributors to draw out important trends, describe the most impactful variables, and grasp collective outcomes like gender equality or social mobilization.

DEFINING THE MENA

As necessary with any introductory framework, let us first define the regional terrain to divulge the most elementary geographic, demographic, and political details. This will set the stage for social inquiry. The societies unpacked in this volume are located in the Middle East and North Africa region, which stretches across the three continents of Europe, Africa, and Asia (Map 1.1 and Map 1.2).

The phrase "Middle East" (also known as "Near East") traditionally refers to the geographic region bounded in the north by Turkey, to the east by Iran, in the south by Yemen, and in the west by the Red Sea. The term itself is socially constructed, coined by British and American strategists in the early twentieth century partly to distinguish this area from the "Far East," meaning China, Japan, and other Asian countries abutting the Pacific Ocean. More recently, scholars often use "Middle East" or "Mideast" as a broad term that covers not just this geographic cluster but also North Africa, another spatial cluster bounded by Morocco in the west to Egypt in the east, with the Mediterranean Ocean to the north and the Sahara Desert to the south. As a result, the Middle East and North Africa – or the MENA region – captures the virtual entirety of the Arabic-speaking world, plus Israel, Turkey, and Iran. Because such terms have been invented, it is telling that only in the latter half of the twentieth century did regional media begin using them fluently. For centuries, Arab cartographers would call this geographic crescent (minus, of course, non-Arab Turkey and Iran) *al-ʿAlim al-ʿArabi* – the Arab world. It took a few decades of imperial intervention to overturn this

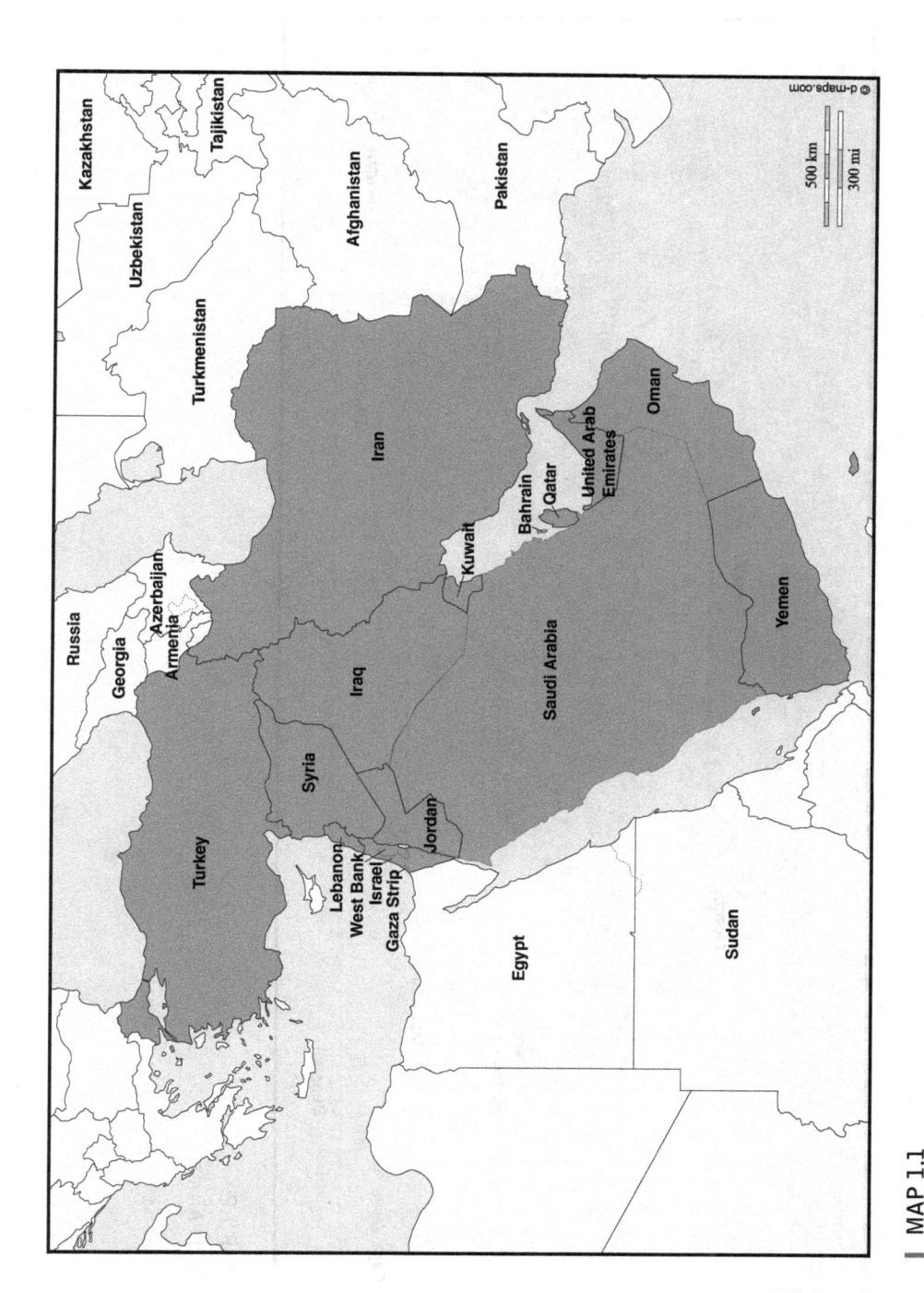

MAP 1.1
The Middle East.

Source: Adapted from D-Maps by Titanilla Panczel.

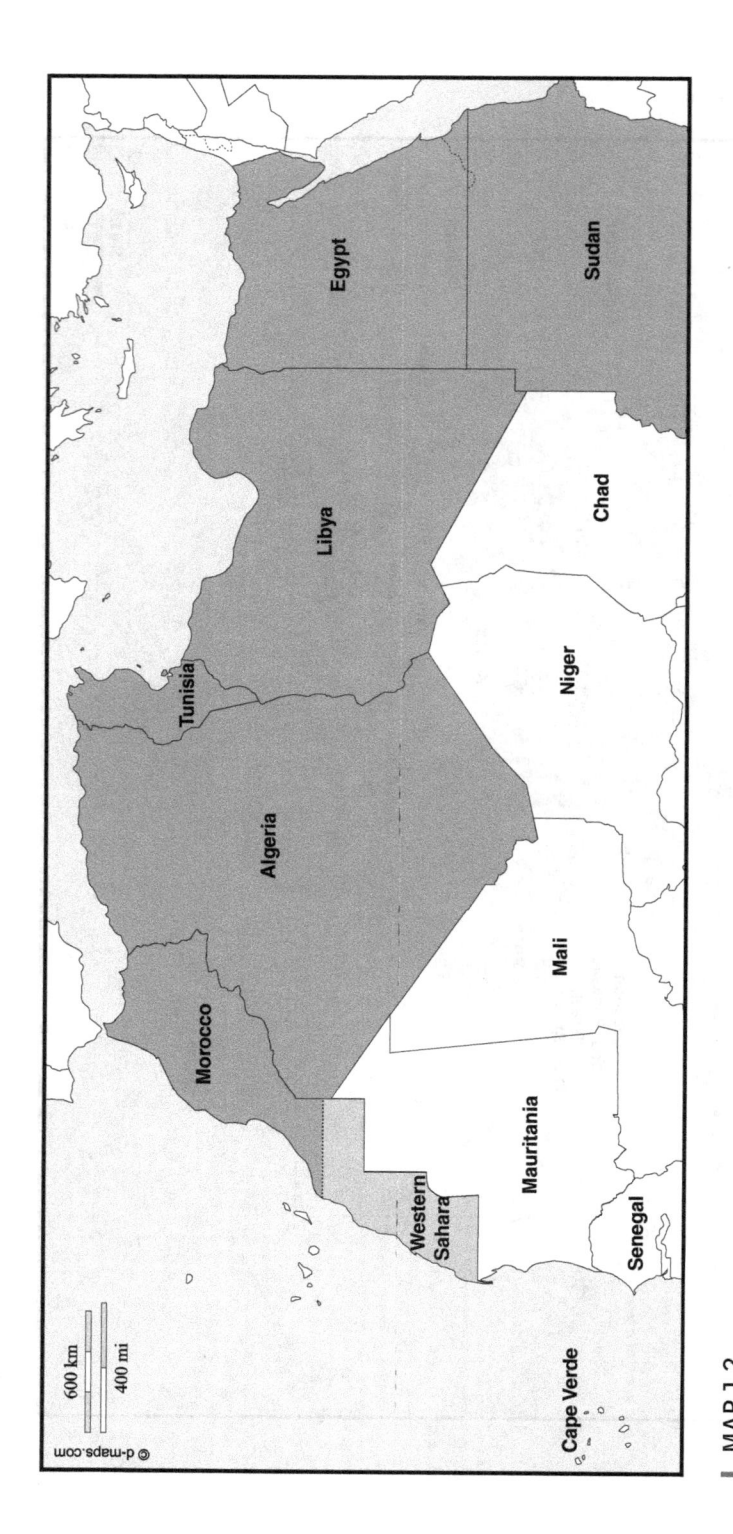

MAP 1.2
North Africa.

Source: Adapted from D-Maps by Titanilla Panczel.

tradition in favor of the Middle East nomenclature, a phrase that more indicates the region's distance from the Western imagination than suggests what rests within. Put another way, Westerners call this region the Middle East, but those in the "Far East" do not call this region the Middle West.

As a broad swathe of topography, the MENA comprises three distinctive subregions. The first is the *Maghrib*, or North Africa; this stretches across the uppermost zone of the African continent and includes Morocco, Algeria, Tunisia, Libya, while Egypt and Sudan are sometimes included in this definition. The term "Maghrib" in Arabic literally means "sunset" and figuratively "west." (Indeed, Morocco's Arabic name is Maghrib as well – fitting given that this land represented the westernmost extent of the old Islamic Caliphates.) The *Mashriq*, also called the Levant in English, begins with Egypt and stretches until Iran. This area includes Israel, the Palestinian territories (West Bank and Gaza Strip), Lebanon, Syria, Jordan, and Iraq. Mirroring the Maghrib, this subregion in Arabic means "sunrise," or "east." The third subregion is the Arabian Gulf, or *Khalij*, which encompasses all the countries residing within the Arabian Peninsula – Saudi Arabia, Kuwait, Bahrain, the United Arab Emirates (UAE), Qatar, Oman, and Yemen. Turkey and Iran are not included in these intra-regional categories, not least because each is among the region's largest countries and the heirs of great empires.

Table 1.1 furnishes some basic demographic and governance indicators for the 21 countries included in this regional definition. As the data show, national populations vary widely in size; principalities like Qatar, with just a few million people, are dwarfed by Egypt with its nearly 100 million residents. The healthy populational growth rates seen in many of these countries hint at the large youth bulge that currently characterizes the generational structure of the MENA as a whole; in terms of age, this is a young region, with nearly two-thirds of the regional population falling under the age of 30. The listing of predominant ethnic groups (which only displays the largest groups totaling 70 percent or more of the population) shows two things. First, Israel, Turkey, and Iran are the only countries where most citizens are not of Arab origin. Put another way, all the countries listed except these three comprise the Arab world, sharing in common the language of Arabic (though with major variations in terms of dialect) and other cultural markers, including religion (mostly Islam). Second, the six Khalij (or Gulf) kingdoms – Bahrain, Kuwait, Oman, Qatar, Saudi Arabia, and the UAE – have large Asian-dominated foreign worker populations; these expatriates staff their economies, and in most of these countries represent the majority of the population, although they are not citizens.

Finally, Table 1.1 divulges the political structure of government in these countries. First, consider Freedom House (FH) scores. FH's *Freedom in the World* index annually evaluates countries on the basis of their civil liberties and political freedoms. Its methodology is often subjective and the data sometimes crude, and by no means can it be called the definitive way

TABLE 1.1

MENA countries – demographics and government, 2018.

	Total population (July 2017)	Annual population growth (percent)	Predominant ethnic groups among residents*	Freedom House ranking (2017)	Type of regime
Algeria	40,969,443	1.7	Algerian Arab	Not Free	Republic (semi-presidential)
Bahrain	1,410,942	2.3	Bahraini Arab (citizens), Asian (foreigners)	Not Free	Ruling monarchy
Egypt	97,041,072	2.5	Egyptian Arab	Not Free	Republic (presidential)
Iran	82,021,564	1.2	Persian	Not Free	Republic (theocratic)
Iraq	39,192,111	2.6	Iraqi Arab	Not Free	Republic (parliamentary)
Israel	8,299,706	1.5	Israeli-born Jewish	Free	Republic (parliamentary)
Jordan	10,248,069	2.1	Jordanian Arab, Palestinian Arab	Partly Free	Ruling monarchy
Kuwait	4,437,590	1.5	Kuwaiti Arab (citizens), Asian (foreigners)	Partly Free	Ruling monarchy
Lebanon	6,229,794	1.2	Lebanese Arab, Syrian Arab	Partly Free	Republic (parliamentary)
Libya	6,653,210	1.6	Libyan Arab	Not Free	Republic (parliamentary)

(Continued)

Morocco	33,986,655	1	Moroccan Arab-Berber	Partly Free	Ruling monarchy
Oman	4,613,241	2	Omani Arab (citizens), Asian (foreigners)	Not Free	Ruling monarchy
Qatar	2,314,307	2.3	Qatari Arab (citizens), Asian (foreigners)	Not Free	Ruling monarchy
Saudi Arabia	28,571,770	1.5	Saudi Arab (citizens), Asian (foreigners)	Not Free	Ruling monarchy
Sudan	37,345,935	1.6	Sudanese Arab	Not Free	Republic (presidential)
Syria	18,028,549	**	Syrian Arab	Not Free	Republic (presidential)
Tunisia	11,403,800	1	Tunisian Arab	Free	Republic (semi-presidential)
Turkey	80,845,215	0.5	Turkish	Partly Free	Republic (semi-presidential)
United Arab Emirates	9,400,145	2.4	Emirati Arab (citizens), Asian (foreigners)	Not Free	Monarchy (federation)
West Bank and Gaza Strip	4,543,126	2.1	Palestinian Arab	Not Free	Republic (semi-presidential)
Yemen	28,036,829	2.3	Yemeni Arab	Not Free	Republic (presidential)

Source: CIA World Factbook (2018); Freedom House (2018), Freedom in the World. * indicates ethnic groups that represent in total at least 70 percent of population. ** indicates no data available due to civil war.

to capture the complexity of a country's high politics. Doing so requires another text altogether, and indeed this book's sister volume takes on this task.[2] For now, however, we must accept these limitations simply to make some quick comparisons and to gain the most basic understanding of governmental institutions.

FH rankings divide countries into three extremely broad categories, namely not free, partly free, and free. "Free" means functional democracies.

In such environs, leaders are elected through free and fair elections, there are legal and active opposition parties, minority groups are protected, and citizens enjoy a reasonable degree of basic equality, rule of law, and expressive and personal freedoms. The media is generally independent of state control. "Partly free" indicates countries in which these pillars are violated in a major way – such as a flawed democracy where a president has tightened his or her grip on power, or an authoritarian regime where the ruler tolerates some exercise of freedom. If elections occur, they are limited or occasionally fraudulent; opposition is legal, but is highly restricted; only some minority groups may be protected; and citizens have some legal and personal freedoms, but many ideas remain strictly off limits. There may be an independent media, but there is also a strong pro-government sector. Finally, "not free" indicates countries where most or all of these tenets are transgressed. These are dictatorships (i.e., autocracies or authoritarian regimes) where elections (if they exist) are heavily rigged, where opposition is either illegal or else suffers severe repression, and where everyday citizens face onerous limits on what they can say, write, and do. Many issues, from religion and minority representation to democracy and women's rights, are tightly controlled by the state; there is little to no independent media.

This three-prong typology is fuzzy, but its utility lies not in the assumption that all countries within each category are identical – they are assuredly not – but rather, that there are meaningful and undeniable differences *across* groups of countries. For instance, Saudi Arabia is many things, but it certainly does not offer more civil liberties and political rights to the average citizen than Tunisia. A more fine-grained approach considers the type of regime (that is, governmental institutions that exercise power) found in each state. Ruling monarchies persist in the MENA in eight countries; they rank fairly low, insofar that unelected kings wield vast executive powers and parliamentary accountability is either limited or absent. The UAE is the only federal monarchy in the world, as it technically comprises seven different principalities ruled by six royal families. A few parliamentary republics, like Israel and Tunisia, are democracies, highlighting the general correlation between elected institutions and political freedom. Iran uniquely stands out in its theocratic structure; it has a presidential system, but ultimate power remains in the hands of unelected Shiʻa clerics. Elsewhere, governments take the form of parliamentary or presidential republics, with varying restrictions on the civil and political freedoms of their societies.

These political structures will not overshadow societal analysis in this volume, but they should be remembered because they set the institutional stage for how many issues play out. For instance, the very large foreign worker populations of the Arabian Gulf kingdoms are kept in political check by conditions of authoritarian rule in which any symbolic or material challenge to the ruling monarchy is met by harsh crackdowns. Likewise, the rentier legacies that contort citizenship and identity are not only artifacts of oil wealth, but also of the autocratic bargains symbolically made between rulers and social forces that claimed to trade political voice for economic protection. In addition, the overall diminished state of democracy in the MENA gives hints about why many leaders worry so much about their expansive youth populations. As the 2011–2012 Arab Spring showed, young citizens deprived of political voice and economic dignity have the meaningful capacity to disobey authority and mobilize for revolutionary change.

HISTORICAL BACKGROUND: A REGIONAL PRIMER

In addition to these vital geographic, demographic, and political features, it is also indispensable to adumbrate the rich and varied history of the MENA region. The purpose is not to retread old narratives (we do, after all, live in an era where Wikipedia is but a click away), or to suggest that there is a hidden message in the majestic arc of human history. The staid reason is that to know where the futures of different societies may lead, it is necessary to first understand from where they originated.

The MENA echoes with antiquity, being the cradle of ancient civilizations such as the Akkadians, Babylonians, and Phoenicians. Judah, Alexander the Great, Carthage, the Romans and the Byzantines – these all exist in the archeological and historical record, as do the milestones they achieved. Among them were the commencement of settled agriculture, the first languages and laws, and the monotheistic faiths of Judaism, Christianity, and Islam. The latter is often interpreted as a turning point in not just regional but global history, because from the inception of Islam through whom Muslims see as God's final Prophet, Muhammad, came the creation of new empires and religious fealties. The year AD 622 marks the beginning of the Islamic calendar because it saw the *hijra* (migration) of the Prophet and his believers from Mecca to Medina; he eventually returned and conquered much of the Arabian Peninsula before passing away in AD 632. This decade began the age of Islamic empires, which for the first centuries took the form of Caliphates – essentially the same notion, except that the title of the leader (Caliph, or *khalifa* in Arabic) explicitly means successor. Succession after the Prophet regarding who might claim the political and spiritual authority to lead the *ummah*, or Muslim community, was a contested issue; bitter disagreements resulted in the great fracture that pitted the minority Shi'a branch of Islam in hierocratic disagreement with the majoritarian remainder constituting what we now call Sunni Islam. The sectarian rift has waxed and waned, and usually resulted in little violent conflict; but it nonetheless remains a doctrinal reality today.

These empires were sprawling. Upon its collapse in AD 750, the 'Umayyad Caliphate had reached three times the size of the Roman Empire, containing not just the MENA but also the Iberian Peninsula in Europe and much of present-day Pakistan, Afghanistan, and Central Asia. The subsequent 'Abbasid Empire was based in Baghdad, and until AD 1258 encompassed a more modest territory, with various splinter dynasties and small emirates ruling over peripheral areas. These centuries embodied what historians call the Golden Age of Islam, characterized at the social level by new advances in philosophy, science, medicine, art, and other realms of knowledge. Some of the oldest universities in the world, which still exist today, were founded in this period, such as the University of al-Karaouine in Morocco (AD 859) and Al-Azhar University in Egypt (AD 970). The 'Abbasids were followed by the last Islamic Caliphate, the Ottoman Empire, which overtook Byzantium and reached the zenith of its power in the late seventeenth century. Based in Istanbul, the Ottoman domain stretched from the MENA deep into the heart of Europe, including Greece, the Balkans and Hungary; it eventually reached the outskirts of Vienna. Contrasting its imperium was the largest Shi'a Islamic empire, the Safavid dynasty, which stretched across modern-day Iran, Iraq, the Caucasus, and parts of Central Asia and Pakistan until its fall in the early 1700s.

The Ottoman Empire decayed over time, however, due to military conflicts as well as internal fragmentation. After the early nineteenth century, Europe's new industrialized powers surpassed Ottoman military, economic, and technological primacy. Despite the empire pursuing political and economic reforms in hopes of reversing its decline, by the late 1800s Ottoman-controlled areas of the MENA region had become frequent targets of European encroachment. At the same time, nationalist awakenings and anti-Ottoman resistance movements erupted in many Arab territories. Even before World War One, most of the Maghrib had become divided amongst British, French, and Italian claims, while many of the smaller tribal sheikhdoms along the Arabian Gulf littoral, such as Kuwait and Bahrain, became subsumed as British protectorates. Iran, then laboring under the royal grasp of the Safavid dynasty's successor, the House of Qajar, similarly had weakened and thereby fell under heavy British and European influence. Symbolizing the fateful intersection of Western strategic interests with MENA local development, in 1908 the British made its first large-scale oil discovery in southwestern Iran.

World War One consumed the Ottoman Empire, resulting in its final demise. In the decade after the conflict, the British and French divided what remained of the Mashriq amongst themselves; the process was the midwife through which Syria, Lebanon, Iraq, and Jordan were born, albeit as protectorates. In Iran, the Qajar dynasty gave way to the country's last monarchy, the Pahlavi crown, in the 1920s, while similarly the modern Turkish republic coalesced in the Anatolian Peninsula as the sovereign replacement to Ottoman power. The Maghrib remained under British, French, and Italian administration, though with some variation. Algeria, for instance, was governed as a territorial part of the French homeland, as compared to the wider autonomy granted to Egypt under British suzerainty. The Arabian Gulf remained largely a British lake, with its principalities attached to British power and southern Yemen serving as a Crown colony under London's direct supervision. Saudi Arabia emerged independently through the forge of internal conquest waged by the House of Saud. British-administered Palestine became an increasing headache during this interwar period; while the global Zionist movement helped a small stream of Jewish settlers arrive, the local Arab population grew much faster, resulting in disruptive conflict, heavy-handed British mediation, and after World War Two an ill-fated United Nations partition that devolved into the first Arab-Israeli War. The result was the creation of Israel sandwiched in between the Palestinian West Bank and Gaza Strip.

The post–World War Two period heralded the independence of all the Arab countries, though at different tempos. Egypt and Iraq were technically independent beforehand, but penetrated by British jurisdictions (such as military bases and transit zones like the Suez Canal). Elsewhere, from 1946 through 1971, all the Arab territories – most of which had experienced Ottoman governance within living memory – graduated from European imposition and entered the international system as sovereign nation-states. The Mashriq came first, with Jordan and Syria attaining independence in 1946. The 1950s saw the Maghrib transit to statehoods, some through arrangement (e.g., Morocco, Tunisia, Libya) and one through the abattoir of war (i.e., Algeria, whose conflict did not end until 1962). The small Arabian Gulf kingdoms came last, with negotiated sovereignty granted by the British in 1971 to Bahrain, Qatar, and the new UAE. At this point, the MENA regional map looked mostly similar to what exists today, though with some changes.

The 1967 Arab-Israeli War resulted in Israel occupying the West Bank and Gaza Strip, while until its unification in the 1990s Yemen was split into northern and southern halves frequently at odds with one another. Sudan went the opposite direction, incorporating a much larger territory until its 2011 fissuring and the creation of (non-Arab) South Sudan.

Though brief, Western imperialism deposited deep social legacies that are relevant to not just the post-colonial era but more generically to how we can understand societal developments across the region today. Most obviously, the cartographic propensity to carve out territorial boundaries without regard to ethnic, sectarian, religious, and tribal coherency underwrote future struggles over national identity once these states became independent. Conflicting claims made by different social groups for recognition or leadership influenced virtually all aspects of post-colonial societies – the discourse of national identity, the allotment of material resources, the role of women, the mechanisms of social mobilization, even the sheer geographic distribution of people across urban versus rural areas. At the political level, however, the interlude of Western hegemony also affected many countries by either installing authoritarian regimes (as in the case of most Arab monarchies, which were strengthened by imperial support) or else leaving behind a cacophony of conflict and poverty that was functionally silenced by post-colonial dictatorships that promised prosperity at the cost of freedom.

In the Arab countries, thus, the politics of authoritarianism in the latter half of the twentieth century coincided with two major forces: first, economic modernization, which proceeded apace through different strategies – oil-fueled rentierism in the Gulf, state-led industrialization in the largest republics, trade-oriented development elsewhere; and second, the societal transformations wrought by urbanization, migration, and mobilization. Outside the Arab world were variations of this formula. Israel's wartime footing and demographic fluctuations girded a burgeoning democratic system; Turkey's republic oscillated between military coups and electoral politics, all the while as a new middle-class emerged; and Iranian society experienced two opposite trajectories, from the secularized stance of the Pahlavi monarchy to the post-1979 revolutionary Islamic Republic. Notably, this spacious generalization of the MENA in the post-colonial decades is the thematic forest containing countless trees of detail. The region experienced a multitude of armed conflicts, including conventional inter-state and internecine intra-state wars; a dramatic ideological journey, with one phase being the rise of Islamist movements and religious extremism in many countries; the ripple effects of hydrocarbon dependence, with the highs and lows of energy pricing buffeting all economies; and continued geopolitical meddling by outside powers, with the US and Soviet Union wooing various regimes to their side with aid and arms as they etched new spheres of strategic influence.

If the MENA's historical trajectory could be periodized into distinctive stages, then the current one initiated with the Cold War's end in 1991 has now stretched onwards for three decades. If the 1950s through 1980s were typified by the promise of post-colonial emancipation and the creation of new states, then the 1990s onwards is the "post-post-colonial" period – an epoch of reckoning and recalibration, as both states and societies have adjusted to hard times. The 1990–1991 Gulf War, the Oslo peace process, the 2003 Iraq War, the 2011–2012 Arab Spring, and various new wars are among the geopolitical earthquakes that have punctuated the regional landscape. Domestically, a frequent occurrence is that many communities have increasingly exercised their voice and agency in response to exclusion from structures of power. Scenes from the Arab Spring, in which popular crowds and individual activists defiantly stood against authority figures, have been seared into the global consciousness. The events of 2011–2012 showed, if nothing else, that social actors across the region *are not silent* in the face of injustice.

Contentious activism is not merely an Arab phenomenon. Over the past decade, the rising crescendo of Turkish civic demonstrations and cultural contestation, swells of demonstrating Iranian urban workers and voters, and the mobilization of Israeli youth over social justice issues all suggest that the populations of the region are confronted with major problems, but also see opportunities for change. The past matters insofar that the challenges that confront different social currents did not crystallize in a vacuum; they are the product of historical choices and antecedent developments, from the political institutions and economic dreams that emerged from imperial memory to the social and ideological entrepreneurship authored by new youths today. *Where do we go from here?* This is the abstruse but inescapable question that this book attempts to answer.

ONE GOAL, THREE THEMES, NINE TOPICS

The diverse analysis within the volume revolves around three core themes that help make MENA populations more familiar and knowable to readers; in turn, each theme comprises a cluster of three chapters. The guiding thread is to take the intellectual path away from the politics of regimes, institutions, and elites, and instead meander through more fruitful avenues of social life – economic trends, points of contestation, opportunities for voice, methods of organization, and the voices of the marginalized. This "bottom-up" approach cannot cover every relevant detail of every population, a mandate that could likely consume a dozen-volume series. Still, it remains loyal to the premise that to know the MENA region from a distance, one must observe how human communities, social relations, and dynamic forces come together within and across arenas of collective action that we call societies. Herein lays the singular goal of this project.

The first theme is *societal structures*. By this, I mean the overarching organization of how routines and behaviors are followed. The three chapters included within this theme explore the rural-urban divide, social mobilization and civil society, and finally the power of identity. Chapter 2's contribution by Rachel Bahn, Tariq Tell, and Rami Zurayk engages the first topic. It sets the tone by exploring the social routines of MENA residents from farm to town, village to city. Emphasizing the rural origins of most societies, including tribal and agrarian communities that are too often ignored in conventional analysis, the authors highlight the cultural and economic shifts made through urbanization and industrialization. The unprecedented growth of new urban centers like metropolitan cities has been transformative, but it has also produced corollary externalities of rural productivity, food security, and migration (both voluntary and forced, as in refugees). The refugee picture is the symbolic, if tragic, encapsulation of the argument: the movement of peoples through perceived boundaries, whether from rural to urban areas or across national borders fleeing gruesome violence, reflects how fast-moving exigencies have outstripped the economic and social underpinnings of their communities.

Chapter 3, authored by Vincent Durac, studies the second topic of social mobilization and civil society. It reviews how citizens in the MENA have struggled to alter the rules and constraints governing their societies through resistance, participation, and organization. It shows the traditions of collective action and even revolutionary power that harken back to the eras of Ottoman and Western imperialism, and then traces the rise of civil society – meaning the associational life between governments, economies, and homes and which comprise all the unique organizations, clubs, and movements that characterize what people often *do* when not studying, working, eating, and sleeping. From the post-colonial period to the current epoch, and through various impediments such as political repression and ideological competition, the analysis underscores the capacity of everyday people to become meaningful actors in voicing their interests and fighting for change.

Chapter 4, by P.R. Kumaraswamy, unloads the concept of identity to ascertain how individuals and groups perceive themselves in the first place within different arenas of societal contestation. It problematizes the definition of identity, including what identity as a variable is supposed to explain. It further highlights how different identities, each carrying historical and emotional baggage, are not always expressed uniformly, and in fact can be malleable and sometimes instrumentalized. Given the sheer number of different identity categories – tribalism, religion, ethnonationalism, refugees, expatriates, youth, and women – the analysis explores how claims made on basis of identity, such as assertions of authority or demands for resources, can produce divergent results; sometimes clashes and conflicts erupt, whereas in other contexts identity contestation fades into the background. In sum, the region contains a multiplicity of collective affiliations that orient how individuals and groups locate themselves versus others.

The second theme is *societal vulnerabilities*. If societal structures reveal the constituting fabrics of social life, then societal vulnerabilities encompass something more external – the economic and material challenges that constrain populations by exposing them to potential harm and dislocation. The three chapters centered upon this theme analyze economic underdevelopment, the legacies of rentierism, and human insecurity from environmental degradation. The first contribution here is Chapter 5, in which Bessma Momani and Morgan MacInnes discuss the arc of economic development in the region. Starting from the post–World War Two years, they discuss the predominant state-led model of industrialization and modernization, which for a brief period of time generated rapid growth and prosperity for many countries. Yet the exhaustion of this costly model, including even the wealthy oil exporters, injected relative deprivation and shocks to many populations. The consequence has been dire, though diffuse across the region. While governments enacted neoliberal reforms and market-oriented adjustments to their official economic policies, societies were forced to adjust to new privations; in the Arab world, and to a lesser degree Turkey and Iran, this has meant stubborn unemployment and rising living costs. Such struggles by the average citizen to put bread on tables and money in pockets makes the 2011–2012 Arab Spring all the more understandable.

Chapter 6, by Hae Won Jeong, traces the social and cultural effects of rentierism. The MENA possesses the world's largest reserves of oil, and its exploitation since the early twentieth century has not only transformed financial and political institutions but also influenced societies as well. Oil wealth generated a complex, interdependent web of social changes that go beyond instant riches. Oil and gas exporters in the Arabian Gulf kingdoms attracted millions of foreign workers who now surpass the citizenry in demographic terms. MENA societies that sent that labor received back their financial remittances; others reaped foreign aid and support. Yet hydrocarbon dependence also distorted notions of citizenship, pushed hyperbolic urban growth, and wasted human capital: in essence, oil was not just a harbinger of riches but also a commodifier of social relations. Though likely irreversible, recognizing these effects across multiple generations may enable us to extract positive externalities as well.

Chapter 7, by Mohamed Behnassi, uncovers the last societal vulnerability through a discussion of environmental change and human conflict. By seeing human security as freedom not just from violence – although that itself is elusive, given the prevalence of armed wars in the MENA – but also fear, hunger, and other dangers not purely rooted in militarized violence, we can appreciate why climate change and ecological degradation is so relevant to entire societies. The region's aridity means that most populations suffer water scarcity; potential environmental impacts of rising temperatures, increased drought, and lower rainfall puts extreme stress on the food supply and public health. Climate change, hence, represents an existential threat to human security, not least because it also raises the propensity for conflict. In the end, unless regional communities adjust to systemic worsening of land, air, and water resources, future prosperity (and perhaps even survival) will be an assumption needing qualification.

The third theme is *societal forces*, meaning the frontiers of change. These refer to major vectors of change and transformation that are reconfiguring entire social groups and shaping public discourse; they are religion and faith, women and gender activists, and finally the rising youth generation. Chapter 8's analysis by Ramazan Kılınç surveys the panorama of religious communities in the MENA, a Muslim-majority region but with Jewish-majority Israel and smaller Christian and non-Abrahamic minorities dispersed throughout. It weighs how religiosity prefigures public attitudes and preferences on social and political issues. It also highlights the mobilizational capacity of Islam, manifest in both efforts to suppress religious movements in the past and the contemporary rise of Islamist movements that range from peaceful service providers to extremist organizations whose violence escapes convenient explanation. Case studies of Egypt, Turkey, Iran, and Saudi Arabia reveal that different Muslim-majority populations have settled upon divergent frameworks of expressing and protecting their creeds and institutions; such diversity is integral to understanding the texture of social life.

Chapter 9, by Lindsay J. Benstead, shifts focus from the realm of faith to the contested domain of women and gender. Often controversial and usually misunderstood, gender roles and equality demands have evolved greatly since the colonial era, and today can be understood by comparing the private sphere (that is, family matters and personal agency) with the public sphere, as manifest in education, employment, and representation. In most countries, we see a gender gap in terms of how women versus men fare – the result of endemic patriarchy, which has declined in recent decades but remains stubborn in areas like economic participation. Likewise, most LGBTQ communities face suppression, forcing adaptation on the margins. Though public attitudes suggest gradually leveling views on gender in many countries, the persistence of inequality is an important puzzle. Explanations for patriarchy are varied, ranging from cultural theories to political economy and social psychology, and need to be carefully considered.

Finally, Chapter 10, by this author, investigates the social and cultural implications of what we call the demographic youth bulge. Most MENA societies are extremely young in terms of age distribution, and the current generation is the most well educated but also well mobilized in regional history; the Arab Spring is but a recent example. Yet while young citizens in the Arab world plus Israel, Turkey, and Iran are agents of change, they also are overcoming bottlenecks in their maturation; among them are failing educational systems, chronic youth joblessness, and political marginalization. In sum, there is dire mismatch between what teenagers and young adults want (dignity, voice, participation) versus what is made available by elderly authorities in their communities and governments. However, youths also share a collective generational experience defined by disconnect from the past, technological interconnectivity, and cultural synergy through art and music. Their movement through public space challenges societal constraints and will continue to define the regional dynamic.

CONCLUSION

There may be no permanent escape from the high politics of governments and powerholders when studying the Middle East and North Africa. Given its representations in global media as well as the heavy legacies of Orientalist optics, there remains a tendency for observers, students, reporters, travelers, and other readers to gaze upon the region and see the regimes, rulers, geopolitics, and foreign policies that seem to determine the course of historical ruptures like the Arab Spring, nuclear proliferation, and violent conflicts. And this is not only expected but necessary: states *do* matter, and engaging the MENA requires absorbing how political decisions and institutional choices are made and remade. Yet as this chapter, and the book as a whole, depicts, *so too do societies matter* – and the social currents that constrain, empower, and change populations comprise the underlying human landscape. By scrutinizing the organizing structures, material vulnerabilities, and forces of change that characterize the region's varied societies, we gain a stronger grasp over not just the region as an object of study but also our own assumptions about how ordinary people live, adapt, struggle, and overcome. Engaging these dynamics is not an easy task, but it makes the Middle East eminently familiar and knowable – and, in no small way, less distant in our collective mind than before. And so, we proceed.

QUESTIONS FOR DISCUSSION

1 What are the most notable problems in how the MENA region seems to be portrayed to foreign audiences through the news media, entertain industry, and other venues of representation?
2 What is Orientalism, and why is it so pervasive despite being identified as a problematic legacy?
3 What are the three sub-regions of the MENA, and what basic traits and features would each cluster of countries be expected to share in common?
4 What is the relative distribution of democracy versus authoritarianism in the region today, and what might be reasons for this?
5 What were the major imperial actors and forces that shaped the evolution of states and societies prior to the mid-twentieth century?
6 After World War Two, how did independence come to the region?
7 All things being equal, what is the payoff of scrutinizing social life and societal dynamics as opposed to topics like politics, diplomacy, and foreign policy?
8 Can tracing the historical origins and development of national societies help explain or predict their future trajectories in the Middle East? How might we test this projection?

NOTES

1 Clifford Geertz, "Which Way to Mecca?" *The New Yorker*, June 12, 2003.
2 See *The Government and Politics of the Middle East and North Africa*, also edited by Sean Yom and published by Routledge.

FURTHER READING

Entire libraries have been filled with books and volumes that inform readers about the global context and historical development of the Middle East and North Africa. Strangely, most references and recommendations gloss over the actual cartographic and physical features of the MENA. Yet these are unavoidable: states and societies can revolutionize their governments or policies but their lands, oceans, and spaces in between remain the same. Hence, first consult National Geographic's *Atlas of the Middle East*, 2nd ed. (Washington, DC: National Geographic Society, 2008), which furnishes breathtaking maps and finely detailed surveys about the region's physical and cultural features – a necessary backdrop to any sustained scholarship. The Perry-Castañeda Library Map Collection, which is online (https://legacy.lib.utexas.edu/maps/middle_east.html), can also fill in the cartographic blanks.

The best general historical readers pay close attention to the cultural, religious, and organizational fabric of social life, while ostensibly remaining fixed upon the major centers of power and macro-level trends like the rise and fall of empires. See, for instance, the following standard "primers" – Ira Lapidus, *A History of Islamic Societies*, 2nd ed. (New York: Cambridge University Press, 2002); Philip Hitti, *History of the Arabs*, 10th ed. (London: Palgrave Macmillan, 2002); Albert Hourani and Malise Ruthven, *A History of the Arab Peoples*, new ed. (Cambridge, MA: Belknap Press, 2010); Peter Mansfield, *A History of the Middle East*, 4th ed. (New York: Penguin, 2013); William Cleveland and Martin Bunton, *A History of the Modern Middle East*, 6th ed. (London: Routledge, 2016); James Gelvin, *The Modern Middle East: A History*, 4th ed. (Oxford: Oxford University Press, 2015); Eugene Rogan, *The Arabs: A History*, rev. ed. (New York: Basic Books, 2017); and Arthur Goldschmidt Jr. with Aomar Boum, *A Concise History of the Middle East*, 11th ed. (London: Routledge, 2016).

Many of these works are anchored in the Arab world, but Turkish and Iranian histories also stretch back many centuries and so have elicited significant study. See, for instance, Caroline Finkel, *Osman's Dream: The History of the Ottoman Empire* (New York: Basic Book, 2007); Douglas Howard, *A History of the Ottoman Empire* (Cambridge: Cambridge University Press, 2017); Ervand Abrahamian, *A History of Modern Iran* (Cambridge: Cambridge University Pres, 2008); and Touraj Daryaee, ed., *The Oxford Handbook of Iranian History* (Oxford: Oxford University Press, 2014). By contrast, Israel is a young state. Accessible works like Daniel Gordis, *Israel: A Concise History of a Nation Reborn* (New York: HarperCollins, 2016) and Benny Morris, *Righteous Victims: A History of the Zionist-Arab Conflict, 1881–2001* (New York: Vintage Books, 2001) give the flavor of its modern rise. There are innumerable others, as each of these non-Arab MENA countries commands its own respected subfield of study within the social sciences and humanities. This sample provides a sample of the scholarship.

Since the early twentieth century, major political events like revolutions, wars, and state formation understandably require elucidation. The most eloquently written text about the region's experience in the modern era is R. Stephen Humphreys, *Between Memory and Desire: The Middle East in a Troubled Age* (Berkeley: University of California Press, 2005). Roger Owen, *State, Power, and Politics in the Making of the Modern Middle East*, 3rd ed. (London: Routledge, 2004) is an aging but still insightful survey of post-colonial developments. For the region's geopolitics and international affairs, see Louise Fawcett, *International Relations of the Middle East*, 4th ed. (Oxford: Oxford University

Press, 2016); Fred Halliday, *The Middle East in International Relations: Power, Politics, and Ideology* (Cambridge: Cambridge University Press, 2005); and Tareq Ismael and Glenn Perry, eds., *The International Relations of the Contemporary Middle East: Subordination and Beyond* (London: Routledge, 2013). US-oriented readers can find great inspiration (but also critique) in Douglas Little, *American Orientalism: The United States and the Middle East since 1945*, 3rd ed. (Chapel Hill: University of North Carolina Press, 2008); Joel Migdal, *Shifting Sands: The United States in the Middle East* (New York: Columbia University Press, 2014); and David Lesch and Mark Haas, eds., *The Middle East and the United States: History, Politics, and Ideologies*, 6th ed. (London: Routledge, 2018).

Recent headline-grabbers, from the Arab Spring to the rise of ISIS, have generated bookshelves of instant knowledge; some may or may not stand the test of time. As of this writing (late 2018), the more entertaining interventions include the following: Robert Fisk, *The Great War for Civilisation: The Conquest of the Middle East* (New York: Vintage Books, 2007); Neil MacFarquhar, *The Media Relations Department of Hizbollah Wishes You a Happy Birthday: Unexpected Encounters in a Changing Middle East* (New York: PublicAffairs, 2009); Bassam Haddad, Rosie Bsheer, and Ziad Abu-Rish, eds., *The Dawn of the Arab Uprisings* (London: Pluto Press, 2012); Joby Warrick, *Black Flags: The Rise of ISIS* (New York: Anchor Books, 2016); Christopher Phillips, *The Battle for Syria: International Rivalry in the New Middle East* (New Haven: Yale University Press, 2017); Robert Worth, *A Rage for Order: The Middle East in Turmoil, from Tahrir Square to ISIS* (New York: Farrar, Straus, and Giroux, 2017); and Marc Lynch, *The New Arab Wars: Uprisings and Anarchy in the Middle East* (New York: PublicAffairs, 2017). All describe the dramatic newsworthy events (revolutions, uprisings, terrorism, conflict, spy-mongering, and the like) in admirable detail, and some even apply a dose of theorizing to it.

Online sources (also available on the companion website)

In the late 2000s, it was easy to recommend a small set of websites and news sources to help intrepid explorers of the MENA to obtain more information and conduct online research. Now, with the informational ecology fractured over social media, zero-day sites, official outlets, fake news, and blogs – all claiming to offer the best, more persuasive picture of regional peoples and events – it is impossible to extract reliable sources from the Internet without some prior pointers. And here they are.

The best regional sources for continuous news coverage of Middle East affairs remain Middle East Online (https://middle-east-online.com), Middle East Eye (www.middleeasteye.net), *Al-Jazeera* (www.aljazeera.com/topics/regions/middleeast.html), and Al-Bawaba Portal (www.albawaba.com). Each does incubate some bias, like all media; so the best strategy is to triangulate the analysis and information received about a particular event or story across all sources, and see where the middle ground lays. Western outlets with regional bureaus also excel but should be treated with the same degree of caution; see, for instance, the *New York Times* (www.nytimes.com/section/world/middleeast), *Washington Post* (www.washingtonpost.com/world/middle-east/), *BBC* (www.bbc.com/news/world/middle_east), *France24* (www.france24.com/en/middle-east), *Reuters* (www.reuters.com/subjects/middle-east), *The Economist* (www.economist.com/topics/middle-east), and *Foreign Policy* (https://foreignpolicy.com/channel/middle-east-africa/). For updated reference information, see the *CIA World Factbook* (www.cia.gov/library/publications/the-world-factbook).

Beyond the news cycle, the best in-depth coverage of social affairs, cultural issues, and popular debates in the region are found in a small but reliable group of dedicated research projects or analytic portals. These include: *Al-Bab* (http://al-bab.com); *Middle East Research and Information Project* (www.merip.org); The Middle East Institute (www.mei.edu/policy-analysis); The Atlantic Council's *MENASource Blog* (www.atlanticcouncil.org/blogs/menasource); the Carnegie Endowment for International Peace's *Sada* periodical (http://carnegieendowment.org/sada); Human Rights Watch's MENA *Team* (www.hrw.org/middle-east/n-africa); and the regular publications of the Project on Middle East Political Science (https://pomeps.org).

PART I

Societal structures

The rural–urban divide, social mobilization, and identities of the region

CHAPTER 2

Social life, from rural to urban

Rachel Bahn, Tariq Tell, and Rami Zurayk

THE RUNDOWN: KEY TOPICS COVERED
- Rural life
- Agriculture
- Urbanization
- Food, water, and sanitation
- Migration
- Refugees

INTRODUCTION

Straddling the crossroads between Africa, Asia, and Europe, the Middle East, and North Africa (MENA) region is a longstanding center of settled farming and more recently urban civilization. The MENA encompasses the Fertile Crescent, where agriculture was born 12,000 years ago and continues to coexist with extensive pastoral nomadism to this day. These rural origins have left an indelible imprint. Despite the images of hyper-developed metropolitanism that dominates Western media, from the skyscraping hotels of Dubai and Doha to the megaprojects of Cairo and Casablanca, the majority of MENA peoples are actually agrarians in the city. By this, we mean transplanted peasants, with one foot in the village which in many ways remains the focus of their social identity and political activity. Yet there is no "typical" social experience in the MENA: to understand it is to span rural, urban, and in-between areas of human activity, joined by important commonalities but also divided by significant distinctions.

This chapter outlines the large structural changes that shape the social routines of MENA residents from farm to city, countryside to town. A brief sketch of the ecological and historical background sets the stage, and establishes the geographic and natural context for contemporary social life. A review of rural-urban population dynamics provides a statistical grounding to the chapter, illustrating the rapid and recent pace of urbanization. Next, the chapter explores the rural areas and dimensions of life; treating towns, villages, and tribal settlements, it highlights the cultural and economic exclusion often faced by communities on the periphery, and how shifts in agrarian life have in turn transformed social structures and relations. The chapter then examines the process of urbanization to problematize how unprecedented metropolitan growth has produced corollary problems in housing shortages, declining education, and infrastructural bottlenecks, even though socioeconomic conditions are generally better in urban than rural areas. This chapter also focuses on the movement of peoples in the form of human migration. On the one hand, the large-scale movement of workers and youths, typically towards both cities (in domestic terms) and the oil-rich economies (in regional terms) has benefited both the receiving countries as well as the countries that send them. On the other hand, the MENA has also experienced extensive forced migration. Wars have generated waves of displaced individuals as refugees, and so this chapter charts their extraordinary salience and challenges.

HISTORICAL, SOCIAL, AND ECOLOGICAL CONTEXT

To understand the power of place – and in particular, the power of *rural* places in the MENA – we must first engage how its social and ecological landscapes changed between late antiquity and the onset of rapid modernization following World War Two. In weaving an alternative account of the region's historical evolution from the history of crops, plagues, and peoples, this chapter embeds its analysis of agrarian change and urbanization into the particularities of historical political ecology, meaning how environmental changes over time have interacted with social and cultural forces to produce inequalities of power.

These particularities are inherent in key features of the arid and semi-arid territory comprising the MENA, the lands stretching from the Atlantic Ocean in the west to the Hindu Kush in the east. The first is a dearth of water due to lack of permanent water resources beyond those stored in the natural water towers of the region's great mountain ranges, or inflows from rivers like the Nile. The chronic lack of easily accessible water had a natural impact on traditional social life: it meant that nomadic herding of animals like camels, sheep, and goats became a leading agricultural technique of harvesting this scarce resource from catchment areas. Other agrarian surplus, such as food crops like wheat, came from intensively irrigated farmlands, which for the most part were concentrated in the great river valleys – the Nile, the Mesopotamian Basin, and Transoxiana to the east of Iran. Despite its aridity, the MENA still became as a hub crop and animal diversity since the Neolithic Revolution. By late Roman times, an integrated trinity of Bedouin, *fellahin* (farmers, peasants, and other agricultural laborers), and "caravan" cities had emerged.

Orientalist scholarship once characterized this preindustrial social structure as a backwards one, where agricultural retardation and social stasis resulted in a broken mosaic of segmented tribes and sects. In historical reality, the conquests of Islam brought about a "Green Revolution" in terms of massively upgrading and diversifying the agricultural practices of these lands. Major periods of decline were linked to outside invasions from beyond the Islamic empires, such as the Turco-Mongol incursions into southern Iraq that devastated its irrigation networks. In Marxist terms, the MENA's segmented social divisions could be said to reflect a class-divided model of pre-capitalist tributary social formation, in which landowners and ruling elites imposed violence and coercion to extract food and other resources from agrarian producers like Bedouin and fellahin. This pattern of inequality and diversity combined with the long-term evolution of the natural landscape conditioned agrarian change in the region until the intrusion of Western imperialism starting in the second half of the nineteenth century.

Another defining environmental feature has been the particularity of energy supplies as dictated by both geography and geology. Before industrialization, this took the form of vast supplies of cheap animal energy drawn from the abundant grazing to be found in the tribal commons that covered the vast, sparsely populated pastures of the mountain and steppe (flat grasslands). In these conditions, animal-based traction was more cost-effective than wind- or water-driven systems, and animal-drawn water wheels more widespread than watermills and windmills. In particular, camel haulage virtually replaced wheeled transport between late antiquity and the arrival of steam-powered transport after the mid-nineteenth century. The efficiency of camel-transport after the diffusion of the North Arabian camel saddle may well have been a key factor in the growth of international trade along such routes as the Central Asian Silk Roads. Its replacement of wheeled transport could also have caused the transformation of the region's cityscapes after the Arab conquests, replacing the grid-like streets and colonnades of late antiquity with the pattern of warren-like quarters and narrow alleys that Orientalists long equated with the "Islamic City," with all of its mysterious exotic backwardness.

In more recent times, the region's urban centers, as well as its economy and socio-political structures, have been transformed by another peculiar energy supply – oil and gas, which gifted mammoth petrodollar surpluses for those countries claiming huge hydrocarbon reserves, especially after the 1973 oil price boom. This has heralded another transformative historical phase. Oil wealth permeated the geopolitics of the MENA after the retreat of Western colonialism following World War Two. Lilliputian but oil-rich "tribes with flags," a term often used to describe the littoral principalities of the Arabian Gulf such as Kuwait and Qatar, existed alongside far larger countries like Egypt and Syria whose revolutionary regimes anointed themselves as the heirs of past empires. Global powers like the US frequently intervened to protect their oil-rich clients. They acted to contain – and, after the end of the Cold War, dismember – recalcitrant states such as the Iraq of Saddam Hussein, which threatened Arabian oil supplies. Indeed, the Arabian Gulf has seen no less than three major wars since the 1980s, namely the Iraq-Iran War, the 1990–1991 Gulf War, and the 2003 Iraq War. All these conflicts involved outside powers and global actors. The area's function as a geopolitical hub controlling the world's largest oil and gas reserves, as well as its strategic location on the crossroads of the Mediterranean and the "New Silk Road" project now encroaching on Western Asia, ensure that, in a broad sense, the MENA never strays far from Western strategists.

As a definitional note, urbanization means the increasing share of a country's population living in urban areas, whether due to natural increase, rural-to-urban migration, or the reclassification of rural areas as urban areas. While the terms "rural" and "urban" are used as if they are starkly defined – an area is typically classified as either rural or urban by national statistical offices – the boundaries are in reality fluid. Administrative areas and definitions may vary by country, with sudden changes in the level of urbanization reflected only at the time of reclassification. In practice, it may be helpful to think of rural and urban as lying along a continuum ranging from rural areas with minimal population to villages, towns, and mid-sized cities, to vast and densely populated metropolitan conurbations.

Evolving rural landscapes and agrarian livelihoods: the Mashriq as archetype

The Mashriq sub-region demonstrates the interactions of the natural environment with socio-political structures. In the past century alone, this area has been marked by empire and colonialism; evolving patterns of agricultural production, pastoralism, and nomadism; and the presence and exploitation of natural resource wealth, all of which continue to impact the lives of its residents.

Ecology has long molded the material culture of Mashriq farming. An array of land- and water-use strategies, including share-cropping, corporate tribal pastures, and communal village lands, have historically prevailed. Agricultural production and agrarian life in the Mashriq transformed under rule by the Ottoman Empire (1516–1918). Settled farming revived during the climatically wet years of the sixteenth century, when the "frontier of settlement" in the Syrian interior moved eastwards into the steppe; but later retreated during the middle period of Ottoman rule (1650–1830), perhaps as a result of the onset of the Little Ice Age and the "tribal breakouts" that accompanied the empire's shifting position in an emergent European world economy.

Conceived as a measure of defensive modernization aimed at restoring the effectiveness of the Ottoman military-fiscal state, the 1858 Ottoman land code fostered the creation of resource frontiers that integrated this agrarian zone into the European world as an exporter of primary products. The growth of early export agriculture – for instance, silk production in Mount Lebanon and cotton in northern Palestine – stood in contrast with more established patterns of land use, such as olive cultivation for local consumption. The growth of grain exports from what is now southwestern Syria and northern Jordan set the stage for the calamity of World War One, in which famine struck during 1915–1918 due to British naval blockade.

The situation of land and peasantry under British and French Mandatory rule (1921–1946) differed markedly from that of Kemalist Turkey, where Ataturk successfully resisted European control. The European powers politically and administratively divided the Mashriq, and in Syria and Trans-Jordan (the predecessor to what is now the Kingdom of Jordan), the geographical base available for agricultural development was eroded further as a result of border agreements with Turkey and Saudi Arabia. Those border agreements reduced arable land available for cultivation and also impeded the natural movement of people. At the same time, these areas were struggling under inflows of Jewish settlers and Anatolian refugees. In northeastern

Syria, patterns of refugee settlement and territorial division undermined the indigenous nomadic economy. Powerful landlords and entitled elites created a privatized land system that was grossly unequal and kept many Bedouin tribes and fellahin impoverished across southern Lebanon, Syria, and Iraq. The Great Palestinian Revolt in 1936–1939 likewise reflected disputes over land and resources, inflamed as well by clumsy British interventions and governance.

During World War Two, a more interventionist colonialism took hold within the Mashriq under the aegis of the Cairo-based Middle East Supply Center, created by the British to regulate commerce and trade in the region. Following the war, however, British policy failed to transition towards development policies that would favor the fellahin or attend to the fallout from the plight of Palestinian peasants. Reflecting demands over water, conflicting Arab and Israeli plans for the River Jordan helped precipitate the 1967 Arab-Israeli War. Following their independence, the Ba'th populist-authoritarian regimes of Iraq and Syria imposed multiple land reforms aimed at redistributing land from wealthy elites and empowering fellahin and other impoverished residents. Yet such "revolutions from above" also sent the nomadism of Bedouin tribes into near-terminal decline, as many common grazing areas were nationalized.

Since the end of colonialism, the rural Mashriq has been buffeted by oil, conflict, and globalization. First, the lure of petrodollars attracted rural migrants from the region to travel and work in the Gulf, resulting in labor scarcities in these labor-exporting countries. Foreign aid by the oil-rich Arab states like Saudi Arabia and Kuwait likewise allowed Syria, Jordan, Lebanon, and by extension Palestinian areas to rapidly build new state institutions, which expanded public employment and contributed to urbanization – further drawing workers and peoples away from rural areas, and reflecting the growing tendency of governments to favor urban consumers living in burgeoning cities over the villager and farmer.

Further downstream, oil wealth indirectly squeezed farm livelihoods, as urbanizing families used remittances (incomes and salaries sent back to them by relatives working abroad, often in the Gulf) to purchase new property and land. While the upstream legacies of rentierism and hydrocarbon dependence are laid out in Chapter 6, close attention here must trace what occurred in lands that had little oil or gas but were nonetheless affected by it. Remittance-fueled urbanization raised real estate prices and triggered urban sprawl, with all the concomitant destruction of the environment this entailed. Traditional farming lifestyles became marginalized further due to new crop technologies and easy access to food imports, which reduced the dependence of societies upon internal food production. In visual terms, new cities began abutting farmlands and agrarian sectors that seldom attracted dense populations before; and in those remaining farmlands, there emerged a dualistic agricultural structure: on the one hand, modern, high-tech, and well-irrigated farms operated, infused with government or private investment and stocked with migrant labor; and on the other, low-tech and productively stagnant farms that were far smaller and run by families and less-skilled workers.

Multiple wars have also influenced the life routines of communities across the Mashriq since the mid-twentieth century. These conflicts range from low-intensity war marked by state terrorism and settler violence, confiscation of land and water, and constraints on the mobility of goods and labor in Palestine; to the prolonged effects of civil war in Lebanon and the destruction brought by warring against Israel in 1978, 1982, and 2006; to the carnage of the Iraq-Iran War of 1980–1988 and the disruption brought by the US-led sanctioning and invasion of Iraq after 1990. Both popular resistance and accommodation to wartime violence have agrarian effects, though these vary across the landscapes of war zones.

A third post-colonial influence is globalization. Like many other developing regions of the world, agricultural markets and producers have been exposed to both external investment as well as global competition. The net result has been to expose the most basic mechanisms of the agrarian economy – pricing, supply, and demand – to powerful forces. This *infitah* (opening) has been driven by the neoliberal ideology of Western donors and international financial institutions, as well as the efforts of a post-populist "state bourgeoisie" aligned with foreign investors (and in the conflict zones with warlords, mafias, and militia leaders) to reverse the effects of land reform and promote capitalist exploitation. Popular resistance to such neoliberalism is apparent in the growth of such social movements as the Palestinian Fair Trade movement, environmental activism in Lebanon, permaculture projects, and ecologically aware food movements.

In sum, the connections between landscape, empire, and food in the Mashriq are enduring. Here, four landscapes – the historically evolved one of accumulated environmental capital adapted to the local ecology, and of endowments held by the class of village-dwelling smallholders created by Ottoman, colonial, and populist land reforms; the oil landscape with its imported technologies and destructive urban sprawl; the war landscape with its persistent violence and displaced people; and the globalizing landscape of agribusiness, real estate speculation, and proliferating organizations – are overlaid together. They reveal the complex evolution of the region's agricultural systems and their impact on the rural economy, the environment, and contemporary lives.

RURAL-URBAN POPULATION DYNAMICS

Rural areas in the MENA have been changing rapidly for several generations. Some have been physically transformed into urban zones, as cities expand and absorb surrounding farmlands and less densely populated corridors. Intermediate cities have taken shape in the areas between and along the corridors linking rural and urban spaces – what are often called extra-urban or "exurbs" in Western parlance. Other rural areas remain less densely populated or outside designated metropolitan zones, but have experienced the encroachment of cities through the flow of goods, services, and remittances, and the adoption of behaviors and attitudes previously found in urban areas. Individuals may move back and forth between rural and urban expanses, from village to city and back again, blurring the line between the two. Many have one foot in the urban and another in the rural, creating hybrid social phenomena. Today, rural areas in the MENA are marked by net outflows of people and materials to urban growth centers. Cities act as a magnet, their opportunities and wealth attracting migrants and draining the human and cultural capital of villages. Rural areas also feed urban consumption, as food (and its constituent nutrients), water, quarried rock, and other materials are drawn to metropolitan centers. Urban areas may return some of these materials in the form of consumer goods or municipal waste; but as not all materials are returned, nutrient cycles become broken and many rural areas become resource sinks.

Still, the inescapable reality is that the MENA *has* rapidly urbanized over the past half century. However, if the region is becoming less rural in character, the rural population has not disappeared completely. Moreover, variation across the region means that the rural population remains significant and important, particularly in some high-population countries. In this section, statistical data is used to explore population dynamics in rural and urban areas to give some scope regarding the movement of peoples and its economic and social effects.

Rural population dynamics

The rural population in the MENA region has more than doubled in absolute terms since 1960, from 94 million in 1960 to 202 million in 2016

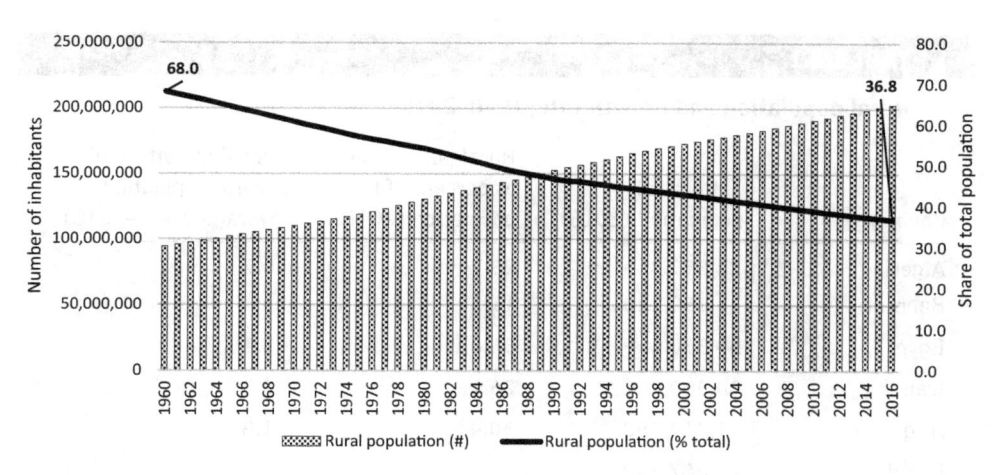

FIGURE 2.1

MENA – proportion of rural population over time, 1960–2016.

Source: World Bank (2018), *World Development Indicators.*

(Figure 2.1). This represents an average annual growth rate of 1.4 percent. However, the rural population has declined as a relative share of the total population, from 68.0 percent to 36.8 percent over that period. By comparison, the region is less rural (or more urban) than the world average, as the MENA's rural population as a share of the total fell below the global figure of 45.7 percent in 2016; but significantly more rural (i.e., less urban) than the developed OECD countries, for which the comparable figure stood at 19.5 percent.

Table 2.1 puts the MENA countries in further comparative perspective, enabling us to grasp not only their rural populations but also how much of their total national populations that rural inhabitants constitute, as well as their growth rate over time. The countries with the most significant rural populations as a proportion of the total population are Sudan, Yemen, and Egypt. In each country, more than half of the population still resides in rural areas. In essence, the most populous countries in the region are also home to the largest rural groups: the rural populations of Egypt, Sudan, Iran, Turkey, and Yemen were reported at 54.3 million, 26.1 million, 21.0 million, 20.8 million, and 17.9 million, respectively, in 2016. The average annual growth of the rural population over the period 1960–2016 ranged from a low of –0.6 percent (decline) in Lebanon – in fact the only country recording an absolute decline – to a high of 7.0 in the United Arab Emirates (Table 2.1).

TABLE 2.1

Rural population and growth rate, 1960–2016

Country	Total rural population (2016)	Rural population as percent of total population (2016)	Annual growth rate of rural population (average, 1960–2016)
Algeria	11,652,313	28.7	0.7
Bahrain	159,120	11.2	3.1
Egypt	54,330,119	56.8	2.1
Iran	20,969,267	26.1	0.7
Iraq	11,312,558	30.4	1.8
Israel	667,718	7.7	0.4
Jordan	1,521,911	16.1	2.1
Kuwait	66,543	1.6	0.6
Lebanon	725,966	12.1	−0.6
Libya	1,337,065	21.2	0.5
Mauritania	1,701,225	39.6	1.4
Morocco	13,869,068	39.3	0.9
Oman	969,554	21.9	1.3
Qatar	17,552	0.7	1.7
Saudi Arabia	5,380,034	16.7	1.2
Sudan	26,119,256	66	2.4
Syria	7,729,548	41.9	1.8
Tunisia	3,757,712	33	0.6
Turkey	20,763,080	26.1	0.2
United Arab Emirates	1,315,914	14.2	7.0
West Bank and Gaza Strip	1,115,998	24.5	2.1
Yemen	17,878,157	64.8	2.4

Source: World Bank (2018), *World Development Indicators.*

Yet when averaged across the region, rural growth rates simply cannot keep pace with the rate of urban population growth. Across the MENA, the average annual rate of rural population growth measured just 1.4 percent during 1960–2016, which explains why rural areas have shrunk drastically over time as a share of total population.

Urban population dynamics

The pace of urban population growth in the MENA region has exceeded that of its rural population in the past half-century, resulting in an increasing level of urbanization. In absolute terms, the total urban population has grown from 44 million in 1960 to 347 million in 2016, a nearly seven-fold increase over the period (Figure 2.2). The population living in urban areas has risen as a relative share of the total population in MENA from 32 percent to 63.2 percent over the period. In comparison to the world figure, the MENA was relatively less urban only until the mid-1960s, after which point its urban proportion has exceeded the global average.

The share of the population currently living in urban areas varies across MENA countries. Currently, the countries with the most urbanized populations include the Gulf countries of Qatar, Kuwait, Bahrain, and the United Arab Emirates, as well as Lebanon and Jordan: in these countries, all of which are geographically small in size, more than 80 percent of the population resides in urban areas. All MENA countries have observed an increase in the proportion of the population living in urban areas over the period 1960–2016 (Figure 2.3). The greatest increases were recorded in countries which began with a lower initial level of urbanization than others in the region, notably Oman (by 61.7 percentage points), Mauritania (53.6 percentage points), Saudi Arabia (52.1 percentage points), Libya (51.4 percentage

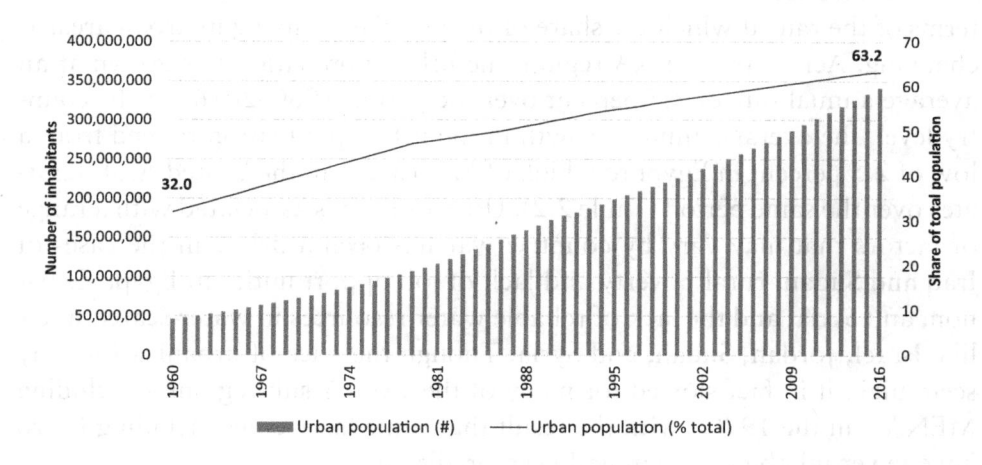

FIGURE 2.2
MENA – urban population, 1960–2016.

Source: World Bank (2018), *World Development Indicators*.

FIGURE 2.3
MENA – urban population as share of total population, 1960–2016.

Source: World Bank (2018), *World Development Indicators*.

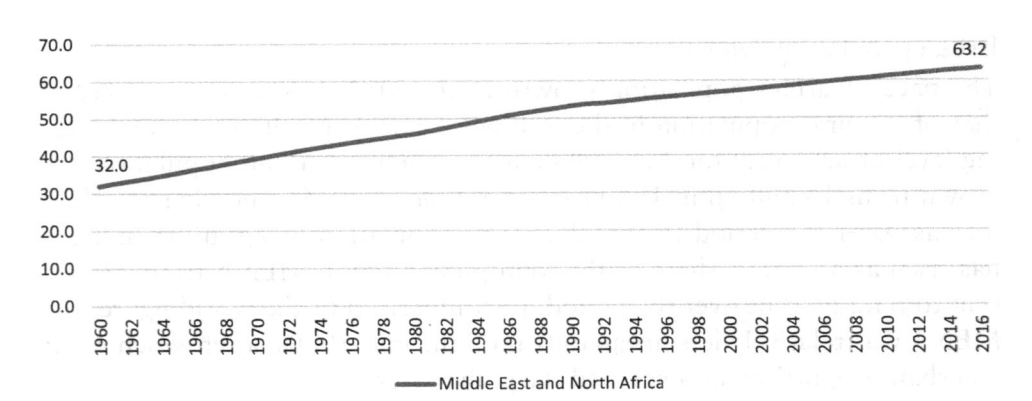

points), and Turkey (42.4 percentage points). By contrast, Egypt, which remains among the least urbanized countries in the MENA region, recorded the smallest increase in urbanization over this period (5.4 percentage points). However, according to the United Nations' Department of Economic and Social Affairs, the population of *every* MENA country will become more than 50 percent urban by 2050.

Urbanization can be measured not only in terms of level, but also in terms of the rate at which the share of the population living in urban areas is changing. Across the MENA region, the urban population has grown at an average annual rate of 3.7 percent over the period 1960–2016. At the country level, the average annual growth in the urban population ranged from a low of 2.5 percent in Egypt to a high of 8.5 percent in the United Arab Emirates over the same period (Table 2.2). Urbanization is associated with a range of factors that may vary by country: war has been a driver in the cases of Iraq and Sudan; rural poverty and lack of job opportunities in Egypt, Lebanon, and Syria; and the lack of reliable water resources in water-scarce states like Israel, Jordan, Sudan, and Syria. Though the pace of urbanization may seem high, it in fact slowed for many of the world's sub-regions – including MENA – in the 1990s, with the result that some large cities including Cairo have fewer inhabitants than had been predicted.

The extent of urbanization can further be considered in terms of the size (actual number of inhabitants) of cities. For example, while Egypt is generally less urbanized than other countries, some 23 million of its people still

TABLE 2.2

Average annual urban population growth rate, 1960–2016

Country	Urban population growth rate (average annual percent change, 1960–2016)
Algeria	3.9
Bahrain	4.0
Egypt	2.5
Iran	3.7
Iraq	3.8
Israel	3.9
Jordan	5.1
Kuwait	6.3
Lebanon	3.5
Libya	4.5
Mauritania	6.8
Morocco	3.7
Oman	3.2
Qatar	6.5
Saudi Arabia	7.4
Sudan	5.5
Syria	5.1
Tunisia	3.3
Turkey	2.8
United Arab Emirates	3.4
West Bank and Gaza Strip	8.5
Yemen	3.6

Source: World Bank (2018), *World Development Indicators*.

live in major urban centers – almost all of them in Cairo (Table 2.3). Conversely, the largest cities in Bahrain and the Palestinian territories (West Bank and Gaza Strip) – each country significantly more urbanized than Egypt in terms of total population – are home to less than one million people.

Finally, urbanization may be reflected in the concentration of population in large cities, and indeed the MENA's population living in large urban

TABLE 2.3

Population living in urban agglomerations and single largest city, 2016

Country	Population living in urban areas with at least one million people	Population of single largest city
Algeria	2,632,469	2,632,469
Bahrain	0	425,062
Egypt	23,990,781	19,127,890
Iran	21,168,007	8,515,571
Iraq	11,841,899	6,810,608
Israel	4,915,270	901,302*
Jordan	1,159,493	1,159,493
Kuwait	2,873,896	2,873,896
Lebanon	2,262,936	2,262,936
Libya	1,128,104	1,128,104
Mauritania	0	990,342
Morocco	7,912,718	3,544,498
Oman	0	865,547
Qatar	0	734,407
Saudi Arabia	14,887,781	6,539,712
Sudan	5,264,922	5,264,922
Syria	9,219,158	3,641,048
Tunisia	2,010,125	2,010,125
Turkey	30,053,995	14,365,329
United Arab Emirates	5,014,712	2,503,700
West Bank and Gaza Strip	0	641,809
Yemen	3,094,124	3,094,124

Source: World Bank (2018), *World Development Indicators*; * includes occupied East Jerusalem.

centers is also growing over time. As of 2016, an estimated 26.3 percent of the region's total population lived in urban areas of more than one million people, which represents a near doubling (by proportion) since 1960. Again, this figure varies widely by country. Approximately 70.9 percent of Kuwaitis but only 6.5 percent of Algerians live in urban areas of at least one million people. In the cases of Bahrain, Mauritania, Oman, Qatar, the West Bank and Gaza, their largest cities (Manama, Nouakchott, Muscat, Doha, and Gaza City, respectively) have populations of less than one million people; therefore, Table 2.3 should be interpreted as zero percent of the population from those countries living in urban areas (including cities and their immediate metropolitan environments) containing more than one million people.

Among the region's 30 largest cities, the World Economic Forum has identified three types that have an important role in shaping urban life in the region: mega-cities, international cities, and hub cities. First, mega-cities are those distinguished by a significant influence on the region thanks to their large population, including Cairo, Istanbul, Riyadh, Baghdad, and Tehran. Their size allows them to act as regional economic drivers, even if their business regulation, infrastructure, and/or soft connectivity (i.e., culture, community, or technologies) remain underdeveloped. Second, international cities like Dubai and Doha are somewhat smaller, and are distinguished less by their traditional status as major population centers and more by their development of advanced, accountable, and competent governance systems, which foster economic success and serve to attract foreign businesses and workers. Third, hub cities such as Amman and Beirut serve a different function: they are gateways to neighboring economies, offering a combination of reasonable business regulation and working infrastructure that facilitate trade and logistics, but whose limitations also prevent them from becoming major international cities or mega-cities.

Rural-urban and national income classifications: who is poor?

In general, rural areas across the developing world tend to be poorer than urban ones. The MENA region fits well into this pattern. Using data from 2016, let us classify these countries into groups according to their relative level of urbanization *and* income, measured as Gross National Income (GNI) per capita. GNI differs slightly from GDP in that the former also includes the incomes, remittances, and value of citizens working abroad. This produces three categories on the rural side: largely rural (more than 50 percent of the population living in rural areas); moderately rural (20–50 percent of the population living in rural areas); or minimally rural (less than 20 percent of the population living in rural areas in 2016). Next, let us divide all countries into four categories of development – low-income (GNI per capita of $995 or less), lower-middle income (between $996 and $3,895), upper-middle income (between $3,895 and $12,055), and high-income ($12,056 or more). This corresponds to how the World Bank classifies countries in terms

TABLE 2.4

Rural populations vs. income levels

	Low income	Lower-middle income	Upper-middle income	High income
Largely rural (>50 percent)	Yemen	Egypt Sudan		
Moderately rural (20–50 percent)	Syria	Mauritania Morocco Tunisia West Bank and Gaza Strip	Algeria Iran Iraq Libya Turkey	Oman
Minimally rural (<20 percent)			Jordan Lebanon	Bahrain Israel Kuwait Qatar Saudi Arabia United Arab Emirates

Sources: World Bank (2018), *World Development Indicators*; World Bank (2018), *World Bank Country and Lending Groups*.

of income level. The result (Table 2.4) is self-evident: all else being equal, urbanization is correlated with income and development. The most rural countries in the region are also the poorest.

RURAL AREAS, AGRARIAN TRANSFORMATION, AND EXCLUSION

Beyond statistics, it is critical that we also unpack social conditions within rural areas, in particular the role of agriculture.

Agricultural employment and value-added

Though modern agriculture was birthed in the Middle East, the region's contemporary physical environment struggles with conditions that make sustained farming difficult in most areas – chronic water shortage, climatic uncertainty, fragile ecologies, and environmental degradation. Seasonal aridity results in parched landscapes, with rainfall less than 100 mm/year across half the region. The low availability of fresh water severely curtails human well-being and security: 17 of 21 countries rank below what international authorities call the "water poverty" threshold, or when a person has access to less than 1,000 cubic meters of water yearly (also known as conditions of water scarcity). The geopolitics of water is critical as most water resources are shared and/or located in conflict zones. Indeed, Egypt, Iraq, Mauritania, Sudan, and Syria depend on rivers and lakes that cross their borders for at least 70 percent of their water needs.

Droughts occur frequently. Historically, droughts have been linked to migration, conflicts, and ecological decline. In recent times, droughts have been exacerbated by greater climatic variability, and prevailing climate change models of global warming suggest an aggravation of droughts and less predictable rainfall in the coming decades. In terms of topology, half the MENA region consists of mountainous land, with thin, calcareous soils and sparse tree cover. Such areas are often too dry for rain-fed farming, and have either been converted to irrigated agriculture supported by pumping water from fossil aquifers located deep underground, or else have been abandoned as agrarian wastelands. The flat grasslands of the steppe cover nearly a third of the region, and once hosted extensive nomadic pastoralism by Bedouin tribes and other groups – a lifestyle which, due to agricultural change and urbanization, has greatly diminished since the 1960s. Camels are often invoked in the popular imagination as the symbol of tribal nomadism (Photo 2.1). An equally productive animal to anchor pastoral economies was the sheep, which scattered rural communities across the Maghrib and Mashriq still utilize for subsistence living (Photo 2.2).

Despite these burdens, farming (and to a far lesser degree, pastoralism) is still important to the livelihoods of many people. For example, agriculture employed nearly 29 million individuals in the MENA as of 2013 (Table 2.5). The region reported an absolute increase in the number of agricultural workers from 2000 to 2013, which was the combined result of rapid population growth and persistence of labor-intensive agriculture, such as the manual picking and harvesting of crops and fruit. However, in following with the trend of ever-rising urbanization, the share of labor within the agricultural sector is declining – a pattern that, according to all authorities that track employment figures like the International Labor Organization (ILO), will continue to diminish for the foreseeable future. The World Bank, whose data are also frequently consulted, also chart this decline: in 1991, 25 percent of all workers in the MENA were employed in agriculture, but in 2017 this had reduced to 18.5 percent, and continues a downward trend. This compounds the overall regional problem of unemployment and relative deprivation that

PHOTO 2.1
Camels and desert in Wadi Rum, Jordan, 2016.

Source: Public domain.
Online: https://pixabay.com/en/camel-wadi-rum-desert-travel-1120371/

PHOTO 2.2
Bedouin herding small sheep flock, 2010.

Source: Public domain.
Online: https://pixabay.com/en/desert-bedouin-goat-mammal-249143/

TABLE 2.5

Employment in the agricultural sector, selected years

Region	Total employment (millions)				Agriculture as share of total employment (percent)			
	2000	2007	2012	2013	2000	2007	2012	2013
Middle East	9.5	10.5	9.9	10.1	22.9	18.6	14.9	14.8
North Africa	15.0	18.0	18.3	18.6	33.8	32.6	30.1	30.0
World	1056.5	1038.1	990.9	1001.4	40.4	35.3	31.9	31.8

Source: ILO (2014), *Global Employment Trends 2014: Risk of a Jobless Recovery?*

Chapter 5 explains; of all the sectors that could generate more jobs to absorb the booming and youthful labor force, agriculture is not one of them.

Within the regional decline of agrarian employment, however, there is considerable variation in its importance across countries. Figure 2.4 presents national-level employment in agriculture, with the floating numbers representing 2017 figures. Employment in the agricultural sector ranged from a high of 75.9 percent of total employment in Mauritania to a low of less than 1 percent in the United Arab Emirates in 2017. Notably, agriculture continues to employ more than a third of the work force in Morocco, Yemen, Sudan, and Mauritania. The overall value added from agriculture as a share of total Gross Domestic Product (GDP), roughly corresponding to how much total economic value is gained from agricultural activities across the entire economy, has fallen in relative terms across the MENA. According to the World Bank, agricultural value added for the entire regional economy has fallen from a high of 46.6 percent in 1962 to just 9 percent in 2017. This confirms our earlier argument: although rural populations and agricultural activity persist, the overall impact of agriculture in terms of workers employed and economic value has diminished over time.

Colonial legacies and agricultural distribution

Agricultural land, or land that could be theoretically used for farming and other agrarian cultivation, accounts for approximately 33.7 percent of the MENA's total land area. Arable land – land actually being worked,

CHAPTER 2 Social life, from rural to urban

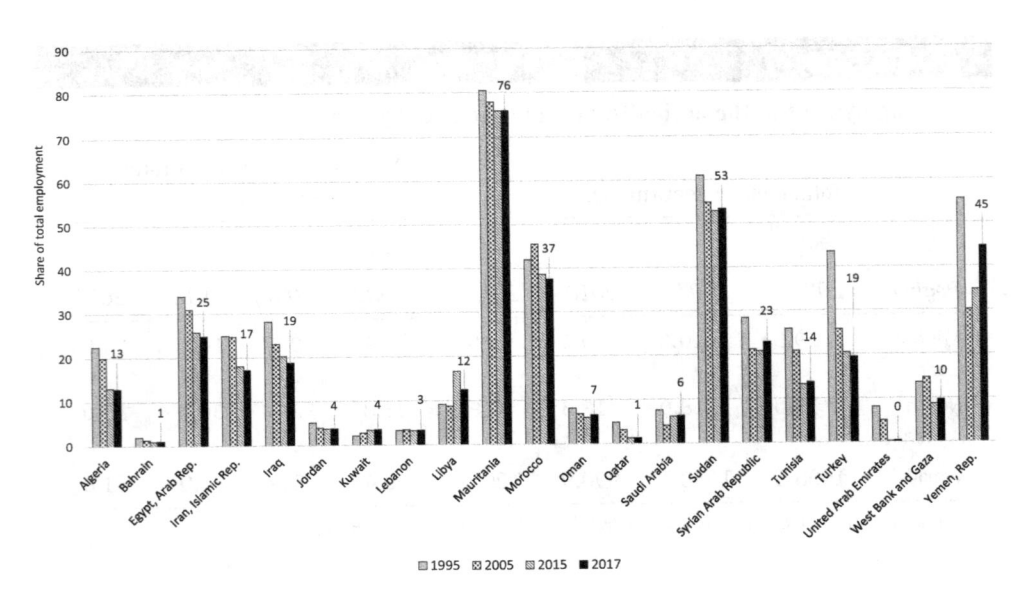

FIGURE 2.4
Employment in agriculture, selected years, 1995–2017.

Source: World Bank (2018), *World Development Indicators*.

ploughed, and harvested on a regular basis for crops, meadows, and gardens – accounted for 6.1 percent.

Ownership and distribution of agricultural land are uneven in MENA, a result of the historical legacies of colonialism and the reversal of the post-independence agrarian reforms with consequences that persist to this day. A major legacy of colonialism in countries with significant agricultural land areas, such as Egypt, Algeria, Iraq, and Syria, was extreme inequality in terms of land tenure, meaning the ownership and use of land. Until the 1950s and beyond, the majority of arable land (variously divided into plots, estates, and holdings) in such environs was controlled by a small wealthy elite class of landlords who were closely allied to the government. Most people working in this sector, including on these vast estates, were fellahin – landless peasants or sharecroppers whose lives were heavily dependent upon the landed elite and political authorities. After the demise of Western imperialism, military coups and political changes resulted in the installation of new republican regimes intending to reverse past trends of inequality. Such governments enacted radical agrarian reforms in the name of social and economic justice, such as the redistribution of rural lands to the fellahin and stronger property rights protections for small farmers. This heralded the demise of the landed elite and a shift in political emphasis upon the masses, as these regimes sought to legitimate themselves by directly appealing to, and sometimes incorporating, these new popular actors.

Such radical schemes did not occur everywhere, and, where they did occur, were not always successful. Land reform was, and continues to be, a complex policy scheme that requires technical expertise, economic planning, and political commitment. One indisputable legacy, however, is the end of vast landed estates owned by a traditional elite of near-feudal landlords. Today, if we count the number of farms, we find most are small. Table 2.6 illustrates this.

As Table 2.6 shows, smallholder agriculture practiced on farms of less than two hectares (roughly, five acres) accounts for approximately 95 percent of all farms by number (not by land area) in Egypt, 87 percent of all farms in Lebanon, 86 percent of all farms in Jordan, and 84 percent of all farms in Yemen. Photo 2.3, for instance, depicts a typical small-size farm in Aswan, in southern Egypt near the banks of the Nile, distinguished by irregular plot size and the modest perimeter of the housing unit and field. However, overall, small farms account for a limited share of total land that is farmed: only in Egypt did small farms of less than two hectares comprise more than 50 percent of agricultural land. The largest gaps between the number of small farms and the share of land they compose are observed in Qatar, Jordan, Yemen, Iran, and Lebanon. For example, small farms of less than two hectares accounted for 74 percent of all farms in Qatar, but occupied only 2 percent of the total agricultural land area. It should be noted that Qatar is an exceptional case: as a tiny peninsular kingdom jutting into the Arabian Gulf, its scarce arable land is dominated by government-owned or government-supported farms.

Urbanization of rural areas

Rural areas across MENA are changing not only as a result of agrarian transformation and shifting patterns of economic activity, but also as a result of interactions with urban areas. These interactions occur in at least three different ways. First, rural areas may become urbanized as a result of the physical expansion of cities. Many of the region's largest metropolitan areas, such as Cairo, have relentlessly expanded into nearby areas (including open deserts) for decades given the congestion and housing shortages found in its traditionally centralized areas. The Cairene experience is telling: many of these half-built areas around the city are sparsely populated – the

TABLE 2.6

Select MENA countries – distribution of farms and agricultural land, by farm size, 2016

	Algeria		Egypt		Iran		Jordan		Lebanon		Libya		Morocco		Qatar		Turkey		Yemen	
	% all farms	% total agri. land	% all farms	% total agri. land	% all farms	% total agri. land	% all farms	% total agri. land	% all farms	% total agri. land	% all farms	% total agri. land	% all farms	% total agri. land	% all farms	% total agri. land	% all farms	% total agri. land	% all farms	% total agri. land
<2 Ha	0.34	0.03	0.95	0.55	0.60	0.06	0.86	0.26	0.87	0.35	0.25	**	0.44	0.07	0.74	0.02	0.35	0.05	0.84	0.26
2–5 Ha	0.23	0.09	0.04	0.18	0.18	0.13	0.07	0.15	0.10	0.25	0.25	**	0.28	0.17	0.06	0.02	0.31	0.16	0.09	0.18
5–10 Ha	0.18	0.14	0.01	0.09	0.11	0.18	0.04	0.15	0.02	0.09	0.23	**	0.17	0.22	0.04	0.02	0.18	0.21	0.07	0.56
10–50 Ha	0.23	0.52	0.00	0.17	0.10	0.43	0.02	0.27	0.01	0.21	0.26	**	0.12	0.39	0.10	0.21	0.16	0.47	-	-
50–100 Ha	0.01	0.11	-	-	0.01	0.09	0.00	0.07	0.00	0.09	0.00	**	0.01	0.07	0.03	0.18	0.01	0.06	-	-
100–500 Ha	0.01	0.12	-	-	0.00	0.08	0.00	0.11	-	-	0.00	**	0.00	0.09	0.02	0.55	0.00	0.03	-	-
>500 Ha	-	-	-	-	-	0.03	-	-	-	-	-	**	-	-	-	-	-	0.02	-	-

Source: Authors' calculations based on Sarah Lowder, Jakob Skoet, and Terri Raney, "The Number, Size, and Distribution of Farms, Smallholder Farms, and Family Farms Worldwide," *World Development* 87 (2016): 16–19. ** denotes no available data.

PHOTO 2.3
Small farm in Aswan, Egypt, 2012.

Source: iStock.
Online: www.istockphoto.com/photo/villages-near-aswan-in-egypt-gm564573992-99005299

product of inflated prices, poor transportation, road mismanagement, and overall absence of land-use planning. It is not coincidental that, in 2018, the Egyptian government announced it would simply build a new capital city altogether nearly 30 miles away from the old city center – an extraordinary solution that suggested that officials had simply given up in reorganizing and upgrading their existing infrastructure and preferred instead to start anew.

In other contexts, such disorganized expansion converts agricultural lands to non-agricultural uses (such as real estate development or industry). Paradoxically, because urban centers often grew in areas with conditions well suited to agriculture such as fertile soils and access to water, this expansion can affect a country's most productive agricultural lands. This has perverse downstream effects: as cities squeeze agriculture from some land, farming in other areas may become more intensive, and thus draw more upon scarce water and other resources.

Incursion of urban areas into the rural space can also occur through a second channel. As transport and communication infrastructure improve, the non-agricultural workforce (i.e., those employed in industry and services) may find it increasingly feasible to live in smaller urban centers or rural areas. These improvements also foster investment in rural areas. Social life in rural areas may become more like that in urban areas, given the easier exchange of goods, services, information, and ideas. Third and finally, domestic incomes and foreign remittances also link urban and rural populations. Many households rely on diversified livelihoods rooted in both rural and urban spaces, generated by multiple individuals engaged in different economic activities but sharing common resources and assets. For instance, a large rural family in Egypt or Morocco may have some relatives employed abroad and others working in Cairo or Casablanca – remittances that can then be saved and invested for their agricultural enterprise. Households can be thereby multi-local.

FOOD IN AN EVOLVING SOCIETY

Given its centrality to social life in both rural and urban settings, food merits special consideration. Issues of food security, food production, and agrarian decline have serious economic and political implications as well. Indeed, food security and food systems in urban environments can be ostensibly linked to political unrest and even revolution. While the connection between food security and environmental degradation is explored in greater detail in Chapter 7, the relationship between agrarian decline and urbanization as structural factors (rather than outside dynamics, like climate change) deserves discussion here.

Food security, food production, and agrarian decline

As defined by the UN and other international agencies, food security means a condition in which all people enjoy physical, social, and economic access to sufficiently nutritious and safe food sources that meet their dietary needs. This is a complex outcome determined by a number of factors. One of the principal factors is agricultural production, which itself is a result of ecological conditions and physical geography (including hydrology, topography, and soil composition). A second factor is the political economy, including both the responsiveness of political institutions and economic opportunities, that shape people's access to a nutritious and healthy diet. Today, both factors combine in the MENA to result in a severe challenge: agricultural production is generally unable to meet local food demand. The region is highly dependent upon imported food, particularly cereals; for this reason, most Arab countries import 50 percent or more of the calories that they consume.

Why is a landscape that as recently as World War Two was capable of meeting local needs now unable to feed its growing population? That is, why has food security worsened over time? A few reasons may provide insight here. First, at the biophysical level, insufficient agricultural production is due to a combination of population growth, limited rain-fed farmland, fragile irrigation systems in areas marked by saline soils, endemic disease, and civil strife. Second, in terms of political economy, the region's agrarian decline has been variously described as the result of market-driven adjustments to water and land resource endowments; a rational adaptation to the presence and effects of oil resources within some countries; a consequence of the loss of agricultural land to urban development; and an outcome of political factors, including the continued subordination of rural laborers, village communities, and agricultural voices to political elites in authoritarian states.

There are other forces, as well, that have weakened the MENA's agrarian environment. These include the current pattern of international agricultural investments; a persistent policy bias towards urban consumers; the impact of oil and remittances on land values and their distribution for rural and urban use; and a general assumption on part of governments that land and property should be geared towards bureaucracy, industry, and commodities – not the traditional ecologies of local producers, such as nomads and fellahin.

Today, those MENA countries that are considered the most rural – Egypt, Sudan, and Yemen – have not yet passed through the agrarian transformation seen in the oil-rich countries, or the transition from an agriculturally based economy to a highly industrialized one with a vibrant services sector. Countries experience and cope with the agrarian transformation and decline differently, depending on their natural resource endowments and whether or not their economy is principally based on fossil fuel extraction. The path of agrarian change is also conditioned by the legacies of colonial domination and the systems of land tenure they produced. The patterns of local governance that crystallized after independence starting in the 1950s also play a key role. Accordingly, the social conditions of agrarian populations (whether peasants or pastoralists, fellahin or Bedouin) may differ from country to country, as does the degree of food security and dependence on food imports. For most countries, however, it is clear that food security will become increasingly dependent on food imports.

Governments and societies disregard this dependency at their own risk. While prolonged food insecurity can result in malnutrition and other devastating social effects, even short-term fluctuations in food security can have strong consequences. In the MENA, variations in food prices have often resulted in conflicts and instability. Long before the Arab Spring, for instance, the shock of suddenly rising food prices caused explosive riots from citizenries that suddenly found themselves struggling to purchase basic necessities such as bread, because governments no longer had the financial resources to subsidize the otherwise high cost of wheat. Indeed, bread riots occurred in Morocco (1981, 1984), Egypt (1977, 1984), Jordan (1989, 1996), Tunisia (1984), and Lebanon (1987). Rising food prices were also linked to the popular uprisings of the Arab Spring, as the basic struggle to secure enough food amidst heightening living costs in other areas motivated many protesters.

Food security and food systems in urban areas

If MENA countries are increasingly reliant on food imports to meet their food demands, they must rely upon rising global agricultural production to meet their increasing aggregate demand. Where food insecurity persists, it is principally the result of insufficient incomes and uneven distribution. The urban poor are particularly vulnerable to rapid increases in food prices. Non-income factors including inadequate infrastructure, substandard housing, failing basic services (especially water and sanitation), and exposure to environmental hazards like pollution also contribute to food insecurity and malnutrition in urban contexts, both globally and in MENA.

BOX 2.1 CASE STUDY – CAIRENE FOOD INSECURITY

Egypt's experience is a seminal case of how a rapidly urbanized and youth-driven society has struggled with food security for generations. Low-income households in Cairo's informal and slum settlements use their daily wages to directly shop for food on a daily basis, buying smaller quantities from higher-priced local shops and street vendors. Those markets and supermarkets offering lower-priced food are located far from their neighborhoods. Coincidentally, this is not peculiar to Egypt: even in American cities like Chicago, Detroit, and New Orleans, "food deserts" can afflict urban poverty pockets, thereby perpetuating conditions of insecurity. Furthermore, Cairene households with limited storage space and lacking a refrigerator may be less able to buy food in bulk at lower prices. As a result, residents

> **BOX 2.1 (CONTINUED)**
>
> of Cairo's informal and slum settlements may pay more for food than residents of wealthier neighborhoods – even as they are least able to afford it. The result is a paradoxical combination of undernutrition and overnutrition. Regarding the former, the dangers of food shortages for the urban poor become most acute when it occurs through slow-moving malnutrition which, unlike large-scale disasters like famines, typically do not warrant the attention of humanitarian organizations. Though hard and reliable data are difficult to find, it is understood that rates of stunting and other signs of nutritional deficiencies have markedly risen among poor Egyptian children under the age of five since the 1990s. Yet the latter phenomenon of overnutrition is increasingly garnering alarm as well given the skyrocketing rates of diabetes – over 15 percent as of 2017, according to the World Health Organization. The reason for the latter is that many struggling families rely too much upon cheap street food or else government-subsidized commodities, resulting in diets extremely high in breads, rice, oil, and other high-calorie but nutrient-poor edibles.

Well-established evidence from across the Global South indicates that higher levels of urbanization are associated with higher incomes and with greater demand for meat, dairy products, vegetable oils, and luxury, processed, and prepared foods. These foods, in turn, are associated with more energy-intensive production and (for many countries) a rising level of food imports. Supermarkets and international food companies hence play an increasing role in meeting this demand, and can introduce changes along the food chain. For example, supermarkets tend to favor larger producers and processors over smaller-scale local producers, such as the family-owned farm. Employment along the food chain tends to shift, with fewer direct producers and more individuals working for the conglomerates that control the processing, wholesaling, retailing, transport, and distribution of food. Studies of the "supermarketization" process in MENA are few, but what evidence we have suggests that this process is indeed affecting food retailing patterns and entire food chains in countries throughout the region. This transformation takes root in urban centers, typically the largest city in each country (e.g., Cairo in Egypt, Casablanca in Morocco, Amman in Jordan), and then gradually penetrating outwards to affect smaller cities and rural areas.

Another direct outcome of urbanization is the shattering of nutrient cycles, one of the pillars of ecosystem integrity. Food harvested from agrarian landscapes is eaten by urbanites in cities that do not have organic linkages to those agricultural lands. Unconsumed or undigested produce such as fruits and vegetables are termed waste, and disposed of – often at great financial and ecological costs – in locations or forms that make it unsalvageable. The nutrients embedded therein exit the system. This failure to close the nutrient cycle also contributes to the impoverishment of soils and reduces water-use efficiency, with deleterious impacts on agricultural yields. Nutrients must then be replaced by their synthetic equivalent, increasing the cost of food production. This process, known as the metabolic rift, is a by-product of the urban-driven food regime in which the consumption is the principal goal with little regard for the mode of production.

Patterns of consumption also have feedback effects onto agriculture. Diets and farming systems evolve simultaneously. As the nutritional transition from traditional diets to Western-type diets takes place in the developing world, farming systems become commodity-oriented, specialized, and less diverse in order to satisfy commercial imperatives. For instance, they may find it more profitable to specialize in a very few products in high demand by major food corporations or international restaurant chains. As a result, even in the MENA, the diet of even rural communities engaged in agriculture are no longer dominated by the foods they produce. Although physically located in the rural world, they have exited the natural cycle and have become alienated from the fruits of their labor.

SOCIOECONOMIC CONDITIONS IN RURAL AND URBAN AREAS

These preceding dynamics, from the historical experience of rural populations to the food struggles of urbanites, highlight unique challenges to the MENA. To further scrutinize this topic – the intersection of economics and social life, or the socioeconomic conditions of everyday life – it is fruitful to compare rural versus urban experience. Certainly, the rapid growth of urban areas has resulted in inadequate housing, infrastructure, and services in many countries. A comparison of living conditions generally reveals, however, a higher standard in urban than rural areas: all else being equal, the average urban neighborhood offers inhabitants better living conditions as a result of economies of scale and proximity to infrastructure and services. The upshot is that socioeconomic inequality not only exists but is persistent.

Living conditions in urban areas

The combination of natural population growth in cities and the influx of individuals from other areas – whether in search of employment or to escape crisis and conflict – has raised pressure on public services (education, health care), infrastructure (roads, lighting, electricity, water and sanitation, waste management), and housing. Even during periods of rapid economic growth, many governments have struggled to meet the needs of ever-expanding cities, a problem that must be juxtaposed against existing deficiencies and environmental fragility.

Housing costs are a major dilemma in the largest MENA urban areas. The high price of land, poor public land management, and rising residential and commercial demand combine to push the ceiling for rents and property prices far above middle-class families. Critically, this is not simply an Arab problem. In Israel, the nearly 150,000 young protesters that demonstrated for social justice in July 2011 demanded, among other things, affordable housing opportunities. In the Arab world, the problem of scarce affordable and safe housing is especially deleterious because it forces many individuals to live in slum conditions. The UN defines urban slums as areas whose inhabitants lack one or more of the following basic provisions: durable and permanent housing that can protect residents against extreme climate conditions; sufficient living space; easy access to safe freshwater; access to adequate sanitation, including usable toilets; and secure tenure or property rights that protect against forced eviction. Photo 2.4 shows a dilapidated slum block in Cairo; note the garbage and crumbling buildings, which still have human habitation despite being disconnected from the major infrastructural grid of the city.

Table 2.7 illustrates the share of urban populations in MENA countries that live in slum conditions. The statistical data vary considerably, but alarmingly high figures are noted for Sudan, Yemen, Oman, and Lebanon. In addition, data are missing for a number of countries though for very different reasons. Housing and urban data for the Palestinian territories of the West Bank and Gaza Strip, for instance, tend to be poor or missing. By contrast, the tiny but wealthy kingdoms of the Arabian Gulf littoral, such as Qatar and Kuwait, are typified by prosperous urban areas whose citizens generally do not live in slum-like conditions comparable to larger, less hydrocarbon-dependent states like Egypt, Morocco, or Jordan. However, these small Gulf kingdoms also host large populations of foreign workers, many of whom live in poorer conditions than citizens – but are also not well counted or serviced by these governments.

Although living conditions remain poor for millions, this is not purely the result of urbanization. Rather, this stems from entrenched inequalities accumulated across the colonial and post-colonial era, and the failure of

PHOTO 2.4
Cairo slum, high view, 2014.

Source: iStock.

Online: www.istockphoto.com/photo/cairo-dirt-and-garbage-gm492599825-40231544

TABLE 2.7

Urban population living in slums, 2014

Country	Population living in slums (percent of total urban population)
Algeria	11.8
Bahrain	**
Egypt	10.6
Iran	30.3
Iraq	47.2
Israel	**
Jordan	12.9
Kuwait	**
Lebanon	53.1

(Continued)

Libya	35.2
Mauritania	**
Morocco	13.1
Oman	60.5
Qatar	**
Saudi Arabia	18.0
Sudan	91.6
Syria	19.3
Tunisia	8.0
Turkey	11.3
United Arab Emirates	**
West Bank and Gaza Strip	**
Yemen	60.8

Source: World Bank (2018), *World Development Indicators.* ** denotes no available data.

government policies and social reform to keep up with the pace of rural decline.

Income and poverty in rural and urban areas

The highest proportion of the rural population falling below the national poverty line (which varies per country) is found in Mauritania, Sudan, and Yemen, where rates exceed 40 percent (Table 2.8). Similarly, a significant proportion of the urban population falls below the national poverty line in a number of countries, notably more than 25 percent in Sudan, Syria, and the Palestinian territories. These figures should be interpreted with caution, however, as official statistics tend to underestimate urban poverty, making inadequate allowances for the cost of non-food expenditures faced by low-income residents (housing, schools, health care). A lack of data makes it difficult to assess living conditions consistently across countries.

Given the discussion and data in this chapter thus far, it should not be surprising that there is more poverty among rural than urban populations. Additional measures confirm this, however. For example, the United Nations Development Programme's annual *Human Development Report* indicated in its 2016 iteration that 29 percent of the rural population in Arab states lived in *multidimensional* poverty – defined as deprivation in terms of not just

TABLE 2.8

Rural and urban populations living in poverty, 2014–2017 (latest available year)

Country	Rural population living in poverty (percent of rural population)	Urban population living in poverty (percent of urban population)
Algeria	4.8	5.8
Bahrain	**	**
Egypt	32.3	15.3
Iran	**	**
Iraq	30.6	14.8
Israel	**	**
Jordan	16.8	13.9
Kuwait	**	**
Lebanon	**	**
Libya	**	**
Mauritania	59.4	20.8
Morocco	14.4	4.8
Oman	**	**
Qatar	**	**
Saudi Arabia	**	**
Sudan	57.6	26.5
Syria	36.9	30.8
Tunisia	**	**
Turkey	6.8	0.6
United Arab Emirates	**	**
West Bank and Gaza Strip	19.4	26.1
Yemen	40.1	20.7

Source: World Bank (2018), *World Development Indicators*. ** denotes no available data, or else negligible amounts.

income and living conditions, but also health and education. Access to education also varies across rural and urban areas: for example, the likelihood of school attendance is lower in rural than urban areas in Egypt, Morocco, and Tunisia. The same holds for health care. In Sudan, for instance, the use of prenatal care was reported to be five times greater by urban than rural women in the mid-2000s. This also accords with global patterns; in general, urban health facilities provide better care than rural facilities around the world. Moreover, as Chapter 9's exploration of gender inequities elucidates, patriarchal subordination due to conservative norms is much more prevalent in rural areas than urban ones.

Access to services and infrastructure in rural and urban areas

Access to infrastructure including electricity, sanitation facilities, and adequate water sources reveal further disparity between urban and rural areas. While most MENA countries offer universal or near-universal access to education, the few that lag behind also exhibit a distinctive pattern. In Libya, Sudan, and Yemen, rural access to electricity measures less than urban access. The same holds with water. The World Bank defines access to basic drinking water as water obtained from an improved source (including piped water, boreholes or tube wells, protected dug wells, protected springs, and packaged or delivered water), provided collection time is not more than 30 minutes for a round trip – rural populations have less access than urban populations with the exception of Turkey, United Arab Emirates, and the Palestinian territories (Figure 2.5). The gaps between urban and rural access

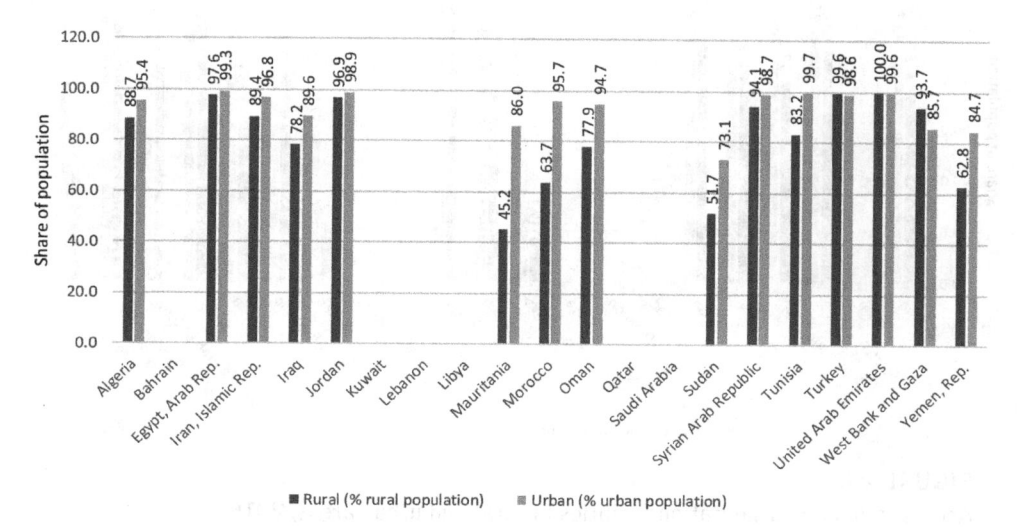

FIGURE 2.5
Access to basic drinking water services in rural and urban areas, 2016.

Source: World Bank (2018), *World Development Indicators*.

to basic drinking water services are widest in Mauritania, Morocco, Yemen, and Sudan. Data are missing for some countries (e.g., Lebanon, Libya) or marginal for others given the tiny size of the agricultural sector (e.g., Kuwait, Bahrain).

Access to basic sanitation facilities provides another measure of divergence between rural and urban populations. The World Bank defines this as the ability to regularly use improved sanitation facilities that are not shared with other households in which waste is taken away and treated off-site through flushable or pump-flush latrines, piped sewer systems, septic tanks, and composting toilets. Here, rural populations suffer from far lower access as compared to urban populations in every country for which data is available except Iraq and the Palestinian territories (Figure 2.6). The gaps are most significant in Yemen, Mauritania, and Sudan.

Rural reactions to urban bias

Strong currents of discontent are found in rural areas throughout the MENA. Such communities suffer social, economic, and political marginalization, and thus often express negative reactions against the perceived urban bias

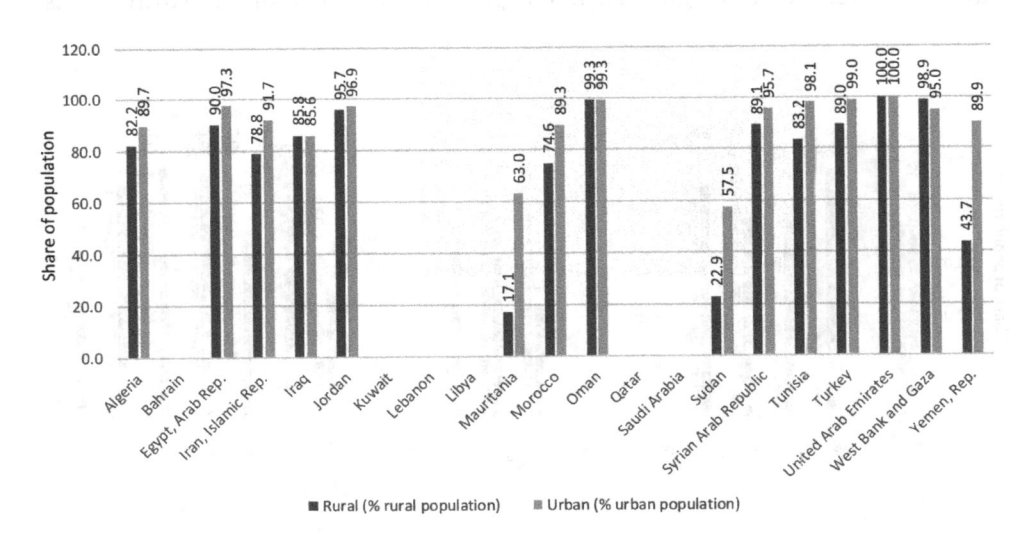

FIGURE 2.6
Access to improved sanitation facilities in rural and urban areas, 2016.

Source: World Bank (2018), *World Development Indicators*.

in which towns and cities generally enjoy better social and living conditions. Historically, such discontent is manifested as opposition to the central government, criticism of the urban liberal elite, and resistance against capitalism. In the current day, it is no coincidence that peripheral rural regions often incubate popular mobilization and uprisings, from the Rif of Morocco to the tribal south of Jordan to the Sa'da region of northern Yemen, where the Houthi rebellion was birthed. Indeed, the 2011–2012 Arab Spring began with Tunisia's Jasmine Revolution, whose spark was not unrest in the capital of Tunis located near the urbanized coastal region but rather the impoverished town of Sidi Bouzid, located nearly 300 kilometers south in the heart of the rural interior of the country.

MOVEMENT AND MIGRATION

Movement and migration are an important story in nearly every country of the MENA. The region has experienced significant displacement of its population in recent decades. Individuals may be displaced across an international border (as migrants or refugees) or within their home country (internally displaced persons). The region also has been the recipient of voluntary migrant flows from other regions, drawing in millions of guest workers from not just other Arab countries but also South Asia and Southeast Asia. The driving factor behind involuntary flows of people is violent conflict, of which the Syrian civil war is the most prominent recent example. Triggering voluntary flows is economic motivation, including the perception among incoming migrants from foreign countries that they would fare better in terms of obtaining employment and earning income in more prosperous Arab states, particularly the oil-rich Gulf kingdoms. Within many countries, migrants moving to cities from rural areas sometimes cite ecological concerns, including the scarcity of natural resources like water due to water sources having been diverted to cities or large farms.

International migration and economic incentives

A closer look at this topic divulges interesting patterns. International migration, commonly defined as the movement of foreign-born people or foreign citizens into a second country, may include both involuntary flows (e.g., those displaced by force) and voluntary flows (those who choose to migrate). Combining both categories, the MENA countries hosted approximately

45.5 million international migrants in 2017, or approximately 18 percent of all migrants globally. International, here, means migrants of both non-MENA origin as well as a MENA country different than the ultimate country of residence. This figure represented a significant increase over 1990, when those figures were 19 million and 12 percent, respectively. One important event was the 1990–1991 Gulf War, when Saudi Arabia, Kuwait, and the other Gulf kingdoms expelled most Yemeni, Palestinian, and Jordanian workers as punishment for their governments' support for Iraq during the conflict. Another trend has been the hydrocarbon-fueled economic growth of these kingdoms, in which demands for labor (especially in unskilled occupations, such as construction, retail, and basic services) has far outstripped their small domestic populations. Table 2.9 charts the total number of migrants living in each MENA country, as well as the top three principal origin countries of those migrants, for 2017.

Two additional issues merit attention: gender and global distribution. First, in terms of gender distribution, international migrants residing within the MENA region are 64 percent male and 34 percent female. The proportion of females ranges from a low of 16 percent in Oman to a high of 56 percent in Palestine. The gender composition of a migrant population may offer some indication as to the motive for movement: when a migrant population is significantly more male than female (e.g., 75–25 versus 50–50 distribution), it may indicate movement of individuals rather than entire families. Second, the flows and distribution of international migration are not even. For example, in 2017, just ten countries globally hosted more than half of all international migrants. Of these ten countries, two are located in the MENA region: Saudi Arabia hosted approximately 12.2 million migrants, while the United Arab Emirates hosted 8.3 million migrants – the majority of them not from MENA countries of origin.

The UN has reported increased movement along certain bilateral migration "corridors" – pathways of migration from one country to a second country – over recent decades, with the MENA growing in significance as a destination. Between 1990 and 2000, only one of the ten bilateral migration corridors was found in the MENA region, from the Palestinian territories (mainly West Bank) to Jordan. Between 2000 and 2010, however, three of the top ten fastest growing bilateral migration corridors flowed into the MENA region: India and Bangladesh to the UAE, India to Saudi Arabia, and Iraq to Syria. The former two comprise migrants crossing borders for economic opportunities, whereas the latter consists mostly of refugees. Between

TABLE 2.9

International migrants per host country, 2017

Host country	Number of migrants	Three top countries of origin
Algeria	248,624	Western Sahara, West Bank and Gaza Strip, Somalia
Bahrain	722,649	India, Egypt, Bangladesh
Egypt	478,310	Syria, West Bank and Gaza Strip, Sudan
Iran	2,699,155	Afghanistan, Iraq, Pakistan
Iraq	366,568	Syria, Turkey, Iran
Israel	1,962,123	Morocco, Ukraine, Russia
Jordan	3,233,553	West Bank and Gaza Strip, Syria, Iraq
Kuwait	3,123,431	India, Egypt, Bangladesh
Lebanon	1,939,212	Syria, West Bank and Gaza Strip, Iraq
Libya	788,419	West Bank and Gaza Strip, Somalia, Iraq
Mauritania	168,438	Mali, Western Sahara, Senegal
Morocco	95,835	France, Algeria, Spain
Oman	2,073,292	India, Bangladesh, Pakistan
Qatar	1,721,392	India, Egypt, Bangladesh
Saudi Arabia	12,185,284	India, Indonesia, Pakistan
Sudan	735,821	South Sudan, Eritrea, Chad
Syria	1,013,818	West Bank and Gaza, Iraq, Somalia
Tunisia	57,663	Algeria, Libya, France
Turkey	4,881,966	Syria, Bulgaria, Germany
United Arab Emirates	8,312,524	India, Bangladesh, Pakistan
West Bank and Gaza Strip	253,735	Israel, Jordan, Saudi Arabia
Yemen	384,321	Somalia, Sudan, Egypt
Middle East and North Africa (total)	45,484,010	India, Syria, West Bank and Gaza Strip

Source: United Nations, Department of Economic and Social Affairs, Population Division, (2017), *Trends in International Migrant Stock: The 2017 Revision*.

2010 and 2017, six of the top ten fastest growing bilateral migration corridors were found in the MENA.

The voluntary aspect of much migration across the MENA reflects an economic logic, as an increasing number of people – both rural populations, and extant urbanites – move to larger cities or other countries for greater employment and income opportunities. The Gulf kingdoms offer a classic example, attracting many millions of South and Southeast Asian migrant workers who in turn remit home much of their wages and salaries. While having shrunk over time, many expatriates in these hydrocarbon-heavy countries are from other MENA countries. As of 2014, for instance, the Gulf Research Center estimated that approximately 330,000 Lebanese, 560,000 Jordanians, and 1.4 million Syrians lived and worked in the Gulf; like many other migrant workers, they remitted home much of their earned income, which in turn infused their home countries with cash resources.

Involuntary migration: refugees and internal displacement

Refugees are those individuals forced to leave their home country to escape war, persecution, or natural disaster. They are an important category of peoples now in the region, as the discussion of identity in Chapter 4 suggests. MENA countries are both the point of origin and the end host of significant numbers of refugees. As of 2017, in terms of destination, the MENA countries accommodated an estimated 6.9 million refugees as of the end of 2016, approximately 42 percent of the global figure (Table 2.10). The MENA countries hosting the largest numbers of refugees include Turkey, Lebanon, Iran, and Jordan, principally as a result of neighboring conflicts like Syria and Iraq. In terms of origin point, approximately 6.7 million refugees were displaced from MENA countries as of 2017, corresponding to 41 percent of all refugees globally. The majority came from Syria. According to the UN High Commissioner for Refugees, an estimated 43 percent of refugees seeking asylum in the MENA region were accommodated and resettled in urban areas and 7 percent in rural areas; the destination of the remaining 50 percent of refugees was unknown. This pattern generally holds across countries with the exception of Mauritania, Sudan, and Yemen, where refugees are more frequently accommodated in rural than in urban areas.

TABLE 2.10

Refugees flows, 2016

Host country	Total number of refugees originally from country	Total number of refugees arriving from other countries
Algeria	3,727	94,232
Bahrain	462	271
Egypt	19,796	213,530
Iran	94,100	979,435
Iraq	316,063	261,864
Israel	495	32,946
Jordan	1,933	685,197
Kuwait	1,021	939
Lebanon	4,740	1,012,969
Libya	8,836	9,310
Mauritania	36,265	74,148
Morocco	2,262	4,771
Oman	38	317
Qatar	29	177
Saudi Arabia	936	140
Sudan	650,407	421,466
Syrian Arab Republic	5,524,515	19,809
Tunisia	1,700	649
Turkey	57,927	2,869,421
United Arab Emirates	112	895
West Bank and Gaza Strip	**	**
Yemen	18,428	269,783
Regional Total	6,743,297	6,919,323
World Total	17,185,327	17,185,327

Source: United Nations High Commissioner for Refugees (2017), *Statistical Yearbook*.

BOX 2.2 CASE STUDY – REFUGEES IN JORDAN

To take a closer look at the complexities of refugee accommodation, consider Jordan. This kingdom has experienced a long history of mass migration due to regional conflicts. During the nineteenth century when the area was under Ottoman rule, significant communities of Chechens and Circassians migrated from the Caucasus. Jordan was created as a British Mandate in 1921. Nearly three decades later, the 1948 Arab-Israeli War would generate a major wave of Palestinian refugees. Another wave of Palestinians came after the 1967 Arab-Israeli War, when the now-independent kingdom lost the West Bank to Israeli occupation. Most of these Palestinian refugees arriving due to these conflicts were offered Jordanian citizenship. Yet another wave came after the Gulf War, when nearly 300,000 Jordanians of mostly Palestinian descent returned to the kingdom from the Arabian Gulf kingdoms after their expulsion. In recent years, conflict has again generated incoming waves of displaced peoples. After the Iraq War, instability and violence in transitional Iraq resulted in nearly a million Iraqis relocating to Jordan, with the greatest numbers arriving in the mid- to late 2000s. Since the start of the Syrian civil war, many Syrians similarly fled violence and bloodshed; of the nearly six million Syrians who left the country between the 2011–2012 Arab Spring and 2018, over a million came to Jordan. Virtually none of these Iraqi and Syrian refugees have been offered Jordanian citizenship, or fair legal opportunities to settle permanently. These refugees have left a tremendous demographic impact: Jordan's 2016 National Census counted 9.52 million residents in the kingdom, of which nearly one-third (2.9 million) were non-Jordanians. Meeting this humanitarian demand has taxed Jordan greatly given its small economy and few natural resources. Already cash-strapped, the government's obligation to furnish education, health care, security, and other public goods to the new population has compelled it to seek more foreign aid to alleviate the cost. Water is another question. This is the second most water-scarce country in the world, falling far beneath the water scarcity line (1,000 cubic meters per capita) with less than 125 cubic meters per person. Providing enough water for the national population during times of peace is a struggle, with water shortages frequently reported during the summer; with millions of refugees, it is close to impossible without massive international assistance and extreme overusage of underground water sources, such as the Disi aquifer bordering Saudi Arabia.

This focus on refugees who cross borders should not obscure another important category of involuntary migrants, namely internally displaced persons (IDPs). Globally, there are twice the number of IDPs as the number of people displaced across borders. IDPs are essentially refugees who do not leave their country: they are forced to flee their homes and communities, but remain within their national borders. Table 2.11 offers a statistical

TABLE 2.11

Internal displacement due to conflict and disaster, 2016

Country	Total number of IDPs due to conflict and violence
Algeria	2,500
Bahrain	0
Egypt	78,000
Iran	0
Iraq	3,035,000
Jordan	0
Kuwait	0
Lebanon	12,000
Libya	304,000
Mauritania	0
Morocco	0
Oman	0
Qatar	0
Saudi Arabia	0
Sudan	3,300,000
Syria	6,326,000
Tunisia	0
Turkey	1,108,000
United Arab Emirates	0
West Bank and Gaza Strip	193,000
Yemen	1,974,000
Regional Total	16,332,500
World Total	40,300,000

Source: Internal Displacement Monitoring Centre (2017), *Global Report on Internal Displacement*.

look at this problem. As of 2017, it was estimated 16.3 million individuals were internally displaced within MENA countries due to conflict and disaster as of 2017. In collective terms, the MENA accounts for approximately 41 percent of all IDPs globally, and its countries account for four of the top ten countries with the most IDPs due to conflict and violence (Syria, Iraq, Yemen, Sudan).

The special case of Lebanon offers both insight and tragedy into IDPs. Lebanon has experienced a series of long-running conflicts including the 1975–1990 civil war, Israel's occupation of southern Lebanon from 1982 until 1990, and the July 2006 war with Israel. These conflicts killed hundreds of thousands of Lebanese, made more than a million homeless, and generated mass migration both within and from Lebanon. The civil war displaced an estimated 28 percent of the country's population, and totally or partially destroyed nearly 200 towns and villages. The Israeli invasion and occupation displaced a further 200,000 Lebanese. As of 2006 – more than 15 years after the civil war formally ended – an estimated 17,000 Lebanese remained displaced, having never returned home. The July 2006 war displaced approximately one million people, or a quarter of Lebanon's population. Around 90 percent of the displaced were able to return to their homes within a week of the ceasefire, although the presence of cluster bombs and unexploded ordnance poses an ongoing threat to returnees.

Environmental migration

An oft-overlooked yet critical aspect of migration is human movements caused by natural disasters and climate change. The UN's International Organization for Migration predicts that by 2050, there will be 200 million refugees worldwide due to environmental degradation and climate change, compounded by rising sea levels. Less dramatically but no less destructive, slow-moving climate change outcomes (such as rising temperatures) can negatively impact agriculture, triggering further incentives for rural populations to leave. Climate models confirm that the MENA region will not be spared from these damages. Already burdened with a fragile ecology and severe water deficiency, it is expected to experience more frequent droughts and rainfall variability. Long-term meteorological data indicate an increase in the frequency of winter droughts over the past 20 years, due to historic cycles as well as man-made climate change. While traditional farming in the region is well adapted to an arid environment, the combination of food system transformation and extreme climactic events are not promising for countries still suffering from, or wrestling with the legacies of, violent conflicts. Absent collective responses, as Chapter 7 will unfurl, the future looks dim.

The consequences of ignorance are dire, because these are not merely social variables; they also shape the political level, too. In Syria, the Arab Spring and civil war were preceded by a vicious four-year drought which, between 2006 and 2010, was considered the worst in four decades. The drought caused acute food shortages in the largely rural and agricultural northeast, and led to a deterioration of the health of the population. Many farmers who were dependent on rain-fed (non-irrigated) production suffered major or complete loss of crops, and many producing livestock lost their herds and flocks. Incomes fell sharply as a result, triggering large-scale migration of more than one million people to the already overcrowded cities in search of employment. Many settled in urban slums and other impoverished areas, exacerbating already fraying social services and increasing political tensions. Those same overcrowded urban centers became hotbeds of angry protests and popular uprisings during the Arab Spring – and frontline battlegrounds during the civil war that followed.

CONCLUSION

This chapter analyzed social life in the MENA region. It explored the dynamics of rural life, including its history and organization; parsed the rapidity and outcome of urban growth; compared the populational trends and economic structure of living conditions in both rural and urban areas; and weighed the import of food security and migration flows. It illustrated the constraints of geography and environment, as well as the promise and perils of urbanization. Particularly important is the fact that the MENA region is now one of the most food import-dependent regions of the globe and may well be the most adversely affected by climate change in the next few decades. The human migration factor is also extremely relevant: masses of people have both circulated around the region voluntarily, in search of work and better lives, and involuntarily as displaced peoples and refugees due to violent conflict. Ultimately, all these structural contexts and constraints matter in understanding how social groups and national populations will cope with new challenges in the coming decades.

QUESTIONS FOR DISCUSSION

1. How have geography and environmental factors shaped the nature of agriculture as both a lifestyle and economic livelihood in the Middle East?
2. How have political and economic forces, including conflict, changed the agriculture sector as a mode of production across the MENA over the past half-century?
3. How do rural and urban areas diverge in terms of living conditions, population movement, employment trends, and social life? Could anything reverse the demographic shift from rural to urban communities?
4. What does the Mashriq, as a particular sub-region of the MENA, tell us about how external factors can influence the rise and fall of rural communities?
5. What variables shape the attainment of food security in the modern world?
6. How have urbanization and food insecurity gone hand-in-hand for many MENA societies?
7. What, if anything, can governments do to reverse food insecurity and make access to nutritious diets more sustainable for their people?
8. What major events and trends have determined the MENA's experience with international migration, including voluntary and involuntary forms?

FURTHER READING

The *Arab Region Atlas of Our Changing Environment* (United Nations Environment Programme, 2013) provides a visual overview of the spatial transformation of Arab geographies, including historical expansion of major cities.

To understand changing patterns in farming activity in a general theoretical sense, readers are directed to the following recent publications: Sarah K. Lowder, Jakob Skoet, and Terri Raney, "The Number, Size, and Distribution of Farms, Smallholder Farms, and Family Farms Worldwide," *World Development* 87 (2016): 16–29; and Leah Samberg, James Gerber, Navin Ramankutty, Mario Herrero, and Paul West, "Subnational Distribution of Average Farm Size and Smallholder Contributions to Global Food Production," *Environmental Research Letters*, November 30, 2016. These help shed quantitative and historical perspective about agriculture, and especially smallholder and family farming in relation to food production and global output. David Satterthwaite, Gordon McGranahan, and Cecilia Tacoli, "Urbanization and Its Implications for Food and Farming," *Philosophical Transactions of the Royal Society* 365, no. 1554 (2010): 2809–20 likewise provides a telling look at how urbanization both affects, and in turn is affected by, change in global agricultural systems and food production.

More specific evaluations of rural life in the MENA are also available. From an ethnographic perspective, Edmund Burke and David Yaghoubian, eds., *Struggle and Survival in the Modern Middle East*, 2nd ed. (Berkeley: University of California Press, 2005) provides telling portraits of peasants, villagers, pastoralists, and tribal communities. Joel Beinin's *Workers and Peasants in the Modern*

Middle East (Cambridge: Cambridge University Press, 2001), also delineates the history and apprehensive experiences of peasants and farmers from the Ottoman period onwards. From a theoretical standpoint, Rami Zuyrak, Eckart Woertz, and Rachael Bahn, *Crisis and Conflict in Agriculture* (Oxford: CAB International, 2018) furnishes a detailed exploration of the intersection of conflict and agriculture, including case studies from the MENA region. Ray Bush, *Family Farming in the Near East and North Africa* (Brasilia: UNDP and FAO, 2016), likewise traces the impact of environmental, infrastructural, and political challenges upon small-holding agrarians in the region. Habib Ayeb and Reem Saad, eds., *Agrarian Transformation in the Arab World: Persistent and Emerging Challenges* (Oxford: Oxford University Press, 2014) highlights the connection between the food security crisis and conditions of agrarian transformation under varying government policies and social movements.

Moreover, Alan Mikhail's edited volume *Water on Sand: Environmental Histories of the Middle East and North Africa* (Oxford: Oxford University Press, 2013), offers useful insights into the unique environment and environmental history of the MENA region, notably the distribution of water, soil, and energy resources, which have shaped both crop-based and pastoral livestock-based agricultural systems, the geographic location of cities, and patterns of industrialization. John McNeill's earlier *The Mountains of the Mediterranean World: An Environmental History* (Cambridge: Cambridge University Press, 1992) explains the historical depopulation of rural, mountainous regions as a result of ecological fragility, population imbalances, and the integration of these regions within the market-based economy. While dated, Bryan Roberts's *Cities of Peasants: The Political Economy of Urbanization in the Third World* (London: Edward Arnold, 1978) explores the implications of economic development on patterns of urbanization as well as social transformations within cities. While the case studies are drawn from Latin America, the themes raised and patterns identified are relevant to the MENA region. Finally, Robert Irwin, ed., *New Cambridge History of Islam, Volume IV: Islamic Cultures and Societies to the End of the Eighteenth Century* (Cambridge: Cambridge University Press, 2010) provides detailed historical information on the MENA region prior to the industrial age. The chapters entitled "The City and the Nomad" and "Rural Life and Economy until 1800" are particularly recommended.

Online sources (also available on the companion website)

All the data cited in this chapter can be found online, and comprise a useful foundation for further research. The World Bank's *World Development Indicators* (http://databank.worldbank.org/data/home.aspx) provides an easy-to-use repository of useful statistical data on a range of topics such as poverty and social conditions, including many of the data series featured within this chapter. Detailed data on employment, including within the agricultural sector, were taken from published reports of the International Labor Organization (www.ilo.org/beirut/publications/lang--en/index.htm), such as its *World Employment Social Outlook* series and its *Global Employment Trends* reports. The United Nations Department of Economic and Social Affairs, Population Division publishes a range of population statistics including on urbanization (https://esa.un.org/unpd/wup/) and international migration (www.un.org/en/development/desa/population/migration/index.asp/). Figures on multidimensional poverty come from the United Nations Development Programme's *Human Development Report* (www.hdr.undp.org/en). Data on refugees were taken from the United Nations High Commissioner for Refugees' *UNHCR Statistical Yearbook* series (www.unhcr.org/en-us/statistical-yearbooks.html), which follows major trends in terms of refugee movement. The Internal Displacement Monitoring Centre (IDMC) regularly publishes reports on internal displacement, including its *Global Report on Internal Displacement* (www.internal-displacement.org/). Finally, the EIU provides a convenient food security index that helps compare the MENA in global perspective (https://foodsecurityindex.eiu.com/)

The *Arab Spatial* website (www.arabspatial.org/) also holds a profundity of maps, charts, and data, and in particular devotes online interactive resources to chart out food security, poverty, and rural development. The Arab Organization for Agricultural Development, a sub-unit of the Arab League, also maintains a website with documentation, yearbooks, and newsletters that may prove useful (www.aoad.org/indexeng.htm).

CHAPTER 3

Social mobilization and civil society

Vincent Durac

THE RUNDOWN: KEY TOPICS COVERED
- Mobilizational concepts
- Civil society organizations
- Colonial resistance
- Workers, students, and women
- Arab Spring
- Post-Arab Spring activism

INTRODUCTION

Social mobilization and contentious politics have been features of MENA societies from the time of the Ottoman Empire to the post-colonial era. Common stereotypes of social life in the region often expressed the assumption that most populations were inherently *passive* in the face of oppressive rule. The greatest challenge to this stereotype came with the Arab Spring of 2011–2012. However, while the events of the Arab Spring have commanded a great deal of attention, it should not obscure the deeper historical reality that grass-roots social mobilization has always existed in the region. By mobilization, we mean how everyday peoples engaged in collective action, advocated their interests, resisted political authority, and protected their communities. The social life of the Middle East and North Africa therefore has been a life of activism, advocacy, and contentiousness, with individuals and groups frequently confronting – and sometimes defeating – structures of power deemed unjust and oppressive.

This chapter focuses on the Arab countries to explore the role of social mobilization and, more recently, civil society. Elements of modern civil society appear throughout the modern history of the MENA region, as this chapter discusses. Anti-colonial resistance against European intrusions drew upon students, workers, women, and other groups, who contentiously pushed back against the entry of European imperialism in various ways. After World War Two, new centralizing authoritarian states, whether republics or monarchies, took power, and they were mostly hostile to the emergence of civil society. Independent social groups were viewed as something to be co-opted and controlled by autocratic leaders. However, this began to change as the end of the Cold War approached, and limited political liberalization created opportunities for citizens to assert new demands. Civil society flourished in many Arab countries from the 1990s onwards, although this did not necessary equate to revolutionary power. The Arab Spring marked a major breakthrough in showing how popular pressures could puncture longstanding dictatorships, giving hope to a future that will likely be marked – as in the past – with continual reformation of everyday people struggling for change.

CONCEPTS AND IMPLICATIONS

Social mobilization and civil society are logically linked concepts that refer to different phenomena but tap the same types of behavior. Social mobilization encompasses situations when individuals and groups engage in collective action in order to engage in sustained and sometimes contested interaction with authority figures, most often to voice their desire for change. The easiest examples include campaigns of popular protest, which involve not just a common purpose and strategy but also the implicit assumption that demanding something from the government – such as human rights, economic justice, or less corruption – might improve the status quo. Mobilization can also result in concrete networks, organizations, and movements designed to maintain these energies and channel the resources of its participants into future episodes of contention. Essentially, by challenging the routines and power of others, maintaining some type of solidarity especially in the face of pushback, and coordinating information and ideas, social mobilization serves as a tool of transformation in the hands of ordinary citizens. There are many forms of mobilized resistance, but the most common are those that capture headlines: protests, strikes, demonstrations, rebellions, sit-ins, occupations, and other types of public action that disrupt the normal flow of social or political life.

Civil society manifests as the sector of public life laying in between the government, family, and economy, and filled with innumerable organizations representing the views of citizens. Such entities include, for instance, non-governmental organizations (NGOs), trade unions, professional associations, religious organizations, advocacy groups, student movements, intellectual circles, artistic cooperatives, social charities, think tanks, and virtually any other kind of collective actor whose purpose is to protect and advocate the interests of constituents with a wider vision of advancing the public good. In many ways, civil society represents the formalized articulation of social mobilization in the modern world: in urbanized, educated, and industrialized countries, individuals are likely to join organizations and groups that not only represent their views but also exist in a legal sense, insofar as possessing a budget, office, network, membership, and website. Civil society, as many researchers argue, is correlated with an extensive array of benefits: the more public associations such as interest groups, student movements, and cultural organizations that a society has, then the more likely those "joiner" citizens will trust one another, work together for joint causes, and diffuse values of tolerance and compromise – outcomes important to democracy.

Civil society organizations, of course, are not coterminous with social mobilization: that is, people can mobilize outside of any formal organization if they believe fighting for change requires drawing upon their private resources and acting informally. To take a frequent example, workers can strike as part of a collective decision from their union, in support of higher wages; or, a subset of those workers can dissent if their union does not agree to strike, and instead independently choose to stop working through informal coordination. Indeed, the Arab Spring indicated the dangers of conflating the two, as the popular uprisings of 2011–2012 were led not by civil society groups but instead by youths and activists who generally were not members of formal parties, entities, or networks that had planned the event for years; rather, they were ordinary citizens spurred into action through spontaneous coordination often done through social media and other informal channels. Typical scenes like that present in Photo 3.1 – youth-led marches and protests rumbling through public spaces, in explicit disobedience to curfews – often drew upon the support of civil society organizations, but were largely led by grass-roots movements. Both of these sources, formalized organizations and informal activism, are important.

PHOTO 3.1
Street march against Egyptian government, 2012.

Source: Photo by elhamalawy is licensed under CC BY-SA 2.0.
Online: www.flickr.com/photos/elhamalawy/8244384675

OTTOMAN-ERA LEGACIES

Long before direct and indirect European intervention in the MENA, the region harbored a rich tradition of resistance and rebellion against political rulers. This was often a response to economic hardship and justice and was especially seen in the last centuries of the Ottoman Empire. In Algeria, for instance, the eighteenth and nineteenth centuries witnessed rebellions led by two Sufi orders against Ottoman rule. Between 1793 and 1805, the leader of the Darqawiyya Sufi brotherhood, 'Abd al-Qadir Ibn al-Sharif, organized a rebellion against the Ottoman-installed governor due to an increase of taxation. However, the rebellion was suppressed and Ibn al-Sharif was forced to escape to Morocco. The Tijaniyya Sufi order was founded by Ahmad al-Tijani in 1782 and likewise resisted the Turkish authorities of Algeria. However, the tribal population was forced to submit and al-Tijani moved to Fez in Morocco. This was not the end of Sufi mobilization, though; al-Tijani's son formed a tribal alliance in the 1820s and attacked the Ottoman garrison at the town of al-Mu'askar in 1827. He was defeated, taken prisoner, and later killed. The hostility between the Tijani order and Ottoman authority is exemplified in the former's belief that the French conquest of Algeria was a fulfillment of al-Tijani's desire for an end to Turkish rule in Algeria, even as that new form of imperial occupation spawned its own anti-colonial resistance movement a century later.

In Egypt, there were several examples of popular defiance against the economic burden imposed on ordinary people. In 1778, for instance, the peasants of Tahta famously refused to pay taxes, resulting in a brief but violent conflict. The short-lived French invasion of Egypt in 1798 was also met by grass-roots struggle. The initial French conquest was followed by widespread protests across the country between 1798 and 1801, when the French withdrew. In Mansoura, 4,000 people mounted an armed insurrection against the occupation. Others mounted non-violent opposition. A French soldier, Sergeant Francois, wrote an eyewitness account on July 19, 1798 of all of the inhabitants of the small village of Shum who refused to provide supplies to the French. French troops then fired on the crowd, killing at least 900 people. Decades later, the introduction of conscription by the new Egyptian ruler promising modernization, Muhammad 'Ali, provoked confrontations. In 1823, a revolt erupted in Minufiyya, a province in the Nile Delta, which was suppressed by troops assisted by six field cannons. The following year, an even greater rebellion broke out involving some 30,000 men and women. Looting, arson, and attacks on local officials were reported; the Cairene government quelled the revolt with a military response that killed 4,000 peasants and townsfolk in a mere two weeks.

Further east, opposition to taxes and the introduction of conscription provided the motivation for a series of rebellions from the 1820s to the 1850s in the Mashriq. In what is now Lebanon, Maronite Christians sought out French protection in the 1820s from the impositions of the Ottoman rule of Acre. The people of Hama and Homs (in present-day Syria) revolted in June 1827 and refused to pay new taxes; several of these oppositionists were subsequently executed. In May 1829, the inhabitants of Baghdad rose up against their Ottoman ruler and put him to death. Another revolt in Lebanon in 1840 was prompted by the introduction of an oppressive system of taxation, but also by the introduction of conscription of peasants into the army. In December 1858, Lebanon witnessed a legendary episode of popular uprising when Maronite Christians rebelled against their feudal overlords in the district of Kisrawan in Mount Lebanon, northwest of Beirut. The peasant movement, which was prompted by grievances against local landlords, noble families, and tax collectors, quickly spread so that by late 1859 almost all of Kisrawan had fallen under its control. The movement was led by a devout Maronite Christian, Tanyus Shahin, and stood on the support of the poor, and probably landless, peasants. The more aristocratic Maronite Church, by contrast, was challenged by a movement that threatened its extensive property holdings as well as its claim to represent the Maronite community. The movement called for the complete political equality of commoners with noble families and their representation at the level of the district.

ANTI-COLONIAL STRUGGLE DURING EUROPEAN ENCROACHMENT

As European advancement into the MENA region assumed greater significance from the mid-nineteenth century onwards, collective action through social mobilization increasingly took the form of anti-European resistance. France began the occupation and colonization of Algeria in 1830, a process that produced 132 years of conflict with a local population which fiercely resented its control. In the course of a meeting in 1827, in the context of an ongoing dispute over contracts for the sale of wheat, the Algerian ruler is reputed to have struck the French consul with his fly-swatter. The incident led to a standoff between France and Algeria and a full-scale invasion of the country three years later. The war of conquest was accompanied by the transfer of most Algerian land, including its richest arable areas, to European colonists. Soon after the French invasion of Algeria, Britain seized 'Aden on the southwest corner of the Arabian Peninsula (what is now Yemen), while continuing to penetrate the Arabian and Iranian shores of the Gulf littoral. In 1881 France occupied Tunisia and established a protectorate; in the following year Britain occupied Egypt. European expansion into North Africa continued with the Italian invasion of Libya in 1911 and the establishment of both French and Spanish protectorates in Morocco the following year.

Far from being atomized and subordinate, communities in these territories engaged in concerted opposition against colonial control. In Algeria, invasion and occupation by the French met with continued difficulties. The son of the head of the Qadiriyya Sufi brotherhood, which had played a leading role in revolts against Ottoman rule, 'Abd al-Qadir, led a rebellion which began in 1832, with the support of important tribes and notables in western Algeria as well as from Morocco. 'Abd al-Qadir's rebellion is significant for a number of reasons. First, it was by far the most successful campaign of resistance to French colonial rule. Second, he succeeded in establishing control over a substantial part of the territory of modern Algeria, which he ran as an independent Algerian state for several years. Third, he justified his campaign against the French on religious grounds, as was indicated by his assumption of the Islamic title of "Commander of the Faithful." However, by the early 1840s, the French began repressing the movement through a scorched-earth strategy which forced 'Abd al-Qadir to seek refuge in neighboring Morocco. The French in turn attacked Morocco and forced its ruler, the Sultan, to sign a treaty to the effect that they would treat him as an outlaw. 'Abd al-Qadir surrendered in 1847; he was taken to Paris and held for five years before settling in Damascus where he died in 1882. During the course of the first 45 years of French rule in Algeria, up to 825,000 people may have been killed directly or indirectly.

The extension of French rule to neighboring Tunisia also met with opposition. Having established initial control, the French withdrew most of their military forces from the country in mid-June 1881. Shortly afterwards, the center and south of Tunisia rose in revolt against French occupation. The most important leader was 'Ali Ibn Khalifa, a tribal leader from the southeast of the country. At the end of June, the townspeople of coastal Sfax joined forces with Khalifa; during the months that followed, tens of thousands of tribal warriors from across the Tunisian south and west (where French authority was weakest) joined the insurgency. However, the dispatch of French reinforcements in the summer changed the course of events. By December 1881, 'Ali Ibn Khalifa had taken refuge in what is now Libya, taking with him an estimated 120,000 tribesmen and their families, signaling the end of the upheaval.

The 1880s also saw significant popular contentiousness in response to British control in Egypt. The background to the establishment of the British protectorate in Egypt was that of economic crisis. The Egyptian ruler, Isma'il (the grandson of Muhammad 'Ali), had spent his way into a debt default by 1876, leaving the way open for European control of the country's finances. Isma'il had run up public debts of £100 million, up from just £3 million when he took office. In 1875, he sold his 45 percent share in the Suez Canal to Britain for £4 million. Bankruptcy forced him to accept both a public debt commission and British and French financial controllers. An army officer, Ahmad 'Urabi, then led a movement against these gestures, and explicitly laid out principles that resonated across the mostly rural society – the rights of native-born Egyptians, the unity of Muslims in the face of Western hegemony, the role of representative government, and the need for a new constitution. 'Urabi and his followers formed an alliance with political notables, but also appealed to the Egyptian public through demonstrations, speeches, and the press. The slogan "Egypt for the Egyptians" reverberated. However, following rioting in Alexandria in which around 50 Europeans and 250 Egyptians died, the British launched a full-scale invasion in 1882. Despite its support among the peasantry and townsfolk, the 'Urabi movement had no strategy for long-term battle, and in August 1882 its forces were routed by the British. Around 2,000 Egyptians and 57 Britons died in the lopsided clash. The British disbanded the rebellion and put 'Urabi and other leaders of the revolt on trial. They were sentenced to death, which was commuted to exile in Ceylon (now Sri Lanka). 'Urabi died in obscurity in 1911 – but again, like other episodes of colonial opposition, the memories of such resistance would linger on.

The scale of European influence in the MENA increased very significantly in the years after World War One, as did Arab societal efforts to resist it. While the Maghrib had come under European domination before the war, the Mashriq and parts of the Arabian Gulf came under direct Western control for the first time. At the 1919 post-war peace conference in Versailles, Britain and France were central to the partitioning of territory that had belonged to the defeated Ottoman Empire into new states over which they established what were known as mandates. The Ottoman province of Syria was carved up into four mini-states – Syria, Lebanon, Transjordan (later Jordan), and Palestine – and a fifth new state of Iraq was created by the British amalgamation of the Ottoman provinces of Baghdad, Basra, and Mosul. Syria and Lebanon came under French control while Transjordan, Palestine, and Iraq were allocated to Britain. Once more, popular organization signaling public anger against such foreign control became a persistent feature of political life.

In Libya, resistance to Italian efforts to establish colonial rule both preceded and followed World War One. Italy first invaded the Ottoman province of Tripolitania in present-day Libya in 1911, meeting resistance from the Sufi Sanusi order, tribal forces, and the Ottoman army. During the first year, over 3,000 Italian soldiers were killed and some 4,000 injured. A treaty between Italy and the Ottoman Empire in 1912 left the locals to fight alone, but even so the Italian army could not control more than a narrow coastal strip until the 1920s. With the fascist takeover of power in Italy under Mussolini, however, the reconquest began anew, as more of the country came under direct Italian governance. A famous rebellion instigated under 'Umar al-Mukhtar, a prominent member of the Sanusi order, derived considerable support from local villages and towns that likewise wished to defy Italian supremacy. In response, the Italian authorities brought to bear the most modern weapons they had – airplanes, artillery, poison gas – and also constructed concentration camps that would eventually hold more than 110,000 people and 600,000 livestock. The latter meant starvation for much of the countryside, and indeed as many as 70,000 may have died due to malnutrition and famine in the consequent years. When al-Mukhtar was finally captured and hanged in 1931, the Italians gathered 20,000 Libyans to witness his execution.

BOX 3.1 CASE STUDY – ANTI-BRITISH RESISTANCE IN COLONIAL EGYPT

Egyptian resistance against British ascendancy occurred not just through violent uprisings but also political activism, foreshadowing a vociferous trend of ordinary citizens contesting the unjust exercise of nondemocratic authority that continues today. One landmark episode occurred a century ago, as the Mashriq was transitioning from a period of Ottoman suzerainty to direct European control. The Revolution of 1919 began in November 1918, when a committee of 14 Egyptian nationalist leaders, led by Sa'd Zaghloul, approached the British authorities with a view to leading a delegation advocating Egyptian independence at the upcoming Versailles peace conference. These political activists called themselves the *Wafd* (delegation), and the party they founded would soon help foster political transformation. Yet in the moment, the British refused; and instead, in March 1919 they deported Zaghloul and his colleagues to Malta. Egyptians responded with a spontaneous, uncoordinated, and unplanned revolt which spread throughout the country. Students in Cairo were the first to act and within two days virtually all were on strike. They were quickly followed by members of the Egyptian bar. On March 11, members of the lawyers' syndicate met and voted to strike. Their refusal to handle cases made it impossible for the business of the state to be handled normally. Demonstrations then broke out in major cities, often resulting in bloody exchanges with the British military. A wave of strikes erupted in Cairo, while in the countryside, peasants joined the movement. Solidarity strikes with the Wafd by railway workers, the government press, tramways, the electric company, the postal service, customs employees, and taxi and carriage drivers paralyzed the country. The Egyptian police and army ceded ground to these demonstrations. Their hands tied, the British released Zaghloul on April 7, but popular pressures continued in support of national demands for the British to leave altogether. This revolt continued and, remarkably, remained almost all unarmed. Mass meetings, often held in mosques, served as the channel through which Wafd leaders broadcasted their messages and directed public groups. On April 16, some 80,000 people jammed into the area around the iconic Al-Azhar mosque in Cairo. The British told the world that Egypt had come to the brink of a Bolshevik catastrophe, and responded with military force: they burned villages, bombed installations, and machine-gunned unruly crowds. The Wafd ironically were no revolutionaries; but the popular sentiment

> **BOX 3.1 (CONTINUED)**
>
> they represented and the sheer simultaneity of protests had put the British on shaky ground. After several more years of tension and disorder, in 1922, the British finally declared an end to the protectorate and Egyptian independence. Though they would still retain authority over key strategic domains, among them the Suez Canal and military bases, at least symbolically the revolution marked a moment of "people power," in which spirited and unremitting insurrections from below compelled one of the mightiest imperial powers to relinquish some of their prerogatives from above.

After World War One, Arab mobilization through renewed activism and the creation of new organizations continued, with many advocates of independence finding their social and political voices. A common theme draws these occurrences together: they involved different coalitions of hitherto unorganized social groups together; they targeted and, in some cases, temporarily defeated European authorities; and in the end, they were all overcome by the superior coercive and financial resources brought by colonial hegemons.

In Iraq, opposition to the British presence was immediate. As soon as British forces landed in the country in 1914, both Sunni and Shi'a *'ulama* (religious jurists and scholars) issued *fatwas*, or religious rulings, declaring a holy war for independence. Early in 1918, a secret society, the League of the Islamic Awakening, was founded in Najaf, with large membership comprising leading religious figures and young journalists. In nearby Karbala, a similar secret society, the National Muslim League, was formed with the objective of activating resistance cells in nearby communities. However, the most important of these societies was Baghdad-based Guardians of Independence, which soon opened branches across the country. The organization represented a coalition of different groups united in their demand for sovereignty and autonomy; it included Shi'a merchants, Sunni teachers, civil servants, the 'ulama, and repatriated Iraqi military officers. By 1920, opposition to British rule had culminated in a national revolt that was only suppressed after the British Minister of War, Winston Churchill, ordered reinforcements from Iran; the number of British troops in Iraq increased from 60,000 in July 1920 to over 100,000 in October of that year. In addition, two squadrons of the Royal Air Force proceeded to attack Iraqi forces through heavy bombardment, essentially bombing villages and towns where suspected oppositionists were operating. The rebellion was over in November, although as in Egypt Britain opted to rule more indirectly through the installation of a friendly monarchy.

In Syria, anti-French attitudes likewise sparked and lit the flames of resistance. The French occupation of Latakia in November 1919 prompted an uprising led by an 'Alawite tribal leader, Sheikh Salih 'Ali. As discussed in Chapter 8, the 'Alawite sect is a syncretic branch of Islam related to the Shi'a. Their defiance came to an end with an agreement between the Turkish and French governments in 1921. Yet not long after, another city – Aleppo, a traditionally vibrant center of commerce and trade – expressed similar conflict. Opposition here was organized by Ibrahim Hananu, a one-time Ottoman bureaucrat and landowner. In the summer of 1919, Hananu founded the League of National Defense, a guerrilla force with 680 recruits. Their work commenced as a rural uprising but gained the support of urban notables and other Syrian nationalists when the French occupied Aleppo in July 1920. The insurgency grew to 5,000, and controlled much of northwestern Syria by November. However, when Turkish supplies and funding dried up, the French were able to wipe out the movement, forcing Hananu to escape to neighboring Transjordan to the south – another mandate, like Iraq, that was created with a pro-British monarchy in place. Within five years, Syria witnessed another, more unified uprising as tens of thousands of people rose up; but like the British in Iraq, the French utilized military firepower to bombard rebellious towns from the ground and air, and coercively bulldoze any group that stood in their way.

Outside the Mashriq, another sustained challenge mounted at the grassroots level to European penetration came from the Rif mountains of northern Morocco, where, between 1921 and 1926, 'Abd al-Krim al-Khattabi led a revolt against Spanish and French colonization. 'Abd al-Krim's father, a judge, began organizing local tribes against the Spanish after the latter established a protectorate overlaying much of the Rif province; 'Abd al-Krim and his brother assumed leadership over the coalition upon their father's death in August 1919. In April 1921, he was elected by 50 *sheikhs* (tribal leaders) as their chieftain, and his guerillas inflicted a major defeat upon Spanish forces in July 1921, which lost from 10,000 to 21,000 troops. Following the titanic clash, and further Spanish losses, the Moroccan movement declared the province free of European rule and called the fledgling country the "Republic of the Rif." In response, the Spanish and French powers regrouped and sought to wipe out what had become the most blatant threat to European colonization in the Arab world. Organizing several hundred thousand troops that outnumbered 'Abd al-Krim's force by four to one, and fielding tanks, artillery, aircraft, and chemical weapons, the European alliance reconquered the liberated Rif territory and eliminated the would-be nationalist movement. In May 1926, 'Abd al-Krim was forced to surrender and was exiled to the French island of La Reunion. In 1947, on his way to France, he managed to escape and lived in Cairo until his death in 1963.

Workers and grievances

On European terms, the nineteenth and early twentieth centuries witnessed the incorporation of MENA economies into a global economic order. Most states in the MENA were penetrated by a variety of outside parties vying for commercial, cultural, or strategic influence. Indeed, long before European military power was felt in the region, its economic power had begun to shape lives. The resultant dislocation of local producers, traders, farmers, shopkeepers, and other local actors prompted mobilization in response in many parts of the region.

These economic grievances were considerable. A walkout by coalminers in Turkey during the nineteenth century in the coastal city of Zonguldak represented the first documented strike by daily wage-earners in the Ottoman Empire. The first labor union, the Ottoman Workers Society, was established in 1894 in state factories and was immediately banned. As a result, 53 strikes took place up until 1908. Yet in 1908 alone, there were 138 strikes, partly linked to broader political unrest and partly due to declining economic conditions, including stagnant pay. Elsewhere in the region, early strikes involved workers protesting poor wages in Damascus in the 1870s; coal heavers in Egypt's Port Said in 1882; and porters working on the docks of Beirut, Istanbul, and Salonica in the early 1910s. In 1907, the cab drivers of Cairo organized a strike that involved thousands in response to heavy-handed attempts at the regulation of their trade by British colonial authorities. The success of the strike led to a wave of others, resulting in the establishment in 1909 of Egypt's first trade union for Egyptians, the Manual Trade Workers Union. The trade unionist movement spread. On the eve of the World War One, under the influence of communist ideology, workers in small plants and in the public sector began to organize new solidarity groups. Cigarette factory workers in Alexandria and Cairo walked out to demand better wages in response to rising prices. After the war, the heirs of this early workers' movement supported the Wafd national uprising, making the impact of wage-earners and daily laborers felt even in the halls of colonial power.

Women's mobilization

The late nineteenth and early twentieth century also witnessed the flourishing of movements devoted to enhancing women's rights across the private and public spheres in the MENA region. A landmark figure was Qasim Amin, who in 1899 published the controversial book *Liberation of Women*. Yet equally prominent were women, many from elite backgrounds (and thus possessing substantial resources), who also imprinted their ideas upon this early ferment of new thinking regarding gender roles and equality. Also, in Egypt, for instance, Maryam Nahhas Nawfal published the first female-authored biographical dictionary of women in 1879. In Ottoman-era Turkey, Fatime Aliye published *Muslim Women*, a work that among other things attacked the practice of polygamy. Around the same time, a number of literary journals directed at women's interests were published.

Moreover, the ascendancy of women's rights activists should not only be measured by the rise of dedicated organizations to this cause alone. Then, as is now, girls and women participated in many nationalist movements against Ottoman and European rule, driving forward popular protests. In Iran, women helped fuel the Tobacco Revolt of 1891, and also sustained the 1906 Constitutional Revolution. During these episodes, Iranian women organized strikes and boycotts of foreign goods, and formed human barriers to keep soldiers away from male demonstrators. In Egypt, likewise, women joined the Wafd-led nationalist revolt in 1919. In the countryside, peasant women burned fields and engaged in acts of sabotage; in cities, urban women boycotted British shops and demonstrated in the streets. After the arrest of Sa'd Zaghloul, his wife took his place in addressing public meetings. In Iraq, women took part in the 1920 uprising, and in 1924 created their own organization, the Women's Awakening Club, to promote female education and political participation. In the same year, the Egyptian Feminist Union was established by a group of activists to promote women's social rights, and to campaign for suffrage and legal equality. In these early years, the majority of women, poor and rurally based, were hardly affected by changes in the legal system or by new educational and employment opportunities; these advocacy organizations were generally small and limited to wealthier women. Yet they nonetheless represented the first expressions of those demanding gender equality during a time of multiple, cross-cutting oppressive structures of patriarchy and imperialism.

FROM EUROPEAN CONTROL TO INDEPENDENCE

Direct European control of the MENA region came late in comparison with colonialism in other parts of the world. Despite its long-lasting effects, it came to an end in a matter of decades, culminating in the last gasp of Western imperialism – World War Two. Although the UK and France emerged from the war on the winning side, both were left economically devastated. France had also experienced military occupation at home, which significantly eroded the notion of its own superiority that projected onto its colonies and mandates. On the other hand, the US emerged from the war as the dominant global power in economic, technological, and military terms. The Soviet Union was also poised to assume a much greater role in international politics. Neither of the emergent superpowers had an interest in assisting the Europeans to maintain their colonial empires. During this interlude, societal activism and new forms of civic mobilization continued – but often infused with powerful nationalist discourses. These would come of age during the turbulent transition towards independence, and the social legacies left behind would continue to shape (and in some cases, change) the new post-colonial regimes that took power.

In Iraq, for instance, the British installed a friendly monarchy under King Faisal after the revolt of 1920 – a royal autocracy that hailed from their wartime allies, the Hashemite dynasty, which ruled the Hijaz region of Saudi Arabia. (Around the same time as the Iraqi monarchy's formation, the British would ensconce another Hashemite scion as ruling monarch of their other major Mashriq mandate, the Emirate of Transjordan.) In 1924 a constituent assembly was elected and a treaty regulating Iraqi relations with Britain was signed. The 1930 Anglo-Iraqi Treaty provided for a 25-year alliance in which the two countries would consult each other on matters of foreign policy. Britain would also retain use of military bases and provide training for the Iraqi army. In 1932, Iraq became independent and joined the League of Nations. Jordan was the only other state to negotiate the end of its mandate. In neighboring Transjordan, opposition to the much lighter British presence was limited, as Emir 'Abdullah (King Faisal's brother) enjoyed somewhat wider support among the mostly tribal populace. In 1946, the mandate became independent as the newly renamed Hashemite Kingdom of Jordan, although Britain likewise retained its right for military basing and also partly controlled the Arab Legion – Jordan's land army.

In the other mandate territories, the situation was more complex. In 1926, Lebanon acquired a constitution with a framework for electoral politics. Lebanese political leaders began to prepare for self-rule during World War Two as French influence began to wane. This culminated in the 1943 National Pact in which Maronite Christian and Sunni Muslim leaders agreed to share power in a future Lebanese state. The French granted independence after World War Two, and swiftly departed afterwards. In neighboring Syria, French policy was more conciliatory following the revolt of 1925, which continued sporadically for another two years. In 1925 a new political organization emerged – the National Bloc – with strong elements of continuity from the landowners, urban elites, and government officials that held power during the Ottoman era. Far from a revolutionary group, the Bloc provided cover for a new political order on more peaceful terms. In 1928 elections to a constituent assembly led to victory for Syrian nationalist voices. In 1930, the French High Commissioner promulgated a new constitution which made Syria a parliamentary republic, with France retaining control over foreign affairs and security. Successive French governments alternated between support for ending the mandate versus retaining control of Syria. World War Two brought about change. Elections in 1943 reified victory for Syrian nationalists, and the French began reluctantly to transfer power to the Syrian government. Under pressure from Britain, the French withdrew from Syria which, together with Lebanon, joined the United Nations in 1946.

In Egypt, as has been noted, Britain declared the end of the protectorate in 1922, although the county was far from autonomous from British influence. Elections in 1924 led to victory for Sa'd Zaghloul, and his *Wafd* movement formed Egypt's first parliamentary party. In 1936 the Anglo-Egyptian treaty gave the country slightly more independence, but the British still retained responsibility for the Suez Canal, leading to tensions that would not be resolved until after the Suez Canal War two decades later.

The outcome of the war was also crucial to the course of events in the Maghrib. The first anti-colonial, nationalist party in Tunisia was created in 1919. A successor, the *Destour* (Constitution) Party, crystalized the following year with the aim of securing the protectorate's full emancipation from French subordination. By 1934, this party split and a new one, the Neo-Destour, pursued more aggressive tactics. In nearby Morocco, new nationalist sentiments emerged in the 1920s following the defeat of the Rif rebellion. By the 1940s, one of these new groups, the *Istiqlal* (Independence) Party, began working with the Sultan, Muhammad V, who began to make demands for the end of the protectorate. After the war, the French responded to both Tunisian and Moroccan nationalism from these parties, and increasing the political elite, with a combination of repression and offers of limited sovereignty. However, events elsewhere proved decisive. More significant French interests in Indochina (encompassing Vietnam, Laos, and Cambodia) came under threat. Anxious about the prospect of fighting a new global war to defend its empire, the French government negotiated with both the Tunisian

Neo-Destour and the Moroccan Sultan; the two countries became independent in 1956. The Algerian path to independence was far more violent. The presence in the country of one million Europeans (given its overall population of ten million) along with the fact that Algeria was treated not as a protectorate or colony, but an overseas province – and thus an integral part – of the French homeland ensured the French government's rejection of any claim to independence. In 1954, the nationalist Front de Liberation Nationale (FLN) was established, and a war of independence ensued. The civil conflict lasted eight years and cost hundreds of thousands of lives; only with French withdrawal did the country win its independence in 1962.

Finally, the Arabian Gulf states arrived to their independence in a distinctive way. While Saudi Arabia was formally established in 1930 and never experienced Western colonial intrusions, the littoral countries graduated from their status as British protectorates relatively peacefully. The isolationist Sultanate of Oman became independent in 1951, although British interests would loom heavily over the emergent state in subsequent decades, culminating in military involvement during the Dhofar Rebellion in the late 1960s. Through diplomatic negotiations, Kuwait became independent in 1961; Bahrain, Qatar, and the principalities that would form the United Arab Emirates did so in 1971. The southern part of Yemen centered around 'Aden won its independence in 1967 after years of unrest and mutinies, while the northern part more resembled Saudi Arabia in never being formally encroached by a European power.

This historical review of the post-colonial transition is meant to provide the backdrop to the political regimes that came to characterize much of the MENA during the post-war period. As various states became sovereign, the new regimes – whether republican or monarchical, and whether coming to office by force or through peaceful transitions – were authoritarian in nature. This would have dire consequences for patterns of social mobilization and civic activism, as the later sections will illustrate. Whereas before, political consciousness and everyday resistance targeted external authorities drawn from the wider imperial sphere, now suppression came from national governments, many of whom would see the organizational expression of contentious politics – trade unions, political parties, student movements, women's rights groups, and the like – as threats to their dominance.

These regimes varied in their trajectory. In Egypt, the Free Officers coup of 1952 ended the monarchical line founded by Muhammad 'Ali at the beginning of the nineteenth century. By the mid-1950s, the new republican regime of Gamal Abdel Nasser was espousing a new ideology of Arab

Nationalism – a fusion of socialism, pan-Arabism, and regional identities – while clamping down on societal resistance to the new order. In 1958, Iraq's Hashemite monarchy was overthrown by the military as well, with the consequent republican regime likewise claiming the mantle of anti-Western Arab Nationalism as its orientation. By the 1960s, both Iraq and Syria were led by a variation of this ideology, the Ba'th (Renaissance) movement as articulated in its mass parties. In North Africa, post-colonial political life was dominated, at least in the cases of Tunisia and Algeria, by the same political groups that led anti-colonial movements. In Tunisia, the Neo-Destour under the leadership of Habib Bourguiba assumed a dominant position and undertook a series of secularizing reforms, suppressing those who defied its orders. In Algeria, the FLN likewise became the chief political party apparatus.

As Chapter 5's discussion on political economy divulges, these core republican states harbored an autocratic social contract that in places like Egypt, Syria, and Yemen became known as *dimuqratiyyat al-khubz* (democracy of bread). This unwritten understanding required the government to undertake social and economic reforms, including the development of the national economy, in return for political obeisance. Variants of this bargain – prosperity for loyalty – also sprung up in most other Arab states, though with local variations; the oil-fueled rentier kingdoms of the Arabian Gulf, for instance, underwrote a more extreme version of this with hydrocarbon revenues, whereas resource-poor states like Lebanon, Morocco, and Jordan supplemented this rentier arrangement with other concessions. Across the board, however, post-colonial governments in the Arab world sought to contain opposition in various ways: forcibly mobilizing societies into compulsory parties and associations; integrating existing groups into state-based organizations; penalizing independent movements and critics with repression; and carefully constructing their legal systems and public spaces to make it difficult for an autonomous civil society to activate in ways that could generate meaningful contestation in the realm of ideas and politics.

SOCIAL MOBILIZATION IN THE POST-COLONIAL ERA

In general, the history of social mobilization in the post-colonial Arab world, from the 1950s until the end of the Cold War, is a history of state impositions, authoritarian rule-making, and punctuated frictions between society and authority. Yet it would be remiss to overly generalize; the collective action of citizens was never eliminated so much as rechanneled and co-opted – and even then, dictatorships found their publics to be filled with contentiousness. Echoing a theme introduced at the chapter's start, popular energies pulsed throughout public spaces even during an era of autocratic rule.

Student awakenings

The period from the end of the nineteenth century to post-colonial independence saw the spread of mass education and, especially, the establishment of new universities across the MENA. With these developments come the first instances of sustained youth activism through student-based mobilization. In essence, young citizens became tenacious players in civil society. In Egypt, after the proclamation of the country's first constitution following the country's grant of (nominal) independence from Britain, student politics acquired a new significance. Students played a prominent role in protests against continued British influence in the country, and the Wafd party sought to incorporate many into its new nationalist movement. However, in the context of a lively, if sometimes chaotic and violent, multiparty political system, students associated with the Wafd were not the only ones active. Anti-Wafd clubs opposing the Wafd's liberal ideals also attracted Egyptian students, spreading both Nazi and fascist literature through youth movements. Communists and the Muslim Brotherhood also reached out, co-opting some university-based groups to expand their activities across the country. On the eve of the 1952 military coup which brought the old monarchist political order in Egypt to an end, hundreds of university and high school students marched to the Foreign Ministry to present resolutions that combined nationalist and communist objectives, demanding that the Foreign Minister denounce Western imperialism and declare support for the Communist-inspired World Peace Movement.

Likewise, in Iraq during the 1930s, youths acquired public visibility in Baghdad and other cities as student protests against British influence became a feature of urban life. Iraqi students also fueled political agitation after World War Two. In 1952, massive youth protests rocked Baghdad, resulting in violent police clashes. Their demands for an improvement in the conditions of university learning, and more widely the elite-oriented educational system, reached much of the urban public, particularly since issues of education were tied to national independence. Iraqi students denounced Western interests and called for the withdrawal of British troops as well as greater economic provisions and clean political elections under the monarchy. On November 23, opposition leaders and workers joined the protests. A police station was attacked and four policemen killed, following which martial law was declared and much of this civic uprising crushed.

Back in Egypt, student movements continued to be a feature of public life and civic activism following the 1952 coup and the rise of the Nasserist regime. The massive expansion of secondary schooling and university education in Egypt mirrored the rapid increase of literacy in most other Arab countries under the authoritarian social contract. Yet this presented a dilemma to nationalist regimes like the Nasserist one. On the one hand, literate young citizens were useful raw materials for political mobilization in terms of carrying ideological banners and espousing support for the new political order. Yet on the other, their very unpredictability and openness to other ideologies, including opposition, made them a potential threat. The result was a strategy of constricted pluralism. At many Egyptian universities through the 1970s, varying political groups representing formal political parties and beliefs, such as Communism, Nasserism, and Islamism, were active. Yet until the Mubarak-led regime in the 1980s, Egyptian students suffered severe constraints on how broadly they could mobilize outside the official framework of government-organized conferences, institutions, and venues. While these blockages were relaxed in the 1980s, Islamist youth movements became increasingly frequent targets of state repression; for instance, security officers began curtailing the activities of many Islamist groups on campuses. As a result, from the 2000s onwards, Egyptian student organizations found it much safer to mobilize around not domestic political problems but foreign policy issues, such as the controversial 2003 Iraq War and the ongoing struggles of the Palestinians. Two rare exceptions were the youth groups *Kifaya* (Enough) and the April 6 movement, whose bold advocacy for democracy and human rights preceded and influenced the popular uprisings that would ultimately unseat the Mubarak dictatorship in the Arab Spring.

Labor mobilization

If students posed a social challenge to many post-colonial regimes in the Arab world, then workers and their unions represented a direr political rival. Especially in the 1950s and 1960s, most countries possessed far more wage-earners working in shops, farms, guilds, refineries, and factories than literate youths in schools. Most governments sought to co-opt and absorb organized labor early on, thereby precluding the creation of truly independent workers movements that could strike, protest, and thereby paralyze the state and economy.

For instance, Nasser often spoke of creating a triumphant alliance between the army, workers, peasants, and industrialists. The Egyptian government thus proclaimed its desire to improve the living standards of the laboring masses, and to join trade unions and labor federations established by the government. Members of the state-organized trade federation received a range of benefits – job security, higher wages, health care, unemployment insurance, pensions, and access to consumer cooperatives – in exchange for their integration into the apparatus of the revolutionary state. For the most part, strikes disappeared as an expression of protest. Yet those that did take place were suppressed by the regime. In August 1952, for instance, the new military regime suppressed striking textile workers, who desired better working conditions and an independent union. The Egyptian army suppressed the demonstrations, killing several and arresting hundreds.

In 1957, the Nasserist regime authorized the establishment of the Egyptian Workers Federation (EWF) while ensuring control over the composition of its leadership, which made the union little more than an appendage of the authoritarian state. The EWF was subsequently reorganized as the Egyptian Trade Union Federation (ETUF), but remained essentially the same organization. Until 1986, the president of the ETUF was also the Minister of Labor; under such political guidance, the federation could not mount meaningful campaigns of resistance or activism.

Likewise, in Algeria, the post-colonial regime under Houari Boumédiène purged all independent union leadership in 1967, including the General Confederation of Algerian Workers. In its place was a new corporatist policy of forced political integration. Reforms introduced in 1971 meant that every major workplace would have an elected assembly of workers that would be subject to governmental tutelage. In neighboring Tunisia, the General Confederation of Tunisian Workers (UGTT) represented the most powerful independent social organization upon the country's ascent to independence in 1956, and indeed played a major role alongside the Neo-Destour in pressuring the French for national sovereignty. However, under the rule of Habib Bourguiba (whose presidential tenure lasted until 1987), the UGTT became penetrated by regime elites; its leadership was occasionally removed, and in general the group worked closely with the new Tunisian state.

These patterns of control and co-optation of potential worker mobilization also took place in the monarchies, but with an emphasis on the former. In the Arabian Gulf kingdoms, for instance, trade unions were either banned altogether (often after rulers suffered early unrest, such as Bahrain) or else, in the exceptional case of Kuwait, legal yet tightly organized by regimes.

Several reasons account for this, among them the superior resources of these oil-fueled monarchies; the weaker basis of labor interests, given the propensity of rentier regimes to give blanket assurances of public employment and generous social benefits that erased many of the hardships suffered earlier; and finally, the thinner legacy of historical worker-based activism, as most prominent anti-colonial resistance movements that drew upon wage-earners too place in the Maghrib and Mashriq. Outside the Gulf, the royal autocracies of Morocco and Jordan likewise sought to shape their labor confederations, but as civic organizations they enjoyed more autonomy from authoritarian dictates than most other countries.

As Chapter 5's discussion of bread riots and fiscal austerity illustrates, though, not even top-down regulation could prevent workers from rebelling when economic conditions deteriorated. When the social contract and authoritarian bargain became unsustainable in the 1970s, resulting in severe cutbacks in public spending – and thus the removal of subsidies that had long made flour, sugar, and other basic goods affordable to even the simplest of laborers – the result were outbursts of public anger. Workers led or participated in many of these episodes, doing so outside the framework of their mandatory labor organizations. During Egypt's unrest in 1977, for instance, workers from the Helwan steelworks factory declared a strike, gathering in Tahrir Square in the center of Cairo in solidarity with other youths, laborers, and protesting citizens. Government installations and police stations were attacked, while banks, casinos, and shops selling luxury goods were attacked before the military suppressed the turmoil and restored order. The same pattern occurred in every other case of bread rioting, such as Tunisia, Morocco, and Jordan; workers stood at the forefront of political resistance in petitioning for economic justice, and they deliberately bypassed existing political channels and organized mandates to do so.

Women's mobilization

Despite their central role in anti-colonial agitation, women's rights movements suffered marginalization following the achievement of independence across the region. In Iraq and Egypt, women gained access to the public sphere through nationalist uprisings yet found themselves excluded from politics after independence. In Algeria, women were vital to the Algerian national movement during the war for independence, with many taking up arms alongside men. In this way, they traversed from the private sphere to the public sphere through the exigencies of struggle – a conduit of temporary empowerment alluded to in Chapter 9's discussion of gender roles. Yet in the post-colonial years, women were often expected to retreat back into the private sphere and assume back their traditional roles. Mirroring its strategy with workers, the Algerian government created the *Union Nationale des Femmes Algériennes* (National Union of Algerian Women), a state-affiliated organization intended to absorb the energies of female activists in order to support the centralized autocratic regime.

More so than labor unions, though, women's movements began flexing their muscle and engaging in concerted collective action starting in the 1980s. In Morocco, for instance, women's rights groups often drew upon interpretations of feminism inflected through Islam, which made them not just distinctive from Western feminist groups but also sufficiently indigenized to give them credibility when desiring gender equality. The Moroccan campaign to reform the Personal Status Code, climaxing in the 2004 declaration of a new law, began in the early 1990s. Furthermore, though not in the Arab world, the Turkish experience provides a parallel instantiation of gradually escalating women's mobilization. Turkish women began to form new organizations in the 1980s to promote gender equality and women's access to the public sphere, consciously seeking to overturn the earlier generation's absorption and co-optation by the Kemalist state. In 1986, Turkish women from Istanbul and Ankara famously united to petition the government to implement the UN Convention on the Elimination of All Forms of Discrimination against Women (CEDAW).

THE POST-COLD WAR RENAISSANCE OF CIVIL SOCIETY

From the early 1990s onwards, the end of the Cold War wrought significant changes in political dynamics as democratization became a buzz phrase across the MENA region. Processes of political liberalization were embarked upon by both republican and monarchical regimes, although the substance of such liberalization was highly variable from context to context. Liberalization, here, means the relaxation of repression resulting in greater political diversity and pluralism, such as the lessening of censorship or legalization of opposition parties; yet it stops short of democracy, because key levers of power (such as executive authority and military control) remain in the hands of unelected rulers.

Such liberalization proceeded in many Arab countries throughout the 1990s. For instance, parliamentary elections were restored or allowed with greater opposition competition in Morocco, Tunisia, Egypt, Jordan, Lebanon, Kuwait, and Yemen. The Algerian experiment was aborted following the military's annulment of a successful Islamist electoral victory there in 1992, and in other countries very unique historical events coincided with liberalization, such as the liberation of Kuwait after the 1990–1991 Gulf War, the 1990 unification of northern and southern Yemen, and the 1990 end of the Lebanese civil war. Yet the overarching factor was growing pressures from the global arena combined with burgeoning expectations from social forces for kings and presidents to allow for more civil liberties and political freedom. Even in the more conservative Arabian Gulf kingdoms beyond Kuwait, there were glimmers of increased participation and contestation. For instance, in March 1999, Qatar held its first elections to a 29-member Municipality Council; women were allowed not only to vote but also to stand as candidates for election. Bahrain held parliamentary elections in October 2002 in which both men and women over the age of 21 voted – the first such national legislative contest since 1973.

Driving this liberalization, and in turn benefiting from it, was a renaissance of civil society, as the loosening of previous restrictions on basic freedoms of public assembly, organizational establishment, and individual expression resulted in a flurry of citizens creating new interest groups. Such civic engagement is another reflection of the spirit of social mobilization that infused public spaces in past generations. According to a UN estimate given in 1995, the numbers of civil society organizations across the region increased from 20,000 in the 1970s to 70,000 in the mid-1990s alone, with 14,000 in Egypt alone. Today, a quick glance at the official rosters of licensed organizations released by various governments indicate the extent to which individuals founded new entities in support of their interests and advocacy. Algeria possesses over 90,000 registered associations; Egypt now has over 40,000; Tunisia has 21,000; Yemen has 7,000; Lebanon has 8,500; Jordan has over 5,100; and the West Bank and Gaza Strip contain over 3,600. Also playing a vital role has been the increasingly active and critical media sector. While Arab governments still retained ultimate control over official news agencies and publishing houses, in many countries an independent media was able to crystallize, resulting in various publications – daily papers, weekly magazines, monthly journals, and so forth – that helped catalyze new organizations and highlight existing ones. Today, the saturation of social media helps play this role in continuing to give visibility to new and old civic groups.

In general, contemporary civil society organizations in the Arab states can be divided into six primary types. One is the religious sector, dominated by Islamist organizations. Some are political; others emphasize charitable enterprise, doctrinal propagation, and social relations. The second consists of service providers that furnish goods and activities that would normally be given by governments; these include educational foundations, employment assistance, health care initiatives, anti-poverty networks, cultural diversity programs, and other entities that seek to improve the quality of life at the grass-roots level. The third encompasses membership-based organizations, which require certain criteria to join and aggressively protect the interests of constituents. These include, for instance, labor unions, student movements, professional syndicates (e.g., the national bar associations comprising all practicing lawyers), and chambers of commerce.

The fourth variant of civil society organizations entails cultural entities that primarily intend to promote solidarity and activity-based awareness, such as artistic cooperatives, literary societies, youth networks, and sports clubs. Environmental activism, of the type discussed in Chapter 7, falls into this bracket, as do many issue-oriented social awareness campaigns led by young citizens. The fifth type is more controversial – it includes pro-democratic organizations, such as human rights monitors, political reform groups, and other entities often associated with democratic opposition under authoritarian regimes.

The sixth and final category is more specious, for it comprises *regime-created* organizations designed to look independent but which in reality are not autonomous from state control. Some ceased to exist after the Arab Spring, simply because their patrons (the regimes) also ceased to exist. These included, for instance, Egyptian charities chaired by Suzanne Mubarak, the wife of former president Hosni Mubarak, as well as medical and employment foundations run by Leila Trabelsi, wife of former Tunisian president Zine 'Abidine Ben 'Ali. Others persist, especially in the kingdoms; every monarchy runs a parallel sector of royally funded charities, foundations, and institutes, which often dwarf non-royal civil society organizations in funding and visibility.

It is telling that many visitors to these countries do not recognize the scope and activities of civil society organizations because despite being public entities, their activities are relatively quiet and mundane – drawing in members and some interested bystanders, producing ideas and achievements that do not necessarily make national headlines, and yet operating to achieve their particular interests. Contrast, for instance, the scene in Photo 3.2 – a Human Rights Watch press conference at the Egyptian Press Syndicate in Cairo, which denounced the dangers to migrants, refugees, and asylum-seekers

PHOTO 3.2
Human Rights Watch holding press conference, Egypt, 2008.

Source: Photo by elhamalawy is licensed under CC BY-SA 2.0.
Online: www.flickr.com/photos/elhamalawy/3025162116

coming to Egypt – to that in Photo 3.3, which shows a group of Egyptian youths making handicrafts under the auspices of a sustainable work NGO. Both are part of civil society; both take place in the public arena; and both can appear quite invisible to those outside their audiences.

The regime-created entities aside, a number of domestic and international factors help explain the extraordinary rise in civic activism seen in the region during the 1990s. Internally, the expression of social organization has been driven not just by increased state tolerance, but also structural forces. Urbanization, for instance, naturally generates a propensity for collective action; all else being equal, more educated citizens living in close proximity to one another tend to create more common groups. Workers, for instance, may coordinate strikes and bargain for higher wages when there is a critical mass of them. Education, too, matters immensely – student movements, after all, are sparked into action where a sufficient number of high school and university learners congregate in common spaces and circulate ideas. In many Arab

PHOTO 3.3
Handicraft workshop for Egyptian youth, 2011.

Source: Photo by maltman23is licensed under CC BY-SA 2.0.
Online: www.flickr.com/photos/maltman23/6223965879

countries, the rise of Islamism was also vital after the 1980s. Islamist movements, from the large Muslim Brotherhood to local charities and service providers, thrived in the fluid networks connecting religiosity to activism, and they comprise a significant portion of civil society. Finally, there was simply greater awareness on part of many Arabs about their meaningful capacity for action. The impact of the dramatic images from the Berlin Wall's crumbling in 1989 and the triumph of people power catalyzed new willingness on part of many segments of Arab societies to mobilize around old and new ideals. This "demonstration effect," as many scholars termed it, suggested a degree of transnational linkage that governments did not understand – namely, that their own public audiences could be cognitively swayed and even inspired by events occurring in seemingly distant lands.

Internationally, local civil society development was spurred by a variety of external factors. In the 1990s, major international players including multilateral institutions like the UN and World Bank, regional organizations like the European Union, and the remaining global superpower in the US all converged upon the belief that a healthy civil society sector was important for democratization, or at the very least good governance in terms of citizens holding their rulers accountable and enhancing the quality of life across society. Thus, whether through the prioritization of democracy promotion through diplomatic protocol and economic aid, or else international support programs providing grants and training to local activists, these global actors did not hesitate to support new civil society organizations in the Arab world. For instance, in 2002, the US created the Middle East Partnership Initiative through the State Department. Four years later, the EU established the European Instrument for Democratization and Human Rights, a platform whose specific mission aimed to strengthen civil society organizations emphasizing human rights and democratic participation.

BOX 3.2 CASE STUDY – THE MEPI FOREIGN AID PROGRAM

In 2002, the US State Department began operating the Middle East Partnership Initiative (MEPI). Building on earlier experiences but also embodying the then-prevalent belief among American policymakers that the US needed to spearhead democratization in the Arab world by empowering local actors, MEPI's mission was simple: reach out and directly empower, through funding and training, civil society organizations and private-sector businesses that stood for political reform, good governance, and ultimately democracy. It also hosted various educational activities, including exchanges that brought students from the MENA region to the US for leadership training. MEPI was not a revolutionary program, as its architects – including Secretary of State Colin Powell – framed the initiative as an incubator for long-term political change, not a short-term instigator. The roster of mostly Arab civil society groups that have received MEPI support since 2002 numbers over a thousand, ranging from tiny start-ups to large foundations. They include groups like anti-corruption watchdogs in Iraq, anti-littering activism in the Palestinian territories, voter registration and education networks in Lebanon, student technology forums in Tunisia, youth entrepreneurship in Algeria, academic research projects in Jordan, media training workshops in Morocco, and women's and children's rights advocates in Yemen. The impacts seem impressive when judged by the views of recipients, and indeed today MEPI alumni gatherings and networks abound in these countries. However, critics have duly wondered about MEPI's purpose and effectiveness. Many saw MEPI as inherently contradictory: the US needed good strategic relations with nondemocratic regimes in the Arab world, especially during the Global War on Terror, which made MEPI not so much a transformer of civil society but merely a public relations gimmick designed to

> **BOX 3.2 (CONTINUED)**
>
> sidestep thorny issues about human rights and democracy promotion. Indeed, MEPI's major regional offices were initially established in Tunis, Tunisia, and Abu Dhabi, UAE – two countries that until the Arab Spring were among the most closed dictatorships of the region and hence paradoxically frowned the most upon social mobilization and civil society. Yet while the ongoing MEPI project may invoke political and moral hazards, it also underscores the pluralism and activism present in many Arab civil societies – leaving the issue still uncertain.

Of course, it is critical to not overplay the promise of civil society. Some Arab countries remained extremely hostile to social mobilization; after the 1980s, their regimes neither liberalized nor tolerated much growth in new independent associations. Even after the Cold War's end, for instance, it was clear that Syria, Libya, Sudan, and most of the Arabian Gulf kingdoms excepting Kuwait and, to a lesser extent, Bahrain would not be joining within the regional wave of civic activism. Their regimes remained typified by high degrees of repression, absence of legal opposition, and antipathy to any kind of social mobilization not directly stoked by rulers themselves. Furthermore, even countries that remained cautiously open to civic engagement still allowed authorities the singular power to suppress any organization that posed a perceived political threat. In most Arab countries with active civil societies, for instance, interior ministries and associational laws govern the registration and operation of civil society groups. It was, and still is, relatively easy for officials to "find" financial irregularities in an NGO, or to locate errors in an initial application for registration, as an excuse to shut down the entire enterprise. Finally, civil societies themselves were hardly unified arenas of coordinated action. Some civil society organizations remained so dependent upon foreign funding that they lacked domestic credibility; this also made them vulnerable to political crackdowns. Others were little more than one-person shows, possessing an office and website but little by way of actual productivity. Moreover, there developed – and remains today – deep mistrust between Islamist and non-Islamist organizations, often resulting in competition between the two camps over ownership of certain issues such as educational provision and health care access.

CIVIL SOCIETY AFTER THE ARAB SPRING

The renaissance of Arab civil society in the 1990s embodied a welcome return of social mobilization in many countries across the region. Although it represented an extraordinary scope of public activism that many previously did not think possible in the region, civil society did not herald revolution or democratization. Importantly, neither did it encompass the full capacity of everyday peoples to mobilize and resist political authority. Civil society organizations are formal legal entities that, registered with authorities, activate around the interests of members. Yet the history of social mobilization is also a history of anonymous citizens choosing to congregate, protest, and contest structures of oppression *without* needing a formal structure to do so. In the late 2000s, researchers were slowly becoming aware that more and more demonstrations and unrest occurring in the Arab world seemed to emanate not from the offices of NGOs or on the orders of professional associations, but rather through spontaneous decisions made by aggrieved peoples needing to express their anger and frustration. By the late 2000s, for instance, Egypt was witnessing an increasing degree of wildcat strikes – that is, strikes occurring outside the official mandate of ETUF and other state-appointed bodies governing workers – that occurred through spontaneous, everyday coordination by wage earners unhappy with their conditions. In 2006, the country experienced 222 strikes, none of them officially allowed by the government; the number increased to over 700 in 2009.

It took the 2011–2012 Arab Spring, however, for the point to be finally hammered home. In no popular uprising did civil society organizations lead the way. Civil society groups participated in these youth-led movements for change, and helped sustain their collective action through supporting the push for democracy; but in every case of peaceful insurrection – and especially in the iconic revolutions that toppled leaders in Tunisia, Egypt, Libya, and Yemen – mass protests resembled more the fiery resistance movements of the colonial era, when citizens grouped together informally and launched campaigns of revolt demanding their dignity and freedom. Put another way, the uprisings were informal rather than formalized; and they were led not by well-trained directors of human rights organizations, for instance, but instead by rebellious youths who simply chose to disobey autocratic rules.

The mobilizational landscape since the Arab Spring has been mixed, marked by highs and lows. Excluding Libya, Yemen, and Syria, as the wars and conflicts raging in these countries have tragically decimated many social and political organizations, authoritarian regimes have generally turned against civil society. Tunisia stands as the bright exception. Having undergone a tentative democratic transition, old and new civil society groups – ranging from the UGTT and other workers' movements to new social, cultural, and gender equality forces – have acted to keep the elected government honest. They have highlighted the need for greater economic development in rural areas, aggressively defended human rights and women's empowerment when necessary, and pressured political figures to not fall back upon the corruption and abuses that marked the previous era of dictatorship under Ben 'Ali.

However, most other governments have either maintained or restricted further their legal frameworks to prevent future large-scale protests, with destructive effects upon civil society. A combination of legal suffocation plus political repression has operated in force. For instance, in 2015, Jordanian authorities revoked the registration and licensing of the Muslim Brotherhood after ordaining a newer, less contentious Islamist organization; they transferred much of the Brotherhood's local financial assets to the new group, thereby signaling their willingness to intervene within large established civic entities in order to prevent meaningful political opposition from mobilizing. Human rights monitors in Bahrain and Kuwait have suffered closure under highly questionable charges of financial improprieties or allegations of disturbing public order. In Algeria, a new law on associations gave the government newer discretionary powers to revoke the charters of any civic entity. Yet Egypt has cracked down upon its large civic sector with fury; not only was the Muslim Brotherhood banned after the July 2013 coup, but new laws banned NGOs from any foreign funding and performing any activity deemed remotely political, such as conducting research surveys or training political parties.

Though imperfect, one measure of declining civil society memberships can be found in by comparing Arab Barometer public opinion surveys between its first iteration in 2008 and its latest wave in 2017. Exploring results for five countries – Algeria, Jordan, the Palestinian territories, Lebanon, and Morocco – regarding the question of whether respondents were members of any organization or formal group, we find fewer people reporting any kind of membership after a decade punctuated by the Arab Spring and subsequent chilling effects (Figure 3.1). Only in Morocco did the proportion of organizational membership rise; and in Algeria and Lebanon, the level of "joiners" halved – a drastic reduction.

However, this does not mean the end of civil society. We have strong evidence that mobilization continues, just around different issues and under new restrictions. Some of the most aggressive environmental activism in the history of the region, such as Lebanon's #YouStink movement and Algerian anti-fracking campaign mentioned in Chapter 7's discussion of environmental impacts, have occurred despite many countries actively discouraging or penalizing spontaneous, grass-roots congregation. As in the past, authoritative impositions to limit the potential of peoples to mobilize are their own

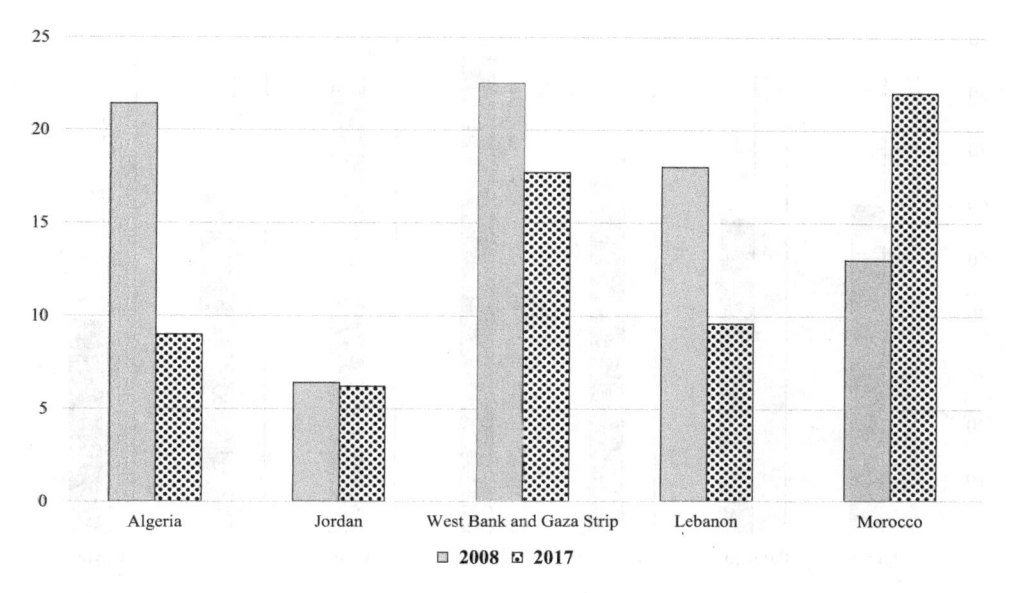

FIGURE 3.1
Self-reported membership in civil society organizations before and after the Arab Spring from Arab Barometer, 2008 vs. 2017.

Source: Arab Barometer, Wave I (2006–2008) and Wave IV (2016–2017).
Online: www.arabbarometer.org. The survey question was: "Are you a member of any organization or formal group?"

worst enemy: over time, citizens and groups learn to adapt to, and work around, such rules – or else flagrantly ignore them altogether, as in the case of the Arab Spring. Indeed, the strength of the 2011–2012 uprisings was their origins in informality rather than formal groups like the Muslim Brotherhood or pro-democracy NGOs. It is easy to prohibit a student movement based at a university; it is difficult to prevent those students from communicating on Facebook, Twitter, or SMS messages.

For instance, consider Figure 3.2, which compares Facebook usage and perceptions of civil society freedom from the latest Arab Barometer results in 2017. There is substantial variation in how people perceive their freedom to join civic groups and independent organizations, ranging from a high of 86.5 percent in Lebanon to an unsurprising low of 38.9 percent in Egypt; but overall, the majority of these Arab countries believe that the *opportunity* to participate in civil society still exists. Likewise, Facebook membership is quite high across the board, with an average of 81 percent reporting having a Facebook page. Of course, a Facebook page alone does not an

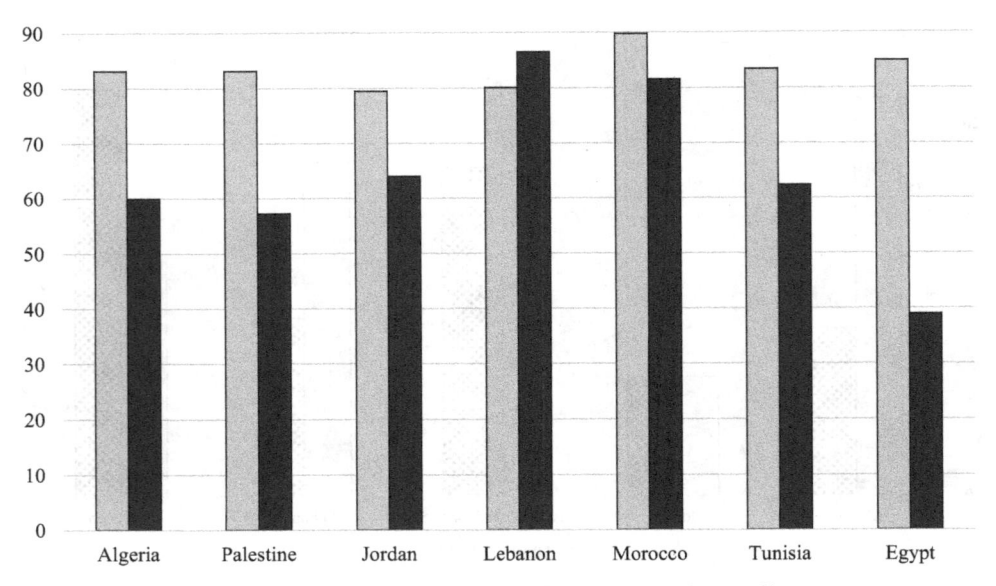

FIGURE 3.2
Facebook usage and perceptions of civil society freedom from Arab Barometer, 2017.

Source: Arab Barometer, Wave IV (2016–2017).

Online: www.arabbarometer.org. The survey question reflected in the second of the data bars for each country: "To what extent do you think the freedom to join civil associations and organizations is guaranteed in your country?"

activist (much less revolutionary) make; but insofar that Facebook represents a realm of social communication and online coordination important for real-world action, this statistical finding suggests that some capacity for renewed collective action does persist, despite the best efforts of rulers to deter any contentious behavior through harsher laws and repression. In other words, the incendiary raw materials are still present – it may simply take another spark to ignite them.

CONCLUSION

The social history of the MENA region is a history of social mobilization and the emergence of civil society. As this chapter showed, across the Arab world, ordinary citizens have collectively engaged in resistance, advocacy, and contention to advance their desires for as long as there have been authoritative structures of oppressive power. The evidence here from the Ottoman Empire to the turbulent decades of European imperialism validate this. In turn, social mobilization has been shown to be not a univalent dynamic produced purely through public action, but also shaped by social, economic, and political responses. Thus, the transition to post-colonial sovereignty and the rise of new authoritarian regimes in the Arab world was marked by the suppression or manipulation of many civic formations that could have formed the basis of an independent and autonomous public sphere, one that might have directly challenged rulers. The end of the Cold War marked a renaissance of social activism and civil society, as individuals formed and joined an incredible spectrum of interest groups ranging from religious organizations, such as the Muslim Brotherhood, to service providers, professional associations, cultural forums, and pro-democracy entities. While governments found ways to contain or deflect such pressures from below, they were not prepared for the Arab Spring, which temporarily overlaid the formal landscape of civil society with a torrent of *informal* mobilization originating from that which rulers could not police directly – the emotive calculations of ordinary citizens, who sought to shatter the boundaries of organized politics and instead directly enact their demands. Though nervous authorities since have sought to clamp down further on the margins of civic action, the history of the region and the prolonged engagements of many people with issues of importance suggest that the question of future social mobilization, and perhaps another Arab Spring, should be framed in terms of not *if* but *when*.

QUESTIONS FOR DISCUSSION

1 What were the primary goals of social mobilization during the Ottoman and European periods of imperialism?
2 How did workers and wage-earners manage to find success in demanding economic rights early on, given their very weak material and financial position?
3 What specific obstacles have women's rights groups faced in advocating for gender equality over time?
4 Why did so many authoritarian rulers see this legacy of social mobilization, and the potentiality of civil society, as threats during the 1950s and 1960s?
5 How were social forces and civic actors co-opted, absorbed, and otherwise neutralized during the Cold War?
6 In the post–Cold War years, what types of civil society organizations emerged during political liberalization in the Arab world?
7 Is international support, including foreign funding, a viable mechanism to empower citizens to resist authority or fight for their interests?
8 What might the future of civil society in the Middle East look like, as the Arab Spring fades into the historical background?

FURTHER READING

There are excellent volumes that survey the history of social mobilization and popular resistance in the MENA region, from colonial (including Ottoman) times to the present day. Two are Charles Tripp, *Power and the People: Paths of Resistance in the Middle East* (Cambridge: Cambridge University Press, 2013), and John Chalcraft, *Popular Politics in the Making of the Modern Middle East* (Cambridge: Cambridge University Press, 2016). Ilan Pappe, *The Modern Middle East* (London: Routledge, 2010), puts some of these struggles in the context of urban, rural, cultural, and women's history. Michaelle Browers locates the conceptual underpinnings of public discourse and civil society in the intellectual ferment of political philosophy and ideology in her *Democracy and Civil Society in Arab Political Thought: Transcultural Possibilities* (Syracuse, NY: Syracuse University Press, 2006). A thoroughly modern and enlightening study of activism today is Asef Bayat, *Life as: How Ordinary People Change the Middle East*, 2nd ed. (Stanford, CA: Stanford University Press, 2013). Joel Beinin and Federic Vairel, eds., *Social Movements, Mobilization, and Contestation in the Middle East and North Africa* (Palo Alto: Stanford University Press, 2011) provides another contemporary look at forms of anti-state resistance and group activism.

The question of civil society – including not just its origins but its democratizing potential, or lack thereof – has also occupied many studies, with the overall consensus hovering between cynicism and caution. The foundational work is Augustus Richard Norton, ed., *Civil Society in the Middle East*, vols. 1 and 2 (Leiden: EJ Brill, 1995–96), which set the stage for a generation of scholarship. Though hopeful, consequent research was less persuaded that civil society alone could revolutionize the Arab world. See, for instance, Sheila Carapico, "NGOs, INGOs, GO-NGOs and DO-NGOs: Making Sense of Non-governmental Organizations," *Middle East Report* 214 (2000): 12–15; Sean Yom, "Civil Society and Democratization in the Arab World," *Middle East Review of International Affairs* 9, no. 4 (2005): 14–33; Vickie Langohr, "Too Much Civil Society, Too Little Politics: Egypt and Liberalizing Arab Regimes," *Comparative Politics* 36, no. 2 (2004): 181–204; and Amy Hawthorne, "Middle Eastern Democracy: Is Civil Society the Answer?" Carnegie Papers No. 44 (2004). Others have pushed back, noting the boundaries of change and adaptation are constantly shifting: see Benoit Challand, "The Counter-Power of Civil Society and the Emergence of a New Political Imaginary in the Arab World," *Constellations* 18, no. 3 (2011): 271–83; and Francesco Cavatorta and Vincent Durac, *Civil Society and Democratization in the Arab World: The Dynamics of Activism* (London: Routledge, 2010).

Zooming out, a theoretical primer that puts regional mobilization in perspective by defining contentious politics and forms of collective action is Charles Tilly and Sidney Tarrow, *Contentious Politics* (Oxford: Oxford University Press, 2007). The earlier Doug McAdam, Sidney Tarrow, and Charles Tilly, *Dynamics of Contention* (New York: Cambridge University Press, 2001) provides a similar framework. One work that applies these concepts to the question of revolutions is Jeff Goodwin, *No Other Way Out: States and Revolutionary Movements, 1945–1991* (New York: Cambridge University Press, 2001); another is Kurt Schock, *Unarmed Insurrections: People Power Movements in Nondemocracies* (Minneapolis: University of Minnesota Press, 2005), which focuses on the moral and political impacts of nonviolent activism.

Back to the MENA, there are many rigorous works that investigate specific realms of social mobilization. For instance, women's movements command attention in Fatima

Sadiqi and Moha Ennaji, eds., *Women in the Middle East and North Africa: Agents of Change* (London: Routledge, 2011), and Valentine Moghadam's *Modernizing Women: Gender and Social Change in the Middle East*, 3rd ed. (Boulder, CO: Lynne Rienner, 2013). Workers and organized labor have also elicited a strong tradition of scholarship. Specific events are scrutinized in great detail in journal articles; see, for example, Ellis Goldberg, "Peasants in Revolt: Egypt 1919," *International Journal Middle Eastern Studies* 24, no. 2 (1992): 261–80, for the legendary Egyptian 1919 Revolution and the nationalist awakening. Joel Beinin, *Workers and Thieves: Labor Movements and Popular Uprisings in Tunisia and Egypt* (Stanford, CA: Stanford University Press, 2015) examines how worker resistance has evolved from the post-colonial era of subordination by dictators to more emancipatory, small-scale uprisings. A longer history of the working class in the region is found in Zachary Lockman, ed., *Workers and Working Classes in the Middle East: Struggles, Histories, Historiographies* (Albany, NY: SUNY Press, 1994). Likewise, close historical analysis of student mobilization can be found in Jordi Tejel Gorgas, "The Limits of the State: Student Protest in Egypt, Iraq and Turkey, 1948–63," *British Journal of Middle Eastern Studies* 40, no. 4 (2013): 359–77, and more specifically in Egypt within Ahmed Abdalla's *The Student Movement and National Politics in Egypt: 1923–1973* (Cairo: AUC Press, 2008).

Finally, there is a plethora of work analyzing the Arab Spring and its effects upon civil society and ordinary activism. Most are edited volumes with many contributions, such as Lina Khatib and Ellen Lust, eds., *Taking to the Streets: The Transformation of Arab Activism* (Baltimore, MD: Johns Hopkins University Press, 2014); Fahed al-Sumait, Nele Lenze, and Michael Hudson, eds., *The Arab Uprisings: Catalysts, Dynamics, and Trajectories* (Lanham, MD: Rowman and Littlefield, 2015); Marc Lynch, ed., *The Arab Uprisings Explained: New Contentious Politics in the Middle East* (New York: Columbia University Press, 2014); Adam Roberts, Michael Willis, Rory McCarthy, and Timothy Garton Ash, *Civil Resistance in the Arab Spring: Triumphs and Disasters* (Oxford: Oxford University Press, 2016), and Fawaz Gerges, ed., *Contentious Politics in the Middle East: Popular Resistance and Marginalized Activism beyond the Arab Uprisings* (New York: Palgrave Macmillan, 2015). Asef Bayat's *Revolution without Revolutionaries: Making Sense of the Arab Spring* (Stanford, CA: Stanford University Press, 2017) is another insightful intervention.

Online sources

Online research on social mobilization and civil society in the MENA can vary in quality. While there are many essays and articles online *about* these topics, the capacity to truly dig deep and learn more about these entities from the inside can vary across countries since not all popular movements, grass-roots campaigns, and formal organizations have made their homes online. Often, a simple Google search or random forays into social media like Facebook or Twitter can reveal the kinds of youth-driven activism or societal congregations forming around the latest issues (and to facilitate that, online tools like TweetTracker [http://tweettracker.fulton.asu.edu/#] abound). Otherwise, there is no master directory or listing for social mobilization and citizen movements in the MENA; because most governments are not democratic, maintaining a database like this would be self-defeating. Freedom House's trilogy of annual reports – Freedom in the World, Freedom of the Press, and Freedom on the Net – at least presents penchant views into how well activists and citizens are able to advance their interests outside of the state, with profiles of every country (https://freedomhouse.org/).

Still, for general research into civil society, there are more concrete resources. A start would be Arab NGO Directory (https://arab.org/directory/), which lists many civil society organizations across the Arab world. Another is the World Association for NGO's global directory listings, which narrows by sub-region (www.wango.org/resources.aspx?section=ngodir). The International Center for Not-for-Profit Law maintains a Civic Freedom Monitor forum that tracks how associational laws and political regulations are affecting civil society groups across the world, including the MENA (www.icnl.org/research/monitor/). The USAID Civil Society Organization Sustainability Index covers general trends regarding survival, health, and financing for civil society groups (www.usaid.gov/middle-east-civil-society). The CIVICUS Monitor also covers the region in evaluating whether conditions for social and civic mobilization remain open or closed (https://monitor.civicus.org/).

Identity, its power and pull

P.R. Kumaraswamy

THE RUNDOWN: KEY TOPICS COVERED
- Defining and measuring identity
- Origins of identity
- Homogeneity versus diversity
- Minority rights and claims
- Tribalism and ethnonationalism
- Identity-based conflict

INTRODUCTION

Who am I? The enigmatic philosophical question searching for identity is extremely pertinent to the Middle East and North Africa (MENA). Generally, social scientists define identity as one's self-conception as it relates to others, resulting in social categorization and differentiation. They connote particular roles and expectations, and provide a sense of purpose and normative rules that govern the boundaries of appropriate behavior. Today, we witness that individuals and groups in the MENA have multiple identities in terms of religious beliefs, ethnic compositions, national sentiments, tribal affiliation, cultural norms, linguistic preferences, and other distinctive traits and practices. Though predominantly Arab and Islamic, there are considerable variations and deviations within the dominant ethnic and religious composition. Furthermore, in political terms, the region does not adhere to a single ideology or system of governance; since the demise of Ottoman and Western imperialism, its regimes have spanned the gamut of governance, ranging from conservative monarchies and familial dynasties to radical republics run by presidential dictators and military strongmen. Yet there is one constant: in general, the response of a dominant group practicing a *particular* identity has been hostile when a subordinate group mobilizes and advances a very different self-conception. In examining identities in the Middle East, we must explore their diversity and multiplicity, take care in their measurement and definition, understand the historical trend towards homogenization, and engage the consequences of conflict when groups advancing and seeking an identity that does not "fit" within an existing political order run against the tall walls of social resistance.

DIVERSITY AND MULTIPLICITY

Individuals never have a single, immutable identity. From the cradle to the grave, their identity evolves with age and maturing of the body, mind, and soul. Gender is an inseparable component of identity, but it also progresses and transforms with time. Family status, geographical origin, preferred language, social class, level of education, chosen profession, religious beliefs, economic conditions, and place of residence considerably influence the identity of an individual. A citizen of a country is more than a social security number, and simultaneously carries a host of non-conflictual as well as conflictual identities.

The American identity, for example, indicates not only gender, religion, or race but also a sense of loyalty to, and rootedness (usually indicating residency) within, a particular sovereign state. There is room within this identity marker to indicate if the person is native-born American or a naturalized citizen, a condition critical to run for the highest elected office in the country. The assimilationist American culture, however, did not prevent the Japanese-Americans being interned during the World War Two. In times of political tensions and conflicts, even full citizens are made to feel differently and their "American-ness" becomes subservient to other aspects of their identity, such as race or gender.

As conglomerations of individuals, nations and states are complex and carry considerable overlapping and often conflicting identities. An Egyptian is not just a citizen but could be a male Coptic Christian working in a private-sector company in the vast and sparsely populated New Valley in southern Egypt. Likewise, a Saudi could be a Sunni Muslim woman living in the Shi'a-majority eastern province unable to transfer her citizenship to her children because she married a non-Saudi Arab Sunni Muslim man. Each adjective and signifier describing these individuals could be justifiably drawn out and used as indicating some meaningful aspect of not only their lives, but also their self-conceptions that enable them to feel affinity and belonging to others sharing that same trait – and inversely, distance from those who exhibit divergent or opposite traits.

Much like individuals, collective actors such as groups, nations, and states invariably carry multiple identities simultaneously; some work in harmony and contribute to national growth and welfare, but often the diversity they bring is seen as harmful and destructive. The multiplicity of identities is not the issue, but their perception and treatment by the society and state are problematic. Acceptance is a virtue rarely practiced. If diversity is the norm, why are multiple identities denied and even abhorred? The reason has to be located in the pressures towards homogeneity.

MEASURING AND OBSERVING IDENTITY

Social scientists have long wrestled with the question of how to measure identity, either at the level of individual or collective actors like ethnic groups. Not only do hundreds of definitions exist, but there has been little agreement on the best method of ascertaining how intensely these identities are felt at the cognitive level; how durable and resilient they are over time; and why some identities are privileged over others, especially during periods of crisis and change. Issues of measurement are critical because identity is not merely a concept but a *variable* – an independent factor assumed to cause individuals and groups to act in certain ways, and to hold certain beliefs. It conversely denotes that the cleavages between those identity-holders and others are grounds for disagreement and conflict.

For instance, to argue that ethnic minorities are more likely to engage in popular mobilization or violent revolt when under attack from oppressive majoritarian governments suggests, for instance, that ethnic identity somehow binds these individuals together and enables collective action. To exposit that female citizens are more likely to vote for, or feel solidarity with, women parliamentarians, leaders, and notables is to imply that the female gender as an identity influences political preferences and choices. To suggest that citizens in nation-states attacked by other countries will band together and join the military in celebration of their patriotic loyalty insinuates that some latent national identity during periods of crisis and peril enables new institutional routines and social behaviors that would not otherwise happen during periods of stability and peace. To claim that two religious communities drawing holy inspiration from dissimilar sacred traditions are more likely to fight over shared land, than if that land was occupied by a single religious sect, is to infer that spiritual disagreement that insists the other is wrong can make violence a more attractive option than peaceful coexistence, even if the latter is a far more rational strategy in terms of reducing costs for all involved.

While we cannot resolve the thorny question of measurement here, it is nonetheless critical to remember that not only does identity *exist* in a concrete sense, its use as an explanation for various social, economic, and political outcomes should be accompanied by some effort to measure and define it. One promising possibility is to first map out all the different identities that *could* shape preferences and behavior, something done later in this chapter in the context of the MENA, and then ascertain all the different social purposes, normative rules, modes of contestation, and relational understandings that flow from any given self-conception. This requires asking certain questions, such as these: what are the perceived goals of an individual or group claiming to hold a certain identity? What are the unspoken principles and criteria that must be met for an individual to belong to this identity category? How has any given identity been contested or debated, both by its holders and by outsiders? And how does this identity differentiate the "Self" from the "Other," the insider from outsider?

While it would take a far larger volume to chart out these useful interrogatives, they are worth considering in future forays into identity-oriented research in the region. Scholars conducting such work tend to employ one of two methodologies. The first is surveys and polls, which query individuals about their attitudes, preferences, beliefs, and values – responses that help us ascertain which identities they prioritize and how they may overlap or disconnect from one another. For example, the Arab Barometer project since 2006 has polled societies across the region on a battery of questions. In the latest (fourth) wave, which took place during 2016–2017, respondents were asked about which of the following single, mutually exclusive choices they most closely identified with: country of birth, religion, ethnicity (e.g., Arab), region (e.g., Maghrib, Mashriq, Gulf), local community or city, and tribe. On average, 45.2 percent chose country and 27.9 percent chose religion. Nearly 9 percent chose tribe, while the remainder choices all garnered below 5 percent. Yet there were considerable variations in the countries, as Figure 4.1 displays in four selected cases – Jordan, Lebanon, Morocco, and Egypt. In Jordan, for instance, few picked country, suggesting weak degrees of nationalism and nationalistic identity in the Hashemite Kingdom.

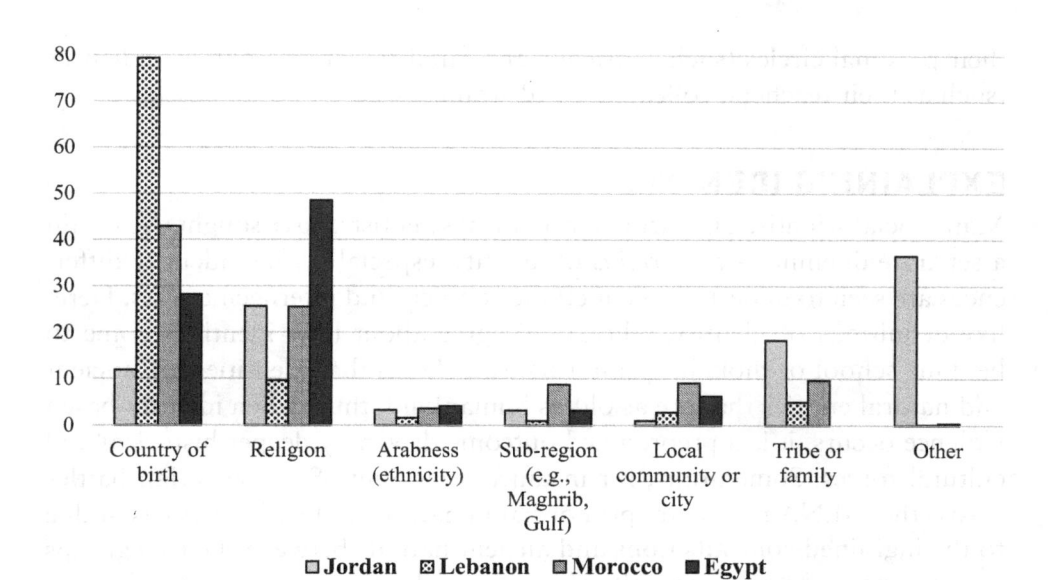

FIGURE 4.1
Revealed identity choices through Arab Barometer, 2017.

Source: Arab Barometer, Wave IV (2016–2017).

Online: www.arabbarometer.org. The survey question was: "If you were being asked to identify yourself, with which of the following would you most closely identify?"

The inverse applies to Lebanon, where nearly 80 percent did so, and even Morocco where about 43 percent did the same. In Egypt, nearly 50 percent picked religion, signaling more intense religious identities in this most populous Arab country, which stands in contrast to Lebanon, where just under 10 percent selected their faith. Few across the board picked ethnicity, sub-region, and local community or city; interestingly, nearly 20 percent in Jordan selected tribe or family.

The second technique is field-based observation and qualitative interviewing, where researchers immerse themselves in the cultural context of societies and slowly observe how individuals and groups interact with one another. They pay close attention to the language and vocabulary used, symbols and images summoned, points of controversy and harmony, and the general tenor of social relationships. Since the late 2000s, social media has become a rich field of inquiry as well, as youths and others often express and articulate fragments of their identity online in ways that could not otherwise be observed. In this manner, observant researchers can make inferences regarding how social actors are explicating their self-conceptions – both to their personal circles (such as friends and families), and to public audiences (such as their teachers, colleagues, and strangers).

EXPLAINING IDENTITY

Many social scientists, in particular political scientists, have sought to explain a separate dilemma – the *origins* of identity, especially when identity differences are seen to underlie violent ethnic conflicts and internecine wars. Here, like definitions of identity, scholars disagree about how identities come to be. One school of thought, primordialism, claims that identities are ancient and natural entities that are as old as humankind; thus, when identity-based violence occurs, it is a preordained outcome driven by deeper historical and cultural forces. Some argue, for instance, that Sunni-Shi'a sectarian battles across the MENA region are primordial in nature, and will always exist due to the ingrained contradictions and ancient hatreds between the two groups that can never be overcome. It is easy to see how primordialism influences public perceptions of MENA conflicts today – Christian-Muslim, Palestinian-Israeli, Sunni-'Alawite, Saudi-Iranian, Moroccan-Algerian, and so forth. According to this essentialist canon, these axes of bloodshed will always exist and elude resolution because they are so deeply embedded into the region's cultural DNA that they should be seen as natural phenomena, not man-made events.

Another school of thought, instrumentalism, claims the opposite: identities may indeed reflect preexisting affiliations and traditions, but they are highly open to outside exploitation. Governments may amplify a given identity to wage war against another, stoking up sentiments to mobilize its population and gain further legitimacy. Thus, an instrumentalist would argue that it is not inherent differences between identities that causes sectarian conflict, but rather the ways that rulers and elites manipulate them for their own ends. For instance, in 1975, King Hassan of Morocco organized the Green March, a mass demonstration to force Spain to surrender control over what was then known as Spanish Sahara, a territory abutting the kingdom's south. Proudly calling for patriotic Moroccans to mobilize in support of the crown and nation, over 350,000 Moroccans entered the territory. While Moroccan sovereignty over this area remains contested today, the Green March was notable because, by fueling Moroccan nationalism, the monarchy buttressed its popular legitimacy and turned public attention away from the economic and political problems faced at home. In doing so, the Moroccan regime manipulated national identity by making an area of land, about which few

Moroccans earlier had known, now seem integral to the public's sense of nationhood and dignity. Today, this area, labeled as Western Sahara on many maps, is thus considered by the Moroccan state as part-and-parcel of its territory despite that much of the international community still sees it as occupied land.

A third school, constructivism, goes further in arguing that identities altogether are simply inventions of society and peoples who need to create categorical differences against an "Other" for greater political and economic purposes. Many scholars have gravitated to this approach over the past two decades to explain puzzling conflicts. For instance, the modern country of Yemen was split into two territories prior to its unification in the early 1990s. The northern part was ruled by a monarchy during 1918–1962 that hailed from Zaydi Islam, a sect of Shi'a Islam. It enjoyed Saudi support in its losing war against a military uprising, and was extinguished in 1970. Yet Saudi Arabia militarily intervened into Yemen in 2015 to push back the country's takeover by the Houthi movement, whose leaders and supporters also hailed from Zaydi Islam. Whereas Saudi Arabia's conservative Wahhabi Islamic clerics saw little trouble sponsoring the pro-Saudi Zaydi monarchy in the 1960s, they declared the Houthi rebels and all of Zaydi Islam as heretics worthy of millennial destruction a half-century later. Such extreme incongruity suggests that identities, or at least their perceptions, are so permeable as to be susceptible for complete reinvention when it suits entrepreneurs and authority figures.

Primordialism, instrumentalism, and constructivism offer very different takes on the origins of identity, and how they evolve over time. In truth, identity conceptions may require insights from all three approaches. Primordialism, for instance, reminds us that divergence between individuals and groups has existed in the past, and may reflect elemental traits that require recognition. Instrumentalism warns us that such differences do not innately predetermine any outcome, from conflict to peace, because those identities can be instrumentalized. Finally, constructivism shows that, in some cases, identities altogether can radically change over time – yet to their adherents appear just as primordial as they did decades or centuries ago.

HOMOGENIZING TENDENCIES

Traditionally societies have often viewed diversity as divisive. For every "Self" there is an "Other" – and those "Others" were sometimes seen as enemies until they adopted the norms, conventions, and conceptions of the "Self."

For instance, the spread of Christianity was accompanied by religious wars and subjugation, a topic that has elicited as much academic study as it has tenacious and controversial debate. In modern times, the schisms of Christianity as expressed by the Protestant Reformation and other rifts resulted in further bloodshed aimed at eliminating pluralism and diversity within Christian communities. Likewise, during the first expansion of Islam during the seventh century, the Prophet Muhammad conducted military campaigns to help convert unbelievers into the new faith, resulting in the formation of the first of several great Islamic empires. And similar to Christianity, there exists substantial tension regarding the question of how Islamic texts and scholars have treated believers of other faiths across time and space.

This homogenizing tendency and aversion to diversity manifests also in the era of contemporary colonialism. Western imperialism during the eighteenth and nineteenth centuries played a crucial part in fermenting this trend, because European powers often exploited ethnic and religious cleavages of their Middle East holdings, such as British treatment of Sunni, Shi'a, and Kurdish communities in Mandatory Iraq after World War One. They privileged and empowered certain Sunni tribes, often at the expense of numerically larger Shi'a communities and other rival Sunni tribes, while also alternatively entertaining and suppressing Kurdish demands for autonomy. Even after Iraq became nominally independent in 1932, British interests in the kingdom required not just close relations with the ruling monarchy – a Sunni one that was implanted by British fiat in 1921 – but also continued societal divisions that prevented unified nationalism and weakened overall resistance to British interests.

Indeed, European powers followed a divide-and-rule policy, but it should be remembered that they did not create identity-based divisions in the Middle East anew so much as reshape and sometimes amplify them. The British-backed Great Arab Revolt during World War One, for example, was primarily an intra-Sunni affair, yet featured Arab tribes and elites, including then-ruler of Mecca, insurrecting against the Ottoman Sultan – a position that was customarily treated as the seat of the Caliph, and thus steward of the old Islamic empires, of which the Ottomans represented the last iteration. Elsewhere, anti-Western uprisings in favor of national independence often enabled minorities within the same colonial territory to unite with majorities despite past tensions. Examples include the role of Christians in Egypt and Syria against the British, Berbers in Algeria against the French occupation, and Baha'i community in Iran during the 1906 Constitutional Revolution.

Many mainstream narratives and histories overlook these moments of cross-communal unity in favor of the more dramatic episodes of internal conflict and minority struggles that occurred afterwards. Internal divisions that were critical for colonialism could not be overcome let alone eliminated, and the post-colonial monarchies and republics that ruled most of the MENA starting in the 1950s onwards struggled to accommodate such pluralism and diversity. This resulted in efforts to create new national identities, which was as much the selective remembrance of history and rewriting of the past as it was the wholesale invention of new ideas, themes, and values to celebrate national unity. Even the three non-Arab countries – Iran, Israel, and Turkey – were challenged in this regard. During key points of state formation or reformation, namely the post-1925 years of Iran, the post-1948 period in Israel, and the post-1923 republican consolidation of Turkey, these governments prioritized through formal systems of education, language, and governance or else informal cultural discourse a single national and exclusive identity: Persian-Shi'a for Iran, Jewish for Israel, and Turkish for the republican successor the Ottoman Empire.

Reasons for this homogeneity are not difficult to fathom. If the exploitation of internal differences were instrumental in the furtherance of Western possessions in the Middle East, their departure usually accentuated and worsened these regnant cleavages. One reason was artificial boundaries. In the Mashriq, post-Ottoman cartography mostly followed the 1916 Sykes-Picot Agreement and the 1920 San Remo Convention, which imposed a British-French geopolitical condominium that disregarded natural geographical considerations. In some new countries like Iraq and Lebanon, this process amalgamated different sectarian and religious forces together under a single fragile flag, while in Jordan and Syria it contrived new national identities by claiming to have discovered historical traditions that legitimated these political orders. Post-Italian Libya, too, artificially incorporated different groups into a single entity that in the post-Arab Spring era has proven extraordinarily vulnerable to fragmentation and violence. Moreover, some ethnonational groups like Kurds or sprawling tribal confederations like the Bani Khalid were divided amongst different states. Likewise, imperial economic interests resulted in the ceding of some areas to these new political entities like the oil-rich Mosul from Turkey to Iraq.

Besides the artificial boundaries and population composition, leadership selection was driven by extraneous considerations. In some, rulers from outside were imposed upon; for instance, the Hashemite family – which had backed the Great Arab Revolt during World War One, and ruled the holy

Islamic city of Mecca at the time – saw its scions installed briefly in Syria, and then in Iraq and Jordan, the latter of which is still ruled by this dynasty. Vocabulary and nomenclature had to be imported from the colonial and imperial lexicon. Turkey, the successor state of the Ottoman Empire, faced a different challenge as it was never formally colonized. Yet it inherited the legacy of an empire that had previously expanded into vast swathes of land outside the Anatolian peninsula, including the Mashriq, Arabian Gulf, North Africa, and Eastern and Southeastern Europe. The defeat and demise of the Ottomans after World War One not only dispossessed it of Arab holdings but also created existential debates with often traumatic consequences about what Turkish-ness signified for the new republic.

This broaches another important aspect of contemporary identity in the MENA – nationalism and national identity. The emergence and evolution of nationalism, or the general belief that one's nation should not only see its interests privileged abroad but also gain and maintain sovereignty and independence over a territorial homeland, was central to Westphalian political order and the development of modern Europe. Only somewhat through the rise of the European Union has recognition of diversity across countries been blunted, or at least accommodated, through the creation of an inclusive pan-European common identity and supranational institutions. A very different process unfolded in MENA countries that were Muslim-majority.

Upon attaining sovereign independence, largely during the 1950s and 1960s, many of these states faced an inherent contradiction between the Islamic concept of a global community of believers transcending time and space (*ummah*) versus the territorial nation (*watan*) that was very much bounded by time and space. Since its birth in the seventh century, Islam spread its message of universalism across social barriers and territorial limits, boundaries, and impediments. The need for community guidance after the death of Prophet ushered in the institutional position of Caliph that continued until the termination of the Ottoman Empire. Throughout constant power struggles and dynastic warring, the seat of Caliph remained the symbolic head of the global ummah. Nationalism is anathema to this conception of a timeless and unbounded Islam. As an ideology rooted in one indivisible territory, nationalism has divided Muslims and created rivalry, conflict, and animosity.

The ummah-watan tension also worked in the opposite direction. Singular communities that found themselves fractured across different post-colonial territorial entities due to imperial cartography felt themselves to be "one people" despite, or perhaps because of, these divisions. Their numerical status as minorities and their marginalization within the boundaries where they lived facilitated the rise of a new national consciousness and demands for a territorial homeland. In this sense, a "ummah-like" counter-nationalism that desires to break down borders has come to typify some minority populations in the MENA. Though all of them attained political maturity or shape, some degree of collective identity exists among groups as diverse as Berbers in North Africa, Bedouins in many areas, Kurds in the Mashriq, Palestinians, Shi'a in the Mashriq and Arabian Gulf, and even some Christians.

Confronted with their fragile composition and future uncertainty, many post-colonial MENA states with Muslim-majority populations sought to distance Islam from their national self-conceptions, though they never denied or eliminated this cultural and religious aspect of identity. For instance, the Turkish Republic was spearheaded by Mustafa Kemal Ataturk, who founded its post-Ottoman political order and aspired to transform the new country into a European power. The new regime introduced massive social and cultural changes, among them significant secularization by removing expressions of Islam and Islamic piety from the public sphere, as well as switching the Arabic script used for Ottoman Turkish to a Latin-based alphabet for a new, modern Turkish language. No longer would Turkey be considered the "sick man of Europe," as the dying Ottoman Empire was commonly denigrated during the late nineteenth century. Turkey's April 1987 application for full membership into the EU was the culmination of this process – a process that has now changed dramatically, given Turkey's governance by an Islamist political party since 2002 and its head, Tayyip Recep Erdogan. During this Erdogan-ruled period, Turkey has rediscovered its Islamic and Middle Eastern heritage, and reoriented back to the Muslim world and the MENA region. The closest Arab analogue to the Turkish trajectory was Tunisia under its two long-serving presidents of Habib Bourguiba (1956–1987) and Zine 'Abidine Ben 'Ali (1987–2011); Bourguiba in particular fancied himself as the Arab equivalent of Ataturk, and likewise implemented many secularizing measures that emphasized a Tunisian nationalism modestly devoid of any Islamic emphasis.

BOX 4.1 CASE STUDY – DHIMMI PARADIGM

One interesting historical window into how identities collide and coexist is the *dhimmi* paradigm, whereby under shari'a and Islamic jurisprudence, Muslim-majority societies offer limited protection to the followers of other two Abrahamic faiths.

BOX 4.1 (CONTINUED)

Historically, Islam's second Caliph (that is, the Prophet's second successor) 'Umar, codified the Prophet's treatment of Jews and Christians, and through the Charter of Mecca formalized an arrangement whereby the followers of other *ahl al-kitab* (People of the Book, meaning Jews and Christians) would be allowed to keep their faith, livelihoods, and properties as dhimmi minorities governance. Such protection is conditional upon dhimmi groups recognizing and adhering to Islamic rule, and to accept a host of social and political constraints that would prevent their own sacred traditions from infringing upon the manifest truth of the Qur'an and Islam. Seen within the context of seventh-century tribal Arabia, the notion that Jews and Christians would obtain a new identity as protected minorities problematizes the relationship between the Islamic "Self" versus "Other." Whereas previously the "Other" was interpreted by hardliners as unbelievers who needed to be converted or conquered, now the identity category of dhimmi enabled some degree of accommodation. Indeed, even despotic Muslim rulers could not be accused of being anti-dhimmi, as this would make render his rulership as violating the covenant of Caliph 'Umar. This was in contrast to the harsh treatment of Muslims by medieval Europe, as well as European attitudes towards Judaism well into the twentieth century.

What were the benefits and weaknesses of this approach, which sought to foreclose identity-based conflict by essentially sequestering the "Other" into a protected category? On the one hand, it created a sense of toleration and adaptation that enabled non-Muslim communities to retain their religious self-conception and social norms – spaces of autonomy hardly given to Muslim communities when they faced the advances of Christian armies during periods of European expansion, such as the Reconquista of Spain. Indeed, it outlawed violence such that because these Abrahamic faiths fell under categorical recognition and protection, they could not be subject to certain injustices. On the other hand, such an arrangement was frozen in time, and unable to address new social changes across the centuries, such as when Jewish or Christian groups desired greater political voice due to their increasing economic status. Moreover, the dhimmi framework reflected early Islamic thinking and extended no protection to non-Abrahamic faiths such as Hinduism and Buddhism, which far predate the birth of Islam in the seventh century.

However, other Muslim-majority countries settled for a more moderate course by anchoring their new national self-conceptions upon Islam, which became an easy marker of identity. They mentioned Islam in their constitution; some fixed Islam as the official state religion, or cited Islamic law (*shari'a*) as a source of law and the legal system. This held true for both republican and monarchical regimes. Ruling presidents of republics during the latter half of the twentieth century, including prominent leaders like Gamal Abdel Nasser of Egypt, Saddam Hussein of Iraq, Hafiz al-Asad of Syria, and Muammar al-Qaddafi of Libya, all legitimated themselves by either invoking Islam and shariʻa or else employing its language to buttress their interpretation of their nationalistic ideologies. They did so despite being nominally secular republican regimes.

Several of the monarchies pursued a slightly different pathway. The ruling dynasties in Jordan and Morocco, the Hashemite and ʻAlaouite houses respectively, claim Prophetic descent and trace their lineage to the tribe to which Prophet Muhammad belonged. The ʻAlaouite dynasty stakes its claim to Fatima, Muhammad's daughter, and her husband, Ali. The Hashemites trace their original lineage to Hashim ibn ʻAbd Manaf, the great-grandfather of the Prophet who died in 497, more than a century before Hijra, the beginning of the Islamic calendar. Meanwhile, the location of Mecca and Medina, Islam's two holiest cities, enabled the Saudi monarchy to christen itself as the Custodian of the Two Holy Places and thus embed a notion of Islam and Islamic authority into the discourse of Saudi nationhood and identity. Across the Gulf, the Islamic Republic of Iran that took power after the 1978–1979 revolution declared – unlike the Pahlavi monarchy that preceded it – Shiʻa Islam as not only its state religion but the moral and social foundation of the Iranian nation.

Israel, the only non-Muslim majority state in the Middle East, is a unique case. Formally, it has no state religion and legally recognizes five religions, namely Judaism, Christianity, Islam, Druze, and the Baha'i faiths. Yet it has privileged Judaism in its state symbols, customs, and holidays, and its national identity has become increasingly less inclusive over time. While always situating itself as the homeland of the Jewish people, Israel's government over the past decade has increasingly emphasized the Jewish aspect of its national self-conception, and has struggled to evolve into an entity with which non-Jewish residents and citizens could identify.

Thus, a century after the redrawing of boundaries and emergence of new states, the Middle Eastern countries have struggled to develop an inclusive national identity that recognizes and accepts religious, ethnic, or other forms of pluralism. The superimposition of a homogenizing identity that distinguishes a dominant "Self" and sets aside a marginalized and sometimes challenging "Other" and opens up a lively debate about minorities and their distinctiveness from the majority population.

DIVERSITY OF IDENTITY: CONTEXTUALIZING CATEGORIES AND CLAIMS

While individual groups have long been studied, major credit for seeing them within the broader regional context in contemporary scholarship goes to historian Albert Habib Hourani. As the new post-colonial Middle East was emerging at the end of the World War Two, Hourani paid special attention to groups of people who were left out of the Arab mainstream in many Arab countries, with their identity claims – and often demands for recognition, if not incorporation and independence – swiftly suppressed. Though important and crucial, Hourani's approach of seeing minorities only as non-Arab and non-Sunni groups was quickly overtaken by newer forms of identity contestation and identity claims by other collective actors. Thus, if one looks at the regional tapestry of societies today, it is possible to observe various broad collective identities, namely tribalism, religiosity, ethnonationalism, refugees, expatriates, youths, and women. These identities are neither impermeable nor immutable. They are not necessarily mutually exclusive, either: one can be tribal *and* Arab *and* Muslim *and* young, but not cannot be Muslim and Christian – or Arab and non-Arab – at the same time. Moreover, the importance of a particular identity is contextual and does not indicate their preference or priority over others. The discerning researcher must look at specific cases of conflict and cooperation, and question what factors and variables are influencing a social actor at a particular moment to induce the prioritization of one identity over another.

Tribalism

Despite the evolution of territorial nationalism, many communities in Arab countries often see, and relate to, one another through the prism of tribalism. In the Mashriq and Arabian Gulf in particular, much of domestic societies belong to a tribal group, confederation, or clan. In the broadest sense, a tribe (*'ashira*) is a group of people belonging to the same lineage living in a specific territory, and whose kinship ties by blood are imagined and considered to play a powerful role in shaping each member's preferences, relations, and behavior. In practical terms, tribes are assemblies of extended families with a shared history and common set of social practices. They can be deeply attached to the land where they dwell or roam. In the Arab world, many tribes consisted of sedentary populations living on arable land for generations; traditionally many *fellahin* (peasants) in such rural geographies had some tribal affiliation or kinship. Nomadic Bedouin, by contrast, often migrated across considerable distances given their pastoral economic production. Though the largest confederations originate from the Arabian Peninsula, the Bedouin came to inhabit every sub-region of the MENA, from the Maghrib to Mashriq to the Gulf.

Whether sedentary or nomadic, tribes were natives of the land long before the arrival of Islam, modernity, or nationalism – the product, as Chapter 2 explicated, of the underlying agronomic and geographic constraints of human settlement across much of the region. While the advent of Islam was a transformative event, the Muslim faith alone hardly created many of the practices, rituals, and norms that tribal members came to associate with tribalism, and it is important to note that tribal identity thus extends far beyond religion. For instance, patriarchy, or male domination in the family and the marginalization of women in society, is often identified with Islam, but its broad presence in the Middle East also reflects deep-seated tribal hierarchies that, in pre-Islamic times, subordinated female roles in favor of male authority. Indeed, the dichotomy between the Islamic teaching and the practice of its adherents are the result of tribal influences upon the society.

In a broader sense, social histories across the MENA are often about the rise and fall of tribes and their constant contestation for power, position, and possessions. In countable terms, there are hundreds of large tribal confederations and groupings across the region. Some ruling monarchies reflect this by assuming some traditional tribal role. Classical Islamic texts, for instance, often described the ideal ruler as one who sought and secured the allegiance of major notables and tribal leaders in return for an oath of allegiance (*bay'a*). This pact was a critical component of leadership legitimacy. In Morocco, the 'Alaouite monarch traditionally holds a ceremony that involves him pledging the bay'a. To a different extent, the Saudi monarch also performs the provisions of bay'a, and indeed this practice was institutionalized in Saudi Arabia in 2007 with the formation of the Allegiance Council. Elsewhere, tribal identities are inherent. For instance, Qatar's ruling family, the Thani clan, hail from the Banu Tamim tribe, while Kuwait's Sabah dynasty belongs to the 'Utub tribal confederation that originally roamed and settled in the eastern part of the Arabian Peninsula. Yet tribalism also influences political practices in some republics. For example, until his overthrow following the US-led invasion of Iraq, Saddam Hussein was seen by outsiders as a leader of one minority group in a sectarian Iraq (Sunni Arab Muslims); but he also belonged to a tightly knit tribal group from his native town of al-Tikrit, a sub-clan of the larger Al-Bu Nasir tribe whose social relations and political loyalties helped Saddam establish his repressive apparatus and political institutions during the 1970s and 1980s. In that sense, loyalties borne out of identification with a common tribe strengthened a non-monarchical state.

However, the winds of change and modernization have severely undermined the coherence of the tribal identity. In search of education, employment, and better opportunities, many tribes have gradually transitioned out of geographical sameness and social homogeneity, towards fates of urbanization and assimilation. The oil boom of the 1970s resulted in a large-scale migration to urban centers across the region but especially in the oil-rich Gulf kingdoms. In Saudi Arabia, for example, only about 15 percent of the citizens live in rural areas, the same proportion now found in oil-poor Jordan, where urbanization likewise has marginalized and reduced the ways that tribal communities in rural areas often distinguished themselves from cities and towns.

In many cases, the city environment has transformed social order and large extended families. The basis of tribal order has given way to closely knit nuclear families that rarely interact with the wider clan or tribe except for festivities or family events. Tribalism flourished when there were day-to-day engagements that reminded members of blood and kin, a core mechanism that transmitted tribal identities; but this is not feasible in the concrete jungles of the metropolis. Urbanization has weakened these constitutive norms and social purposes – and also diluted endogamous marriage, the core basis of the tribal order. Social media engagement with the far-off world has become more attractive than the immediacy of the tribal setting. The notions of "honor killing" against women are principally a reflection of tribalism, but such practices have become increasingly outlawed due to pressures not only from the international community but from within, as urbanized social forces in Arab countries condemn such practices.

Yet tribal identity and the political preferences and behaviors that reflect it have not disappeared entirely. They often crop up during national upheavals and crises. Upon its inception in 2015, for instance, the Houthi rebellion in Yemen was driven mostly by tribal forces knit together by both political and kinship ties. The civil war proceeded thus primarily as a fight between them and an opposing central government backed by various tribal clans, among them the Hashid confederation, which also played a prominent role in fostering Yemen's original civic uprising during the Arab Spring. In sum, though considerably weakened, tribal identity is prevalent in many MENA countries and is a prominent marker of internal discourses.

Religiosity

As the cradle of the Abrahamic faiths, the MENA has followers of Judaism, Christianity, and Islam. Excepting a very brief period of Lebanese history, Christians were never a majority population in any part of the region, and their number has dwindled considerably during the twentieth century. Countries which had significant Christian populations such as Iraq and Lebanon have witnessed a substantial exodus to the West. Indeed, traditional

Christian towns with biblical importance, like Bethlehem in the West Bank and Nazareth in Israel, are now demographically non-Christian. Despite this, as Chapter 8 explains, the region still plays host to Christian denominations reflecting theological and ethnic variation. This includes Coptic Christians in Egypt, Maronites in Lebanon, and smaller groups of other Christian denominations such as Armenian, Greek Orthodox, and Chaldean communities across the Mashriq.

Jews are the second prominent non-Muslim identity. Countries like Iran, Iraq, Morocco, Turkey, and to a lesser extent Yemen had large, historically rooted, culturally vibrant, and resourceful Jewish communities. Their *dhimmi* treatment (discussed earlier in the chapter) enabled them to survive and flourish under various Islamic empires. The emergence of Zionism and Jewish nationalist aspirations undermined this centuries-old benevolent but unequal social contract. Thus, after the formation of the Israeli state, a combination of factors including domestic hostility and affiliation with the renewed Jewish identity resulted in large-scale emigration to Israel from other MENA countries. Interestingly, the process of globalization has resulted in a new Jewish presence in some of the Gulf Arab countries either as citizens (Bahrain) or as temporary expatriate populations (UAE). How these new small communities reconcile Jewish identity with residence in non-Jewish environs is a topic of worthy future study. Yet even the notion of a singular Jewish identity is problematic. Within Israel proper, immigrating Jewish residents often assume new categorical sub-identities within Judaism, such as Ashkenazi, Sephardic, Mizrahi, Falash Mura (i.e., Ethiopian and Eritrean), and Russian Judaism. Here, tensions have thus emerged between the predominant transnational Jewish identity with more parochial ones focusing upon race, language, and origin.

An equally significant challenge lays in defining the identity of the MENA's majority population of Muslims. It would be fallacy to assume that being Muslim is equivalent to citizenship of particular nation-states like Saudi Arabia, or that identification with Islam as both faith and cultural system is the most important overarching identity for Muslims.

First, the universalism of Islam – and with it, the homogenizing tendency that situates all Muslims as members of a timeless ummah – has clearly come into conflict with heterogeneity in the form of various sects that have branched out from Islam over time, some of which have become powerful minority streams while others have evolved into independent religions. The Shi'a faith belongs to the former category, and the roots of this branch date back to political conflict following the death of Prophet Muhammad in

AD 632. Differences emerged over his succession, namely who would lead the Muslim community. The mantle of the Caliph initially fell on Abu Bakr, the Prophet's close companion and father-in-law. He was later succeeded by other companions – 'Umar and 'Uthman – and finally 'Ali, the Prophet's cousin, in AD 656. The followers of 'Ali disputed this succession line, especially after this Caliph's assassination in AD 661 and the short-lived reigns of his sons, Hassan and Hussein. This early political divergence resulted in the formation and development of the Shi'a sect, replete with a doctrine and belief system that differed substantially from the majority Muslim community which we now deem Sunni Islam.

Though a distinct branch of Islam, Shi'a Muslims only compose a demographic majority in three states – Iran, Iraq, and Bahrain. Elsewhere they are either virtually non-existent (such as in most Maghrib countries) or else represent a minority. As a minority group, Shi'a Muslims have experienced varying degrees of incorporation. For instance, the Shi'a minority constitutes about a quarter of the Kuwaiti population yet generally enjoys political and legal equality. In Syria are found 'Alawites, who represent a small sect within Shi'a Islam. They have become especially prominent because the ruling Asad family and regime hail from this traditionally marginalized group, and since their time in power 'Alawite symbolism and networks have been elevated into the heart of the Syrian state and military. For instance, upon becoming president in March 1971, Hafiz al-Asad amended the Syrian constitution, which required the president of the republic to be Muslim. Yet many Syrians, including its majority Sunni population, did not consider the 'Alawites as Shi'a much less Muslim. To circumvent the problem, in July 1973 al-Asad induced Musa al-Sadr, a leading Shi'a cleric in Lebanon, to issue a *fatwa* (religious edict) declaring 'Alawites to be Shi'a – and thus Muslim. In turn, the rise of the 'Alawites and their struggle to fuse their communal identity with a broader Islamic one underscores the multiplicity of Shi'a identification, for there are in fact many small sects that have branched out from Shi'a doctrine over the past millennium, including Zaydi and Isma'ili communities, whom many other Muslims reject.

Shi'a Muslims represent up to 15–20 percent of Saudi Arabia's population of over 30 million yet generally suffer economic, political, and religious discrimination. They are concentrated in the same eastern provinces as some of the densest oil fields. The ongoing Saudi-Iranian rivalry, which has waxed and waned since the Iranian Revolution but has reached a high point of tension since the early 2010s, is often interpreted as a clash of competing sectarian identities. Iran's Shi'a Islamic self-conception stands on one side, while on the other is Saudi Arabia, which situates itself as the keystone to Sunni Islam despite that its particular brand of Muslim faith is Wahhabism, a particularly orthodox and conservative subset of Sunni Islam. Many Wahhabi texts argue that the Shi'a are not true Muslims, and are instead *kafir* (non-believers).

Yet it is difficult to pin down the Saudi-Iranian rivalry as one that purely reflects sectarian identity differences, since each country also has very material competing goals, such as control of the Gulf waterway and dominance in proxy conflicts such as the Syrian and Yemeni civil wars. If one were to ask Saudi versus Iranian citizens to name their most important identity, not all would reply with Sunni (or Wahhabi) versus Shi'a Islam. It has been suggested, thus, that religious identities are very prone to manipulation by governmental elites. Such instrumentalization has been critical in fueling sectarian warfare, and illustrates that rather than essentialist and primordial, identities can be exploited, amplified, and influenced by political strategies and geopolitical pressures. After all, if Sunni and Shi'a Muslims subscribed to competing Islamic identities that *by definition* require intractable conflict, there would be far more violence and bloodshed in the MENA region. Saudi Arabia and Iran would have already gone to war, and Shi'a communities would be under perennial siege by Sunni majorities elsewhere.

Ethnonationalism

Ethnicity is defined as a group of people that share the same general ancestral background, and whose members affiliate with one another through similarities such as common languages, historical traditions, cultural values, and social practices. Arabs represent the largest ethnic group in the MENA region, and comprise the vast majority of the region's over 400 million people. Only in Israel, Turkey, and Iran, whose conceptions of nationhood do not coexist with Arabness (that is, they are not Arab states), do Arabs represent a demographic minority.

Arab identity has undergone various historical permutations over the centuries, in close interaction with religion and other indigenous forces and also in reaction to Ottoman and Western imperialism. Among its core identity markers is language (Arabic) and other basic values and practices. However, in the post-colonial era nation-states have served to fracture a coherent sense of Arab identity that can transcend geographic barriers. For instance, during the 1950s and 1960s, the political ideology known as Arab Nationalism became popular in many Arab countries, and among its tenets aimed to create a pan-Arab state encompassing the entire Arab world. Yet appeals to such regional or transnational Arabism did not succeed in erasing state boundaries imposed by colonialism; among the few efforts was the short-lived political union between Egypt and Syria during 1958–1961. That experiment fell apart because Arabness alone was insufficient to fuse two non-contiguous countries. Another instrument to enshrine Arab identity was the Arab League, which was founded in 1945 and serves as the regional organization linking all Arab countries together. Yet the Arab League too has faltered in fostering enduring unity. It has struggled at times to contain conflict between its Arab members, such as failing to prevent Iraq in 1990 from invading Kuwait. The homogenizing tendency within pan-Arab discourse therefore has been challenged in accommodating the political reality of Westphalian order, which entails the creation of territorialized nation-states whose borders are both imagined cartographically and fixed geopolitically.

Moreover, there are other divisions with the Arab ethnic group. For instance, Arabness is not the same as being Muslim, as Christian communities exist in many Arab states. Violence against Coptic Christians in Egypt can be interpreted as conflict *across* religious lines but *within* a single ethnic group. Indeed, like religion, it is often difficult to ascertain the influence and power of Arabness. Arabs in Morocco, Oman, Egypt, and the Palestinian territories may celebrate their common heritage, but these states are not moving towards common cultural and political union simply on basis of that shared identity. Arab identity, however, is commonly referenced during conflicts that pit some Arab group against a non-Arab group, such as conflicts against Israel or more recently the Saudi-Iranian rivalry, which implicates not just religious differences that are imagined and real but also an Arab versus Persian dynamic.

Yet at the least, Arabs represent a broad and variegated ethnic category whose members do mostly inhabit sovereign nation-states. The same cannot be said for other major ethnic groups in the region, such as the Berbers who are concentrated in Algeria, Libya, and Morocco. These peoples resided in these territories before Arabization and Islamization. They speak a distinctive language and have cultural practices and historical traditions different from Arabs. Many communities long struggled for recognition in these Maghrib countries, and only recently have some (such as in Morocco) been granted linguistic and educational autonomy that bolsters their sense of identity. It is unlikely they will attain an independent nation-state of their own, however.

Perhaps the same can be said of Kurds, a non-Arab ethnic group split across eastern Turkey, northern Syria, northern Iraq, and northwestern Iran.

Kurdish campaigns for independence over the past century, some waged violently and some peacefully, reflect an important aspect of modern ethnic identity – it is often consonant with demands for national independence. Herein lays the ethno-nationalistic basis of identity, in which the achievement of sovereignty and creation of a political statehood is seen as the ultimate expression of ethnicity. The closest approximation to a national state for Kurds today is the autonomous Kurdistan Region in Iraq, a statelet with its own governing institutions and flag (Photo 4.1). As a keystone of identity, the Kurdistan Region is often framed as the foundation for a future permanent Kurdistan that could unite all other Kurdish national groups in the region.

In other cases, minority communities coexist with majority ethnic groups that define the boundaries of nationhood. For instance, the Islamic Republic of Iran's constitution offers limited protection to "Recognized Religious Minorities," which besides Judaism and Christianity includes the pre-Islamic Zoroastrian faith. The Turkish understanding of a non-Turkish "Other" is anchored in the 1923 Treaty of Lausanne, which only explicitly promised

PHOTO 4.1
Kurdish flag as used in Kurdistan Region of Iraq.

Source: iStock.
Online: www.istockphoto.com/photo/kurdish-flag-gm116380692-5199914

protection to "Turkish nationals belonging to non-Muslim minorities" – a category that pointedly excludes the Kurds. In other countries, minority identities are accepted so long as its holders accept their political marginalization, such as the practice of non-Muslim faiths by expatriates in the Gulf kingdoms.

> **BOX 4.2 CASE STUDY – JORDAN AND IDENTITY**
>
> There are exceptional circumstances where national identity assumes a peculiar character due to internal contestation and demographic change caused by completely exogenous factors. For instance, the Hashemite Kingdom of Jordan presents a challenge to debates about what ethnonationalism means in the context of Arabism and other identities. After the 1948 and 1967 Arab-Israeli Wars, Jordan absorbed millions of Palestinians from the lands west of the Jordan River, primarily what we now call the West Bank. It offered them Jordanian citizenship – something no other Arab country that absorbed Palestinian refugees, such as Lebanon and Syria, chose to do. Yet today, there rages intense controversy about the true size of the Palestinian population in Jordan, a sensitive topic tinged with memories of the 1970 civil war known as Black September, which pitted Palestinian guerilla forces against the Jordanian military. Having hosted and to some degree assimilated Palestinians as citizens, the Jordanian government has struggled to accommodate advocacy of Palestinian nationalism, which would create an independent Palestinian state in historic Palestine which overlays much of modern Israel. If an independent Palestine were to emerge tomorrow, some evoke fear about what would happen next: would Jordanians of Palestinian origin stay in the kingdom or move to the new state (as some would prefer)? Furthermore, if they choose to stay, could Jordanians of Palestinian origin overcome much of the lingering political and social discrimination they face? Thus, in terms of ethnonational identity, Jordan presents a fascinating additional dimension despite its outward appearance of being a uniform Middle East country with an ethnically Arab and predominantly Sunni Muslim population. In such an environment, the otherwise innocuous question, "*Min wayn inta* (Where are you from)?" can carry loaded social and political implications about how an ordinary citizen is supposed to draw the boundaries of identity and national belonging.

Refugees

Though not often discussed, it is important to discuss the existence of a refugee identity because the MENA region has a considerable refugee population displaced by violent conflicts. The Palestinians are the most prominent example, and their plight is linked to the non-realization of an independent Palestinian state. At the end of the 1948 Arab-Israeli War, the Palestinian refugee population was estimated at 600,000–700,000 – a number that increased to over five million in 2015. (This figure does not count the Palestinians who became Jordanian citizens.) Most of these refugees live in UN-run camps in the West Bank, Gaza Strip, Jordan, Lebanon, and Syria. As noted above, Lebanon and Syria have refrained from naturalizing their Palestinian refugees despite many living and working there for generations, having been dispossessed of their homes in wars more than a half-century ago. Researchers of Palestinian refugees have noted the complexity of their identity: many articulate simultaneously strong nationalist sentiments regarding Palestine and resigned expressions of being stateless people.

Another refugee category consists of Syrians. As of 2019, six million Syrians have been forced to leave their homeland due to the civil war; most have fled to neighboring countries like Turkey, Jordan, Lebanon, and Iraq. While their host governments have struggled to accommodate them given the resources needed to ensure their safety and security, their host societies present a different problem. Given the intertwining conception of these newcomers as both Syrians (that is, a different nation) *and* refugees (that is, a stateless people), locals in these countries have reacted in varying ways. Some treat them as outsiders and foreigners, while others have sought greater assimilation – often by invoking overarching identity themes, such as Arabness or Islam, to justify their accommodation.

Expatriates

The presence of large expatriate communities in the wealthy Gulf kingdoms is a significant addition to debates about how different identities coexist and create varying patterns of conflict or cooperation. Though non-citizens, their presence is considerable. In Saudi Arabia, the most populated among them, expatriates make up nearly one-third of the total population and 55 percent of the workforce. In most other kingdoms, expatriates actually comprise the vast majority of the population. For instance, over 88 percent of Qatar's population of 2.6 million are non-Qatari residents. These expatriates have sought economic opportunities in states infused by hydrocarbon wealth, and themselves exhibit considerable diversity. For instance, in the Emirati metropolis of Dubai, one finds a profundity of expatriates from both Western and Asian countries, working in both unskilled and highly skilled positions. As non-citizens, their rights and privileges are minimal, though Western expatriates tend to receive better treatment – both financial and social – than those arriving from South and Southeast Asia.

These foreign migrant workers contribute to ethnic diversity, even if their own identities as foreigners remain muted against political and legal systems that ostensibly remain oriented to national citizens. For instance, a significant portion of the expatriate community in the Gulf kingdoms is non-Muslim, including not only Christians and Jews but also non-Abrahamic faiths such as

Hinduism, Buddhism, and Sikhism. This has resulted in host countries finding ways to accommodate their religious and cultural needs. In Saudi Arabia, strict adherence to Wahhabi Islam inhibits public worship of non-Muslim faiths, but private and non-visible congregations are tolerated. Bahrain, Kuwait, Oman, Qatar, and the UAE all allow non-Muslim places of worship for the benefit of the expatriate community. Some have been constructed on the land donated by ruling monarchs, and include churches, Hindu temples, Sikh gurudwaras, and Buddhist temples. Some of them exist as independent structures while others are part of larger complexes of non-Islamic faiths.

As a resident population, expatriates have come to define and shape the demography of these host kingdoms. They do not have citizenship rights, although notably Qatar agreed to begin granting a small number access to permanent residency starting in late 2018. Yet it would be reasonable to assume also that as strong communities, they will increasingly voice their unique identities in the coming years.

Youth

Although discussed in Chapter 10, youth identities compose a critical part of the MENA region's mosaic. The Arab Spring protests which began in Tunisia in December 2010 catapulted Arab youth to the center stage as not only a social force but a political actor, with a particular generational identity. The World Bank defines "youth" as those between the ages of 15 to 24, although a broader definition would include those between 15 to 29. Nearly a third of the MENA region's population falls in this expanded category, and in most countries, they represent the fastest growing segment of the population. Youth primarily led the Arab Spring protests during 2011–2012; they came to symbolize demands for dignity through employment, democracy, and reforms.

Gender

Though also discussed in Chapter 9, female identity composes a vital part of the region's social terrain. While gendered inequality is endemic across the world given the prevalence of patriarchy, many post-industrial societies have begun grappling with issues of gender *fluidity* – including the recognition that unlike some identity categories like tribe, ethnicity, or (youth) generation, one can choose a gendered position. For most MENA societies, the primary issue remains gendered inequality. Excepting Israel, the region's countries feature certain patterns of inequity: women have less access to economic resources, suffer from less political representation, possess fewer legal rights, and often occupy positions of social subordination. At the same time, vibrant women's movements celebrating the identity of girls and women have arisen across civil societies.

DYNAMICS OF IDENTITY-BASED CONFLICT

Many conflicts across the MENA region emanate from or are linked to seemingly incompatible identity claims. Indeed, since the Arab Spring, three civil wars in the region – those of Libya, Syria, and Yemen – have a strong identity component, insofar that battles for power and the mobilization of supporters for competing factions has required the assertion of at least one of the aforementioned social categories. Central to identity-based violence, to return to this chapter's early passages, is the assertion of a proud "Self" and the targeting of an "Other" whose identity is seen as not only incongruent with, but *threatening* towards, the integrity of the Self. Thus, one predictor of conflict is the presence of mutually exclusive identities as discussed in preceding sections, which create distance between communities and enable identity holders to imagine their rivals as focal points of animosity, discrimination, and even violence.

Another predictor is when identity conflicts concern indivisible assets. For instance, the primary component of the long-running Palestinian-Israeli conflict concerns ownership of land: whereas Zionism sees the land upon which Israeli stands as integral to modern Judaic aspirations, the Palestinian national movement confers possession of such territory as similarly integral to its own self-conception as a dignified and freestanding people. The city of Jerusalem is central to this; it is the third holiest place for Muslims after Mecca and Medina; it is the second most sacred place for the Christians after Bethlehem; and it played an imperative role in stoking the Zionist movement as the site of important Jewish temples and memories. What makes this issue so tense is that land is an indivisible asset, but is so intricately embedded in competing national identities that resolving the conflict will require either expropriating land from one side in favor of the other (e.g., a "one-state" solution), or else finding a compromise to enable two different nation-states to coexist side-by-side (the "two-state" solution).

Possession of land, and ultimately the transformation of such territory into independent and sovereign nation-states that house entire ethnic groups, is also key to understanding historic conflicts involving Berber or Kurdish identity. While Morocco and Algeria have made some adjustments in their political model that no longer call for the complete suppression of Berber identity in its educational, cultural, and linguistic aspects, the Kurdish situation is more intractable, for each state that hosts Kurdish minorities has historically sought ways to contain them, believing that they threatened national unity.

This highlights a problem raised earlier: the failure to develop an inclusive national identity by MENA countries for whatever reason – colonial hangover, shortsightedness, political imperatives, fears over instability – means that identity-based differences are prone to outside manipulation or reconstruction, which may play upon primordialist conceptions and thus result in conflict. This is true for Turkey and Iran, the two Muslim-majority but non-Arab states, as well: their exclusion of various "Others" (such as Kurds) in their sense of nationhood and national identity has paved the way for tensions.

Is there hope? The MENA is the regional site of such diverse and multiple identities that perhaps conflict would be highly likely, if not inevitable, for simple statistical fact. If, for instance, there are dozens upon dozens of "Self" versus "Other" dualities, it should not be surprising if at least some result in bloodshed. The non-inclusive nature of many national identities is worrisome, but identity discourses and conceptions also change over time. That they are open to outside exploitation and re-invention also suggests that at the very least, identity-based differences that seem to be intractable can in reality also be nudged towards accommodation and compromise with the right political interventions.

CONCLUSION

This chapter explored the diversity and multiplicity of identity in the MENA region. It unpacked the definition of identity, noting its varieties, and also briefly touched upon the methodologies and analytical frameworks that scholars use to employ identity as an explanatory variable when understanding complex outcomes such as ethnic conflict, territorial divisions, and international disputes. It then touched upon the perennial tug-of-war between the homogenizing tendency of majorities as pitted against the existence of pluralism across society. Such tensions manifest in various ways in the post-colonial MENA, such as the cleavage between a timeless and boundless ummah versus the very bounded and territorialized notion of nation-states. It reviewed the primary axes of identity today, among them tribalism, religion, and ethnonationalism. A case study of the dhimmi framework and insights about the dynamics of identity-based conflict enable us to further grasp the complexities and challenges inherent when engaging the social life of a region with an incredible degree of diversity.

QUESTIONS FOR DISCUSSION

1 How should we define identity?
2 From where does identity originate, and how do different identities form over time?
3 What is the homogenizing tendency we witness historically, and how has it been challenged by diversity and pluralism latent in MENA societies?
4 How can multiple and overlapping identities exist – must individuals and groups always prioritize a single enduring self-conception?
5 In the modern MENA region today, what are the primary categories and sources of identity for individuals and groups?
6 What types of relationships, institutions, and policies might allow mutually exclusive identities to coexist with one another peacefully?
7 Why have so many MENA states been reluctant to accept, admit, and accommodate minorities that desire cultural or linguistic recognition?
8 When does identity cause conflict? Are there predictors and signs worth remembering?

FURTHER READING

The pioneering work on how identity in the Middle East has been historically conceived, especially for minorities, belongs to Albert Hourani, *Minorities in the Arab World* (London: Oxford University Press, 1947). This classic is still central to our understanding over how diversity and pluralism have evolved over time vis-à-vis religious, ethnonational, tribal, and other identities in the region. More recent works on minorities in the region include Will Kymlicka and Eva Pföstl, eds., *Minority Politics in the Middle East and North Africa: The Prospects for Transformative Change* (London: Routledge, 2018); Paul Rowe, *Routledge Handbook of Minorities in the Middle East* (London: Routledge, 2018); Joshua Castellino and Kathleen Cavanaugh, *Minority Rights in the Middle East* (Oxford: Oxford University Press, 2013); and Ofra Bengio and Gabriel Ben-Dor, eds., *Minorities and the State in the Arab World* (Boulder, CO: Lynne Rienner, 1998).

Religious identity in the context of a Muslim-majority region has also elicited rigorous research across multiple disciplines. A recent addition is Heather Sharkey, *A History of Muslims, Christians, and Jews in the Middle East* (Cambridge: Cambridge University Press, 2017). Another is Bernard Lewis's *The Multiple Identities of the Middle East* (New York: Schocken, 2001). P.R. Kumaraswamy's essay, "Islam and Minorities: Need for a Liberal Framework," *Mediterranean Quarterly* 18 (2007): 94–109, invokes the dhimmi paradigm introduced in this essay. Another enlightening read is Laura Robson, *States of Separation: Transfer, Partition, and the Making of the Modern Middle East* (Berkeley, CA: University of California Press, 2017), which explains how the deliberate creation of non-Muslim minorities in Israel, Turkey, and other former Ottoman territories occurred through European strategies and diaspora politics. A telling reader is Ibrahim Saad Eddin, *The Copts of Egypt* (London: Minority Rights Group, 1996), which charts out the origins and status of one well-known religious minority. Jewish minorities prior to the creation of Israel have also attracted meritorious research; one readable study is Avigdor Levy, ed., *Jews, Turks, Ottomans: A Shared History, Fifteenth Through the Twentieth Century* (Syracuse, NY: Syracuse University Press, 2002), which surveys the ways that Jewish minorities in Ottoman Turkey expressed, protected, and advanced their cultural identity.

From a theoretical perspective, there are several extremely useful handbooks and readers that can provide guidance through the process of defining, conceptualizing, measuring, projecting, and ultimately incorporating identity as a meaningful variable in social research. One is Rawi Abdelal, Yoshiko M. Herrera, Alastair Iain Johnston, and Rose McDermott, eds., *Measuring Identity: A Guide for Social Scientists* (Cambridge: Cambridge University Press, 2009). Another is Margaret Wetherell and Chandra Talpade Mohanty, eds., *The SAGE Handbook of Identities* (London: Sage, 2010), which draws upon politics, sociology, philosophy, psychology, and anthropology to unpack the meaning and implications of identity claims. Seth Schwartz, Koen Luyckx, and Vivian Vignoles, eds., *Handbook of Identity Theory and Research* (New York: Springer, 2011) similarly breaks down identity as a social construct, as does Peter Burke and Jan Stets, *Identity Theory* (Oxford: Oxford University Press, 2009), which seeks to parse out a theory of identity and how identities vary between persons, groups, and roles. Rogers Brubaker and Frederick Cooper, "Beyond 'Identity,'" *Theory and Society* 29 (2000): 1–47 provides a new perspective.

Ethnonationalism and national identities rest upon a vibrant tradition of anthropological and historical inquiry. How we define ethnicity and nationalism is an intertwining question because, as the following authors suggest, the collective answer draws upon the same responses to insecurity and desire for exceptionalism in the modern world. See, for instance, Benedict Anderson, *Imagined Communities: Reflections on the Origin and Spread of Nationalism* (London: Verso, 1983); Ernest Gellner, *Nations and Nationalism* (Ithaca, NY: Cornell University Press, 1983); Rogers Brubaker, *Ethnicity Without Groups*, new ed. (Cambridge, MA: Harvard University Press, 2006); Eric Hobsbawm, *Nations and Nationalism Since 1780*, 2nd ed. (Cambridge: Cambridge University Press, 2012); Paul Brass, *Ethnicity and Nationalism: Theory and Comparison* (Newbury Park, CA: Sage, 1991); and Donald Horowitz, *Ethnic Groups in Conflict* (Berkeley, CA: University of California Press, 1985).

Online sources

The nature of identity makes online scholarship somewhat hollow: many journal articles and essays can be found through databases such as JSTOR, but in terms of concrete *data*, the pickings are slim because a great deal of this research is qualitative – requiring careful historical understanding, field-based immersion through personal interactions, and patient observation over time. However, there are still a few places online where one can glean some insight about the ways that residents in the MENA ascertain their different identities. Pew Global contains a multitude of global surveys and opinion polls, and some of them regularly ask individuals around the world (including the MENA) about their preferences regarding, for instance, national attachments and religion (www.pewglobal.org/). The Arab Barometer survey project raised in this chapter presents all of its data and results online (www.arabbarometer.org/). A dizzyingly exhaustive reference online for all types of identity-oriented scholarship is SAGE's Encyclopedia of Identity (http://sk.sagepub.com/reference/identity). A quantitative source of data can be located in the Ethnic Power Relations Dataset (https://icr.ethz.ch/data/epr/), which provides several statistical and geospatial modes of measuring ethnic groups (as an identity category) across the world, including the MENA.

PART II

Societal vulnerabilities

Economic development, rentierist legacies, and environmental conflict

CHAPTER 5

Economic development
Bread, jobs, and beyond

Bessma Momani and Morgan MacInnes

THE RUNDOWN: KEY TOPICS COVERED
- State-led industrialization
- Neoliberalism
- Bread riots
- Non-inclusive growth
- Unemployment
- Divergent development

INTRODUCTION

This chapter discusses the challenge of equitable economic development throughout the Middle East and North Africa (MENA), focusing primarily on the Arab countries. Beginning in the post–World War Two era (a deliberate cutoff to maintain a modern focus), it evaluates the paths taken by the region's various economies following independence. Particular attention is paid to economic sectors that profoundly shaped the well-being of rapidly growing populations, such as agricultural production, industrial investments, and government services. Initially, a state-led economic development model prevailed throughout the region, characterized by import substitution and protectionist barriers to trade, the nationalization of key sectors of the economy, generous subsidies to energy and housing, and the provision of widespread employment by way of an enlarged public sector. Up until the 1980s, this development model proved successful, in improving material living standards, health, and education. During this time, the MENA enjoyed

145

high rates of economic growth, exceeding many of the world's other developing regions.

However, by the 1980s the state-led economic strategy had exhausted itself, exposing regional populations to rising food prices, inefficient production, a bloated public sector, and rising debt. The high growth and rising living standards to which many societies had become accustomed in the 1960s and 1970s vanished, and the MENA began to fall behind other regions in economic development. In response, many countries embarked upon economic and institutional reforms to pursue greater integration with the world economy. Yet such liberalization policies of openness were stymied by political factors, leaving the process of reform incomplete and results inconsistent. Reactive policies and strategies available to MENA governments, as well as those proposed by multilateral entities like the International Monetary Fund (IMF) and World Bank, have sought to address these challenges, but with unequal results for both national economies and social life. This failure to reinvigorate economic growth and provide sufficient employment opportunities for burgeoning populations inevitably gave rise to disaffection and protest among the masses. Relative economic deprivation played a major role in igniting the Arab Spring and fueling the violent conflagration which has since consumed much of the Middle East.

As in other developing regions, the MENA region and the Arab world in particular have also seen the emergence of a large informal economy, and its implications for employment and living standards are examined. The chapter then provides an overview of how different economies in the region have experienced markedly different trajectories in the past few decades, with a widening rift evident between the resource rich and sparsely populated countries of the Arabian Gulf, and the region's more populous but resource-deprived nations. In closing, it reflects on the contemporary economic challenges faced by these countries.

POST-WAR ECONOMIC TRAJECTORY

How should a state organize its economic affairs to provide jobs for its people, generate economic growth to improve standards of living over time, and structure its economic relations with the rest of the globe so as to remain competitive? These are not easy questions to answer. Certainly, the discipline of economics has not always been in unanimous agreement about which economic model works best to provide bread, jobs, and opportunity. In common with much of the developing world, MENA governments have gone through various phases in their adoption of different economic development models. Some of the development models used by these regimes were indigenous ideas, but often they were borrowed from other countries or international organizations, and highly influenced by donors and corporations. We can see phases when MENA countries adhered to the standard pattern of economic development common throughout the developing world, while at other times the region went against the grain of conventional thinking. Of course, as this chapter demonstrates, economic development cannot be easily divorced from politics.

The politics of the region often shaped how MENA governments designed their economic programs, and changing economic development models were more often than not determined by the region's political realities rather than economic rationality. Whether a country chooses to promote a given industry, liberalize its exchange rate, sign a trade agreement, welcome foreign investors, or impose tariffs and taxes on certain goods can have significant political effects on particular groups and individuals. Vested interests can also shape government decisions, and who wins out in policy choices can often be better explained by politics than by economics.

The state-led development model

After World War Two, many developing countries adopted a state-directed development model characterized by heavy government intervention and regulation, attempts to deliberately direct the growth of infant industries, the nationalization of many private entities in key economic sectors, tariffs and protections that favored local producers and state-owned enterprises, and reforms to break up the concentrated ownership of agricultural land. Developed countries also witnessed relatively substantial economic intervention by the state during this time period, providing models which could be imitated by aspirant developing nations. Although popular in other regions during the immediate post-war era, the MENA region was particularly enthusiastic in its embrace of state-led economic development, falling behind only the socialist economies of Eastern Europe in the level of state direction of economic affairs.

Imbued with a newfound sense of nationalism, post-colonial MENA governments used state-led economic development models to assert their sovereignty and autonomy. Referred to as import-substitution industrialization (ISI), the economic logic was to manufacture goods for the domestic market which had previously been imported from the colonial powers in order to generate local employment and allow national industries to progress up the value chain, using these early profits to become more sophisticated and advanced over time. Among the MENA countries which adopted an import-substitution industrialization plan were Turkey, Iran, and the largest Arab states – Egypt, Algeria, Syria, and Iraq. These countries possessed relatively substantial populations capable of supporting an industrial strategy which relied on a large and growing domestic consumer market in order to employ the growing urban working class.

> **BOX 5.1 CASE STUDY, PART I – EGYPT DURING THE BOOM YEARS**
>
> An illustrative example of statist development can be found in Egypt. The country gained independence from Britain in 1922, and became a republic following a military revolution in 1952. Egypt's executive was (and remains) headed by a president, armed with sweeping powers and usually the rubber-stamped approval of the Egyptian legislature. Following the 1952 coup, Egypt was ruled by the Arab Socialist Union (ASU), a political party grounded in Arab Nationalism and socialist ideologies, in a single party system ruled by President Gamal Abdel Nasser. Under the ASU, Egypt pursued an agenda of land redistribution and the nationalization of banks, factories, and firms. University graduates had easy access to jobs in the bureaucracy or public sector upon graduation. Accordingly, the public sector became the economy's primary buyer and seller.
>
> At the same time, the banks of the Nile, long the breadbasket of impressive empires, had turned their bountiful farmland to more profitable enterprises than bulk cereals. For instance, at the beginning of the twentieth century, three-quarters of Egypt's exports consisted of raw, unprocessed cotton. Rather than exporting the cotton to be processed in more developed economies such as Britain or France, Egypt's leaders decided to take advantage of its large population by employing them in a state-owned textile industry. There was an inherent logic in this; Egypt had the largest population in the Arab world, and the textile industry was labor-intensive, meaning that this was a relatively efficient way of generating employment. To this end, ISI measures were engaged: private textile producers were nationalized and protectionist measures enacted to shield domestic factories from foreign competition. One example was tariffs, or taxes on imports. By increasing the price of imported fabrics, clothes, and other textiles, the government could induce Egyptians to purchase locally made varieties instead. The same ISI policies of statist investment into domestic industries protected from global market pressures held for a broad array of other industries, from foodstuffs to more advanced goods and inputs like iron, steel, fertilizer, cement, and paper. Through the mid-1960s, the strategy seemed to work. In 1963, Egypt's GDP growth rate peaked at nearly 10 percent – an astounding figure seldom seen outside the most developed countries at the time, whether Western or Communist.

To support the growing role of the state, the public sector also expanded. The public sector encompassed the economic domains that were partly or wholly controlled by governments. This included the bureaucratic civil service positions charged with carrying out government functions and implementing regulations. It also included jobs in constructing and maintaining public infrastructure in transportation, communication, and other areas; public services such as the police and military; and state-owned enterprises, or firms where the governments retain majoritarian or total ownership. Increasing numbers of people came to work in this sector, whose newly expanded role in guiding political and economic administration required a relatively educated and urban population.

Hence, investment in education, urban infrastructure, and the state bureaucracy were intertwined. Reducing illiteracy and making access to education universal was a major theme in many of these countries' development through the 1950s through 1970s. High school graduates were often able to find decent employment in major cities, working in public agencies, departments, and offices. Universities were built by the state to help educate the new cadre of public-sector workers while becoming important sites for building a sense of national identity. A system of using standardized high school exit exams to rank and sort students into various subfields and universities granted the state further control over the education system.

As ruling coalitions in the MENA – meaning not only governments but also their core supporters – came to rely on the support of both industrial and public-sector workers, many leaders found it politically sensible to increase their wages and dispense more and more state benefits in the form of rent control, free university education, and subsidized food and energy. Though an expensive ruling formula, this made good political sense. Authoritarian regimes needed popular backing and legitimation, and in the absence of democratic participation, economic prosperity functioned as a substitute.

And indeed, the state-directed (often termed "statist") development model pursued in Egypt and other MENA states through ISI appeared successful throughout the 1950s and 1960s. New industries were created, diversification away from agriculture took place, jobs were plentiful in the industrial sector, and urbanization proceeded. A strong state apparatus was created to manage and direct this, fusing political support for the industrial policy with populist governments in the manner of the Nasser regime in Egypt. As shown in Figure 5.1, the MENA experienced the world's highest rates of economic growth as measured in Gross Domestic Product (GDP) per worker during the 1960s and compared favorably with other developing regions into the

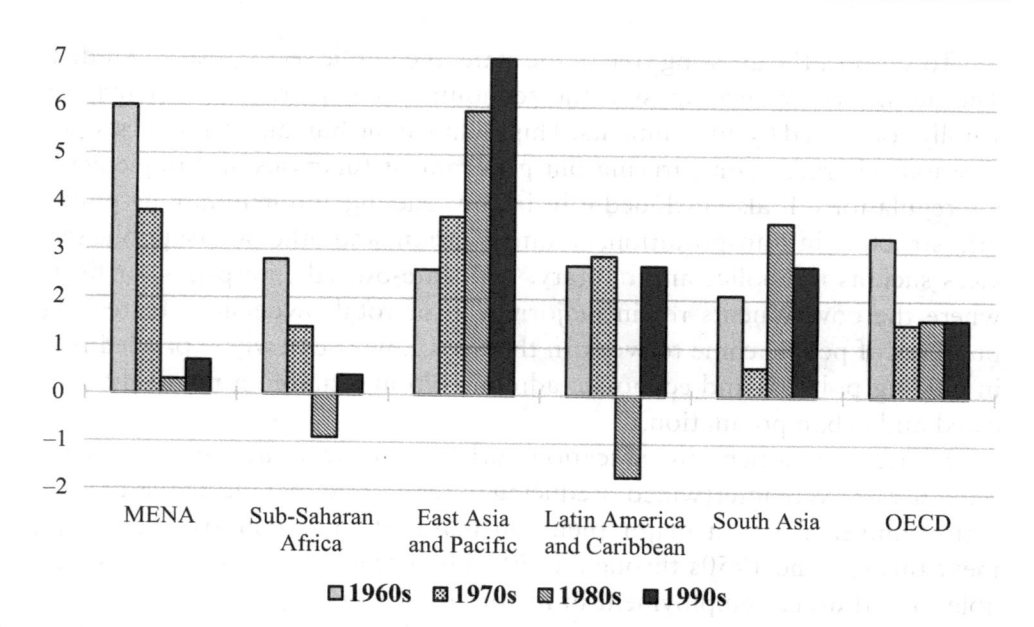

FIGURE 5.1

MENA vs. global regions – GDP growth per worker (percent), 1960s–1990s.

Source: Data from Tarik Yousef, "Development, Growth, and Policy Reform in the Middle East and North Africa since 1950," *Journal of Economic Perspectives* 18, 3 (2004): 91–115.

1970s. Most countries in the region were able to maintain unemployment rates close to those found in advanced economies. This economic expansion allowed for tangible gains in poverty reduction and life expectancy by the 1990s. According to the World Bank's 1995 report, *Claiming the Future: Choosing Prosperity in the Middle East and North Africa*, in 1990 only 5.6 percent of the MENA's population lived on less than a dollar a day (a global standard indicating extreme poverty), compared to 14.7 percent in East Asia and 28.8 percent in Latin America. Average life expectancy at birth rose from 46.7 years in 1960, to 58.7 years in 1980, finally to 73.5 years as of 2016. The primary education completion rate rose from 49 percent in 1970, to 73 percent in 1985, and 91 percent in 2016. By these standards, we can conclude that most societies in the Middle East advanced considerably over these decades, and we can also conclude that though benefits were uneven, the quality of many lives improved.

Stagnation and the limits of state-led growth

Yet as Figure 5.1 also shows, robust productivity growth tapered off over time: the MENA economies in the 1990s were not roaring as they were decades earlier, especially not compared to the more advanced economies of the Organisation for Economic Co-operation and Development (OECD). Over time, the products offered by state-owned companies – from food to steel to leather – became relatively expensive compared to imported goods that could be imported (factoring out overvaluation of currencies which made the foreign products artificially expensive), while the public sector became bloated and unproductive. The monopolistic nature of the ISI model and high tariffs all contributed to poor quality control and produced less than desirable consumer goods. The expected shift to an export-led strategy where these consumer goods could become sophisticated and high-quality enough to be sold on the international market, as had been the case with the "Asian Tiger" economies of Hong Kong, Singapore, South Korea, and Taiwan by the 1980s, did not materialize for the MENA.

Moreover, the agricultural sector was often neglected during the heyday of statist development. As a consequence of overvalued exchange rates used to protect the industrial sector, there was less of an export market for MENA agricultural goods, harming the profitability of farmers. Agricultural goods were often heavily subsidized in order to benefit urban workers, leading many farmers to leave their fields in search of work in burgeoning cities. A number of MENA countries, such as Egypt, had once sustained bountiful harvests and exported great quantities of food to the rest of the world. The ISI period saw agricultural production decline as there was less and less profit to be made. Many countries which had once been net exporters of food became net importers. This drained governments' coffers of foreign exchange and often forced them to borrow from foreign banks and governments simply to purchase food.

The Arab republics in particular, such as Algeria, Egypt, Syria, and post-1958 Iraq, also ideologically pursued development policies inspired by socialist principles. This went hand-in-hand with ISI, resulting in extremely high financial drain by the 1970s. The costs of subsidized consumer goods, foodstuffs, energy, and the public wage bill were all absorbed by the government, while there was little in the way of consumer or income taxation to contribute to state budgets. Indeed, most regional governments refused to impose adequate tax policies due to both political sensitivities and lack of foresight. State-run companies were anointed the engines of growth yet begun to sputter given their lack of competition. Workplace conditions did not incentivize productivity, and managers were hardly motivated to generate profits. Government support was politically motivated because even when state-run companies were bleeding money and profits, public funding was necessary to keep alive these symbols of national development. Moreover, the prevailing social contract produced a highly empowered and vocal working class that was increasingly committed to keeping the statist development model intact and unchanged. Workers were directly connected to ruling political parties, akin to unions that were led by the state. Consequently, the urban working class became highly politicized and came to expect ever more extensive government subsidies, especially during periods of high inflation.

Crucially, while only the largest Arab republics attempted large-scale industrialization through ISI, the notion of providing public employment, social goods, and other welfarist measures through state-run development came to also characterize smaller Arab countries that similarly could not rely upon oil exports for wealth, in particular Morocco, Tunisia, and Jordan. Across the board, by the 1970s these governments' national financing became increasingly stressed as they were forced to spend at high rates without adequate taxation and other domestic revenues. Perhaps the greatest drain outside ISI-driven economic investments, however, was the public sector. In many countries, it was seen as an innate right for citizens to obtain a government job upon graduation from high school or university, which was even mentioned in constitutions. Public-sector jobs were perceived as relatively secure positions with many extra benefits, including subsidized housing, preferential prices, and generous health packages.

From a political perspective, maintaining ever-expanding payrolls for the civil service, educational sector, and even military made sense. Such policies were seen as maintaining popular support for ruling presidents, parties, and kings. They redistributed resources to rapidly expanding urban centers where the new middle classes demanded jobs. And they kept the social contractarian promise of prosperity and livelihood in return for political obedience and stability. This political reasoning held even despite that such economic institutions often became overrun with superfluous personnel and worsening inefficiencies. Indeed, in many bureaucracies and ministries, corruption and favoritism became rampant as managers and elites sought jobs and contracts for families and friends. The solution from the perspective of government planners was starkly inadequate: continue hiring and bump up wages to keep the public workforce happy, while borrow from domestic banks and foreign lenders to close the budgetary gap.

The bottom falls out
The global economic environment starting in the mid-1970s was one of rapidly rising prices, particularly commodities like oil, food, and raw materials.

Arab oil-exporting states enacted an oil embargo of Western countries as a direct result of US support for Israel in its 1973 war with the Egyptian-led Arab armies, while global demand elsewhere continued to increase. While Western audiences recognize this period as the global energy crisis, the oil-exporting countries, particularly the Gulf kingdoms of Saudi Arabia, Bahrain, Kuwait, Oman, Qatar, and the United Arab Emirates (UAE), remember it as a time of rapid enrichment due to skyrocketing energy prices. Much of their newfound wealth was deposited into commercial banks, US Treasury bills and other bonds, or direct investment in the US, but oil-exporting countries also began to invest in building their national infrastructure and creating rentier economies.

This had profound implications for the region, as Chapter 6's investigation of rentierist social and cultural legacies explains. Here, economic patterns come into focus. When statist development began in some MENA countries in the 1950s, the rapid accumulation of wealth by the oil-exporting states two decades later became intricately tied to the region's collective economic stability. These mostly monarchical countries became massive importers, providing reliable markets for regional exporters. In expanding their economies and public sectors, they provided not only universal employment for their citizens but also work opportunities for other Arab nationals, millions of whom relocated to the Gulf for work opportunities – and in return remitted back their salaries, which infused these "labor-exporting" states like Lebanon, Jordan, and Yemen. In addition, hydrocarbon rents were also redistributed regionally through Arab foreign aid; for instance, the oil-rich kingdoms sent billions of dollars to Egypt and Jordan during the 1970s, in solidarity with their wartime footing as "front-line" states against Israel. Finally, most Arab countries were able to obtain oil and gas from regional producers at below-market rates; this helped keep energy prices low, while oil-rich kingdoms like Kuwait could simply absorb the losses.

This all changed in the early 1980s. Due to the energy crisis starting in the mid-1970s, global markets suffered from an oil surplus characterized by falling demand and ever-rising production. Oil prices plummeted during the 1981–1986 period, which created devastating ripple effects across the region – and especially Arab states – that were already beginning to feel the burden of ISI's self-defeating inefficiencies, overstocked public sectors, and public debt. The oil price shock generated a host of economic ramifications that touched every MENA economy: labor-exporting states lost remittance income, oil-exporting states lost energy revenues, trade patterns were disrupted, imports and consumption declined, Arab foreign aid dried up, and indebted governments suddenly faced financial realities. The solution for many countries like Morocco, Tunisia, Egypt, Algeria, Jordan, Lebanon, and Turkey was to turn to the world's lenders of last resort – the World Bank and IMF – and seek out emergency loans to avoid complete economic collapse.

Thus, the state-led development model persisted beyond the point at which its economic weaknesses had become apparent, owing to its perceived political merits. It was exceedingly difficult for MENA governments to tackle redundant labor in the public and industrial sector. The constituencies who would be adversely affected were quite skilled at mobilization through their unions, professional associations, and political parties, and could take to the urban streets to protest. Fearful of regime in stability, the governments of the day more often than not backed away from reforms which would incur the ire of these interest groups. Instead of restructuring, governments continued to borrow heavily from outside sources and, as is often the case in autocratic regimes, use the military and security services to clamp down on public protests against rising prices and costs of living. Indeed, Morocco, Egypt, Tunisia, and Jordan all experienced what we now term "bread riots" during the 1980s, as government efforts to cut costs by reducing food and fuel subsidies (which raised prices overnight in many cases) ran against angry publics whom were not financially equipped to deal with skyrocketing living costs.

The social costs of this laggard arrangement would become apparent decades after these bread riots. The legacies of state-led development meant that by investing heavily into creating an educated middle-class in urban areas wedded to government jobs and public services, these governments had few answers when financial hardship forced them to pull back, reducing the promise of employment and prosperity given a generation earlier in return for political quiescence. The eventual response given the dissolution of this social contract was the rejection of quiescence and mobilization for change.

BOX 5.2 CASE STUDY, PART II – EGYPT DURING THE BUST YEARS

Egypt's halcyon years of rapid growth came crashing to a halt during the 1970s, the product not only of conflict and military expenditures but also the internal exhaustion of its economic model of ISI. By the early 1970s, the cash-strapped government was caught between two unenviable choices: raise more domestic revenues through taxation, which would be extremely controversial, or else cut the public spending and government involvement, hoping that market forces

BOX 5.2 (CONTINUED)

could rescue the economy. Anwar Sadat ascended to the Egyptian presidency in 1971 following Nasser's death, and chose the latter. With rising debt and suffocating finances, Sadat abandoned the socialist ideology of the ASU years, implementing a period of *infitah* (or "Open Door") policy in 1974, aimed at partially liberalizing the Egyptian economy – that is, reducing state spending, privatizing some industries, and encouraging foreign investment. However, this agenda met with limited success given resistance by bureaucrats, elites, and political institutions that had invested so much in the earlier statist model.

Unable to procure the credit necessary to maintain food imports, Egypt was forced to sign a loan arrangement with the IMF in 1977 valued at $146 million. This required the reduction of subsidies in order to contain government expenses, resulting in price increases on consumer goods like bread. Yet the urban poor and middle classes alike had grown accustomed to cheap bread to meet their most basic dietary needs. In January 1977, riots exploded in the streets of Cairo. These anti-government bread riots resulted in 73 deaths and thousands of arrests, and required the Egyptian army itself to fan out and restore order. Unable to withstand the political repercussions of this attempted policy reform, the Sadat government revoked the price changes, and the economic reform program stalled. This symbolized the incredible difficulty of altering two generations of calcified popular expectations that had been built around a narrow social contract; when the government sought to renege on its end of the deal and liberalize the economy, societal forces needed some other compensation – if not material alleviation, then perhaps political and democratic rights. Yet the latter was not forthcoming, which induced the Egyptian regime to shy away from further economic overhauls that were direly necessary. Three more decades of stagnant policies that prioritized political survival over financial sustainability followed under Sadat's successor, Hosni Mubarak, until the Arab Spring and revolution came to Cairo in 2011.

Neoliberalism and globalization

By the 1990s, most MENA governments came to the realization that they needed greater external support from foreign governments and international financial institutions as a way to weather the hard times. Yet financial relief from the IMF and World Bank came with painful conditions, known as structural adjustment policies. Some of the policies which the IMF and World Bank expected of borrowers included exchange rate liberalization, devaluation of currency, restrictions on budget deficits, decreased interest rates, increased energy prices, lower government subsidies, revised labor laws that favor employers, the implementation of sales and income taxes, privatization and selling of state-owned enterprises, banking liberalization, trade liberalization, the removal of rent control, and ease of foreign investment. In essence, following the Washington Consensus template borrowed from the canon of neoliberal economics, they desired countries to cut back government involvement in the economy, lower spending and raise taxes, and open up economies to global forces. Most also joined the World Trade Organization, and some like Jordan and Morocco later pursued free trade agreements with the European Union and the United States. The assumption shared by many technocrats was that an overgrown state apparatus was "crowding out" the private sector, and therefore MENA governments needed to step back and allow the private sector to be the engine of economic growth. The goal was to encourage the MENA countries to outgrow the old statist model and integrate with the globalizing economy through free trade, foreign investment, and harmonized practices, even if such policies exposed national populations to the material pain of adjustment.

However, such reforms did not turn Turkey, Iran, and the Arab states into Asian Tigers, led by export-oriented industries that could lead globally competitive economies. The aforementioned case study of Egypt presents perhaps the most important reason: economic change creates political losers, and few governments – least of all authoritarian regimes that rely upon some type of popular legitimation – wish to bear the wrath of urban publics who are deprived of access to all the pillars of past prosperity, from welfarist measures to public employment. While all MENA countries that accepted IMF and World Bank loans were forced to implement some neoliberal reforms, such as privatization of state-owned companies and lowering trade barriers, such measures were either rolled out partially or else not accompanied by corollary austerity (that is, cutbacks in public spending).

A closely related factor is corruption, as powerful elites – officials, magnates, politicians, generals, and other operators – have worked to exploit market-oriented economic reforms. High levels of cronyism have allowed elite businesses connected to rulers to receive access to cheaper land, subsidized energy prices, lucrative license deals, special financial arrangements, or inside information. For instance, the privatization of state-owned assets often went to these well-connected elite families – something especially seen in pre-revolutionary Egypt, Syria, and Tunisia, where the extended families of their ruling presidents themselves became inordinately wealthy by capturing key sectors and taking advantage of new rules. Thus, many liberalization reforms resulted in a transfer from state ownership to crony elite ownership.

Another reason for poor regional performance in an era of neoliberal globalization is structural. The monumental 2002 *Arab Human Development Report* (AHDR), a landmark study commissioned by the United Nations

Development Programme, pointed to three fundamental deficits in the Middle East: a deficit of political freedom, a deficit of gender equality, and a deficit of knowledge creation. Ameliorating the latter means incubating a private sector to attract technology transfers and encourage innovation. Yet with high tariff barriers, excessive bureaucratic red tape, and weak links to global financial markets, the region outside a few pockets of excellence (such as Israel, Istanbul, and recently a few Gulf littoral cities) has proven inhospitable to foreign investment that could spur such domestic entrepreneurship and local knowledge generation. Moreover, perceptions of regional insecurity and conflict make it difficult to woo international investors and educators.

Undoubtedly, the MENA has needed foreign investment to provide technology and technical knowledge that can create labor-intensive new industries, augment the technical and post-secondary education sector, and upgrade infrastructural development projects needed to meet urbanization challenges such as transportation, housing, food security, and waste management. There is simply not enough capital and expertise available domestically to sustain the level of production and employment necessary to satisfy the region's booming youth population. However, despite decades of attempted neoliberal reforms, MENA economies lag in their efforts to attract foreign investment. In fact, the World Economic Forum reports that the entire region attracts no more than 1 percent of global foreign investment and roughly 2 percent of foreign investments that flow to non-Western developing states.

Finally, the engine of economic growth in successful developers has been export-oriented development – that is, the creation of industries and sectors specifically designed to produce goods and services for global competition. This has been seen most pointedly in the East Asian economies, starting with the Asian Tigers in the 1970s, and more recently with China. Indeed, until the 1970s, MENA economies compared favorably to South Korea, Taiwan, Hong Kong, and Singapore in terms of GDP growth and per capita income. The divergence occurred starting in that decade, and by the 1990s these four developers had become OECD-level industrialized countries. Their key to success was exports. In some ways, Asian Tiger policies during the 1950s and 1960s resembled the state-led model employed in the Middle East; for instance, infant industries identified as being crucial to future national prosperity were sheltered from global competition through governmental subsidies and trade barriers. Yet governments were also keen to politically and economically pressure domestic industries to improve and become more sophisticated over time, knowing that merely servicing domestic consumers would not suffice for the long term. That degree of institutional discipline, manifest in policies such as making government financial support contingent upon export performance, forced these economies to compete and upgrade. Indeed, many of these four countries' national brands have become ubiquitous in the global marketplace – think cars (e.g., Hyundai, Kia), banks (e.g., HSBC, DBS), technology (e.g., Samsung, Acer), and airlines (e.g., Singapore Air, Cathay Pacific).

The Gulf states and the second oil boom

The picture in the oil-rich MENA economies, and especially the hydrocarbon-heavy Gulf kingdoms, is different in terms of how economic cycles have shaped social routines and the quality of life for most national societies. The Arabian Gulf states benefited from the first oil boom in the 1970s but did not diversify of their national economies, and they were therefore hammered hard during the oil price collapse of the mid-1980s. In the 2000s, however, oil prices rose again after a period of stagnation, and the Gulf kingdoms began to consider the long-term necessity of diversifying their economies. Related to this were regional efforts to both internally harmonize and integrate national policies through the Gulf Cooperation Council (GCC), a regional security alliance created in 1981 but which over time matured into an integrative organization that facilitated coordination. Some achievements, for instance, were a common Gulf customs union in 2003 and a common market in 2008 – benchmarks that greatly reduced trade barriers and began to create shared stances regarding employment, welfare, property rights, business regulations, and other aspects of economic production. This enhanced regional integration has contributed to some impressive years of economic growth and improved intraregional trade, although oil and gas exports have still served as the lifeline of these economies.

Spurred by high energy prices that peaked in the early 2010s, the GCC kingdoms' cash reserves ballooned. In turn, the wealthiest states like Saudi Arabia, Kuwait, and the UAE began to finance not only their domestic investments but also overseas assets, companies, and projects in the OECD economies and East Asia. As measured through their sovereign wealth funds designed to invest surplus oil and gas revenues abroad, such investments are enormous. For instance, as of 2018, the Kuwait Investment Authority holds nearly $600 billion in cash and assets, and maintains (among other holdings) a nearly 7 percent stake of Daimler AG (the German manufacturer of Mercedes-Benz), making it the single biggest shareholder in this firm. At the same time, these kingdoms have also begun underwriting massive domestic urbanization schemes that have transformed the skylines of cities like Dubai, Abu Dhabi, and Doha through unprecedented construction booms, new tourism, real estate development, and banking. Finally, starting in the 2000s, the Arabian Gulf kingdoms began more aggressively investing into the rest of the Arab world, especially the oil-poor states now struggling with financial exhaustion and laggard economies. Gulf monies poured billions of dollars into telecommunication, banking, construction, tourism, and real estate across the region, but especially Morocco, Egypt, Lebanon, and Jordan.

The 2000s oil boom also enabled the richest GCC kingdoms, in particular the UAE and Qatar, to begin carving out a new identity for themselves, undergoing a slow but significant neoliberal shift – a "rebranding" of sorts, promoted by a young, entrepreneurial, and Western-educated class of technocrats and investors. The GCC states have been liberalizing their domestic regulatory space, joining the World Trade Organization, and supporting private-sector investment. Yet while aware of the finite nature of their oil resources, and accepting that new technologies have boosted oil production from other countries (such as the US) while reducing global hydrocarbon demand, these states have struggled to diversify their economies. The UAE has gone farthest, attempting to transform Dubai and Abu Dhabi into a commercial, transportation, and financial hub linking the West to Asia.

NON-INCLUSIVE ECONOMIC GROWTH, RELATIVE DEPRIVATION, AND THE ARAB SPRING

The causes of the political revolutions which swept the Arab world during 2011–2012 are difficult to ascertain with absolute certainty. Uprisings are, by their nature, complex outcomes driven by many variables. However, economic factors played a substantial role in generating the social forces and contentious impulses behind the uprisings. The Arab Spring was not instigated by the impoverished underclass of the Arab world: peasants and the poor were not revolutionaries. Rather, it was literate, unemployed, disenfranchised, and middle-class youth – in essence, the products of historical modernization – that took to the streets to protest. The Arab Spring began in countries that were actually experiencing modest economic growth by the late 2000s: in 2009 and 2010, Tunisia achieved 3 and 4 percent GDP growth, Egypt 4.7 and 5 percent, Libya 1.8 and 5.2 percent, Yemen 3.9 and 7.8 percent, and even Syria 4 and 5 percent. Most of these countries had also attempted to liberalize their economies, at least partially, in response to neoliberal pressures. Thus, the environment in which the Arab Spring arose was not one of particularly severe recession. However, rebellions still transpired in those countries because the diffusion of the gains from growth did not keep pace with the rising expectations of many people. In other words, the region experienced what is known as *non-inclusive economic growth*.

Inclusive growth, as defined by the World Bank, occurs when growth is sustained over the long-term and reaches a broad spectrum of the population across different sections of the economy. Economic growth is regarded as successful when it is diversified across different industries, encompasses various segments of the labor force, manifests in the form of productive employment (including outside the public sector), and is primarily directed to competitive markets. While the Arab world appeared to be experiencing some GDP growth in statistical terms immediately preceding the Arab Spring, it was not inclusive, being constrained by the heavy legacies of statist development from the economic side and the institutional demands of authoritarianism from the political side.

This explains matters at the macro-structural level, but why did this induce Arab peoples in so many countries to revolt? One can identify a widespread sentiment during 2011–2012 that the region's population, led by its enormous youth populace, held high expectations for material prosperity which were simply not satisfied by political and economic systems unable to full the old social contract put into place generations earlier. This is the classic definition of relative deprivation, as used in the early work of political scientist Ted Gurr. Young protesters were literate and knowledgeable, well aware of their potential capabilities and economic potential – but there was a gap between their present circumstances and what they believed they *deserved*. It was not surprising, therefore, to see a common demand among the Arab Spring demonstrators and activists to be one of *karama* (dignity).

To feel relative deprivation, a disgruntled group must make a comparison to others. Arab youths often compared themselves to similarly educated citizens, including the older generation, and questioned why they faced such deplorable economic prospects, such as their unlikelihood to obtain jobs even after university training. In countries like Egypt, unemployment among youths (defined by the World Bank as those between 15 and 24) measured 62 percent in 2011, Yemen 48.4 percent, and Syria 56.9 percent. Perceptions of grinding corruption among rulers and the wealthy interested only in perpetuating the old economic system weighted down by a sluggish public sector were endemic. Anger at nepotism amongst authoritarian elites and their cronies flared. In sum, the educated class of young people created by the MENA's past developmental trajectory had high expectations – but those expectations were never matched by the dimming prospects for economic mobility or political voice.

THE INFORMAL SECTOR

The need to generate greater employment for younger generations has been an urgent priority in the MENA since the 1980s economic decline. Although employment growth has in fact been relatively large in absolute terms, it has failed to keep pace with the expanding population. Under the tenure of the state-directed economic model, most MENA states adopted the convention of lifetime employment, generous pensions, and other substantial benefits for workers. However, these factors render the labor market rigid and inflexible. Today, many companies adhering to labor regulations do not have much freedom to downsize their workforce in the event of an economic downturn or unforeseen costs. As such, firms in generally weak private sectors are hesitant to expand employment even during periods of economic growth. Furthermore, firms must typically deal with heavy regulatory burdens, typified by vast mountains of paperwork, inspections, and contracts. Regulations can asymmetrically disadvantage younger, smaller firms against larger, more established companies which are able to deal with regulatory burdens by hiring administrative staff and legal counsel.

The result has been the creation of a vast *informal sector* of the economy. The informal sector means areas of a national economy where workers and firms operate outside of legal and regulatory supervision. This exists in many aspects of life across the world – think, for instance, of the money made by teenagers who babysit or graduate students who tutor on the side. The problem arises when such informality characterizes such a large chunk of the overall economy that it begins to compete with, and even overtake, the formal private sector (e.g., if that teenager was actually employed at a babysitting company, or if that graduate student ran a registered business that gave tutoring lessons for a legal fee). In the Arab world, where informality looms large, informal employment can be so deeply intertwined with formal economic organizations that disentangling the two can be difficult. Photo 5.1, for instance, depicts a common scene in urban Cairo in the early parts of many days – a bread carrier delivering loaves of freshly baked products. For decades, bakeries that secured subsidized flour, sugar,

PHOTO 5.1
Bread carrier in downtown Cairo, 2007.

Source: Photo by paulk is licensed under CC BY 2.0.
Online: www.flickr.com/photos/paulk/3167762218

and other products through official distribution channels could not operate informally; they were registered buyers and producers, and often their prices were monitored as well. Yet while the bakery itself was a formal company, many of the people it employed, including bread carriers given cash wages or stipends for their daily runs, worked off the books, earning no formal incomes but still contributing to the company's operations, economic output, and food distribution.

A large informal sector is commonly taken as a sign of ill health in an economy. As the World Bank outlined in its 2014 report, *Striving for Better Jobs: The Challenge of Informality in the Middle East and North Africa*, informality can undermine economic productivity and development. The sorts of occupations found in the informal sector tend to be low-skill jobs, requiring little education, and affording meager opportunity for training and skills upgrading. Workers in the informal sector operate without legal contracts, and do not contribute to, or benefit from, social security such as pensions or health insurance. Incomes in the informal economy are generally lower (even for workers with similar skillsets), and employment security more precarious, than is the case with formal employment. Moreover, working conditions are quite often sub-standard, potentially unsafe or hazardous. The swollen size of the informal sector is problematic from the perspective of governments as well, since economic activity which transpires in the informal sector goes undeclared and untaxed, resulting in losses to government revenues. This in turn induces the state to try to compensate by levying heavier taxes on those companies which operate openly in the formal portion of the economy, further adding to the incentive to seek refuge in the informal sector. In the MENA region, a significant portion of informal employment takes the form of service-based jobs in transportation, retail, tourism, agriculture, and construction. The ranks of the informal workforce are drawn disproportionately from younger generations, and include an incredibly diverse array of work that make economies operate – construction workers, vehicle drivers, miners and fishermen, cooks and clerks, street vendors, waste pickers, hotel cleaners, and the like.

As the same World Bank report notes, the firms which operate in the informal sector are a combination of small companies which forego official registration and operate entirely beneath the regulatory radar, and other (typically larger) firms which do most of their business in the formal sphere, but also engage in some informal activities. Informal employers like construction companies, restaurants, and tour operators must expend a portion of their time and resources concealing their operations or bribing officials. The desire to escape the reach of law discourages firms from taking advantage of the opportunities available to formal businesses, such as obtaining bank credit and judicial protection. Still, operating informally remains an attractive option for many companies, allowing them to circumvent registration, taxation, and regulations. Another factor pertinent to informal economics is state capacity, meaning its legal power and capabilities to regulate, punish, and reorganize society. This affects a firm's decision to operate informally in two ways: firstly, by increasing the likelihood that those who operate outside of the law and refuse to comply with regulation will be punished; and secondly, by increasing the quality and quantity of the state services which firms in the formal sector can make use of, further decreasing the appeal of informality.

The final problem with informal economics is one of macroeconomic reform. MENA governments received inordinate advice from consultants, planners, aid donors, and multilateral institutions like the World Bank and

IMF to upgrade their economies through the pathways aforementioned, for instance, emphasizing export-oriented industries, reducing corruption, attracting foreign investment, and generally harnessing the potential of their vast human (and especially youth) resources. Yet if a large share of their workers and businesses operate in the shadows, sequestered from the reach of formal policies, top-down reforms will simply fail to reach much of the populace and the overall economy.

The MENA economies have some of the largest informal sectors in the world. The regional informal economy constitutes a larger share of total economic activity than is the case in developed countries and most post-Soviet states, but a smaller share than in East Asia, Latin America, or Sub-Saharan Africa. In the *average* MENA country, the informal economic sector encompasses one-third of the entire GDP and two-thirds of the total labor force. This trend is especially evident in countries with large rural populations and high population densities, such as Yemen and Morocco, while it is far lower in oil-rich countries with small populations, such as the UAE and Qatar. Consider Figure 5.2, which provides statistical data between 2000 to 2007. The horizontal axis shows that the percentage of workers not contributing to social security – a common measure for the size of the informal economy, since working in unregistered businesses means not contributing to pension and insurance plans. The figures are austere; approximately 90 percent of the Yemeni labor force works informally, as does 76 percent in Morocco, nearly 66 percent in both Lebanon and Iran, 50 percent in Tunisia, and 45 percent in Egypt. The vertical axis of Figure 5.2 illustrates the other side of the equation: the informal sectors contribute a hefty percent of overall economic output, ranging from a low of under 20 percent in Syria and Iran to a high of nearly 40 percent in Tunisia. Hence, both in terms of numbers employed and the overall output, the informal sector looms large in regional economies.

Still, there are some positive aspects of informality. The informal sector can be a site of innovation and entrepreneurship. Unencumbered by the onerous level of regulation faced by actors in the formal sector of the MENA region, informal businesses and workers often exhibit a comparably high level of flexibility and creative energy. Many companies begin by operating informally and transition to the formal economy once they have grown and expanded to sufficient size to contend with regulatory burdens. Small firms commonly operate informally to avoid the costs of worker benefits and taxes, while larger registered firms may still underreport the extent of their operations for these same reasons.

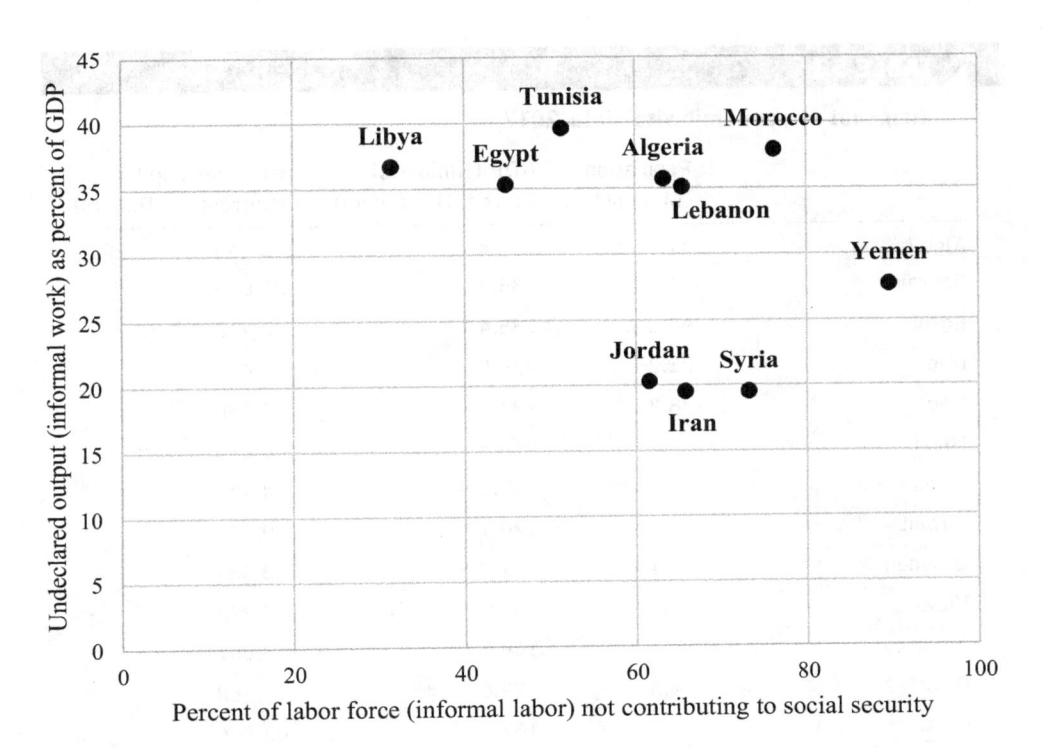

FIGURE 5.2
MENA countries – size of informal economic sectors, 2000–2007.

Source: Data from World Bank, *Jobs for Shared Prosperity Jobs for Shared Prosperity Time for Action in the Middle East and North Africa* (Washington, DC: World Bank, 2013).

DIVERGENT DEVELOPMENT

While this chapter has described shared regional patterns and challenges for the MENA, it should be noted that the region exhibits also sharp divergence in economic outcomes. Even a casual glance at these countries illustrates the sheer variation of population, economic output, and incomes per capita, the latter of which is a crude proxy for relative wealth. Table 5.1 lists these data, and illustrates how a myriad of factors – historical legacies, resource endowments, demographic content, and so forth – have shaped each economy today.

The World Bank often divides the MENA economies into three categories: 1) resource-rich, labor-importing countries; 2) resource-rich, labor-abundant countries; and 3) resource-poor countries. As per Table 5.1, the most prosperous area of the MENA region (excluding Israel) is the resource-rich, labor

TABLE 5.1

Snapshot of economic vital data, 2017

	Population (Millions)	GDP (Billions of Current US Dollars)	GDP Per Capita (Current US Dollars)
Algeria	41.3	170.4	4,123
Bahrain	1.5	35.3	23,655
Egypt	97.6	235.4	2,413
Iran	81.2	439.5	5,415
Iraq	38.3	197.7	5,166
Israel	8.7	350.8	40,270
Jordan	9.7	40.1	4,130
Kuwait	4.1	120.1	29,040
Lebanon	6.1	51.8	8,524
Libya	6.4	51	7,998
Morocco	35.7	109.1	3,007
Oman	4.6	72.6	15,668
Qatar	2.6	167.6	63,506
Saudi Arabia	32.9	683.8	20,761
Syria	18.3	**	**
Tunisia	11.5	40.3	3,491
United Arab Emirates	9.4	382.6	40,699
West Bank and Gaza Strip	4.7	14.5	3,095
Yemen	28.3	18.2	643

Source: World Bank (2018), *World Development Indicators*. ** indicates no data available.

importing countries of the Arabian Gulf – essentially the GCC, or Saudi Arabia, Kuwait, Bahrain, Qatar, Oman, and the UAE. Indeed, at purchasing power parity, the IMF and the Word Bank estimate that Kuwait, the UAE, and Qatar rank among the ten wealthiest countries in terms of per capita income in the world. Indeed, Qatar ranks as the highest, outpacing even the US. These high levels of income are the consequence of accruing a oil and natural gas wealth, which is then divided among a small population (before the fall of the Qaddafi regime in 2011, Libya also witnessed this phenomenon to a lesser extent). The Arabian Gulf constitutes the world's single largest source of oil, and its beneficiary kingdoms offer unparalleled universal welfarist measures in terms of free education, health care, and public-sector employment that can still accommodate most citizens' demands. Unemployment rates are the lowest in the MENA region, but it is notable that few GCC citizens are employed in the private sector given the small size of the non-oil economy and the still-attractive option of government-related work.

Yet paradoxically, most Gulf kingdoms have also benefited from economic prosperity as characterized by rapid urbanization and new commercial development. Their small local populations were never able to fill these labor demands. Instead, they have long relied upon migrant workers, or expatriates, to take up these jobs. Approximately half the entire GCC population consists of migrant workers, and in some states, foreigners outnumber nationals by a wide margin. As displayed in Figure 5.3, a staggering 94 percent of Qatar's workers, and just under 90 percent of its population, are

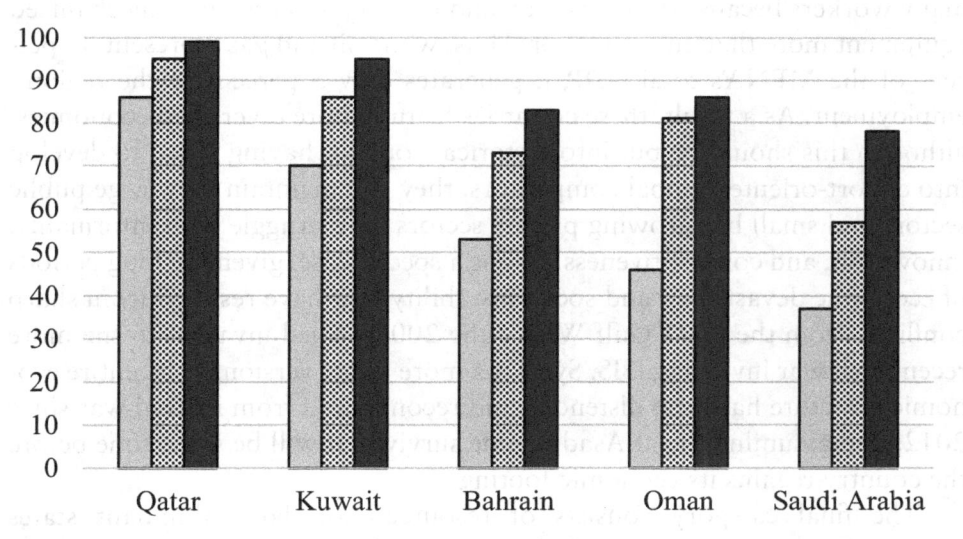

☐ Non-nationals as a percent of population (latest year available, 2010–2016)
▨ Non-nationals as a percent of employed population (2015)
■ Non-nationals as a percent of non-public sector employment (2010)

FIGURE 5.3
GCC kingdoms – non-nationals in population and employment, 2010–2016.

Source: Data from Gulf Labour Markets, Migration, and Population Programme (2018).
Online: http://gulfmigration.org

non-national (that is, foreign-born). The bulk of these migrant workers come from South and Southeast Asia, while a smaller flow originates from other MENA countries. It is a common arrangement for such expatriates to send a portion of their income back to their families. Illustrating the wide-ranging economic effects of oil, such remittances have become a crucial source of income for households across the world, from Morocco and Jordan to Bangladesh and the Philippines.

The second category of economic outcomes stems from resource-rich, labor-abundant countries. Essentially, this means Iraq, Iran, Algeria, and to a lesser degree Syria, which have some oil and gas resources (and thus earn some revenues from their export). But they have far larger populations than the Gulf kingdoms, and most followed the model of statist development in the past to a close degree given the higher difficulty of sustaining universal employment and welfarist schemes resembling the generous arrangements found in the GCC. Another factor is that though hydrocarbon industries is a vital economic activity, it is not labor-intensive. It simply does not employ many workers because the extraction and refining of oil requires mechanized equipment more than human labor. Thus, while oil and gas represent 36 percent of the MENA's total GDP, it generates only 5 percent of the region's employment. As a result, these countries feature more diversified economies, although this should be put into historical context: having failed to develop into export-oriented global competitors, they still maintain very large public sectors and small but growing private sectors that struggle with informality, innovation, and competitiveness. Iraq is a special case, given the long periods of economic devastation and social instability that have resulted from sharp conflicts, from the 1991 Gulf War to the 2003 US-led invasion to the more recent civil war involving ISIS. Syria is a more tragic version, as its entire economic structure has been distended and reconfigured from its civil war since 2012; and assuming the al-Asad regime survives, it will be some time before the country regains its economic footing.

The final category consists of resource-poor, labor-abundant states such as Egypt, Lebanon, Jordan, Morocco, Tunisia, and the Palestinian territories. Lacking much oil and gas resources, these countries are densely populated by regional standards and feature among the lower incomes per capita. Nowhere is this more evident than Egypt, with a population near 100 million crowded along the banks of the Nile. As of 2018, its GDP per capita stands at around $2,413 – less than an eighth of Saudi Arabia's and under 4 percent of Qatar's. Egypt, Jordan, Morocco, and Tunisia pursued statist development to a close degree, with kings and presidents inaugurating ambitious development schemes from the 1950s and 1960s onwards that were characterized by public employment, rapid urbanization, some domestic industrialization, and the promise that such a social contract would continue unabated. They were, not coincidentally, also hit hardest with the regional economic recession from the mid-1980s onwards; remittances and foreign aid from the oil-exporting kingdoms like Saudi Arabia and Kuwait dried up, and they could not compensate with greater trade given the uncompetitive nature of their industries. While these economies did recover somewhat, their struggle to provide economic opportunities manifested in the 2011–2012 Arab Spring and in the ongoing challenges to satisfy the aspirations of their youth populations. They also remain highly vulnerable to regional trends, such as oil price shocks; as a common Jordanian refrain goes, when the oil-rich Gulf sneezes, the Hashemite Kingdom catches the cold.

The differential effects which the Arab Spring and recent conflicts have had on MENA economies cannot be understated. Anarchic civil wars and breakdowns of state institutions in countries like Syria, Libya, and Yemen have destroyed the economy due to the decline of industry, sheer violence and loss of life, and flight of capital. Yemen's GDP contracted 59 percent between 2013 and 2016, while Libya's GDP declined 38 percent from its 2010 peak.

CONTEMPORARY CHALLENGES: THE CASE OF UNEMPLOYMENT

Arab youths are plagued by chronic unemployment and underemployment. Job creation in the MENA is largely entrusted to the government, which is tasked with pivotal roles in economic management. Despite attempts at liberalization, public-sector employment remains disproportionately large, however. As Figure 5.4 shows, the MENA region as compared to other key global regions has the largest public sector as measured by the proportion of government spending dedicated to the wages of government-related workers. These figures only count civilian rather than military salaries, and also do not include the lifelong pensions guaranteed to teachers, civil servants, bureaucrats, and other public-sector retirees. Though these data are spotty across the MENA, we know adding these figures up often means that a shockingly high degree of a national budget is essentially already spent each year on simply maintaining the livelihoods of current and retired employees under

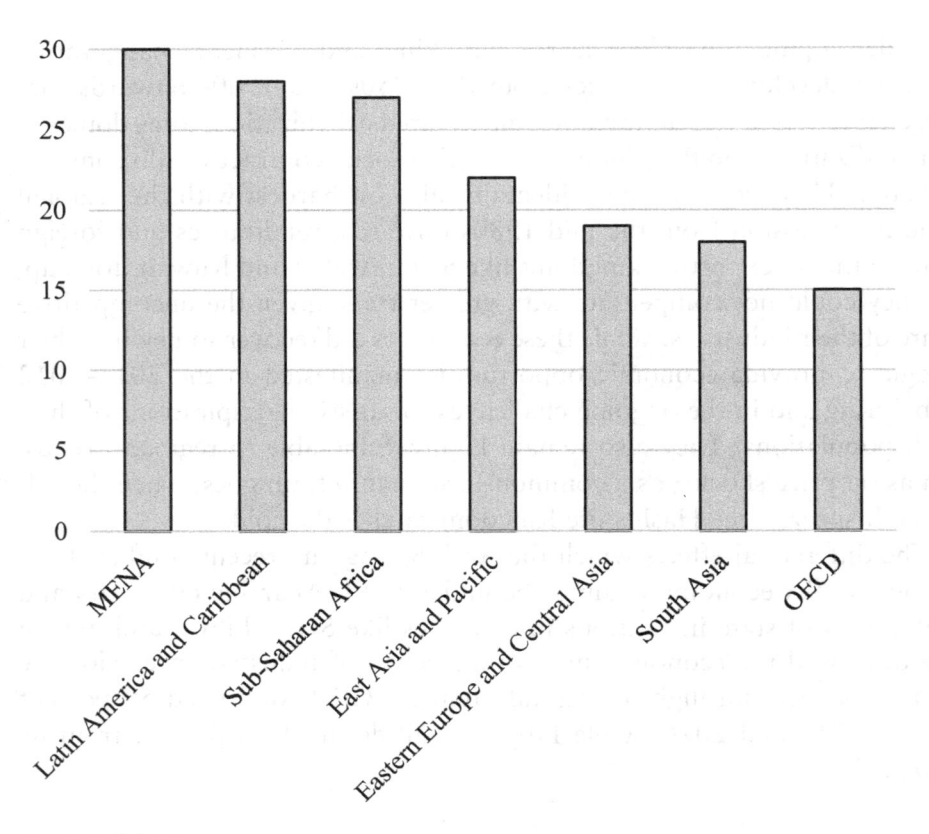

FIGURE 5.4
MENA vs. global regions – size of public sector by Government Wage Bill, 2016.

Source: Data from World Bank, *Size of the Public Sector: Government Wage Bill and Employment* (Washington, DC: World Bank, 2016).

the government's responsibility. For instance, two-thirds of Jordan's 2018 national budget of nearly $13 billion was devoted to civilian and military salaries and pensions.

Outside the smallest oil-rich GCC kingdoms, if the public sector can no longer be relied upon as a job generator, where else can employment originate? Agriculture is not the answer, given its general decline over time as well as the marginalized role played by rural populations and producers now. Existing industries have some potential, but many economists point to services in some form – retail, financial, transportation, and so forth – as a potential job creator. Yet the problem here combines informality with competitiveness; too many service jobs already fly under the radar, while leading formal businesses that have broken out and become profitable on a regional and even global scale (such as Jordan-based Arab Bank, Qatar-based Al-Jazeera media, and Kuwait-based Zain telecommunications group) tend to hire in highly skilled positions for which there is intense competition.

Part of the problem may rest in the cultural psyche of many Arab societies, in which the availability of high-paying, office-based work – a remnant of statist development and public-sector employment – has become such an entrenched desire that positions requiring lower levels of skills, such as retail and construction, are immediately rejected as viable occupations. This "culture of shame," as some economists term, remains a severe impediment to matching youths to jobs in countries like Jordan and Tunisia. In such countries, as Chapter 10's analysis of youth joblessness and demographic pressures divulges, unemployment is paradoxically higher among the best educated. University graduates often have a higher unemployment figure than those that just finished primary school, partly because of a lack of skilled positions across the economy and partly because university graduates cannot conceive of working in jobs involving any kind of manual labor or basic servicing, such as retail.

Most MENA economies also wrestle with the problem of low female participation in the workforce due to a variety of social, familial, and cultural pressures, as well as government policies (such as insufficient maternity leaves) that often discourage women from seeking long-term employment. In the OECD countries, the female labor participation rate – which the World Bank defines as the percentage of women aged 15 years and up who enter the workforce and look for jobs – stands at 51.3 percent; by contrast, the MENA region's figure is 20.6 percent. In some countries, the rate is even lower; Algeria, for instance, has a 15.2 percent female labor participation rate. An absence of women from the workforce robs a country of productivity; it prevents vital talent and skills from reaching the economy, while also reinforcing patterns of patriarchy that gender inequality. This provides some clues into the formal gender inequalities witnessed in many Arab countries plus Iran, as engaged by Chapter 9.

Finally, while many in the region point to the oil-rich Gulf kingdoms as models of development, given the surreal level of technology-fueled urbanization that has transformed cities like Dubai and Abu Dhabi, this too cannot be the answer. Economic development in the Arabian Gulf is the product of unique structural and historical factors, the least of which is geological luck, that cannot be replicated elsewhere. It is also remarkably easier for governments to offer near-guaranteed public employment and generous welfarist protections when the population of national citizens is tiny, as in Qatar and the UAE; and even then, as Chapter 6's discussion lays out, the long-term consequences on rent-based development on social relations can be highly distorting.

The path forward will require a combination of policy creativity and political flexibility. Economic planning over past generations was as much a product of political imperatives as it was technical rationality, and divorcing both governments and societies from long-held expectations about the boundaries of their social contract will require meaningful change emphasizing the *inclusive* aspect of development. The Arab Spring gave a hint of this democratic potential. Policy creativity comes into play with more innovative reforms that capitalize on youth populations, reduce social and gendered inequalities, link informality to the overall economy, emphasize export-oriented growth and industrial competitiveness, reduce public-sector overhead, and kickstart the private sector with the promotion of entrepreneurship, smarter regulations, and national prioritizing. It is telling, however, that popular expectations are not especially high. See Figure 5.5.

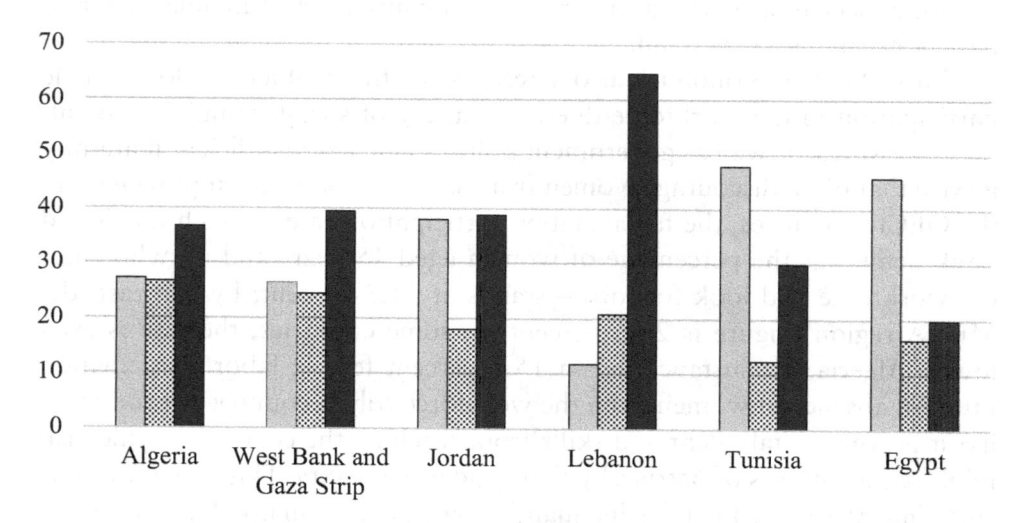

□ Somewhat or much better   ▨ Almost the same
■ Somewhat or much worse

FIGURE 5.5
Economic expectations from Arab Barometer, 2017.

Source: Arab Barometer, Wave IV (2016–2017).

Online: www.arabbarometer.org. The survey question was: "What do you think will be the economic situation in your country during the next few years (3–5 years) compared to the current situation?" The responses ranged from don't know, much worse, somewhat worse, almost the same, somewhat better, and much better.

Whether the MENA region and especially the Arab world can take this step forward is unclear, but economies (and thus societies) cannot be imprisoned in the dustbin of underdevelopment forever. In 1960, war-torn South Korea's per capita income was barely $160, one-tenth of Egypt's during that heyday of statist development and ISI. Sixty years later, their outcomes have starkly diverged – not because history willed it, but largely due to the economic initiatives and policy implementation of planners who staked the future upon the capacity of their society to commit to change. The same could very well happen in the Middle East, with the stakes never higher for everyday people than they are now.

CONCLUSION

In the post-war era, post-colonial MENA countries looked to chart their own course on the international stage, and many adhered to a state-led development model involving ISI and a politically driven set of economic projects. This resulted in measured gains regarding education, employment, and economic growth, but austerity and recession from the mid-1980s onwards signaled the exhaustion of this strategy. From that point, the pathways of various regional economies meandered into vastly different directions, ranging from the wealthy hydrocarbon-heavy Gulf kingdoms to less prosperous, labor-abundant countries like Tunisia, Egypt, and Jordan. Outside the narrow band of the richest GCC states, the region today faces a major crisis in terms of inclusive economic development, which cyclically results in social unrest and political resistance. While oil exporters face their own challenges in terms of diversification, most other states are attempting to attain consistent, self-sustaining growth in the long run. The most immediate concern is reducing dependence on the public sector as a source of employment, and encouraging the creation of private-sector jobs that can provide for the region's large youth cohort.

QUESTIONS FOR DISCUSSION

1 What was the statist model of economic development, and how did in manifest in the MENA region starting in the 1950s?
2 What caused the exhaustion of statist development, and how did both governments and societies react to economic crisis from the mid-1980s onwards?
3 At the same time, why did certain other developing countries in the world, such as the Asian Tigers, begin to outperform the MENA and achieve industrialized success?

4 Why is non-inclusive economic growth so devastating to populations with large youth generations?
5 How does a large informal sector help or hurt an overall economy?
6 Why would relative deprivation related to economic underachievement have political consequences?
7 What are various categories of economic outcomes we see in the MENA region today, and what makes each distinctive?
8 Would it be advisable for the region's economies (and thus social groups as well) to pursue outside advice given by global actors, such as the IMF and World Bank?

FURTHER READING

There are excellent general surveys of the region's economic history and prevalent strategies, which combine theoretical narratives with case studies of specific countries. Social dynamics and demands coincide with political constraints and impositions in these studies (thus the notion of *political* economy), which include Melani Cammett, Ishac Diwan, Alan Richards, and John Waterbury, *A Political Economy of the Middle East*, 4th ed. (London: Routledge, 2015); Roger Owen and Şevket Pamuk, *A History of Middle East Economies in the Twentieth Century* (Cambridge, MA: Harvard University Press, 1999); and Rodney Wilson, *Economic Development in the Middle East*, 2nd ed. (London: Routledge, 2010). Though these works tend to emphasize the Arab world, there is excellent non-Arab scholarship as well: for Israel, see Paul Rivlin, *The Israeli Economy from the Foundation of the State through the 21st Century* (Cambridge: Cambridge University Press, 2010); for Turkey, Şevket Pamuk, *Uneven Centuries: Economic Development of Turkey since 1820* (Princeton, NJ: Princeton University Press, 2018); and for Iran, Homa Katouzian's *The Political Economy of Modern Iran: Despotism and Pseudo-Modernism, 1926–1979* (London: Palgrave Macmillan, 1981); plus Suzanne Maloney's *Iran's Political Economy Since the Revolution* (Cambridge: Cambridge University Press, 2015).

More contemporary issues of economic growth and social well-being since the twentieth century, which pay attention to variations across MENA countries due to different types of resource constraints and demographic endowments, also abound. Examples include Marcus Noland and Howard Pack, *The Arab Economies in a Changing World* (Washington, DC: Peter Institute for International Economics, 2011) and Paul Rivlin, *Arab Economies in the Twenty-First Century* (Cambridge: Cambridge University Press, 2009), which were the state-of-the-art prior to the Arab Spring. Excellent post-2011 interventions include Magdi Amin et al., *After the Spring: Economic Transitions in the Arab World* (Oxford: Oxford University Press, 2012); Ahmed Galal and Ishac Diwan, eds., *The Middle East Economies in Time of Transition* (London: Palgrave Macmillan, 2016); and Bahgat Korany, ed., *Arab Human Development in the Twenty-first Century: The Primacy of Empowerment* (Cairo: American University of Cairo Press, 2015). There are also robust article-length works, such as Tarik Yousef, "Development, Growth, and Policy Reform in the Middle East and North

Africa since 1950," *Journal of Economic Perspectives* 18, no. 3 (2004): 91–115; Felina B. Duncan and Zulal S. Denaux, "Determinants of Economic Success in the Middle East and North Africa," *Global Journal of Business Research* 7, no. 5 (2013): 25–34; and Samir Makdisi, Zeki Fattah, and Imed Limam, "Determinants of Growth in the MENA Countries," in *Explaining Growth in the Middle East (Contributions to Economic Analysis, Vol. 278)*, eds. Jeffrey Nugent and N. Hashem Pesaran (Amsterdam: Elsevier, 2007). Indeed, other essays in this edited volume will prove enlightening as well.

Many authors also put the MENA in global perspective, discerning an abrupt change in the region's economic growth and societal trajectories since the 1980s and believing that external variables like trade and globalization can help explain this. See, for instance, Hassan Hakimian and Jeffrey Nugent, *Trade Policy and Economic Integration in the Middle East and North Africa: Economic Boundaries in Flux* (London: Routledge, 2005); Clement Moore Henry and Robert Springborg, *Globalization and the Politics of Development in the Middle East*, 2nd ed. (New York: Cambridge University Press, 2010); and Laura Guazzone and Daniela Pioppi, eds., *The Arab State and Neo-Liberal Globalization: The Restructuring of State Power in the Middle East* (Reading, UK: Ithaca Press, 2012). At the same time, rigorous works parse out specific controversies and issues regarding the variables underlying the region's growth potential. Multilateral aid pressures and neoliberal conditionalities are explored in Jane Harrigan and Hamed El-Said, "The Economic Impact of IMF and World Bank Programs in the Middle East and North Africa: A Case Study of Jordan, Egypt, Morocco and Tunisia, 1983–2004," *Review of Middle East Economics and Finance* 6, no. 2 (2010): 1–25. The distorting social effects of public-sector employment in Arab countries are likewise unpacked in Ragui Assaad, "Making Sense of Arab Labor Markets: The Enduring Legacy of Dualism," *IZA Journal of Labor and Development* 3, no. 6 (2014). The World Bank's *Striving for Better Jobs: The Challenge of Informality in the Middle East and North Africa* (Washington, DC: World Bank, 2014) tackles the question of informal unemployment head on, much like its other excellent reports and studies of regional development, which can be found online (below).

Online sources

There is a colossal trove of economic data on the MENA online, thanks to the resources of the multilateral institutions. The World Bank maintains its *World Development Indicators* which, as noted in Chapter 2, tracks (among other things) economic trends since 1960 (http://databank.worldbank.org/data/home.aspx). It also allows, for public access, its library of books and volumes about Middle East economic and social development, including some of the reports used in this chapter (https://openknowledge.worldbank.org/handle/10986/2168). The ILO also maintains detailed information about employment trends (www.ilo.org/beirut/lang—en/index.htm). The IMF's work, including its Finances Dataset, are also available online (www.imf.org/en/Data). Beyond quantitative data, there are excellent periodicals too that track regional economic developments; among them are the World Bank's *MENA Economic Monitor* (www.worldbank.org/en/region/mena/publication/mena-economic-monitor), the GCC-oriented Gulf Labour Markets, Migration, and Population Programme by the Gulf Research Center (http://gulfmigration.

org/), and the OECD's own programs and materials on the MENA Region (www.oecd.org/mena/). *Middle East Economic Digest* serves, as well, as one of the more insightful running periodicals about regional developments, particularly in the business world (www.meed.com/). For more advanced academic research, consult the Cairo-based Economic Research Forum, including its conference proceedings and academic papers (https://theforum.erf.org.eg/).

CHAPTER 6

Social and cultural legacies of rentierism

Hae Won Jeong

THE RUNDOWN: KEY TOPICS COVERED
- Hydrocarbon energy
- Rentier state theory
- Urbanization
- Citizenship
- Expatriate populations
- Human capital and knowledge

INTRODUCTION

Since the British Royal Navy's decision to convert its fuel from coal to oil on July 2, 1910, the Middle East and North Africa (MENA) region has assumed vital geostrategic importance, and its "black gold" became a major political, economic, and diplomatic pivot for international actors coveting its control. In July 1928, the Red Line Agreement enabled the American, Anglo-Persian, British-Dutch, and French partners of the Turkish Petroleum Company (TPC) to create an international oil cartel. Over the next several decades, Western firms dominated the oil industry; for instance, TPC and Standard Oil of California obtained concessions for oil exploration from Iraq and Saudi Arabia in 1925 and 1933, respectively. The 1950s marked a turning point in terms of MENA governments beginning to gain control over the flow of their energy revenues, as signified by the nationalization of the oil industry in Iran and in the decades after in the other major oil exporters. While fluctuating oil and gas prices since the 1970s have resulted in fortunes being made and lost for many countries, this era – one marked by state ownership over hydrocarbon finances, which in turn diffuses across the MENA region in obvious and hidden ways – continues today.

The result is rentierism, a concept that is woven deeply into prevailing studies of the MENA region, and which occupies this chapter. Rentierism refers to a broad set of interconnected social, cultural, and economic processes that characterize the development of the MENA region. The notion of "rents" here manifests as the by-product of exporting oil and gas by hydrocarbon-rich countries. They appear in three primary forms: as the tremendous financial revenues accruing to governments, the foreign aid those governments in turn circulate across the region, and finally the remittances sent back by foreign workers in these economies back to their home countries. These financial linkages connect the MENA countries to one another, and internally generate political and social relations of dependency within national populations that comprise the rentier social contract. The entire region's social development has been transformed by this phenomenon. By exploring the meaning of a *rentier state*, we can trace the long-term effects of rentierism across all the different sub-regions of the MENA, from the Maghrib to the Mashriq and back to the Arabian Gulf, the latter of which holds the preponderance of oil and gas resources. Various topics, in particular urbanization, citizenship, and human capital, illustrate these societal legacies. Turkey and Israel are mostly excluded from this analysis as their economic orientation and productive mechanisms largely fall outside the realm of rentierism. The underlying theme is that by itself, hydrocarbon endowments are not an inherently positive or negative factor; it is *how* they are exploited, deployed, and redistributed that shape the social life of the region. And for better or for worse, rentier states have tended to utilize them in ways that make sense in ensuring short-term stability but leave behind destructive long-term legacies.

RENTIER STATE THEORY (RST)

The theoretical paradigm used to study both governments and societies in oil- and gas-rich countries is rentier state theory (RST). Often invoked by political scientists, sociologists, historians, and economists, RST describes many of the ways in which influxes of hydrocarbon wealth permeate the political institutions, social relations, and economic structure of well-endowed countries.

The keynote term of RST is *rent*. Rent is a technical economic concept, but in practical terms it is defined as the income gained by the differential exploitation of a natural resource owned by some political actor, such as a government. The MENA region is characterized by both energy rents and strategic rents. The former refers to what most people commonly conceive as oil wealth – the financial flows garnered from the sale of oil and gas, which is produced and exported from a national territory. Other natural resource rents exist, however; for instance, other developing countries may have mineral rents from diamond, copper, and gold deposits. The fundamental trait about such natural resource rents, whether from energy assets or minerals, is their origin: they are gifted by geology. Today, the MENA countries most dependent upon their large oil and gas assets, but also stable enough to consistently produce and export them, are considered archetypal extractors of energy rent; these include the Arabian kingdoms, namely Saudi Arabia, Kuwait, Bahrain, Qatar, Oman, and the United Arab Emirates. Algeria and Iran are sometimes included in this category, although their economies are less reliant upon this commodity. Libya and Iraq, as well, could be considered, but have been stymied over the past decade by instability and war.

Figure 6.1 provides a snapshot of this rentierism in the MENA region; using the data of 2016–2017, the figure illustrates the percentage of all goods exports that hydrocarbon fuels (e.g., oil and gas) comprise for most MENA countries. As the data show, countries like Iraq, Libya, Algeria, and the Gulf kingdoms are extremely dependent upon energy exports. Suddenly removing oil and gas from their trading portfolio would hurt economies that have not yet diversified into other sectors – not to mention governments as well, as their revenues are heavily dependent upon energy sales given their national control over these industries. The UAE is an exception; though traditionally classified as a rentier state, over the past decade it has managed to branch out into other industries such as finance, transportation, and real estate development.

Strategic rents are different. They refer to the financial benefits extracted from the exploitation of a country's location and development. Most purveyors of strategic rents are countries that are not reliant upon energy rents; that is, they benefit not from geology but geography, because they play on the territorial and geopolitical interests of outside actors. For instance, Egypt gains strategic rents from the use of its Suez Canal, as it charges passing ships a toll in order to pass across its maritime territory. Saudi Arabia, to a lesser extent, benefits from the commerce and consumption derived from the millions of Muslim pilgrims that travel to the kingdom every year for the *hajj* pilgrimage. Foreign aid and remittances are also strategic rents. Countries like Jordan and Morocco attract enormous volumes of foreign aid

FIGURE 6.1

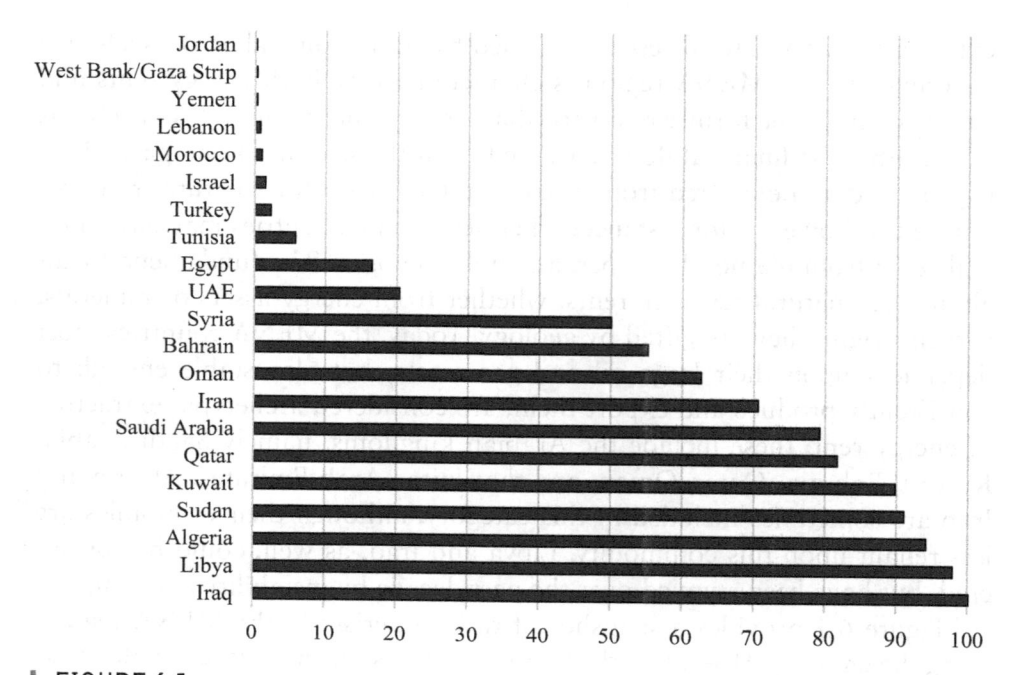

MENA countries – oil and gas as percent of all exported goods, 2014–2017 (latest available year).

Source: World Bank (2018), World Development Indicators.

from Western allies who wish to ensure that these pro-Western kingdoms remain stable and secure during a time of regional conflict. Likewise, labor-abundant countries Yemen and Lebanon enjoy rents in the form of remittance flows, predicated upon the fact that hundreds of thousands of their citizens have traveled abroad to work in booming oil-rich economies, such as Saudi Arabia or the UAE, and hence send back their salaries.

The classic version of RST was based upon the notion that because rents represent financial resources that flow into a country outside of conventional economic productive activities, they often distort social and economic development. The result is a destructive and unsustainable social contract. A rentier state has an economy that is substantially supported by external rents, such as energy rents or strategic rents; those revenues then accrue to governments, putting immense financial power in the hands of political rulers. The underlying assumption is that a rent becomes a bargaining chip for rulers, as it cements the interdependent relationship between state and society.

Governments become allocative, meaning that their primary role is not so much to produce economically but rather allocate and redistribute the exogenous monies flowing into their coffers. Therefore, they generally tax less, or not at all, which furnishes them autonomy from societal pressures typically found in countries where governments are dependent upon citizens paying their taxes. The refrain "no taxation without representation" becomes "no taxation, no representation," because citizens who do not surrender their income or property to rulers also have little claim to political voice; hence, these states are expected to be more authoritarian and less democratic. Likewise, such rent-driven governments can repress more, because the financing needed to build robust militaries or security services come not from the domestic populace but the outside world.

Related to the financial and political impact of rents is the cultural and social dimension. Many theorists of RST argued that rentierism can exacerbate *neopatrimonialism*, or a mode of social relations in which interactions between individuals and groups are defined by clientelism and patronage rather than equality and reciprocity. Put another way, rentierism can contribute to a culture of dependency. Financial wealth that falls into the treasury of rulers enables them to treat social groups, from the single citizen to collectivities such as labor unions, not as meaningful partners but instead units to be controlled by making them dependent upon their allocations of wealth and resources. Inversely, from the perspective of the ruled, obedience comes not from the belief that the government is truly legitimate, but the brute force of dependency upon state largesse for jobs, protections, and other goods. This long-term reliance gives patrons considerable control, rendering citizens into *clients*.

Such logic has been applied to the richest rentier states in the Arabian Gulf with small populations, such as Qatar and Kuwait, where regimes provide cradle-to-grave welfarist benefits, from education and health care to financial protection and jobs, which supposedly render these citizens mere clients of governmental largesse. This also hints at the weakness, however, of rentier states: because governments and citizens begin to see rentier distribution as an economic entitlement, short-term benefits such as rapid economic growth soon generate faster growth in *expectations* for more. Yet if the flow of rents is disrupted, such as during economic slowdowns or oil price collapses, the result can be severe dissent and unrest from those who consider these entitlements as birthrights. Indeed, as Chapter 5 argued, it was the exhaustion of the old state-led social contract fueled by rentier economics that in many countries convinced many youths to mobilize during the 2011–2012 Arab Spring due to relative deprivation. The promises of economic prosperity made by rentier governments and consequent belief of many citizens that their livelihood depends upon a vertical distribution of patronage from their governments left many societies in a perilous state: when regimes were no longer able to fulfill their side of the rentier social contract, the result was resistance, rebellion, and demands for voice.

Since the 2000s, our knowledge of rentierism has grown immensely. Scholars of the MENA now understand that rents do deposit heavy legacies over states and societies, but the effects vary across cases and often in counterintuitive ways that turn the logic of RST upon its head. The "neo-RST" phase of theory development has enriched our knowledge of rentierism by exposing these wrinkles. For instance, that some oil-rich autocracies suffer revolution and overthrow (such as Libya in 1969 and Iran in 1979) while others soldier on even during oil price fluctuations (such as Algeria, Kuwait, or Indonesia) suggests that regimes can invest their rents in institutions and strategies that may insulate them from popular unrest. Moreover, the commerce and wealth created in the economy by outside rents do not necessarily create loyal businesses and corporate firms; some may have close relations with rulers, while others challenge them.

Inversely, while the neo-patrimonial effects of rentierism were long assumed to suggest that the bureaucracies and governments of rent-dependent states were inefficient, fragmented, and corrupt, in reality one often finds pockets of excellence and efficiency even in the most oil-steeped countries like Saudi Arabia. Finally, the relationship between rentierism and authoritarianism is highly problematic and complex. There are plenty of examples of countries that derive much of their wealth from oil and gas exports which are also thriving liberal democracies, from Canada to Norway. Nondemocratic MENA rentier states are not equally repressive; political opposition is legal and active in Kuwait, for instance, but more restricted in Bahrain and Qatar. Counterfactually, it is also unclear whether the mere presence of rents is what prevents democracy: had the UAE or Saudi Arabia, for example, not enjoyed the geological gift of oil deposits in the 1950s, would they be flourishing democracies today? Answering this question is purely hypothetical, but it nonetheless points to the problems of making simplistic causal claims.

MATERIAL IMPACTS UPON POPULATIONS

Rentier dependence has subjected the development of many MENA economies to a boom-bust cycle, rather than a steady trajectory. As a result, many regional economies have struggled with several weaknesses, of which the greatest is the governmental tendency to spend their way out of trouble (such as public-sector employment, expensive consumer subsidies, and other goods) – a habit sustainable to most only by high energy prices or foreign aid inflows, two variables that often fluctuate wildly.

For instance, the sharp decline in oil prices from a peak of $115 a barrel in June 2014 to less than $40 a barrel in December 2015 pummeled the budget of the Arabian Gulf kingdoms, forcing many to cut back subsidies and other public spending in the face of declining financial revenues. Fuel prices rose by 80 percent in Saudi Arabia and Kuwait; one Kuwaiti newspaper, *Al-Qabas*, even surmised that retrenching subsidies could include putting an end to other cradle-to-grave benefits, such as the free health care and educational standards that have traditionally come with Kuwaiti citizenship. In addition to cutting social spending, Saudi Arabia and the UAE became the first two Gulf kingdoms to introduce a 5 percent Value Added Tax (VAT, a form of indirect taxation) on goods and services on January 1, 2018. The rest of the GCC, including Bahrain, Kuwait, and Oman have pledged to implement this VAT – a radical change given that these states have seldom needed to tax their citizens in the past.

Related to this fiscal frailty is the inclination of governments to tightly control central banks and monetary policy, such as pegging the national currency to a fixed rate; this allows leaders to protect their economic domains from volatility by keeping out foreign exchange fluctuations, but it also is highly inefficient and often expensive. When Egypt acceded to pressures in 2016 by the International Monetary Bank (IMF) to float (that is, unpeg) its Egyptian pound currency, in return for consideration of a $12 billion loan, the effect was dramatic. As often happens after long periods of fixed rates, the Egyptian currency dropped in value, and prices for many basic goods like food and electricity rose.

Strategic rents, namely foreign aid and remittances, have likewise cast long shadows over their receiving economies. The MENA region receives considerable foreign aid from global powers like the US and EU, as well as multilateral institutions like the IMF and World Bank. However, often neglected is that Arab oil exporters (such as Saudi Arabia and Kuwait) can circulate foreign aid as well to fellow regional states, aid that is essentially repackaged oil rents but now used for developmental purposes, such as financing food systems and building infrastructure. According to the World Bank, the Arab countries historically fell into three categories of recipients in terms of how much developmental assistance they received during 1970–2010 from other

Arab (and oil-rich) states: the first group includes Bahrain, Syria, and Oman, which received more than 70 percent; the second group of Morocco, Yemen, Lebanon, and Jordan accounted for 20–40 percent; and the third cluster received 10–20 percent, including Egypt, the Palestinian territories (West Bank and Gaza Strip), Somalia, Sudan, Turkey, Mauritania, and Djibouti.

However, from 2011–2015, this pattern reversed, as Table 6.1 shows. While the wealthiest rentier states in the region, especially hydrocarbon exporters like Qatar, the UAE, and Saudi Arabia, continue to furnish developmental assistance to other countries around the world, nearly 60 percent was devoted to the MENA region, plus Pakistan. Egypt, by far, accounted for the lion's share of Arab aid, receiving over $2.6 billion, or 33.5 percent, followed distantly by Morocco, Jordan, Yemen, and Sudan – an order that makes sense given that their regimes struggled during this period with popular unrest partly driven by economic demands from citizens suffering relative deprivation.

Remittances have equally profound implications for the labor-abundant MENA countries that send migrants to work abroad. In 2017, the World Bank reported that remittances accounted for 6.3 percent of Gross Domestic Product (GDP) in Morocco, 9.6 percent in Egypt, 11.1 percent in Jordan,

TABLE 6.1

Top recipients of Arab developmental assistance (foreign aid), 2011–2015

	Amount (in millions $US)	Share (Percent)
Egypt	2,624	33.5
Morocco	373	5.8
Jordan	337	5.3
Yemen	322	5.0
Sudan	181	2.8
Pakistan	123	1.9
Mauritania	103	1.6
Lebanon	87	1.4
Tunisia	83	1.3
West Bank and Gaza Strip	72	1.1
Total	4,305	59.7

Source: Organisation for Economic Co-operation and Development (2017), *Trends in Arab Concessional Financing for Development*.

15.3 percent in Lebanon, and 18.4 percent in Yemen. In plain terms, the cash sent to these countries from expatriates working abroad, especially in the oil-rich Arabian Gulf kingdoms, represented a sizable chunk of the economic productivity of these countries. Households that receive money from relatives working abroad can purchase more goods and services, and often those remittances can alleviate poverty as well by giving families a boost in their consumption and savings. Local banks likewise benefit. Furthermore, unlike foreign aid, remittances go straight to families and individuals rather than through governments, although ultimately governments can benefit – they not only enjoy a stronger overall economy, but also can extract more taxes from the incomes and activities produced by remittance-boosted households.

The oil price decline that came after December 2015 had mixed effects given these rentier networks of dependence. Countries dependent upon hydrocarbon exports like the Arabian Gulf kingdoms, Algeria, Iraq, and Libya were negatively impacted, and countries that need remittances from their workers within those economies like Egypt, Jordan, Lebanon likewise suffered. However, because these labor-abundant countries also import their energy as they have few gas and oil reserves, they also benefited from cheaper costs. The modest recovery of oil prices starting in January 2018 swung the pendulum back, advantaging one set of MENA countries over another. While falling oil prices are expected to relieve fiscal constraints of the oil-importing economies and increase the availability of cheaper consumer goods, in the long run it would hurt the labor-abundant, energy-importing countries by restricting the remittance flows of cash and financing that their economies have come to rely upon. Clearly, reliance upon hydrocarbon exports makes an economy extremely vulnerable to global price fluctuations, since the forces that shape the cost structure of oil and gas lay far outside the borders of these producers.

Economic diversification

The pervasiveness of rent-seeking behavior, the macroeconomic volatility of the MENA region (including the vulnerability of all countries to energy price variations), and the prospect for peak oil (meaning the point at which oil reserves and extraction begin to irrevocably fall) raises the concern of economic sustainability. While economic diversification does not automatically lead to economic competitiveness, low oil prices have pressured many MENA governments to cut back their public spending, especially expenditures on food and fuel subsidies, based upon very conservative estimates of global energy markets. (One exception lies in the labor-abundant, energy-importing states like Jordan and Lebanon, which somewhat benefit from cheaper energy costs – but simultaneously get pummeled by falling remittances.) According to the World Economic Forum's annual *Global Competitiveness Report*, in 2017 Egypt showed remarkable progress in diversifying its economy, while the UAE's diversification strategy enabled it to remain one of the region's most competitive economies despite its historical origins in oil dependency.

However, it is telling that after the 2014–2015 decline in oil prices, many of the wealthiest energy exporters in the MENA began to launch ambitious economic reform agendas that promised to transform both the economy and society by shifting human capital away from hydrocarbon dependence. Saudi Arabia's Vision 2030, Kuwait's Vision 2035, and Bahrain's Vision 2030 are all examples of sweeping, top-down government strategies that have pledged to create new industries and export sectors, while moving citizens away from public employment and towards private-sector entrepreneurship and excellence. Abu Dhabi Vision 2030's strategy for promoting non-oil economics is predicated on developing an export-oriented economy and small and medium-sized enterprises – that is, private businesses that may not be giant corporations because they employ no more than 250 people, but nonetheless are the drivers of commerce and services.

The precise initiatives however are catered to the specific needs and interests of individual states. Yet interestingly, energy importers have also sought to strengthen their economic competitiveness by investing in human capital and innovative fields. Through Vision 2020, Tunisia is seeking to attracting more foreign investments and develop its tourism sector to its fullest capabilities. Egypt's Vision 2030 identifies education and human development as the main pillars of development alongside natural resources development (water and energy security), as well as urban planning and environmental development. Jordan's Vision 2025 emphasizes education and youth entrepreneurship, arguing that the kingdom may not have much oil or water but does have an abundance of young talent. Lebanon's Sustainable Development Goal 2030 is committed to reducing the social and economic disparities between governorates and the urban and rural areas.

Often lost in economic diversification models, however, are the concomitant changes in social life that must occur. Economic diversification is often a coded phrase meaning that governments are seeking to escape the constraints of rentierism. However, as the preceding discussion suggests, rentierism is more than simply dependence upon oil sales – it envelops the region in a complex interlocking web of social and financial dependence. For the Kuwaiti government to declare that the kingdom should move beyond its reliance upon oil revenues may express a realistic belief that hydrocarbon wealth will not last forever. Yet it also means that it must convince citizens to stop seeking near-guaranteed employment in the public sector, such as government-related work, and instead work in a private sector that is currently staffed by foreign migrants. This requires changing not just jobs but *preferences* as well – values entrenched by past generations confronted with guarantees of state generosity. It means that foreign workers in Kuwait may no longer have their positions, or at least may suffer the possibility of return; that in turn implies less remittance incomes for labor-sending countries like Egypt and Lebanon, as well as Asian countries like India, Pakistan, and the Philippines. Such long-term impacts are not well theorized, partly because the future is uncertain but partly also because no single government can fully map out how its actions within a rentier region will precisely affect other countries.

URBANIZATION

While RST describes the effects of rentier dependence upon economic development, the social fabric of the MENA has also been shaped by this dynamic. Consider urbanization. Modernization theory assumed that urbanization was an inevitable part of every society's developmental ascent upwards, with rural and agricultural populations leaving behind their agrarian lives in favor of increasingly agglomerated towns and cities, which in turn represent the greatest economic and political centers. Along the way, these societies also industrialized, creating new sectors of manufacturing and production. Theories of modernization and industrialization are modeled after the Western experience, particularly countries like the US, United Kingdom, and Germany, which began this process at various points in the nineteenth century. Later in the twentieth century, the same occurred with newer industrializers in Latin America, as well as East Asia. However, the MENA region presents something of a riddle: many societies urbanized *without* industrializing. Rentierism again here plays something of a role. Economic modernization and rapid urbanization occurred in oil-rich states like Saudi Arabia, Kuwait, and the UAE without those countries also developing a separate industrial base. Other MENA countries, such as Morocco, have resembled a bit more the standard pathway; lacking energy resources, such states have experienced urbanization alongside some industrial development.

As Chapter 2 noted, urbanization in the MENA has been fueled by various factors, among them population growth, government planning, forced sedentarization, refugee displacement, the decline of rural productivity, and the natural migration of people in search of new economic opportunities. The magnitude of the urban-rural divide and the rate of urbanization, however, is markedly different across the region. According to the World Bank, the MENA's urbanization rate (that is, the percentage of the population living in towns and cities) did not reach 40 percent until the 1970s. From then until the 2010s, the growth of urban areas proceeded at an extremely brisk pace, which raised a host of new social issues and challenges, among them food and water security, educational and health care provisions, increased energy consumptions, and generating sufficient employment opportunities for an increasingly young population.

There are considerable nuances in urbanization patterns across countries, based upon not just their populations but also their access to energy rents. Nowhere has the intersection of rentierism and urbanization been more intense than in the oil-rich Gulf kingdoms. Property development, infrastructural expansion, and new construction fueled by the oil-dependent economy has rendered especially the small littoral principalities, namely Kuwait, Bahrain, Qatar, and the UAE, as the most urbanized sub-region in the MENA. Their population growth has been energized by the influx of migrant workers coming from labor-abundant countries. This has made possible the fantastical level of construction that has transformed the skylines of these tiny principalities and turned what were once modest towns into metropolitan complexes, as symbolized by the towering commercial centers of Dubai (Photo 6.1) and other Gulf cities.

Gulf cities are not immune to the dark side of excessive urbanization, but these problems are most acutely felt in the urban areas of oil-poor countries in the Maghrib (e.g., Morocco, Tunisia) and Mashriq (e.g., Egypt, Lebanon, Jordan). In many large cities like Casablanca, Cairo, Tunis, Beirut, and Amman, housing shortages and high living costs have resulted in informal urban settlements – neighborhoods that suffer high food and water insecurity, but are also often dependent upon remittances from local households who have relatives working in the Gulf economies. Informal settlements are defined as residential zones in which local residents do not have formal property claims, through leasing or ownership, over the land and buildings in which they live. According to UN-Habitat, Cairo has the highest rate of informal settlements (62 percent) followed by Syria (38 percent) and Jordan (16 percent).

PHOTO 6.1
Dubai skyline, 2016.

Source: iStock.
Online: www.istockphoto.com/photo/spectacular-skyline-of-dubai-uae-futuristic-modern-architecture-of-a-big-city-at-gm669045142-122234777

Rates of urbanization will continue to grow. As of 2017, according to the UN Department of Economic and Social Affairs' Population Division, a number of MENA countries (Libya, Israel, Lebanon, Jordan, and the six Gulf kingdoms of Saudi Arabia, Kuwait, Bahrain, Qatar, Oman, and the UAE) featured urbanization rates of 80 percent or more. Some, like Kuwait, are almost entirely urbanized, with only a tiny fraction of the population reported to not live within a major urban neighborhood or agglomeration. However, for other countries, rates of migration to cities and towns will continue to grow at a steady pace. Figure 6.2 uses the same UN data and shows the projection of urbanization through to 2050 of four Arab countries that had among the lowest urbanization rates in 1960 – Yemen, Sudan, Morocco, and Egypt. As the figure illustrates, by 2050 all four will be solidly upon a trajectory of upward increase, with Morocco in particular experiencing

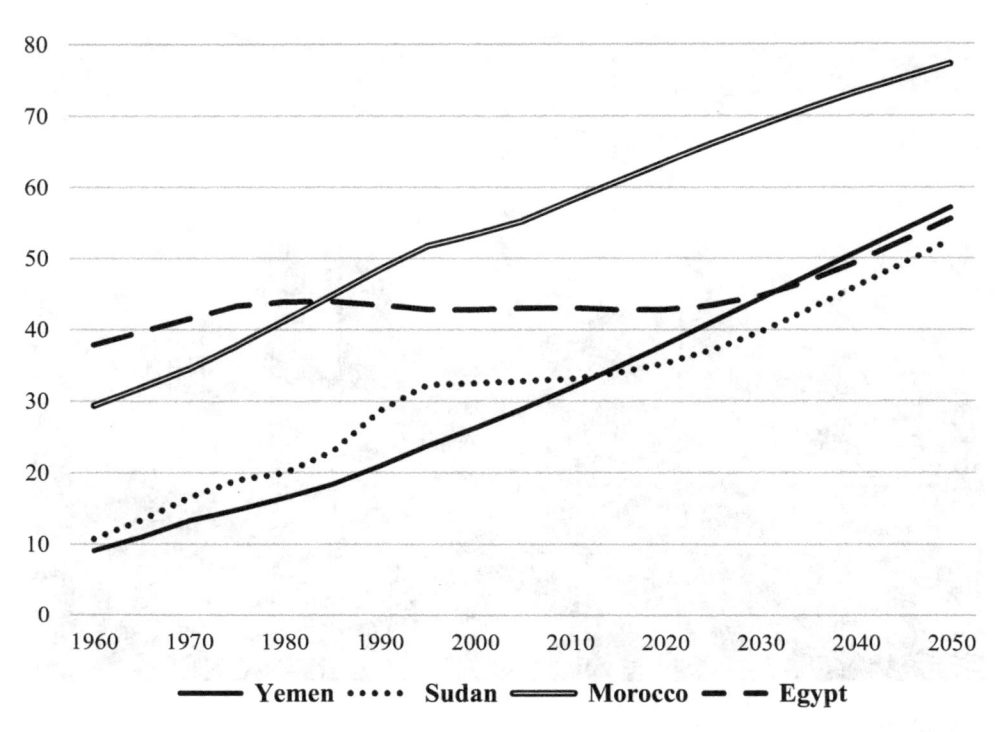

FIGURE 6.2
Yemen, Sudan, Morocco, and Egypt – projected urbanization through 2050.

Source: United Nations, Department of Economic and Social Affairs, Population Division (2018), World Urbanization Prospects: The 2018 Revision.

extremely high rates. Note that these four countries are not energy-based rentier states, but through all the ways explicated earlier such as foreign aid and remittance flows are linked to the oil and gas production of hydrocarbon-based exporters like Saudi Arabia and Kuwait.

Semi-informal and informal settlements deserve closer attention, as these represent the dark side of urbanization. Informal neighborhoods across the MENA region are constrained by a combination of supply-side housing bottlenecks and inadequate government housing policy. In Cairo, informal settlements in agricultural lands have been the dominant mode of urbanization since the 1950s: rather than a centrally planned city creeping outwards, migrants from rural areas went *inwards*, and began living on the then-outskirts of Cairo, only to see their neighborhoods swallowed up by the ever-expanding growth of the metropolis with each successive generation. One innovative mapping project undertaken by the German Federal Ministry for

Economic Cooperation and Development, the Participatory Development Programme, shows that informal settlements in Cairo are truly sprawling and encompass 60 percent of the total urban population – 12 million people that live in underserved and densely populated zones that feature poor social services and general neglect.

MENA governments recognize this, and some have embarked on massive development schemes. For instance, Egypt's Cairo 2050 plan entails introducing spatial planning and new urban models to optimize housing distribution, infrastructural development, and land use, with the goal of lessening informal settlements. In an effort to accommodate rising demands for housing, the government intends to upgrade infrastructure and redistribute population in oversaturated districts to less densely populated ones. Similarly, Lebanon and Morocco's National Spatial Strategy Initiatives seek to reduce population congestion in Greater Beirut and Grand Casablanca, respectively, by developing secondary cities and towns that will draw people away from city centers.

Such promising yet uncertain agendas stand in sharp contrast to the type of urbanization schemes found in the contemporary Gulf kingdoms. For instance, Abu Dhabi in the UAE comes across as a comparatively better-planned metropolitan area that has been continually recrafted by the government, whose planners enjoy access to ample oil revenues to finance reconstruction and rezoning projects. Among the most ambitious examples of this is Masdar City, a planned "mini-city" development that its architects claim will be among the eco-friendliest examples of urbanization in the MENA region, as it will rely heavily upon solar energy and have little net carbon impact. In summer 2018, likewise, the Saudi government announced that it would construct a futuristic urban zone called Neom – a $500 billion city in the desert that would have unparalleled automation and technological prowess. Whether such a project is sustainable or simply reflects wild science fiction dreams remains to be determined, but one resource the Saudi government possesses that remains beyond reach of aid-dependent states like Jordan is its oil reserves. In some ways, such a scheme embodies the rentier ecology of the region: oil revenues will underwrite the government's directed construction of such a mega-city, while the workers actually building it will finance their home economies and family households in countries like Egypt, Yemen, and Pakistan by remitting back the wages earned from their labor.

One hidden impact of urbanization, especially in the Gulf, that is often lost upon observers outside the region is health. Certainly, excessive informal settlements carry inherent health risks to residents; shantytowns and squatted buildings are unsafe, access to clean water and fresh food is scarce, and sanitation systems are lacking. Yet in the heart of rentierism, the packed wealthy cities of countries like Kuwait, Qatar, and the UAE, lurks another challenge with devastating impacts upon community well-being – *overconsumption* resulting in obesity, diabetes, and hypertension. According to the United Nations Development Programme, up to 40 percent of the population under 18 years of age in the Gulf kingdoms are overweight or obese. Kuwait typically ranks as among the most obese countries in the world, with doctors performing 5,000 bariatric interventions (i.e., stomach stapling surgeries) annually. Furthermore, according to the International Diabetes Federation, likewise, as of 2016, five of the six Arabian kingdoms (Saudi Arabia, Kuwait, Bahrain, Qatar, and the UAE) rank in the top 16 countries in the world with the highest diabetic incidence rates, with Saudi Arabia occupying the highest spot at seven. Oman is not far behind at 29. While the reasons vary across countries, the common ones include lack of exercise due to sedentary lifestyles, reliance upon vehicular transportation, and excessive eating of unhealthy foods such as from fast food chains.

When it comes to reproductive health, social and cultural barriers even in urban areas means that women – particularly those in informal settlements – face serious disadvantages. This applies to virtually all MENA countries. In the least developed states like Sudan and Yemen, an extremely high proportion of girls marry between 15 to 19 years of age. Sex education is virtually absent in many educational systems. In 2014, Egypt's Population Council conducted a national youth poll that queried 10,000 young people between the ages of 15 to 29 about various social issues, among them whether they recalled discussing puberty with a family member. Only about 34 percent of respondents responded in the affirmative, with just 21.4 percent of boys and young men doing so. By contrast, only a fraction reported receiving such information in school; even among the best-educated cohort, those with a university degree and often the products of private schooling, just 15.6 percent reported receiving some type of school curriculum that contained information about puberty.

THE MEANING OF (RENTIER) CITIZENSHIP

Social and cultural aspects
Citizenship construction in the MENA region is construed along three dimensions: economic provision, social identity, and cultural development. RST

tells us that many governments have treated citizenship as entirely reflective of the first dimension, as rentierism creates relations of dependency and hierarchy rather than reciprocity and democracy. For some observers, there are no citizens in a symbolic sense in rentier states, only clients of governmental patronage. This passes too for resource-poor MENA countries, which exhibit rentier qualities given their dependence upon strategic rents like aid and remittances. Thus, the social contracts found in these countries since the inception of the post-colonial period of state-building and independence after World War Two was one where regimes were expected to provide education, health care, employment, housing, and other entitlements and protections in return for patriotism and loyalty, all in the name of the greater nation. Such arrangements are rampant throughout the region; they are found in even the most energy-poor states like Morocco and Jordan. They are not markedly distinctive than those found in the cradle of rentierism, the Arabian Gulf kingdoms; the only difference is that the latter can often afford to pay for it.

BOX 6.1 CASE STUDY – RENTIER CITIZENS OR CLIENTS?

In purely legal terms, citizenship simply describes the status of being a citizen, meaning a naturalized or native-born member of a state who is granted a wide array of political rights in return for pledging some type of allegiance to the government. It is a judicial term. Yet citizenship also has deeper meaning in terms of the identity, sociability, expectations, norms, and purposes that are expressed by mere fact of possessing its juridical underpinnings. In Western countries, citizenship as discussed in the public sphere means precisely this – the legal basis for *belonging* to a country or national community, of articulating loyalty to the government, in return for receiving its protection and care. Citizens, therefore, should feel strong attachments to their country. Yet in the MENA region, and especially the Arab world, we do not find such connections predicated upon imagined belonging or legal verticality. Figure 6.3 illustrates results from the Arab Barometer's survey undertaken in 2016–2017 in its fourth wave, which queried respondents about what they identify with most strongly; among the choices were country of birth, religion, ethnicity (i.e., Arabness), region, local community, and tribe or family. These categories were mutually exclusive; respondents had to pick only one. The graph shows results for only the option of country of birth, and indicates that the average result across nine groups of respondents – Jordan, Egypt, Algeria, Tunisia, Morocco, the Palestinian Territories, Lebanon, and Syrian refugees in both Jordan and Lebanon – was just 45.2 percent. There is also considerable variation, with less than 12 percent of Jordanians expressing country as their primary point of identification, as compared to the

BOX 6.1 (CONTINUED)

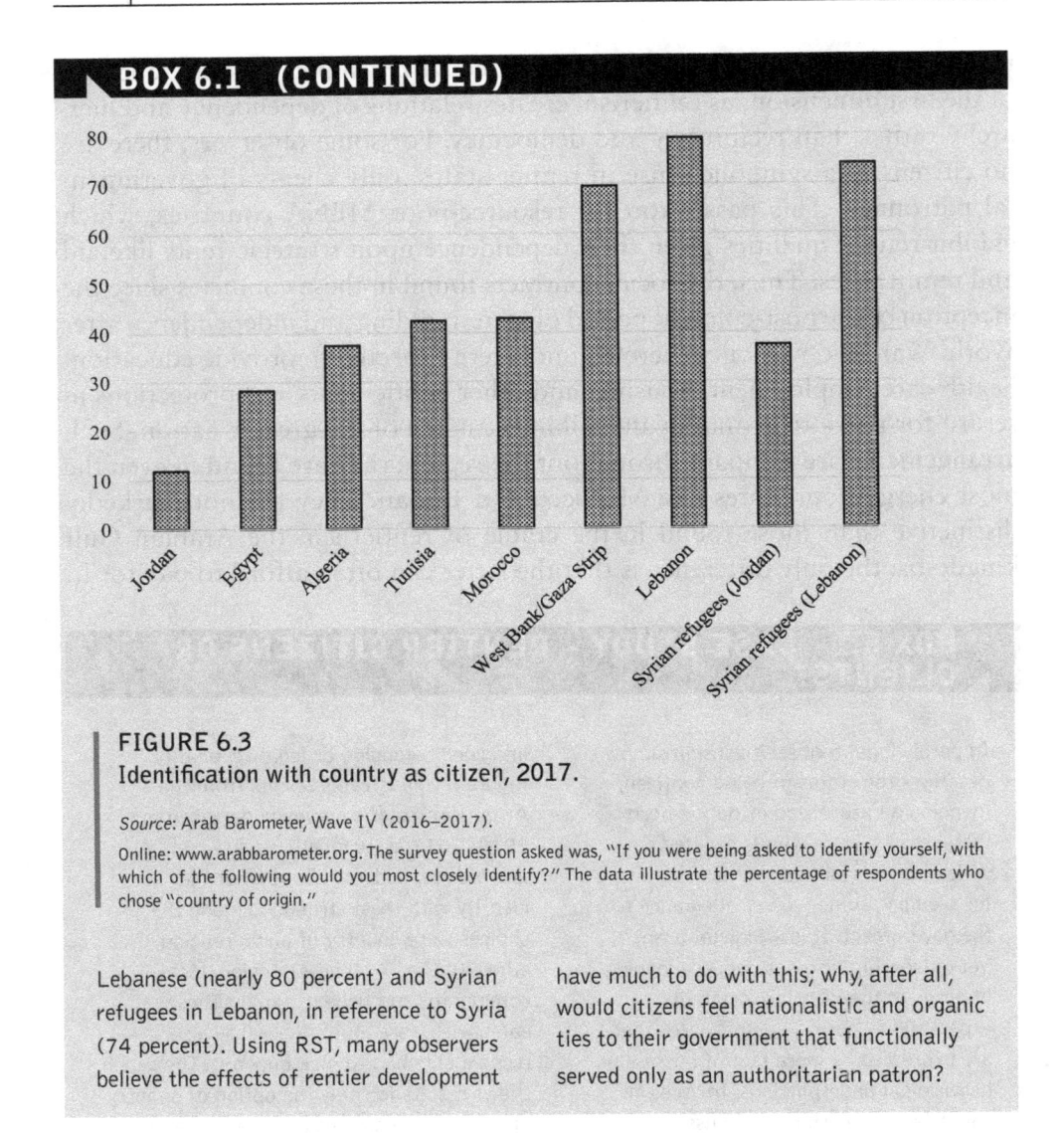

FIGURE 6.3
Identification with country as citizen, 2017.

Source: Arab Barometer, Wave IV (2016–2017).

Online: www.arabbarometer.org. The survey question asked was, "If you were being asked to identify yourself, with which of the following would you most closely identify?" The data illustrate the percentage of respondents who chose "country of origin."

Lebanese (nearly 80 percent) and Syrian refugees in Lebanon, in reference to Syria (74 percent). Using RST, many observers believe the effects of rentier development have much to do with this; why, after all, would citizens feel nationalistic and organic ties to their government that functionally served only as an authoritarian patron?

Given the rapidly expanding costs of economic provisions that most countries can no longer afford, many governments are instead embarking upon new efforts to revitalize social capital and national pride, often through programs that combine economic development with some type of top-down social mobilization that links with civil society and voluntary associations. Morocco and Jordan, for example, have increasingly promulgated new projects focusing upon civic engagement and public service in hopes of fostering a sense of citizenship among youth that is not dominated by purely material or economic demands. Over the past two decades in Jordan alone, the monarchy has launched a litany of such citizenship-driven projects such as "We Are All Jordan" and "Jordan First," which sought to overlay the extant Palestinian-Transjordanian communal divide with a new discourse focusing upon loyalty to the Hashemite crown, pride in belonging to Jordan (however artificially constructed), and a greater sense of belonging to local communities.

By contrast, constructing a new conception of citizenship infused with social and cultural notions of modernity, pluralism, and coherence is more difficult in a country like Lebanon or Yemen, whose internal ethnonational and sectarian divides have long eluded the establishment of a centralized state resting atop a unified societal foundation. Likewise, many MENA states are protective regarding the conferral of citizenship to those who are not born on their soil but instead have parents who hail from that country. Only a minority of countries worldwide grant automatic citizenship to those born on their territory regardless of the circumstances of birth and the nationality of parents; these include states as varied as the US, Pakistan, and Brazil. In most other countries, the nationality of parents is a key determinant of citizenship. While the MENA countries generally recognize as citizens anyone who are born to citizen fathers regardless where they are born, the situation is far more complicated and problematic when only the mother is a citizen. Israel, Algeria, Egypt, Morocco, and Tunisia are unique in that their nationality laws automatically grant citizenship to children born to citizen mothers, regardless of the father. In most other Middle East countries, a mother who is a citizen cannot pass on nationality to children at all, or only in the rarest of circumstances.

Furthermore, contestation over citizenship is inflected by rentier legacies in more direct ways. For instance, because most MENA regimes remain authoritarian in nature, and are also inexorably related to past economic development promises, there is an inevitably political aspect to citizenship discourse. Citizens, according to this perspective, should not simply be loyal to their country in a patriotic sense, but also *obedient* to authority figures that furnish them with all the entitlements and goods (or least attempt to) that accompany the autocratic social contract – education, protection, and ideally employment. It is not coincidental that ruling elites worried about grass-roots protests during the 2011–2012 Arab Spring in Bahrain and Syria, for instance, claiming that many demonstrators in their countries were foreign agitators rather than citizens – because true Bahrainis or Syrians would never rebel against their rightful rulers. Moreover, many countries possess groups of people for whom the cultural definition of citizenship rings hollow. Some are minority groups that have long resided in these countries even prior to their modern post-colonial formation, and so are national citizens, but only recently have been allowed linguistic, educational, and political parity with the majority. Examples include the Berbers of Maghrib countries and the Kurds of Turkey. Others are longtime residents who have lived in the country for generations, and yet have never been granted citizenship due to both social and economic reasons, such as the large *bidun* (Arabic meaning "without [nationality]") community in Kuwait.

The Gulf aspect

The rentier kingdoms of the Arabian Gulf often express their collective identity under the umbrella banner of a *Khaliji* (Gulf) identity, which as Chapter 1 pointed out constitutes one of the three primary sub-regions of the MENA. Rentierism here has deposited a major artifact: citizens of these states are simultaneously residents of hydrocarbon-dependent exporters that have offered the most generous economic and welfarist benefits in the past, and have the highest degree of urbanization; and yet they also share pre-oil cultural similarities that are construed in religious, tribal, and geographic terms. For instance, the homogeneity of the Khaliji identity is reflected in attires that vary slightly in terms of coloration and style but generally abide by the same basic requirements. For instance, in the Gulf states, the conventional garb for men is the *thawb* or *dishdasha*, a full-length long-sleeved tunic, topped with a *ghutra* (also known as a *shimagh*), a headdress fashioned from a scarf, which is held in place with an *aqal* (or cord). Photo 6.2 shows a Kuwaiti variant of this.

Traditionally, women in the Arabian Peninsula and Gulf states donned the *abaya*, a full-length outer garment resembling a long cloak that draped over their entire bodies, alongside the *shayla*, a usually black hijab that covers the hair or else a *niqab*, which covers the face except for the eyes. Photo 6.3 illustrates an Emirati woman wearing the abaya and shayla, but not niqab. These attires are distinctly stylized to their nationality, which set themselves apart from foreigners in cultural terms.

The belief that Saudi, Kuwaiti, Bahraini, Qatari, Emirati, and Omani citizens shared closer historical and cultural bonds than those of other Arab countries, not to mention Iran, Turkey, and Israel, helped instigate the creation of the Gulf Cooperation Council (GCC) in 1981. Though originally established as a security alliance against Iran and, later, Iraq, the GCC has

PHOTO 6.2
Gulf traditional male garb in Kuwait, 2010.

Source: Photo by @N04 is licensed under CC BY-SA 2.0.
Online: www.flickr.com/photos/92278137@N04/9783079684

facilitated various forms of social and cultural citizenship integration, among them reciprocal entry rights across the GCC for fellow citizens, as well as future plans to create a common currency and other forms of regional union. While such schemes were interrupted starting in 2016 by the widening Saudi-Qatari rivalry as it played out in diplomatic and economic conflict, the underlying impetus of the GCC remains: members of these affluent societies produced by oil and gas wealth believe their citizenship constructions are closely aligned. The rentier aspect is especially important when considering Yemen, which lays on the southern part of the Arabian Peninsula abutting Oman and Saudi Arabia. Yemen, too, is a Gulf state, yet as it did not share in the pathway of rentier development and social formation under monarchical regimes in the past, is generally considered outside the imagined boundaries of GCC citizenship.

PHOTO 6.3
Gulf traditional female garb in UAE, 2015.

Source: Photo by @ frosch50 is licensed under CC BY 2.0.
Online: www.flickr.com/photos/frosch50/23811041572

Moreover, some Gulf kingdoms are increasingly focusing upon what political scientists call "soft power," or rebranding their international identities and images – partly to modernize their notions of citizenship at the domestic level, and partly to filter out how the world appears to citizens at the systemic level. Among the two key points of expenditure are the cultural industry and future-oriented projects. Examples of the former include recent efforts by the UAE, Qatar, and increasingly Kuwait and Saudi Arabia to rebrand their countries as touristic destinations, playing upon their heritage as sites of ancient civilizations or else playing up the cosmopolitan and modern dimensions of their urbane environs. Examples abound. In keeping with the aims of enriching heritage and strengthening the tourism industry, UAE has opened a branch of the French Louvre in Abu Dhabi. Qatar will host the FIFA World Cup in 2022. Bahrain's Authority for Culture and Antiquities designated the staid city of Muharraq as the capital of Islamic culture in

2018. Also, in 2018, Saudi Arabia announced it would soon open Mada'in Salih – a well-preserved ruin from the pre-Roman Nabatean civilization – to the world, in hopes of making the kingdom recognizable as a site for cultural and archeological tourism. All these projects, of course, are funded by rents.

The exclusionary boundaries of rentierism

The oil boom in the 1970s financed major development projects across the Arabian Gulf oil exporters, attracting an enormous flow of migrant laborers and expatriates from the Arab world, the Indian subcontinent, and Southeast Asia that soon came to staff the local economies. Today, the result are relatively small populations with large communities of foreigners, almost all of whom have no path to citizenship in an obdurate working of rentier logic. As Figure 6.4 shows, the ratio of foreigners to citizens varies across the kingdoms but is particularly imbalanced in favor of non-nationals in the UAE and Qatar by a nearly 9:1 ratio. The demographic imbalances have far-reaching implications for social and economic growth, as well as citizenship construction. The *kafala* (sponsorship) system is required for all migrants

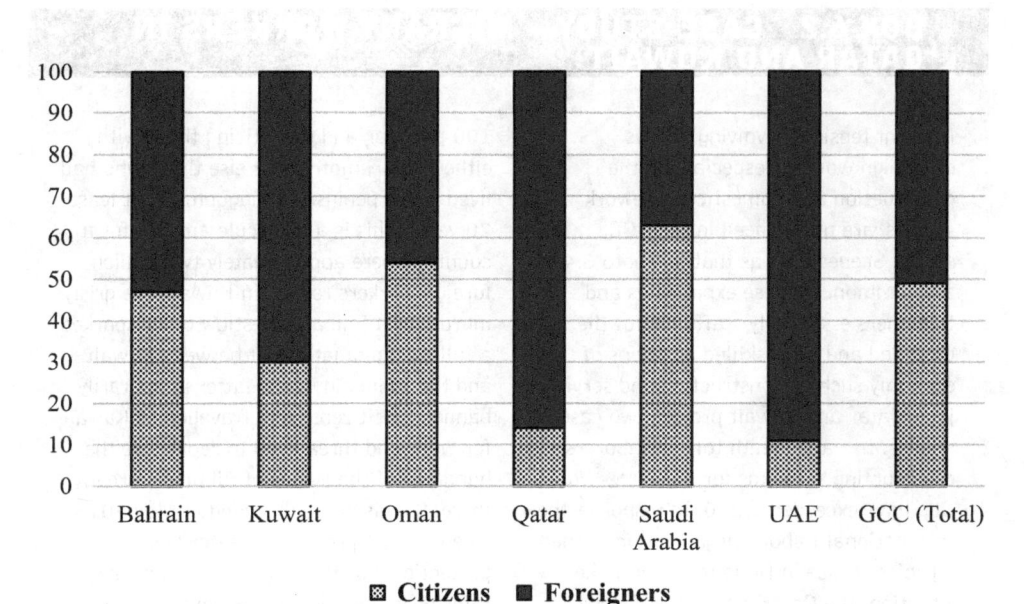

FIGURE 6.4
GCC states – ratio of citizens vs. foreign residents, 2015–2017 (latest available year).

Source: Gulf Research Center (2018), Gulf Labour Markets, Migration, and Population Programme.
Online: http://gulfmigration.org

seeking employment in the Gulf, meaning that any workers wishing to reside in these kingdoms must have a local employer or sponsor (*kafil*). Such a system is often exploited, however, as sponsors have inordinate power over their workers in terms of mobility and salaries; in the worst cases, physical abuses and labor violations abound.

Moreover, labor migration to the Gulf kingdoms does not lead to naturalization. A major reason flows from prevailing conceptions that foreigners cannot claim "ownership" to the economic and social benefits of the rents fueling the rest of the country. Citizenship in this sense is more *exclusionary* than inclusionary, as it signals not so much abstract bonds of patriotism and loyalty but rather a political status: citizens deserve all the welfarist protections, social privileges, and economic beneficence of their geological endowments. As such, it must be safeguarded as a nontransferable right of locals. Such inscribing of hard boundaries of identity that separates citizens as a national "Self" against a foreign, non-citizen "Other" is discussed in more detail in Chapter 4.

BOX 6.2 CASE STUDY – MIGRANT WORKERS IN QATAR AND KUWAIT

Migrant tensions involving abuses of foreign workers, especially in the construction and domestic housework sectors, are pronounced in the GCC states. Scenes such as that in Photo 6.4 are common, as these expatriates and foreigners essentially staff most of the unskilled and semi-skilled positions of the economy such as construction and service jobs. Qatar and Kuwait provide two case studies. In Qatar, death tolls of laborers constructing stadiums for the 2022 World Cup have exceeded 1,200. In response, the International Labour Organization opened a project office in Doha to monitor the situation. The Qatari government slowly began to improve working conditions while introducing in 2018 a new proposal to offer permanent residency to its foreign workers, albeit in the tiniest numbers – just 100 per year, and prioritizing those with either Qatari mothers or else those who had lived in the peninsular kingdom for at least 20 years. This is a miniscule amount for a country where approximately two million foreign workers reside. In Kuwait, the grisly murder of a Filipa domestic worker sparked a full-on diplomatic spat between Kuwait and the Philippines. The latter temporarily banned its citizens from traveling to Kuwait for work and threatened to repatriate the hundreds of thousands of Filipinos already there; the dispute only ended in May 2018 when Kuwait promised greater legal protections for these workers. Piecemeal reforms in other kingdoms have also occurred. For instance, Qatar and Bahrain abolished their kafala systems in 2016 and 2017, respectively, although foreign workers must still be documented and

BOX 6.2 (CONTINUED)

PHOTO 6.4
South Asian construction workers in Dubai, 2010.

Source: Photo by @ rufuskahler is licensed under CC BY 2.0.
Online: www.flickr.com/photos/rufuskahler/4266165065

monitored to a close degree – and similarly still lack the political freedoms and social mobility of citizens. That foreign labor is receiving some modicum of protection suggests that international pressure and greater awareness have had some effect. It is still unlikely, however, that foreigners will enjoy an easy path to citizenship in these archetypical rentier states, where citizenship is not simply a marker of identity but instead a social status that guarantees lifelong benefits.

HUMAN CAPITAL AND EDUCATIONAL DEVELOPMENT

A final legacy of rentierism can be found in the realm of human capital and educational development. Human capital refers to the social and economic value inherent to an individual's capabilities, including his or her skills, knowledge, and productivity. As discussed earlier, an economic implication of rentierism stemmed from the tendency of many MENA governments to install large public sectors that offered government-related work, typically in the civil service, administrative bureaucracy, military and security institutions, or else state-owned companies, as a key piece of the rentier social contract. Yet as Chapter 5's discussion of the exhaustion of this model elaborated, not only does this place the onus of responsibility for economic development upon government planners, it also means that citizens simply do not develop the skills necessary to staff key positions in the rest of the economy.

For instance, faced with shortages of teachers, most Gulf kingdoms have long featured educational payrolls filled with Arab instructors at the primary and secondary schooling levels (mostly Egyptians, Syrians, Jordanians, and Palestinians) since the 1970s. Moreover, the grand urbanization and modernization schemes launched by some states like Saudi Arabia and the UAE require skilled and competent citizens to man them; but it is unclear whether the relations of dependency and vertical hierarchy cultivated by rentierism can be overcome. For instance, the UAE generally reports a very high literacy rate among adults, between 95 to 99 percent. Yet it is also acknowledged that simple functional literacy does not equate to skills acquisition, awareness of literature and theory, or even the ability to function in complex work environments, especially in the private sector. Perhaps partly for that reason, in 2016 the UAE launched a nation-wide "law of reading" program that sought to make reading a routinized aspect of Emirati life: government employees were to read at work, coffee shops were mandated to offer books to customers, and even babies were to be given reading bags filled with material upon birth.

Educational development offers another window into modern struggles from past decisions regarding the allocation of resources. While Chapter 10's discussion of youths in the MENA tackles the deeper problems regarding inadequate schooling systems found across the region and equally in both resource-rich and resource-poor countries, it bears mentioning here that the wealthiest rentier states in the Gulf have undertaken an interesting strategy that combines cultural reorientation with creative rebranding. In recognizing the need to diversify their economies and invest in human capital, the GCC kingdoms have invested in new "education cities" – conglomerate urban zones filled with well-funded institutes, universities, and schools, many of which are branches of Western institutions attracted by financial and political interests.

For instance, the Qatar Foundation sponsored the construction of Doha's Education City, which currently holds not just various Qatari schools, research centers, and academies, but also branches of Virginia Commonwealth University, Cornell University's medical school, Texas A&M

University, Carnegie Mellon University, Georgetown University's School of Foreign Service, Northwestern University, and European institutions like University College London and HEC-Paris, a business school. Most of these universities abide by agreements that reserve a large number of spots for Qatari citizens. Similar arrangements can be found in the UAE, such as Dubai's International Academic City and Abu Dhabi's own international educational complex, as well as Saudi Arabia's Education Zone of its King Abdullah Economic City. The branch campuses of Western institutions hosted by the GCC states furnish a viable alternative for Gulf nationals and Arab migrants who wish to educate their dependents in a competitive, yet culturally compatible environment.

However, critics have questioned whether such a strategy will generate the human capital and innovation necessary to transcend a rentier system. For instance, Qatar is governed by a ruling monarchy, has no elected legislative institutions, and features little tolerance for political dissent or legal opposition. Yet many American universities operate under a model of liberal arts education, one where critical expression and political freedoms are taken as givens. At the gleaming branch campuses of Western institutions, both professors and students are reminded they reside on Qatari soil and so abide by Qatari law – compliance that theoretically stifles one of the major selling points of American-style immersion and education. Whether such a contradiction can be overcome represents the latest challenge presented by the long shadow of rents and rentier statism.

CONCLUSION

The social and economic development of MENA countries is deeply intertwined due to rentierism, which not only connects most states to one another but has also transformed the most basic routines of everyday life. RST and its theoretical corollaries inform some of the immediate impacts, among them lack of economic diversification, diminishment of democracy, arrangements of dependency, and cultural habituation into regarding citizenship as a bundle of entitlements. The downstream effects of these rents include not just the revenues themselves from oil and gas sales that accrue to the MENA governments that own these industries, but also the foreign aid flows they circulate to other countries, as well as the remittances sent back home from migrant workers working in rent-fueled economies. This puts constraints upon what we might consider the normal trajectory of industrialization and urbanization, and introduces a host of negative externalities. At the same time, because rentierism also often turns citizens into clients, it leaves many societies unsure about what citizenship fundamentally means – especially in an era of declining economic returns and future uncertainty, as embodied by the Arab Spring. While the GCC kingdoms alone possess the resources necessary to engage in cultural orientation, national rebranding, and educational upgrading, it remains to be seen whether these are viable strategies that are sustainable in the long run given that hydrocarbons are not a renewable resource. In the end, the enduring lesson from this engagement is that rentierism has left a long legacy that continues to buffet MENA societies with the unintended consequences of easy money.

QUESTIONS FOR DISCUSSION

1 What are the basic tenets of rentier state theory (RST), and to what extent have these assumptions been challenged over time?
2 How does the rentier social contract differ from the traditional relationship between democratic representatives and national societies?
3 How are strategic rents different from energy rents?
4 What are the negative externalities of urbanization, particularly those seen in rentier societies?
5 At the cultural level, how has rentierism affected the construction of citizenship and the meaning of national belonging outside the Arabian Gulf?
6 Within the Arabian Gulf kingdoms, why is citizenship often exclusionary and protected in relation to foreign workers?
7 Are strategies to improve human capital and educational quality in the core rentier states of the Arabian Gulf effective?
8 Is there any escape from rentier legacies, or do these countries simply wait until the oil and gas run out?

FURTHER READING

The seminal sources that provide solid theoretical and empirical grounding on RST include the classic Giacomo Luciani and Hazem Beblawi, eds., *The Rentier State* (London: Routledge, 1987) and Giacomo Luciani, ed., *The Arab State* (Berkeley, CA: University of California Press, 1990). At a cultural level, a canonical text that explores how rentier dependence generates a "mentality" within individuals is Khaldun Al-Naqeeb, *Society and State in the Gulf and Arab Peninsula* (London: Routledge, 1990). Thereafter, Jill Crystal's *Oil and Politics in the Gulf: Rulers and Merchants in Kuwait and Qatar* (Cambridge: Cambridge University Press, 1990) and Jacqueline Ismael's *Kuwait: Dependency and Class in a Rentier State* (Gainesville,

FL: University of Florida Press, 1993) capture class formation and class dynamics in an archetypal rentier society. More recently, Adam Hanieh's *Capitalism and Class in the Gulf Arab States* (London: Palgrave Macmillan, 2011) takes a neo-Marxist approach in understanding how, at the social level, oil and gas riches have amplified patterns of domination and hegemony. Cross-regional studies that establish links between rentier development and other social and political outcomes also include Michael Ross, *The Oil Curse: How Petroleum Wealth Shapes the Development of Nations* (Princeton, NJ: Princeton University Press, 2013) and the earlier Terry Lynn Karl, *The Paradox of Plenty: Oil Booms and Petro-States* (Berkeley, CA: University of California Press, 1999). At a less scholarly pace, Daniel Yergin's *The Prize: The Epic Quest for Oil, Money & Power* (New York: Free Press, 1992) is an entertaining foray into the early struggle by various actors for the MENA's hydrocarbon wellsprings.

At the more micro-analytic level, recent studies have taken RST further to explore how rentierism has influenced the formation of new social groups, political interests, and business classes; that is, it is not merely political but socializing as well. See, for instance, Michael Herb, *The Wages of Oil: Parliaments and Economic Development in Kuwait and the UAE* (Ithaca, NY: Cornell University Press, 2014); Steffen Hertog, *Princes, Brokers and Bureaucrats: Oil and the State in Saudi Arabia* (Ithaca, NY: Cornell University Press, 2010); Justin Gengler, *Group Conflict and Political Mobilization in Bahrain and the Arab Gulf: Rethinking the Rentier State* (Bloomington, IN: Indiana University Press, 2015); and the much earlier but still relevant essay by Hootan Shambayati, "The Rentier State, Interest Groups, and the Paradox of Autonomy: State and Business in Turkey and Iran," *Comparative Politics* 26, no. 3 (1994): 307–31. A fascinating addition is Courtney Freer, *Rentier Islamism: The Influence of the Muslim Brotherhood in Gulf Monarchies* (Oxford: Oxford University Press, 2018), which suggests a counterintuitive relationship between religion and rentierism.

The literatures on intra-regional dynamics of institutional and urban development of rentier states have been published alongside works on migration studies in the MENA region. Nazih Ayubi, *Over-stating the Arab State: Politics and Society in the Middle East* (London: I.B. Tauris, 1996) is a landmark volume that combines historical and sociological approaches focus on the notion of neopatriarchy. Nelida Fuccaro's *Histories of City and State in the Persian Gulf: Manama Since 1800* (Cambridge: Cambridge University Press, 2009) focuses on urban developments in Bahrain by situating the work against the wider context of spatial and sociopolitical trajectories of port towns in the region. Farah al-Nakib's *Kuwait Transformed: A History of Oil and Urban Life* (Stanford, CA: Stanford University Press, 2016) examines the history of urbanization in Kuwait City and the social implications of urban transformation in an oil-based economy.

Regarding migration studies, Abdulhadi Khalaf, Omar AlShehabi, and Adam Hanieh, eds., *Transit States: Labour, Migration and Citizenship in the Gulf* (London: Pluto Press, 2015) provides a broad spectrum of analysis on history, politics, and sociology of migration including core issues covered in the remit of this chapter. Annika Kropf and Mohamed A. Ramady, eds., *Employment and Career Motivation in the Arab Gulf States: The Rentier Mentality Revisited* (Berlin: Gerlach, 2015) provides an incisive view into how rentier-inflected attitudes can shape economic and social preferences of citizens in the context of large expatriate populations and migrants. Calvert Jones, *Bedouins into Bourgeois: Remaking Citizens for Globalization* (Cambridge: Cambridge University Press, 2017), explores how educational systems are likewise shaped by the confluence of rentier economics, social transformation, and foreigners.

Other references on education, social relations, and human capital in rentier states include up-to-date publications such as Yew Meng Lai, Abdul Razak Ahmad, and Chang Da Wan, eds., *Higher Education in the Middle East and North Africa: Exploring Regional and Country Specific Potentials* (Singapore: Springer, 2016), which addresses higher education reforms in the MENA region that seek to improve access and upgrade the quality of education. Another edited volume on higher education include Dale F. Eickelman and Rogaia Mustafa Abusharaf, eds., *Higher Education Investment in the Arab States of the Gulf: Strategies for Excellence and Diversity* (Berlin: Gerlach Press, 2017). This reference covers a broad range of topics such as bridging gender gaps in higher education, enhancing the soft power of higher education, and confronting the challenges facing public health and natural science education.

Online sources

Online portals, many maintained by multilateral institutions and intergovernmental organizations, provide crucial data and insights into the issues discussed here. The World Bank publication series on *Global Economic Prospects: Economic Outlook for the Middle East and North Africa* (most recently online at www.worldbank.org/en/region/mena/publication/gep-2018, but also easily accessible with Google searches) and *Gulf Economic Monitor* (www.worldbank.org/en/country/gcc) are regularly published, and present ample data and a comprehensive overview of the latest economic forecasts as they relate to hydrocarbon constraints and dependence. The Oxford Institute for Energy Studies (www.oxfordenergy.org/) also presents a wealth of studies and findings regarding the social and political implications of rentier dependence. The World Bank's *MENA Development Reports* – nearly two dozen of them, found online (https://openknowledge.worldbank.org/handle/10986/2168) – also cover many of these issues. The UNDP's *Arab Human Development Reports* (www.arab-hdr.org/) are major studies that chart out how rentier legacies have shaped social issues such as knowledge, gender, and human security. The UNDP also maintains an exhaustive battery of quantitative indices on human development, gender development, and inequality on its data portal (http://hdr.undp.org/en/data), which can be useful in charting out the impact of rents on societal well-being. Within the Gulf, the Gulf Research Center's Gulf Labour Markets, Migration, and Population (GLMM) Programme (http://gulfmigration.org) provides good snapshots of key migration and demographic trends for each GCC state. Finally, a global entryway onto research into migrant and remittance flows is the Migration Data Portal (https://migrationdataportal.org).

CHAPTER 7

Environmental change and human conflict

Mohamed Behnassi

THE RUNDOWN: KEY TOPICS COVERED
- Human security
- Regional conflicts
- Environmental degradation
- Climate change
- Water scarcity
- Social adaptation

INTRODUCTION

Lives and livelihoods of millions of people worldwide, especially in fragile regions like the MENA, are severely threatened by environmental degradation and climate change. The threat is multigenerational: the destruction of ecological systems today can irrevocably inflect the social and economic routines of future generations. This chapter explores the intersection between environmental harms and human security, highlighting how what were once treated as marginal issues for debate – water scarcity, sea level changes, temperature unpredictability, and other risk factors associated with environmental stress – have become central factors that shape the social routines and well-being of many across the region. Conventionally, researchers treated the term "security" as a state-centric one, meaning a stable and safe political order defined by rule of law and protection of rights. Now, however, we understand the term more broadly as *human security*, meaning the elimination of threats posed to human beings from not just conflict and violence, but other areas such as economic poverty, food shortages, preventable diseases, and above all environmental harms – that is, natural and man-made destruction of ecological systems that provide the water, air, land, and resources necessary for healthy life.

This chapter therefore focuses upon how environmental change (including climate change) negatively impacts human security and even instigates conflict. Human security inseparably links social systems and their natural environments, and strives to achieve freedom from not just fear, but also of wants and natural hazards. It shows how emerging risks – such as climatic risks – are raising new and unavoidable questions about the capacity of governments to meet the needs of MENA societies. Perceiving these risks from a human-environmental nexus also enables us to see how they connect to a myriad of issues and areas such as human rights, social adaptation, economic justice, and geopolitical resilience. Its concluding hope is that human societies are capable of making innovative policy responses and technological advances to minimize environmental degradation, with the first step being awareness and the next concerted action.

A THICKER CONCEPTION OF HUMAN SECURITY

Only at the beginning of the twenty-first century have most observers of the MENA countries reached consensus that the effects of environmental and climate change are severely threatening human security. The United Nations Development Programme's landmark 1994 *Human Development Report* set the stage, as it redefined human security to mean relative freedom not just from violence but from fear, disease, oppression, hunger, and environmental destruction. However, much remains to be done in this respect because key scientific and political agendas, nationally and internationally, are still defined by conventional understandings of security that marginalize attention paid to the natural environment in favor of more visible, and perhaps more glamorous, notions. Classic conceptualizations of security, as understood by political scientists, emphasized its military and coercive aspects, such as states waging war or peace with one another. For instance, security during the Cold War meant freedom from nuclear holocaust waged by global superpowers, endangering all; security afterwards could be interpreted as freedom from new forms of physical violence, such as ethnic conflict or non-state terrorism, that endangered entire societies by destabilizing the boundaries of existing nation-states.

In this sense, the traditional conception of security was "hard" – it emphasized how states and countries struggled to reduce the risk of militarized violence, the kind of physical brutalities and casualty-inducing aggression that have long been associated with security discourses. It put attention onto diplomacy and institutions, and of the interaction between politicians and elites at the global stage as they maneuvered their governments throughout the international arena. It warned of the dangers wrought by coercive instruments, from small arms to nuclear weapons, and saw issues of human health or environmental protection as an *effect* of insecurity rather than the cause.

By contrast, the newer view of human security focuses not upon states and governments, but societies and individuals. It views human life not just in terms of casualties and preservation, but through the framework of *quality*: an indigent rural peasant whose economic livelihood has been robbed by water shortages and crop destruction caused by global warming may well be alive in the physical sense, but that person may suffer from such incredible hardship on a daily basis that pronouncing her safe due to nuclear disarmament rings hollow. Human security, in this new paradigm, intends for human beings to not merely survive but flourish, and attain measures of satisfaction and fulfillment that come only by ensuring qualitative well-being. Thus, the state of the physical environment is a component of social life in the deepest way. Its degradation is not simply an effect of insecurity but a *cause* of it.

As Chapter 2's treatment of rural life and the food cycle indicated, environmental security is crucial because modern societies and economies are mutually dependent upon life-supporting ecological systems. Their transformation can affect the health of a community not just in headline-grabbing ways (such as depletion of rivers or pollution of air) but in microscopic and invisible forms, such as the vitamin content of one's daily food after those edibles are manufactured through a complex chain of production involving industrial corporations, international suppliers, domestic processors, and local marketers. At a global scale, the environmental conservation movement over past decades has usefully reminded audiences about what is at stake – the diminishment of water supplies, the depletion of fisheries, the loss of biodiversity, the destruction of agricultural lands, global warming and rising sea levels, and finally ozone depletion and air quality. A major assumption among researchers of environmental security is that such harms are manmade, insofar that we can clearly see how social forces, economic development, and political decisions leave concrete imprints upon the natural world. In turn, because water, air, and land resources are omnipresent, their quality or scarcity inevitably reshapes patterns of private consumption and public routines.

HARD CONFLICTS IN THE MENA REGION

Because this chapter deals with the intersection of the natural world – specifically, environmental problems and climate change – with the well-being of human societies through the creation of conflict, it is necessary to also set the stage by highlighting the modern record of past conflicts in the MENA region. As social scientists know well, the MENA has been no stranger to both interstate violence in the form of conventional wars between rival states, as well as internecine violence in the form of civil wars often waged along ethnic, sectarian, and ideological cleavages. This does not make the region exceptional, given the prevalence of violence in many other regions in the post–World War Two era. What makes the MENA unique is the combination of strategic factors that have sometimes increased the frequency and intensity of violence beyond what might be normally expected: the presence of valuable resources, such as oil; the emotive salience of the Israeli-Palestinian divide; the legacies of colonial occupation and imperialism; and the propensity of outside great powers, such as the US and Soviet Union, to utilize the region as a proxy chessboard, intervening frequently in order to support allied groups and regimes against rival forces deemed threatening to their geopolitical schemes.

Leaving aside cases of Islamist insurgencies and terrorism, a topic explored by Chapter 8, as well as revolutions and military coups, consider Table 7.1. This takes available historical data and common knowledge to list the costliest (in terms of at least 1,000 deaths) civil and interstate conflicts in the MENA since the 1950s. While there remains considerable dispute over the lethality tolls for many of these wars, the overall point is that the region has hosted numerous and often prolonged bouts of armed violence between belligerent actors. One of the costliest, in the form of the Syrian civil war, has only begun to wind down as of 2018.

Though it may seem obvious, it is important to elucidate all the myriad effects upon human rights and basic security that conventional conflicts exert. The introduction of violence destroys lives and families, particularly when civilians are targeted with assaults, rapes, imprisonment, torture, and murder. Economies can be decimated by sustained warfare, depriving many people of jobs and incomes. Damage to infrastructures and housing expose individuals, particularly the weak and vulnerable, to further mental and physical injury. Access to food and drinkable water often turns difficult due to disrupted supply and provision chains, resulting in malnutrition and starvation. Conflict zones also exhibit a higher incidence of diseases, including communicable epidemics easily prevented during peacetime with proper medical care, such as cholera. Displaced communities, sometimes coinciding with entire ethnic or sectarian groups, generate flows of refugees that

TABLE 7.1

Major armed conflicts in MENA, 1945–2018

Year	Conflict	Major combatants	Minimum estimates: civilian + military deaths (as of Apr. 2019)
1948	Arab-Israeli War	Egypt, Syria, Jordan, Lebanon, Israel, Palestinians	16,000
1956	Suez Canal War	Egypt, Israel, France, Britain	3,250
1958	Lebanon political crisis	Lebanon, US, Lebanese opposition	4,000
1962–1970	North Yemen civil war	North Yemen, Saudi Arabia, Egypt	125,000
1963	'Aden Uprising	South Yemen, Britain, Yemeni rebels	2,000
1964–1975	Dhofar Rebellion (Oman)	Oman, Iran, Britain, Omani rebels	11,500
1967	Arab-Israeli War	Israel, Egypt, Syria, Jordan, Iraq	18,500
1970	Black September (Jordanian civil war)	Jordan, Palestinian guerillas	4,000
1973	Arab-Israeli War	Israel, Egypt, Syria	20,500
1975–1990	Lebanese civil war	Lebanon, Israel, Palestinians, Iran, Hizbullah, Syria, France, US, Italy	115,000
1978–2013	Kurdish conflict (Turkey)	Turkey, Kurdish rebels	50,000
1982	Hama uprising (Syria)	Syria, Muslim Brotherhood	10,000
1980–1988	Iran-Iraq War	Iran, Iraq, rebel groups, US	450,000
1987–1993	First Intifada (Israel and Palestinian territories)	Israel, Palestinians	1,350
1990–1991	Gulf War	Iraq, Kuwait, US-led coalition	25,000

(Continued)

Year	Conflict	Major combatants	Minimum estimates: civilian + military deaths (as of Apr. 2019)
1991	Iraqi uprisings	Iraq, Kurdish, and Shi'a opposition	30,000
1994	Yemeni civil war	North and South Yemeni forces	7,000
2000–2005	Al-Aqsa Intifada (Israel and Palestinian territories)	Israel, Palestinians	5,000
2003–2010	Darfur conflict (Sudan)	Sudan, rebel groups	250,000
2003–2011	Iraqi War and occupation	Iraq, US, Britain, various rebels	405,000
2013–2017	Iraqi civil conflict	Iraq, Iran, US-led coalition, Kurdish groups, Islamic State	90,500
2011-present	Syrian civil war	Syria, Hizbullah, Iran, Russia, various rebels, Kurdish groups, Islamic State, US-led coalition	400,000
2011-present	Libyan civil war	Libya, rebel groups, Islamic State	20,000
2015-present	Yemeni civil war	Yemen, rebel groups, Saudi Arabia, UAE	75,000

Source: Uppsala Conflict Data Program (2018), *UCDP Conflict Encyclopedia*; various secondary sources.

require immediate assistance. Finally, even after conflict formally ends, the destruction wrought and weakness of governments afterwards can place undue burdens upon populations already enervated with the externalities of unremitting violence.

The prevalence of conflict in the MENA region is critical to note given the analysis that follows. Environmental damage and climatic variability can worsen existing conflicts and wars by magnifying the particular effects of violence upon human population. Put another way, wealthy regional clusters like Western Europe or North America may see climate change as undesirable in economic terms, but at the very least their constituent states have not engaged in war against one another for many decades – and so in many wars are best prepared for it. By contrast, regions already struggling to find peace and stability are the least-prepared to adapt to such major transformations, and their populations are most exposed to its externalities.

LINKING ENVIRONMENT, CLIMATE, AND CONFLICT

According to traditional notions of security, the natural environment is mostly seen as a separate entity from human societies, and often perceived in terms of its mere capacity to provide resources that meet anthropogenic needs. In this respect, natural resources often represent different interests and values related to their purpose, availability, and market utility. When politicized, especially in times of scarcity, access to and control of these resources may stimulate competition among actors, which may eventually lead to conflicts. These are the key reasons why many observers of environmentally fragile regions like the MENA, sub-Saharan Africa, and South Asia have investigated the environment-conflict nexus in the past. Indeed, it is intuitive to see how conflicts can logically result in insecurity of the hard sort, involving militarized and coercive violence, between countries due to incompatible claims over critical natural goods.

BOX 7.1 CASE STUDY – NATURAL RESOURCES AND CONFLICT

Cynics of environmental security argue that there are few instances of nation-states waging war over natural resources, to the scale often feared in terms of military violence, ecological destruction, and wasted resources. While it is true there has not been any world war over water, in actuality the MENA region is home to a coveted natural good that shows the extent to which natural assets external to human society can generate war: oil, a nonrenewable endowment of geology whose perceptions of scarcity and utility generate incompatible demands for ownership. A major impetus for the 1990–1991 Gulf War was the desire of the Iraqi state under Saddam Hussein to absorb the more massive oil reserves of comparatively wealthier yet strategically weaker Kuwait. Though quickly defeated by the international coalition, the Gulf War's final phase in early 1991 resulted in widespread destruction to water and air resources. Retreating Iraqi forces set fire to many oil wellheads, which burned for months; the black plumes from these over 650 fires could be seen from space. Until the final large-scale burnings were extinguished in November 1991, up to one billion barrels of oil were burnt. The event altered weather patterns, air breathability, and even water quality in the Arabian Gulf for months, while permanently costing Kuwait 1 percent of its total reserves. To put this in perspective, today one billion barrels of crude oil could fuel the global

> **BOX 7.1 (CONTINUED)**
>
> economy for nearly ten days. The Gulf War indicated the extent to which violent conflicts can wreak havoc on ecological systems and human societies, exposing all concerned to a perverse self-perpetuating cycle begun by covetous imperatives to capture goods inherent in the natural environment. While the case of oil may be an extreme one, given that even the normal use of hydrocarbon resources negatively impacts the environment, it is not difficult to see why such battles over a *water* resource, such as a river or aquifer bordering two countries, can be even more devastating due to the potentiality of massive pollution, deliberative soiling, and overuse that inexorably come with the launching of formal conflicts.

Many researchers have questioned the relevance of the environment-conflict thesis and related assumptions, such as whether the scarcity or abundance of natural resources and violence lead inevitably to violent conflicts. On the one hand, thus far, while disputes involving natural resources have a higher chance of transforming into more sustained war, natural resources alone are rarely sufficient to initiate an outbreak of conventional conflict – i.e., a country invading or attacking another, resulting in costly battle. There are few historical cases, for instances, of "water wars." On the other hand, we also know that environmental factors can easily increase the risk of violent conflict, and often become entangled in ongoing wars once their scarcity is revealed. In other words, a sudden shortage of a crucial ecological good necessary for societal functioning can make existing tensions even worse. Thus, while there may be few cases of water wars in human history, there are also few cases of combatant armies or states making *peace* for environmental reasons – that is, due to mutual recognition that continued violence will endanger a precious natural resource.

A recent addition to these diverse types of relations between environment/natural resources and conflict is climate change. Given its severe implications for the availability of natural resources and ecosystemic balance, many analysts have expressed concern over the climate-conflict nexus – that is, the propensity for climate change, and its implications regarding rising temperatures, sea level changes, and increasingly unpredictable weather patterns, to become a security issue capable of escalating latent conflicts into violent outbreaks. For instance, as Chapter 2 discussed, the Syrian civil war was partly caused by a preceding drought whose effects upon the rural sector and agricultural livelihoods spurred social and political changes that fed into the 2011 protests and, later, the endemic violence that followed.

For many developing countries, climate change is best conceptualized as a broad variable that may not only cause disruptions and damages, but often amplifies the effects of preexisting problems such as social inequality, corrupt governance, economic underdevelopment, and physical insecurity. In this sense, climate change regardless of its anthropogenic or natural causes disproportionately burdens the world's most challenged and vulnerable societies, which are least prepared to adapt to changing global conditions. Climate change has the potential to compound existing low-intensity conflicts, spill tensions or clashes into neighboring countries, and create new points of rivalry between competing communities, groups, and even states. Due to inadequate social protection, the weakest parts of society are likely to be the most exposed to the adverse effects of climate change; this includes the poor, indigenous peoples, refugees, women, children, and the elderly. Thus, climatic variability aggrandizes the struggles already faced by these vulnerable segments. In sub-Saharan Africa, for instance, climate-related environmental change such as changing rainfall patterns, unforeseen droughts, changes in vegetation cover, and increasing resource scarcity have generated innumerable small-scale episodes of violence where few existed earlier, such as conflict between livestock herders and farming communities.

On a larger scale, it is easy to see how the downstream effects of climate variations can generate domestic externalities. Leaving aside the dramatized depictions of global disasters often invoked in Hollywood movies, the explanatory linkages are easy to trace when contextualized with specific goods and vulnerabilities in mind. For instance, if droughts or floods cause sudden shortfalls in wheat production, and the price of bread rises so dramatically that governments can no longer afford to subsidize this basic commodity, then public audiences are not immune to social mobilization, collective protests, and other demands for livelihood. For instance, consider the 2010–2011 period, in which global grain prices nearly doubled due to a multitude of environmental blockages in the most prolific grain exporters – drought in Russia, flooding in Australia and Pakistan, and even disruptions in the American and Canadian agricultural heartlands. Over the same period of time, the world also witnessed a near-simultaneous outburst of social protests and rioting in grain-importing countries such as Kenya and Kyrgyzstan. When juxtaposed against this background, the Arab Spring does not look exceptional: far from it, societies with historical memory of food protests in the past (i.e., bread riots mentioned in Chapter 5) were also the sites of the largest popular insurrections, such as Egypt, Tunisia, and Yemen.

Yet, despite this potential, concern over climate change remains peripheral to the prevailing strategic interests and policy frameworks of many countries. One reason is that the links between climate change, security, and conflict are not always clearly established. Another has been the reluctance of some countries, such as the US and China, to throw their economic weight behind global efforts to both recognize and act upon the issue. For this reason, it is still challenging for many observers to see climate change as a potential security threat. Still, even if climate change is not the sole indicator of instability and disorder, empirical evidence and intuitive reasoning both suggest at least that it does not help societies to stabilize and develop. When seen as a "multiplier" of preexisting risks, climate change can interact with other social, economic, and political problems and expose human communities to even more peril. The effects are especially pronounced during periods of conflict that displace peoples (thereby turning them into refugees), undermine food availability, and allow political elites (such as rebel leaders or government officials) to exploit scarce resources.

ENGAGING CRITICISMS OF THE ENVIRONMENT-CONFLICT THESIS

As discussed earlier, the argument that environmental and climatic factors may lead to increased human conflicts and thus degrade the security of entire populations has become a major concern. Some are not convinced, however, and it is important to consider these criticisms. For instance, is the current worry with the environment merely a trendy repackaging of the old Malthusian concern regarding the exponential growth of humanity outstripping a finite supply of resources, thereby ensuring future catastrophe? While the logic may be facially similar, it is important to highlight that resources should not be conflated with environment: the former is a subset of the latter. The invocation of "environmental" issues does not merely involve resources of economic value; rather, it implicates not only the entire natural setting of modern existence but also the issues that neo-Malthusian projections have never considered, such as the fate of polar ice shelves and their consequent effects upon ecological notions (such as biodiversity in the oceans). Moreover, arguments about human growth exposing the scarcity of resources like minerals and oil incubate a major assumption, namely that expectations of abundance will not come to fruition due to overconsumption of those goods due to economic development. Environmental concerns are different, for they are centered upon the entirely separate possibility that constraints upon societies will come not simply as a result of their structural growth but from the natural realm.

Critics also accuse conceptions of environmental security to be overly alarmist, because the underlying problem with scarce resources concerns pricing – a mechanism that can be adjusted or ameliorated through human action. For instance, perhaps the most complex, uncertain, and disruptive problems exist not in nebulous domain of global environmental problems, but simply in specific industries or countries overloading what we call planetary "sinks" – that is, the capacity of major natural formations such as the oceans and atmosphere to absorb pollutants. Accordingly, in most of the cited instances of "environmental" resource scarcities, scarce resources can be altered in price in order to balance supply and demand, illustrating that the real dilemma is economic rather than natural. However, again this misses the mark. Environmental problems are those effects or externalities that cannot be priced or reasonably substituted, because they affect not just the material prosperity of states and societies but rather the mental and physical well-being of individual bodies. Consider, for instance, increasing rates of pollutant-induced cancer, the permanent loss of biological species, and increased global warming. Such issues constitute some of the essential consequences of environmental damage and underscore that many resources can have both economic and ecological functions, such as water and land.

Finally, many critics decry that given the paucity of doomsday-like scenarios involving environmental degradation, such as violent wars over shrinking rivers or entire nation-states disappearing under rising sea tides, concerns over environmental security are exaggerated – perhaps driven by the scholarly need to generate faddish ideas for public audiences, or else misguided by distorted data. Yet as argued earlier, the leading voices in global debates concerning environmental security (and insecurity) do not claim that any single natural variable spells the downfall of human civilization, or is the only causal trigger of conflict and violence. Rather, the current understanding is two-fold. First, all else being equal, environmental harms can amplify the social, economic, and political problems that already afflict many societies; hence a society struggling with poverty may not implode into civil war if droughts destroy the wheat supply, but it certainly will not climb out of poverty. Second, those societies that will be affected most acutely by environmental insecurity already face dire vulnerabilities, because they have been exposed to previous conflicts or suffer from underdevelopment. These include populations in sub-Saharan Africa, South Asia, Central Asia, and the MENA region. Thus, the effects of environmental destruction will disproportionately undercut those countries least equipped to handle them.

ENVIRONMENTAL SECURITY IN THE MENA REGION

The MENA region is characterized as a hyper-arid to arid region with pockets of semi-arid areas. Aridity, in geographic terms, refers to areas that have little to no available water. Hyper-arid areas rarely receive more than 100 millimeters (less than four inches) of precipitation annually; arid zones receive rainfall between 100 to 300 millimeters per year; and semi-arid areas can receive up to 500 millimeters. There are only a few precious temperate zones, such as coastal North Africa and the shores of the eastern Mediterranean, as well as small snow-receiving areas in the mountainous parts of Morocco, Algeria, Lebanon, Iraq, and Iran. Overall, the region overlaps with the world's two largest deserts outside the Arctic and Antarctica. The largest is the Sahara, which extends from the Maghrib eastwards towards Egypt and Sudan, and also southward into Africa. To put the Sahara in geographic context, the desert is the size of the US. The lesser desert is the Arabian Desert, which comprises most of the Arabian Peninsula. The Arabian Desert contains the *Rub'a al-Khali* (Empty Quarter), the longest contiguous sand desert in the world.

Such aridity is a function of precipitation and evaporation, which are in turn caused by dry and descending air currents resulting from oceanic dynamics and atmospheric pressures. Perhaps the easiest way to conceptualize the distribution of aridity is to study a physical map of the planet. The Tropic of Cancer rests beneath the 30th parallel northern latitude; tracing this circle around the globe, we find deserts and drylands with regularity – from the Sonoran and Chihuahua Deserts of North America, for instance, to the Saharan region and Arabian Peninsula of the MENA. Both the Tropics of Cancer and Capricorn (the later resting above the 30th parallel southern latitude) correlate with arid terrains where rain clouds are sparse.

As Chapter 2 accentuated, the climatic constraints of aridity have molded the cultural development and social relations of many populations in this region for centuries. Some of the first permanent farming communities and later urban constructions were found here, and all changed in response to environmental variability. For thousands of years, people of the region coped with climatic challenges by adapting their survival strategies to changes in rainfall and temperature. The more arid the area, the more likely local peoples would engage in pastoral activities, with an emphasis on animal haulage through camel-based nomadism; such Bedouin imagery accounts for the cultural synonymy, in the Western mind, between camels, desert, and the Arab world.

When conditions changed, so did communal productivity: camel herders became cultivators, cultivators moved to more fertile areas, and entire cities were ultimately built based upon the perceived proximity to water supplies. Indeed, the great Islamic cities of the region (Cairo, Damascus, Baghdad) which once served as centers for the classical Caliphates were constructed alongside rivers or in water basins. Newer metropolises today that are booming in size, such as Amman in Jordan, Riyadh in Saudi Arabia, and Ankara in Turkey, have urbanized only because modern hydraulic technology (with the unfortunate side effects of overusage) allow for the piping of water from deep underground or over long distances.

The fear of many environmental security experts today is that climate change and environmental destruction will result in unprecedented extreme conditions, with consequences that are difficult to predict (although, again, they are not likely to be good). What compounds the underlying problem of water scarcity will be not just the anthropogenic factor of a growing population (and its externalities of poverty, pollution, and resource overusage), but also increasing temperatures, rising sea levels, and unpredictability in terms of extreme events like droughts and desertification. This demanding environment makes MENA countries among the world's most vulnerable to climate change. As climate variability increases, so does human vulnerability to it – especially for the poor and those heavily dependent on natural resources, such as farmers and pastoralists. People living in urban centers and those working in tourism must also cope with climatic extreme events and the degraded resources that sustain urban communities or tourist destinations. Gender dynamics and public health systems in MENA countries likewise may also be challenged by climate impacts. If no drastic measures are taken to reduce the impacts of climate change, the MENA region will likely experience the following outcomes: reduced agricultural productivity and incomes, a higher frequency of drought and heat waves, a long-term reduction in already-lacking water supplies, and the loss of low-lying coastal areas to the oceans. This exposure will have considerable implications for human settlements and socioeconomic systems.

The problem of water
Less than 3 percent of the planet's total water is freshwater, of which most is encased as glaciers and ice. Of the remainder left, the MENA has only a fraction. The region's abundance of hydrocarbon resources sharply contrasts to its paucity of available freshwater sources, whether as precipitation, surface inflows (e.g., lakes, rivers), and groundwater reserves such as aquifers.

The MENA holds five of the top ten countries with the most oil reserves, but also eight of the world's most water-stressed countries. According to the UN Food and Agricultural Organization (FAO), the regional average for renewable water availability per capita is just 1,200 cubic meters – six times less than the global average of 7,000 cubic meters per person, and many times less than the regional averages for Latin America and the Caribbean (34,500 cubic meters per capita) and North America (20,300 cubic meters per capita). Compounding the problem, the MENA annually withdraws over 70 percent of its renewable water resources, putting extreme expectations upon the replenishment of rivers and aquifers to maintain this level of extraction. For instance, one study utilizing NASA satellite data suggested that between 2003 to 2010, the Tigris and Euphrates river basins – which stretch across Turkey, Syria, Iran, and Iraq – lost 144 cubic kilometers of water, equal to the volume of the entire Dead Sea.

Not surprisingly, the region's underground sources are extremely taxed; the Arabian aquifer system, which mainly Saudi Arabia and Yemen draw from, is classified as the most over-stressed aquifer system in the world. At current usage rates, the UN estimates the regional average for water availability per capita will drop below 1,000 cubic meters in 2030. To make more precise evaluations, consider that the FAO defines water stress as a dangerous situation when annual water supplies drop below 1,700 cubic meters a person, meaning the ecological system can no longer meet the human demand for water without artificial interventions. Water scarcity is defined as when the figure drops below 1,000 cubic meters per head; and absolute water scarcity means imminent crisis, as water levels drop below 500 cubic meters per person – and so without some kind of massive institutional response, existing economies and societies cannot sustain themselves. As Table 7.2 outlines, the water availability for most MENA countries is extremely low today, and excepting two cases (Iraq, Turkey) can be classified as matching conditions of water stress, water scarcity, or absolute scarcity. When compared to familiar countries like the US, Russia, China, Germany, or Brazil, these levels all suggest that at a regional basis, the MENA is immersed in water crisis.

There are inherent imbalances across the region as well. For one, industries related to urbanization and development consume the vast majority of this resource, and so some of the most water-intensive countries in terms of usage (such as Algeria, Israel, Bahrain, Saudi Arabia, and Kuwait) also happen to have the least volume of available water. Furthermore, some countries have turned to desalinization plants that convert seawater and brackish sources; for instance, the FAO estimates that at least 40 percent of Israel's

TABLE 7.2

MENA vs. select global countries – total renewable water resources per capita, 2014

	Total renewable water (in cubic meters, per capita)	Water level classification (stress, scarcity, absolute scarcity)
Algeria	294.2	Absolute scarcity
Bahrain	84.2	Absolute scarcity
Egypt	637.1	Scarcity
Iran	1,732	Stress
Iraq	2,467	
Israel	220.7	Absolute scarcity
Jordan	123.4	Absolute scarcity
Kuwait	5.1	Absolute scarcity
Lebanon	769.6	Scarcity
Libya	111.5	Absolute scarcity
Morocco	843.6	Scarcity
Oman	311.7	Absolute scarcity
Qatar	25.9	Absolute scarcity
Saudi Arabia	76.1	Absolute scarcity
Sudan	939.5	Scarcity
Syria	908	Scarcity
Tunisia	410.1	Absolute scarcity
Turkey	2,690	
UAE	16.4	Absolute scarcity
West Bank and Gaza Strip	179.3	Absolute scarcity
Yemen	78.3	Absolute scarcity
USA	9,538	
China	2,018	
Brazil	41,603	
Japan	3,397	
Russia	31,543	

Source: UN Food and Agricultural Organization (2018), *Aquastat Database*.

drinking water comes from desalinization programs, while 70 percent of the world's total desalinated water output is produced by the hyper-arid Arabian Gulf kingdoms. However, desalinization is also an energy-intensive process that is not especially efficient. Photo 7.1, for instance, shows a typical desalination plant in the United Arab Emirates. Such facilities must be located nearby power stations, resulting in the by-product of air pollution and carbon emissions – as well as net energy loss – in order to create drinkable water. Traditional desalination is an *industrial* process, and like all chemical industries is not cost-free.

Finally, different sub-regions of the MENA are confronted with varying sources of danger. For instance, in the Maghrib, fast-rising rates of water usage stem from rapid urbanization in countries like Morocco and Tunisia over the past half-century, combined with the agricultural production of these states. In the Mashriq, water scarcity results from the near depletion of overland water sources such as the Jordan River, but also the increased need generated by mass urbanization, refugee flows from conflicts like the Iraqi

PHOTO 7.1
Power and desalination station in UAE, 2012.

Source: iStock.
Online: www.istockphoto.com/photo/power-and-desalination-station-gm144348087-4211245

and Syrian civil wars, and some industrial development. In both regions, though, countries like Egypt, Jordan, and Israel have had to incorporate water concerns into their foreign policy; such "hydro-diplomacy" has forced them to seek sharing agreements with neighboring countries in order to alleviate their water deficiency.

Given that governments cannot will the clouds to drop more rain, and that the aridity resulting from geographic and climatic events is a near-permanent feature of the region, the only solution to water-related crises is better management and conservation of existing resources. This includes plugging key areas of leakage and waste, such as making industries and agriculture more efficient; reducing everyday consumer usage of water; controlling withdrawals from overland and underground water sources to allow for natural replenishment; harvest and preserve what rainfall that does exist; and innovate, such as recycling wastewater and recovering additional lost outflows. The dilemma, much like the broader obstacle to tackling climate change on a global level, is that because water is a transnational good, such collective responses require that countries work with one another – even putting aside preexisting historical, economic, and political rivalries.

BOX 7.2 CASE STUDY – WATER SCARCITY IN YEMEN

Water shortages undermine human security through their impacts upon public health, food production, poverty aggravation, and living costs. In the short term, they can instigate social unrest, as happened to Yemen in 2009. In August of that year, protesters in southern Yemen violently clashed with police, resulting in several casualties and deaths, due to aggressive rationing imposed by the government. Entire districts were left without running water for months. Citizens thus had to turn to buying water from trucks at exorbitant prices, with some reporting that they spent a third of their monthly salary simply securing enough water for their families to drink, cook, and bathe in. The situation in the capital of San'a was hardly better; by that summer, residents reported only sporadic running water flows through the municipal piping system, and similarly turned to buying water from weekly tankers. Popular frustrations magnified not just existing anger with poor government services, but also made more visible the tribal rebellions occurring in the north as well as the spreading violence of al-Qaeda. The causes of this spike in water scarcity were multiple: authorities excessively distributed existing supplies over multiple towns and cities, while excessive drilling of unregulated wells – sometimes for private use, and sometimes for agricultural irrigation – contributed to the near exhaustion of the primary aquifer system.

> **BOX 7.2 (CONTINUED)**
>
> Many profitable farms grew not grains but instead *qat*, a notorious plant whose cultivated leaves are chewed as a mild narcotic; the qat plant has no nutritional value, yet is extremely thirsty and wasteful to grow. A prolonged drought in the north, which made many rural inhabitants crowd into cities, did not help matters; but neither did the government – then under the authoritarian leadership of President Ali Abdallah Salih and his dominant party – as it emphasized security and military spending over more prosaic items like municipal affairs and water conservation. National conditions of water emergency worsened throughout 2010, and the spiraling cost of water from private sellers was among the economic burdens that drove many thousands of Yemenis to the streets during the Arab Spring starting in January 2011. Revolution, in no small part, came from thirst.

MANAGING ENVIRONMENTAL IMPACTS IN THE MENA REGION

Given the imminence of environmental erosion and climatic change, what are the costs of doing nothing across the MENA? As the preceding analysis suggests, climate change acts as an amplifier of risks, insofar that while it may not be the sole cause of political instability, social harms, or economic stagnation, it acts to magnify preexisting weaknesses in states and societies. For instance, high food prices resulting from environmental shocks were not enough to trigger the Arab Spring during 2011–2012; after all, bread riots have happened before in the MENA region. However, it is difficult to brush out pictures of protesters in revolutionary scenes from Tunisia and Egypt – as well as other protest movements, such as in Jordan – where activists and citizens mobilized by waving loaves of bread as a symbolic embodiment of their frustrations about lack of dignity and material injustice. In this way, the interplay between environmental health and other dynamics, such as urbanization, migration, development, and governance, becomes critical. The urbanization element is especially important; as Chapter 6's exploration of the linkage between rentierism and urban development signified, the relentless fueling of metropolitan cities through capital investments or remittances from abroad may seem positive from an economic standpoint, but this also creates massive new burdens upon the underlying environmental resources and ecological elements such as water.

In concrete terms, existing models – taking into account patterns of urban growth, economic production, energy use, and demography – suggest a very dark picture. Though precise figures are elusive, virtually all projections suggest that the MENA region will suffer lower rainfall, increased frequency of drought, more extreme heat, and sea level changes. The heat factor is especially relevant given several record-breaking temperature events. In 2017, the city of Ahvaz in southwestern Iran reported a temperature of 128.7 degrees Fahrenheit (53.7 degrees Celsius) – an all-time high for the country. The year earlier, Kuwait reported a July temperature of 129.3 Fahrenheit (54 degrees Celsius), making it the second highest recorded temperature in modern history. And in July 2018, the township of Quriyat in Oman recorded the world's all-time highest "low" temperature (that is, the lowest point of temperature throughout a 24-hour solar cycle), with a measured reading of 108.7 Fahrenheit (42.6 degrees Celsius). The Max Planck Institute for Chemistry predicts that summer temperatures in the MENA will rise twice as fast as the global average in the coming century, and so these records are likely to be broken.

Finally, environmental issues themselves have become an actionable issue for social mobilization and civic engagement, of the type discussed in Chapter 3. Environmental activism has become increasingly vocal and visible, especially since the Arab Spring. Partly inspired by the international environmental conservation and climate change movement, and also infused by domestic energies from civil society, new social forces have mounted campaigns of protests and awareness that remind policymakers about the costs of ignoring these issues. Indeed, while imperfect, one indicator that marks public frustrations with governments failing to take action regarding major environmental problems, as well as widespread awareness that climatic and environmental issues fundamentally *matter*, are results from polls run by Gallup. For years, the polling firm's global survey included a question regarding the environment: "In [your country], are you satisfied or dissatisfied with efforts to preserve the environment?" As Figure 7.1 indicates, in 2017, while average scores across global regions varied between 40 to 80 percent, the MENA ranked nearly last with just 42 percent satisfaction rate, whereas various sub-regions of Asia ranked highest. For comparison, North America measured nearly 50 percent.

In qualitative terms, we can easily observe many upswells of environmental activism across the region in the 2010s. In March 2015, for example, violent demonstrations erupted in southern Algeria against a shale gas drilling project. While ultimately suppressed, the anti-fracking movement surprised many in highlighting the extent to which local communities recognized the negative impacts of energy extraction. Anti-fracking protests also occurred in Israel

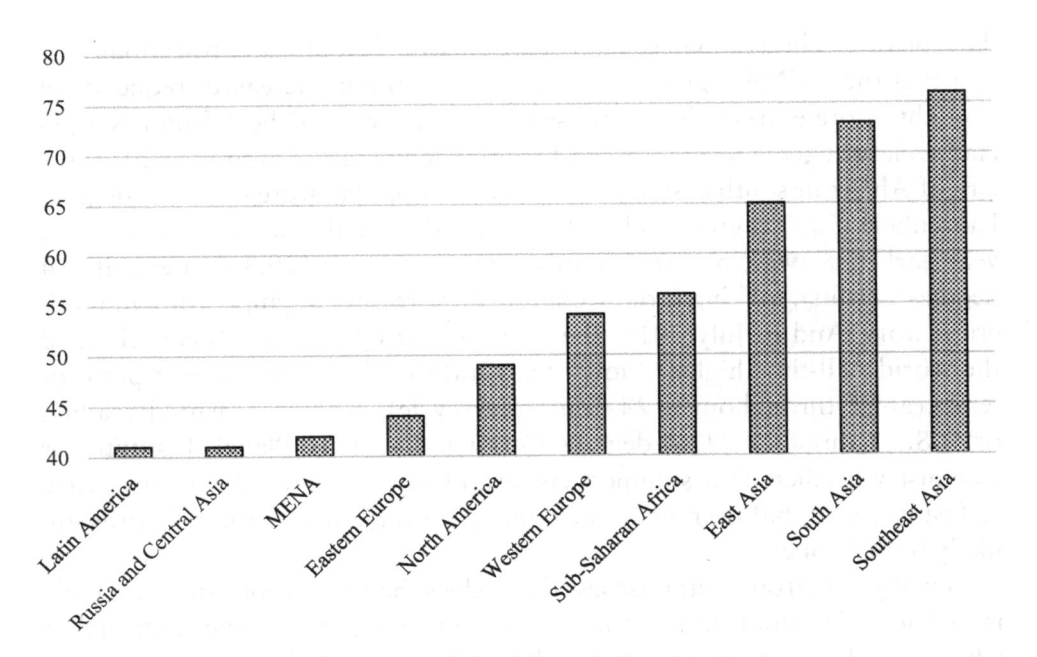

Figure 7.1 MENA vs. global regions: satisfaction with efforts for environmental preservation, 2017.

Source: Gallup (2017), *Gallup World Poll*.

Online: www.gallup.com/topic/world_poll.aspx. The survey question was: "In [your country], are you satisfied or dissatisfied with efforts to preserve the environment?" The illustrative data indicates the proportion of people indicating they were satisfied.

throughout 2012–2013 in Adulam, not far from Jerusalem. From 2008 onwards, Egyptian environmental activists organized numerous protests against fertilizer waste, gas drilling, coal burning, and other harms. In August 2015, likewise, Lebanese youth groups mounted protests under the #YouStink campaign, complaining about the political and institutional lethargy that allowed trash to pile up around Beirut. In Iran, protests over water shortages broke out throughout 2018, as farmers near Isfahan and outlying rural areas complained over malfunctioning pipelines and water pollution from oil and sugar cane refineries. In November 2012, the UN held its annual summit for its Framework Convention on Climate Change in Doha, Qatar; the event went smoothly, but also featured a coalition of Arab and non-Arab environmentalists mobilizing to more aggressively advocate for policy change (Photo 7.2). In November 2016, the UN held the same event in Marrakech, Morocco – a small victory for many Moroccan

PHOTO 7.2
Qatar Climate Change March at UN Conference, 2012.

Source: Photo by Adopt A Negotiator is licensed under CC BY-SA 2.0.
Online: www.flickr.com/photos/adoptanegotiator/8234818066

environmentalists who lobbied for greater political action, and similarly used the event as a showcase for their advocacy.

Struggles for adaptation

Adapting to climate change is not a new phenomenon for the MENA region. For thousands of years, peoples across this geographic crescent have attempted to accommodate climate variability by adjusting their modes of production and survival to changing conditions, such as variations in rainfall and temperature. To be sure, there are already difficulties of inducing collective action among international states to tackle climate change issues at the global level; consider, for example, the lack of adherence by many states to the greenhouse gas and adaptation targets set with the 2015 Paris Agreement. Yet inaction at the regional level will generate numerous long-term effects that will be felt at the economic level. A UN Environmental Program report in 2014, for instance, projected that developing countries will pay two to three times higher the cost in adapting to changing climatic conditions – such as adjusting agricultural methods or crops in response to higher temperatures, or shifting locations of residential and commercial sites due to changing weather patterns or sea levels.

Adaptation measures are in principle supposed to help increase the resilience of social and ecological systems to absorb the effects of change. In this regard, a vital role is played by governments to adopt international concords designed to address these threats, while implementing them successfully at the domestic level. The governmental duty to protect people from harm, which is universally recognized, inevitably implies the adoption and implementation of robust climate adaptation policies while mainstreaming human security into them. However, governments should be cautious because these policies can potentially infringe upon other human security concerns, such as the livelihoods of existing economic producers. Still, adaptation strategies should be maintained by communities as a key to continuously protecting fragile ecosystems and vulnerable populations from severe impact. Reorienting financial resources to other areas may exacerbate vulnerability. Similarly, disaster risk management should be dedicated to address the particular situation of the most vulnerable and marginalized.

At the micro level, communities can adapt in agile ways. For instance, consider desertification – a destructive process that consumes arable land and destroys agricultural possibility, and is caused by land overexploitation, water exhaustion, and rising temperatures. Photo 7.3, for instance, illustrates the consequences of desertification in Morocco, with unusable plots effectively abandoned in terms of human settlement given the inability of local soils to support sustainable agrarian production. At the local level, strategies exist to stop or alleviate desertification, often by planting certain tree lines to fence off shifting sands and to maintain minimum nutrient levels in the ground. Adaptation, in this context, means ways that populations can protect themselves from the worst effects of environmental degradation or climatic change.

However, adaptation at the *national*, much less *regional*, level is more difficult. Scaling up strategies requires leaders to assess not just the risks of doing nothing but also the costs of various responses, in close consultation with their societies and constituencies. Those adaptation responses run into a political hurdle, however, because most states in the MENA region remain authoritarian rather than democratic. Without popular inputs into policymaking, it will be difficult for ruling elites to singlehandedly estimate the most optimal way to distribute the costs of adaptation fairly, including

PHOTO 7.3
Desertified and abandoned cultivation in Morocco, 2014.

Source: Public domain.
Online: https://pixabay.com/en/donkey-desert-morocco-animal-272070/

compensation for those who stand to lose. Constructing a hydroelectric station on large rivers to reduce greenhouse emissions, for instance, may disrupt the food source or economic livelihood of riverside communities. Requiring efficient means of irrigation through rainwater conservation and solar-powered pumps may entail shifting crop rotations or even the location of agricultural estates. Moderating extreme temperature shifts by planting a particular species of tree in mass numbers to reflect sunlight and reduce stormwater runoff may require rezoning existing urban areas, not to mention the water demands and financial costs of such policies.

Thus, true adaptation always brings costs; there is no singular perfect solution. For instance, in 2018, the Moroccan government unveiled a massive solar power plant in the Sahara Desert with the goal of replacing imported oil and gas with renewable sources. Such a policy seems sensible from an environmental and strategic standpoint; not only does this render the kingdom less vulnerable to oil and gas price fluctuations from its trading partners, it also will reduce its carbon footprint by eliminating many tons of emissions. Yet the project is also water-intensive, since solar energy production requires wet cooling, and its unveiling elicited local criticism regarding the method of land acquisition used by, and poor community relations with, the multinational corporation operating the facility. As this example shows, while the replacement of hydrocarbon fuels with renewables such as solar and wind energy represents one governmental response to environmental pressures, implementing these policies often provokes resistance and pushback when the tradeoffs and costs are not fully revealed to stakeholders.

At a broader level, successful adaptation requires that states work together because environmental injury is a transnational phenomenon; with a few exceptions, the use and abuse of water, land, and air cannot be localized to a single population. However, thus far, there are very few concerted efforts at envisioning adaptation strategies at the regional level. One reason is that environmental policy simply does not occupy a high priority for many governments – something that is shared by many countries across the world, but is especially prevalent in the MENA. While most MENA countries have created environmental agencies or ministries, such political institutions have little weight when countries deal with large-scale strategic issues, such as that of trade, foreign aid, militarization, and refugees. Furthermore, bilateral tensions between neighboring countries caused by strategic disagreement at a higher level, such as Moroccan-Algerian disputes and the Saudi-Qatari divergence, all but foreclose the more basic task of engaging in environmental dialogues. Even temporary agreements to share water resources during droughts can be difficult to reach if countries are not already on excellent diplomatic terms; in 2007, for instance, drought raised tensions between Turkey, Syria, and Iraq when the Turkish government diverted considerable water from the Tigris and Euphrates watershed to irrigate its agricultural sector. Another reason is that several countries have become conflict zones (i.e., Syria, Libya, Yemen); merely picking through the aftermath of these wars and fully understanding how communities have been affected will require substantial reconstruction.

However, instances of coordination do exist, such as Israeli-Jordanian collaboration on water-sharing and water conveyance. The 1994 peace treaty between these two countries opened the door for long-term water management, including withdrawal rights for the Jordan and Yarmouk rivers – virtually the only sources of flowing freshwater between these two countries facing conditions of absolute water scarcity. Despite bilateral work being temporarily disrupted by discord or shocks, cooperation culminated in a 2013 agreement signed between the Israeli, Jordanian, and Palestinian governments. That agreement included a proposal for both a desalinization plant on the Red Sea that would benefit all three populations, replenish the fast-disappearing Dead Sea, and ameliorate existing demands on existing water sources. What distinguishes this particular success is that all the actors involved face critical conditions of water scarcity that are imprinting palpable social and economic effects; that is, concerted action is easier to catalyze when the environmental threat is imminent, existential, and unmitigable.

CONCLUSION

Environmental degradation and climate change greatly threaten human security and development in the MENA region. As this chapter has discussed, by thickening our conception of human security and then understanding inherent risk factors of the region – among them a past record of frequent violent conflict, the existence of vulnerable populations, and the fragility of many states – we can better grasp the challenges and opportunities that lie ahead. As the climate system warms, many of these countries will be the worst affected in terms of their severe implications for their ecological and social systems in addition to their limited coping capacities. The analysis of the region's poor water resources, and the differential imbalance of their use and abuse, underscores this.

Unpacking the nexus between environment, climate, and conflict from both a theoretical and empirical perspective uncovers the necessity of collective action to both recognize and respond to climatic impacts. Climatic change or environmental issues alone may not be (as of yet) the sole drivers of violence and instability, but when conceptualized as an amplifier or multiplier, their long-term consequences are dire. Populations facing agricultural failures, acute water shortages, unlivable urban conditions, and failing infrastructures may incubate unrest and instability for any number of reasons, but these structural deficiencies *do not help matters* and, in all likelihood, make things worse. The path forward, both globally and regionally, requires adaptation and creative responses, but political and strategic impediments have often blocked this pathway. To make the process efficient and sustainable, social adaptation to inevitable climatic shifts will need to be prioritized by MENA countries, lest their vulnerable populations be exposed to more risk factors, with all the accompanying harms and damages this entails.

QUESTIONS FOR DISCUSSION

1. What is human security, and how is environmental security an intricate component of this concept?
2. How does human security differ from past conceptions of "hard" security?
3. What is the record of militarized conflicts in the MENA region?
4. How does climate change increase the risk of human conflict, in terms of causing more political unrest and social violence?
5. How have geography and geology affected the availability of freshwater for most MENA countries?
6. What are the projected impacts of climate change, in social and economic terms, for different types of human communities?
7. Will we see more variants of environmental activism in the future from MENA civil societies, or does this represent a contemporary trend that will not last?
8. Why has collective action needed for regional adaptation to climate change proven so elusive for most MENA countries?

FURTHER READING

The study of the environment, a large interdisciplinary field that only recently has come to the MENA, offers excellent primers regarding environmental conservation and policymaking. Among the most memorable are Jean-Frédéric Morin and Amandine Orsini, eds., *Essential Concepts of Global Environmental Governance* (London: Routledge, 2015); Kate O'Neill, *The Environment and International Relations* (Cambridge: Cambridge University Press, 2009); and Ken Conca and Geoffrey Dabelko, *Green Planet Blues: Critical Perspectives on Global Environmental Politics*, 5th ed. (London: Routledge, 2018). Older foundational works include Arthur Westing, ed., *Global Resources and International Conflict: Environmental Factors in Strategic Policy and Action* (Oxford: Oxford University Press, 1986); Murray Bookchin, *The Ecology of Freedom: The Emergence and Dissolution of Hierarchy* (Palo Alto, CA: Cheshire Books, 1982); and the classic essay by Garrett Hardin, "The Tragedy of the Commons," *Science* 162 (1968): 1243–48.

Within the MENA, there does exist an anthropological and sociological tradition of studying human interactions with ecological systems. See, for instance, Diana Davis and Edmund Burke, eds., *Environmental Imaginaries of the Middle East and North Africa* (Athens, OH: Ohio University Press, 2013); Elizabeth Williams, "Environmental History of the Middle East and North Africa," in *The Oxford Handbook of Contemporary Middle-Eastern and North African History*, eds. Amal Ghazal and Jens Hanssen (Oxford: Oxford University Press, 2015); Alan Mikhail, *Water on Sand: Environmental Histories of the Middle East and North Africa* (Oxford: Oxford University Press, 2013); and, for a much earlier look that connects to premodern geographies of human settlements and agriculture, Arie Issar and Mattanyah Zohar, *Climate Change: Environment and Civilization in* the Middle East (Berlin: Springer-Verlag, 2004). A telling look at Israel's own struggles is Alon Tal, *Pollution in a Promised Land: An Environmental History of Israel* (Berkeley, CA: University of California Press, 2002).

The environment-conflict nexus discussed here remains an ongoing debate, although consensus has settled somewhat over the notion that environmental stress and climate change may not be the single trigger for any violent conflict but nonetheless can greatly amplify and aggrandize risk factors. See, for instance, Jon Barnett, "Destabilizing the Environment-Conflict Thesis," *Review of International Studies* 26 (2000): 271–88; Thomas Bernauer, Bohmelt Tobias, and Koubi Vally, "Environmental Changes and Violent Conflict," *Environmental Research Letters* 7 (2012): 1–8; Nils Petter Gleditsch, "Whither the Weather? Climate Change and Conflict," *Journal of Peace Research* 49 (2012): 3–9; and James Lee, *Climate Change and Armed Conflict: Hot and Cold Wars* (London: Routledge, 2009). Richard A. Matthew, Jon Barnett, Bryan McDonald, and Karen O'Brien, eds., *Global Environmental Change and Human Security* (Cambridge, MA: The MIT Press, 2009) synthesizes this debate and carefully weighs all implications for human security.

More recently, contemporary issues of climate change and environmental activism have arisen among MENA specialists. The current period is one of burgeoning research and new ideas. An analytic framework that defines human security and environmentalism is Mohamed Behnassi and Katriona McGlade, eds., *Environmental Change and Human Security in Africa and the Middle East* (Berlin: Springer-Verlag, 2017). Environmental activism is engaged by Jeannie Sowers in her landmark *Environmental Politics in Egypt: Experts, Activists, and the State* (London: Routledge, 2012), and in other works, among them Jeannie Sowers, Avner Vengosh, and Erika Weinthal, "Climate Change, Water Resources, and the Politics of Adaptation in the Middle East and North Africa," *Climatic Change* 104, no. 3–4 (2011): 599–627. Adaptation is also tackled in Dorte Vener, ed., *Adaptation to a Changing Climate in the Arab Countries: A Case for Adaptation Governance and Leadership in Building Climate Resilience* (Washington, DC: World Bank, 2012). An excellent overview is found in J.P. Evans, "21st Century Climate Change in the Middle East," *Climatic Change* 92, no. 3–4 (2009): 417–32.

Harry Voerhoeven, ed., *Environmental Politics in the Middle East: Local Struggles, Global Connections* (London: Hurst, 2018) presents an excellent array of contributors that evaluate "green" issues and resource conservation. Similarly, Ashok Swain and Anders Jägerskog, *Emerging Security Threats in the Middle East: The Impact of Climate Change and Globalization* (Lanham, MD: Rowman and Littlefield, 2016) provides an excellent and updated survey of climate change as a threat to human security in the MENA. Gawdat Bahgat, *Alternative Energy in the Middle East* (London: Palgrave Macmillan, 2013) weighs the potentialities of solar, wind, and other non-hydrocarbon energy sources. Tony Allen, *The Middle East Water Question: Hydropolitics and the Global Economy* (London: I.B. Tauris, 2001) and Asit K. Biswas and Eglal Rached, eds., *Water as a Human Right for the Middle East and North Africa* (London: Routledge, 2008) explore water stress and water scarcity dynamics. Eckart Woertz, *Oil for Food: The Global Food Crisis and the Middle East* (Oxford: Oxford University Press, 2013) explores how ecological breakdowns have facilitated and quickened the food insecurity felt in many human populations across the region. Similarly, the essay, Sarah Johnstone and Jeffrey Mazo, "Global Warming and the Arab Spring," *Survival* 53, no. 2 (2011): 11–17, connects climate change factors to the 2011–2012 Arab uprisings. Again indicating the region-wide (as opposed to Arab-centric) nature of the issue, Fikret Adaman and Murat Arsel, eds., *Environmentalism in Turkey: Between Democracy and Development* (London: Routledge, 2005), probes how different environmental impacts have elicited social and cultural mobilization.

Online sources

Sizable research materials exist online for the study of MENA environmentalism, climate change, and adaptation. The UN Food and Agricultural Organization's regional portal, for instance, displays a variety of data and publications (www.fao.org/neareast/en/). The FAO's water database also has telling indicators regarding water stress and water scarcity around the world, including the MENA (www.fao.org/nr/aquastat/). The World Bank also devotes a large program to MENA climate change (www.worldbank.org/en/programs/mena-climate-change). The UNDP's Climate Change Adaptation portal also contains useful MENA-related resources (www.adaptation-undp.org/). Climate Action Tracker (https://climateactiontracker.org/) has country-specific information regarding compliance of different states to global climate accords, such as the 2015 Paris Agreement. Finally, there are a rising number of regional blogs and websites dedicated to mobilizing more attention around environmental adaptation and conservation strategies. Examples include EcoMENA (www.ecomena.org/) and Green Prophet (www.greenprophet.com/), the latter of which provides news on all aspects of lifestyles – design, technology, food, architecture, and more – that are sustainable.

017
Societal forces

Religion and faith, women and gender, and youth generation

CHAPTER 8

Religion and faith

Ramazan Kılınç

THE RUNDOWN: KEY TOPICS COVERED
- Major religions
- Faith-based minorities
- Concept of religiosity
- Religious activism
- Islamist movements, peaceful and violent
- Egypt, Turkey, Iran, Saudi Arabia

INTRODUCTION

The Middle East and North Africa (MENA) is the birthplace of the three Abrahamic religions – Judaism, Christianity, and Islam. Religion matters in making sense of not just politics, but social attitudes, societal relationships, and national orientations. If religion was irrelevant, would Saudi Arabia have justified its 2015 intervention in Yemen to its own citizenry through sectarian arguments regarding the threat of Shi'a Islam? Can the emergence of religious extremism be explained without any reference to faith, belief, and sacrifice? Can the Israeli-Palestinian question be separated from the religious attachments of the people involved? Can historical and contemporary civil wars, from Lebanon and Libya to Syria and Iraq, be explained without exploring how religious elites manipulate their traditions to amplify political and material demands? In sum, the ways people engage their faith and piety, the mechanisms through which these beliefs animate social relationships and everyday routines, and the processes through which religious beliefs influence economic and political institutions are important in the Middle Eastern context.

This chapter surveys religion within and across MENA societies. Although the Middle East is home to diverse religious groups, over 90 percent of its people are Muslims, and Islam plays a significant role in social and political activism. This chapter starts with a brief overview of the religious landscape, showing the distribution of different religious traditions. Then, it shows how religion has played a central role in structuring private and public lives, with a focus on charity, social work, education, and health. Finally, it shows how religion influences the public imagination of politics and the participation of different communities in struggles for a better future. It also summarizes the emergence of Islamist and other politically motivated religious organizations with a special reference to bottom-up mobilization. Ending with a cluster of case studies, it offers an analysis of how religious mobilization manifests itself in the national contexts of four prominent MENA countries that often appear in global headlines – Egypt, Turkey, Iran, and Saudi Arabia.

THE RELIGIOUS LANDSCAPE

As the search for the sacred and the worship of the divine, religion is a defining phenomenon in the Middle East. Although Islam gained predominance after the rise of the great Islamic Caliphates from the seventh century onwards, the MENA is also home to diverse religious traditions. Today, more than 90 percent of the people in the region belong to the religion of Islam, although there are significant Christian and Jewish populations in the region as well. Chapter 4's review of identity showed that religion was a major pillar of self-conception; the analysis here will take this argument further by showing the doctrinal diversity and deep roots of faith in the region. Table 8.1 delineates the religious landscape of the entire region in terms of population and affinity.

Islam

Islam is the most widely followed religion in the MENA. Although many observers assume that most Muslims are Middle Eastern, in reality only one-fifth of the world's entire Muslim population resides in this region. While Muslims consider Islam as a continuation of Judaism and Christianity, they believe that Muhammad is the final Prophet of God. The majority of Muslims are Sunnis, but there are significant Shi'a Muslim communities in the Middle East as well. The central tenets of Islam include several interrelated notions, among them the oneness and universality of God; the vast sovereignty and power of God, and thus the duty of believers to worship His creations; the

TABLE 8.1

MENA – religious landscape, 2017

	Muslim population	Percent total	Christian population	Percent total	Jewish population	Percent total	Other	Percent total
Algeria	40,559,749	99	286,786	0.7	410	0.001	122,499	0.29
Bahrain	987,659	70	211,641	15	141	0.01	211,500	14.99
Egypt	86,366,554	89	9,704,107	10	97	0.0001	970,314	0.99
Iran	81,529,435	99.4	246,065	0.3	24,606	0.03	221,458	0.27
Iraq	37,232,505	95	587,882	1.5	11,758	0.03	1,359,966	3.47
Israel	1,469,048	17.7	165,994	2	6,199,880	74.7	464,784	5.6
Jordan	9,961,123	97.2	204,961	2	1,025	0.01	80,960	0.79
Kuwait	2,205,449	76.7	497,448	17.3	575	0.02	171,950	5.98
Lebanon	3,364,089	54	2,523,067	40.5	2,492	0.04	340,147	5.46
Libya	6,427,001	96.6	179,637	2.7	67	0.001	46,506	0.70
Morocco	33,646,788	99	33,987	0.1	6,797	0.02	299,083	0.88
Oman	3,962,774	85.9	299,861	6.5	46	0.001	350,560	7.60
Qatar	1,566,786	67.7	319,374	13.8	694	0.03	427,453	18.47
Saudi Arabia	28,286,052	99	5,714	0.02	286	0.001	279,718	0.98
Sudan	36,225,556	97	**	**	**	**	**	**
Syria	15,684,838	87	1,802,855	10	180	0.001	540,676	2.0
Tunisia	11,301,166	99.1	34,211	0.3	1,140	0.01	67,282	0.59
Turkey	80,683,525	99.8	80,845	0.1	24,254	0.03	56,592	0.07
UAE	4,615,081	76	546,523	9	607	0.01	910,264	14.99
West Bank and Gaza Strip	3,519,001	73	265,130	5.5	867,699	18	168,719	3.5
Yemen	27,784,498	99.1	56,074	0.2	280	0.001	195,977	0.70
TOTAL	481,153,119	93.7	18,052,162	3.5	7,143,035	1.4	7,286,407	1.4

Source: CIA (2018), *World Fact Book*; Palestinian Central Bureau of Statistics (2018), *Annual Yearbook*. ** indicates data unavailable since partition of Sudan into two countries in 2011.

insufficiency of belief alone, and the necessity to actively practice one's faith in life; and the Prophecy of Muhammad, the last of a long line of Prophets (including those familiar to Christians and Jews, such as Abraham, Moses, and Jesus) who carried God's message on Earth. The necessity of practice and worship is expressed through Islam's Five Pillars, to which all Muslims regardless of sect and origin subscribe. Those Five Pillars are the *shahada*, or testimonial declaration of belief in God and Muhammad's Prophecy; prayer; *zakat*, or charity; *sawm*, or fasting; and *hajj*, or pilgrimage to Mecca – the holiest city in Islam, and the birthplace of Muhammad where his first revelations from God occurred. Photo 8.1 illustrates the Ka'ba, the holy structure at the center of the Sacred Mosque in Mecca – in essence, one of the holiest edifices in Islam, as Muslims must face in the direction of the Ka'ba during formal prayer.

Islamic terms are expressed in Arabic, because Arabic is the language of the Qur'an, Islam's holy book whose text represents God's message to

PHOTO 8.1
Ka'ba within sacred mosque in Mecca, Saudi Arabia, 2014.

Source: Public domain.
Online: https://pixabay.com/en/kaaba-islam-the-pilgrim-s-guide-3635723/

humanity. Like other religious traditions, Islam has also generated a rich literature encompassing philosophy, theology, and law.

The Sunni-Shi'a divide within Islam emerged after the death of Prophet Muhammad as a political conflict. Both groups agree on the fundamental creed of Islam, but they diverged over the issue of succession to the Prophet's leadership over the Muslim community: the minority that saw the Prophet's son-in-law, Ali, as the rightful heir became the Shi'a (in Arabic, literally partisans of Ali) while those that did not now occupy the wide category known as Sunni Muslims. This split has not always been historically violent or conflictual, but it has resulted in a Shi'a Islamic tradition whose unique variations on religious doctrine make it stand apart from the majoritarian Sunni Islamic tradition. Today, Iran, Iraq, and Bahrain have majority Shi'a populations, while the Shi'a represent the minority (or are hardly found) in the other MENA countries. Shi'a Islam itself contains various sects; the three primary ones are the Twelver, Zaydi, and Isma'ili groups. These variants all agree upon the primacy of Ali and his heirs as the rightful successor to leadership over the Islamic community, but disagree on the order of his descendants and other theological matters.

By contrast, while it represents the large majority of Muslims worldwide, Sunni Islam is a misleading category. While some see the label as simply denoting Muslims who are not Shi'a, in actuality Sunni Islam encompasses an astonishing variety of doctrines as well, including various schools of jurisprudence and theology. For instance, there are four major schools of Islamic law, or *shari'a*, that interpret Sunni orthodoxy in distinctive ways – the Hanbali, Hanafi, Maliki, and Shafi'i paradigms, and Sunni countries like Morocco, Egypt, and Saudi Arabia subscribe to different ones. There are also many different theological and philosophical traditions, especially from the golden age of Islamic philosophy from the ninth through thirteenth centuries. Sunni Islam also encompasses Sufism and Sufi orders, which practice mysticism and through various rituals and practices seek higher perceptive feelings of spirituality and inner truth.

In addition to these relatively more mainstream Islamic denominations, there are heterodox Muslim groups in the MENA as well. Two such groups are Alevis in Turkey and 'Alawites in Syria. Although Alevis in Turkey follow the teachings of Ali, they do not affiliate themselves with Shi'a Islam strongly. Alevism is a syncretic form of Islam that combines Islamic elements with pre-Islamic local traditions. Alevis have some practices not found in mainstream Sunni and Shi'a traditions; for instance, they have special worship ceremonies that include music and dance. They constitute about 15–20 percent of the population in Turkey. Though often confused with the Alevis, the 'Alawites of Syria constitute a separate ethnoreligious community and practice their own unique variation of Shi'a Islam, differing especially from Sunni theological principles. Upon the eve of the Arab Spring and before the Syrian civil war, they composed 11 percent of the country's population. There are also small 'Alawite minorities in southern Turkey and northern Lebanon.

People of the Middle East found ways to accommodate these denominational differences throughout history. However, these differences have also created political conflicts. In Iran, Iraq, Yemen, Bahrain, and Lebanon, sectarian differences have shaped the political positions and struggles between Sunnis and Shi'a. While the Sunni minority in Iran has often faced suppression, Bahrain and Iraq have been ruled in the post-colonial era (and for Bahrain, well before) by regimes dominated by Sunni elites that often restricted the freedoms of Shi'a. After the Iraqi invasion of 2003, the Shi'a controlled the political process and discriminated against Sunni communities, especially after the withdrawal of American troops in 2011. The recent war in Yemen, escalated through Saudi and Iranian interventions, has been waged around sectarian elements pitting Sunni versus Shi'a identities. In Turkey, Alevis have faced discrimination by the state for generations. In Syria, the 'Alawite minority produced the al-Asad regime, which has ruled Syria since the 1970s and still presides over a war-torn society today.

Christianity

Christians are a small but still significant minority in the MENA region. Most belong to Orthodox Christianity, but there are also Catholics and a small number of Protestants. Egypt, Syria, and Lebanon have the largest Christian populations; Egypt alone has nine million, most of whom belong to the Coptic Christian tradition. The Coptic community has been influential in Egyptian life for many years, and has contributed political figures, business luminaries, and cultural pioneers. Syria has also a significant Christian minority, which constitutes around 10 percent of the population with around 1.5 million. Almost all belong to the Eastern Orthodox tradition, Syriac Christians being the largest group. They have played a significant role in economic life, and likewise have contributed disproportionate numbers of political elites that have served in the Syrian government since the demise of colonialism after World War Two.

Finally, Christians also constitute a large part of the Lebanese population, although the lack of a modern census makes it difficult to ascertain their precise number. Estimates typically put them at between 20 to 35 percent. The largest sect is Maronite Christianity, followed by the Greek Orthodox. Given its confessional system, Lebanon offers its Christian community a strong political voice; the President, for instance, is customarily a Maronite Christian, whereas the Prime Minister is Sunni Muslim and the Speaker of Parliament a Shi'a Muslim. Indeed, Lebanon is a country where even after the 1975–1990 civil war, religious communities often reside alongside in close proximity with one another. As Photo 8.2 shows, in downtown Beirut, one finds a famous Maronite cathedral alongside a prominent blue-domed Muslim mosque.

There are Christians in other MENA countries too, but in fewer numbers. There are approximately a half-million Christians in Iraq, about 1.5 percent of the total population. Iraq is home to several Chaldean (a Catholic denomination) and Assyrian (an Orthodox denomination) communities, as well as small groups of Armenians, Greeks, and more recently Evangelical

PHOTO 8.2
Beirut – St. Georges Maronite Cathedral next to Muhammad Al-Amin Mosque, 2009.

Source: Photo by ordel is licensed under CC BY-SA 2.0.
Online: www.flickr.com/photos/ordel/3642739700

Christians. About 2 percent of the Israeli population, including the West Bank, is also Christian; a fair number of Palestinians and Arabs fall into the Catholic, Orthodox, and other denominations. Turkey and Iran also have Christian minorities but their numbers are slimmer; in both, they constitute less than 0.5 percent of the total population. Of these, the largest segment are Armenians following the Orthodox faith.

As a minority group, Christians in the Middle East are generally wealthier and better educated than the mean. Historically, many played a major role in the development of international trade and commerce, and also collaborated with their governments to protect communal interests. Recent trends in the region, however, have put unprecedented pressures upon Christian communities in many countries. Though data are elusive, it is well established that the overall number of Christians living in countries like Lebanon, Egypt, Iraq, and Syria have diminished over the past decade due to instability, turmoil, and violence, some of it aimed at Christians. The Israeli government's expansionist settlement policies in the West Bank have also created an outflow of Christian Palestinians from the area.

Judaism

Virtually all Jews in the MENA are found in Israel. There remain tiny, scattered Jewish minorities across Iraq, Tunisia, Morocco, Turkey, Algeria, and a few other countries – the remnants of once-thriving communities that mostly emigrated to Israel after its establishment in 1948. About 75 percent of Israel's population is Jewish, and has been periodically infused with mass waves of Jewish immigration from other countries. Generally, they divide into three distinctive groups. Those Jews who are originally from the Middle East are called Mizrahi. Those who originally descended from the Iberian Peninsula, which during the height of the Islamic Empires held a thriving and protected Jewish minority, are called Sephardic. Finally, those who emigrated from Europe to Israel and Palestine starting in the late nineteenth century through the Zionist movement, and later *en masse* after World War Two, are Ashkenazi. The Ashkenazim have long dominated the political and cultural life of Israel despite being the newest group of Jews to enter the Middle East.

Since its inception, Judaism has shaped life in Israel in many ways that extend beyond the country's symbolic identity as the world's only Jewish state. Religiously inspired Jewish political parties have gradually increased their influence on Israeli politics over time, including parties such as Shah, United Torah Judaism, and the Jewish Home. Formal marriage and divorce for the Jews can only be conducted by a rabbi, leading many secular Jews to go abroad for civil marriage licenses. The burgeoning influence of conservative Jewish norms belonging to the Jewish Orthodox tradition has also resulted in increased social segregation against secular-minded Israeli citizens. In these and other ways, non-Jewish minorities – including Palestinian Christians and Muslims – within Israel have often struggled to find adequate accommodation for their belief systems. Most recently, the July 2018 introduction of a new law that officially defined Israel as the national homeland of all Jews generated considerable controversy given its perceived exclusionary bias against non-Jewish Israelis.

MISUNDERSTANDINGS OF RELIGIOSITY AND FAITH

To many outside observers, the MENA region and especially its Muslim-majority countries appear as extremely pious, overly conservative places where deeply Islamic cultures stand frozen in time, hostile to all things Western. In such mysterious environs, the faithful adherents of Islam place extraordinary trust in their religious authorities to guide their path and dictate their social relationships. Moreover, Middle Easterners in this view are extremely hostile to secularism; they crave religiosity and need their faith, so much so that it prevents the normal functioning of economic and political development. Inevitably, this results in authoritarianism and repression, suggesting some relationship between religiosity and regime type.

The problem with such caricatures lays not only in their Orientalist ethnocentrism, an assumption laid bare in Chapter 1, but the ways they traffic in misunderstood concepts that encourage misunderstandings across cultural boundaries. It is not uncontroversial to suggest that there are many pious people in the MENA, insofar as they are devoutly religious; but it is a leap to suggest that faith-based preferences come *prior* to political and social ones. These assumptions must be unpacked systematically.

First: how religious are people in the Middle East? A straightforward question eludes easy answers. It would not be controversial to say that the *average* Muslim in the region, for instance, is probably more devout than the *average* European; but piety alone does not dictate other social, economic, and political outcomes. Most of all, piety varies across countries. Table 8.2 shows the frequency of religious service attendance in selected cases – Iran, Iraq, Morocco, Turkey, and Egypt – with data taken from the World Values Survey, a global opinion polling series that has been conducted since 1981. The data come from its fifth "wave" or round of polls, deployed during 2005–2009; though a sixth and newer wave exists, many MENA countries

TABLE 8.2

Five Muslim-majority MENA countries – frequency of religious service attendance, 2005–2009

	Iran	Iraq	Morocco	Turkey	Egypt	TOTAL
More than once a week	20.3	15.5	84.5	13.7	31	28.3
Once a week	13.5	12.4	5.5	19.9	24.6	16.2
Once a month	9.4	2.7	1.5	1.7	3.8	4.4
Only holy days	22.8	10.4	6.8	23.4	11	14.8
Once a year	6.5	0.7	0.1	3.2	0.6	2.3
Less often	0	5.1	0.6	3.9	9.4	4.4
Never	22.6	38.2	0.2	32.3	19.5	24.3
Missing; not asked by the interviewer	0	13.9	0	1.1	0	3.6
No answer	4.9	0.4	0.8	0.7	0.1	1.5
Don't know	0	0.6	0	0.2	0	0.2
Total number of respondents	2,667	2,701	1,200	1,346	3,051	10,965

Source: World Values Survey (2009). Figures given in percentages, except last row (total number of respondents in survey). The survey question was: "How often do you attend religious services?".

are missing or excluded from the later iteration. The data show that between these five notable Muslim-majority countries, there is remarkable variation among individuals in terms of how often they attended some kind of religious service (e.g., going to mosque for prayer and sermons). A full 84.5 percent of Moroccans reported attending such services more than once weekly, compared to a low of 13.7 percent in Turkey. Moreover, varying portions of each country, ranging from a fraction in Morocco to 38.2 percent in Iraq, reported *never* attending religious service.

The same variability holds for another question, namely how important religion is to an individual. When posed with that interrogative, respondents in these six MENA countries gave somewhat more consistent answers. As Table 8.3 shows, the vast majority of each country, ranging from 74.6 percent in Turkey to 95.6 percent in Iraq, reported that religion was *very* important, while only a relative fraction of each society said the opposite – that religion was not at all important. The puzzle here concerns the source of variation. Iran is an Islamic Republic, governed by a theocratic government ultimately headed by Shi'a clerics; it imposes strict sanctions upon public and private life to ensure that its citizens abide by an orthodox interpretation of Shi'a

TABLE 8.3

Five Muslim-majority MENA countries – importance of religion to individuals, 2005–2009

	Iran	Iraq	Jordan	Morocco	Turkey	Egypt	TOTAL
Very important	78.2	95.6	94.4	90.5	74.6	95.4	88.8
Rather important	16.1	3.3	5.2	7.9	16.6	4.1	8.4
Not very important	3.9	0.4	0.2	1.2	6.2	0.2	1.8
Not at all important	1.5	0.2	0.2	0.2	2.5	0.2	0.7
No answer	0.3	0.2	0.1	0.1	0.1	0	0.2
Don't know	0	0.3	0	0	0.1	0	0.1
Number of respondents	2,667	2,701	1,200	1,200	1,346	3,051	12,165

Source: World Values Survey (2009). Figures given in percentages, except last row (total number of respondents in survey). The survey question was: "How important is religion to you?".

Islam. Yet a significantly lesser proportion of Iranians proclaim that religion is very important when compared to Egypt or Iraq, where virtually all respondents expressed so. Such data show that while the MENA region is likely more religious in terms of measurable indicators than some other regions, it is hardly a monolith of sacrality.

The MENA region, and especially its Muslim-majority countries, are thus places of reliably strong religiosity. What does this mean, though, for governance and politics? An oft-cited conjecture by many outside observers is that very religious peoples in the Middle East must desire theocracy. Here, empirical evidence in varying forms shatters this linkage between social beliefs and political preferences. For one, there are virtually no theocracies in the MENA excepting the case of Iran's Islamic Republic. Theocracy means a political regime in which political authority stems purely from religious institutions, so that religious figures such as priests and clerics *by law* always exercise direct power over all other elected and nonelected offices. It does not mean a political system in which very religious people happen to brandish power; as is often caricatured in the West; after all, there is no statutory exclusion even in liberal democracies against election candidates who happen to be even fundamentalist in their faith.

Neither does it refer to countries where there is an official state religion, which means there is a single faith that the government has historically supported and financed – but which still has no institutional role in determining who has political authority and how policies are made. While most

Muslim-majority countries in the MENA have installed Islam as the state religion (excepting Lebanon), so too does England have a state faith (Anglican Church) as does a slew of other European and Latin American countries that officially support Catholicism. For another, there is no political tradition of establishing strongly religious governments in the MENA that explicitly fuse religious content with domestic and foreign policies. From the most prominent historical dictatorships, such as Nasser's party-state in Egypt, to the most powerful monarchies of the present, such as the House of Saud in Saudi Arabia, most institutional structures of governance have been non-religious in nature – impelled forward not by mandates of faith, but by the very profane desires of a small elite to maintain vast political power.

This broaches a corollary question: does the faith of Muslims preclude supporting values of democracy? Here, the latest reliable public opinion polling data provides evidence for answering this question with a resounding no. Using the Arab Barometer project's latest 2016–2017 wave of surveys across seven Arab countries, we can ascertain directly through revealed public attitudes whether religious identification has any affect upon political preferences. Figure 8.1 shows that clear majorities across all countries

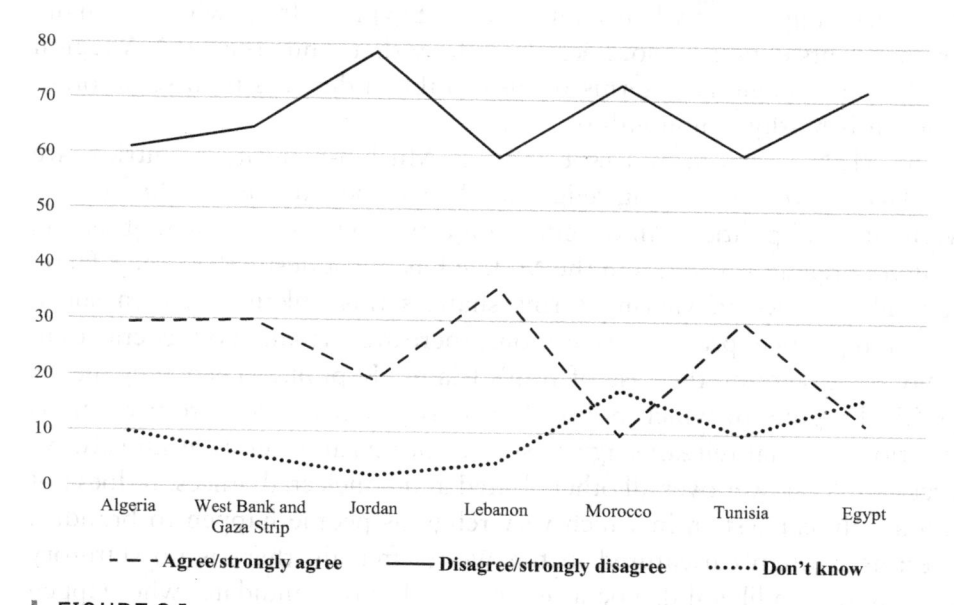

FIGURE 8.1
Compatibility of Islam with democracy from Arab Barometer, 2017.

Source: Arab Barometer, Wave IV (2016–2017).

Online: www.arabbarometer.org. Respondents were asked to strongly agree, agree, disagree, strongly disagree, or respond with "I don't know" in reaction to this statement: "Democracy is a Western form of government that is not compatible with Islam."

did not think that democracy, as a Western form of government, had any incompatibility with Islam, ranging from nearly 80 percent in Jordan to about 60 percent in Lebanon. Moreover, as Figure 8.2 divulges, an overwhelming majority in every country preferred democracy as the best political system; in Morocco and Tunisia, just 10 percent or less did not prefer democracy at all.

Finally, even if many MENA residents are strongly religious but also support democracy, could they still plausibly desire for faith to still play some official role in politics? Again, survey data gives no evidence that corroborates this assumption. As Figure 8.3 shows, Arab Barometer polling results show that an average of nearly 75 percent of respondents across the region did not believe any religious leader should interfere with the decisions of voters during elections. In sum, while religion structures cultural and social life in obvious ways – by furnishing the beliefs, norms, and spiritual orientation of its adherents – there is no obvious conclusion to be made regarding

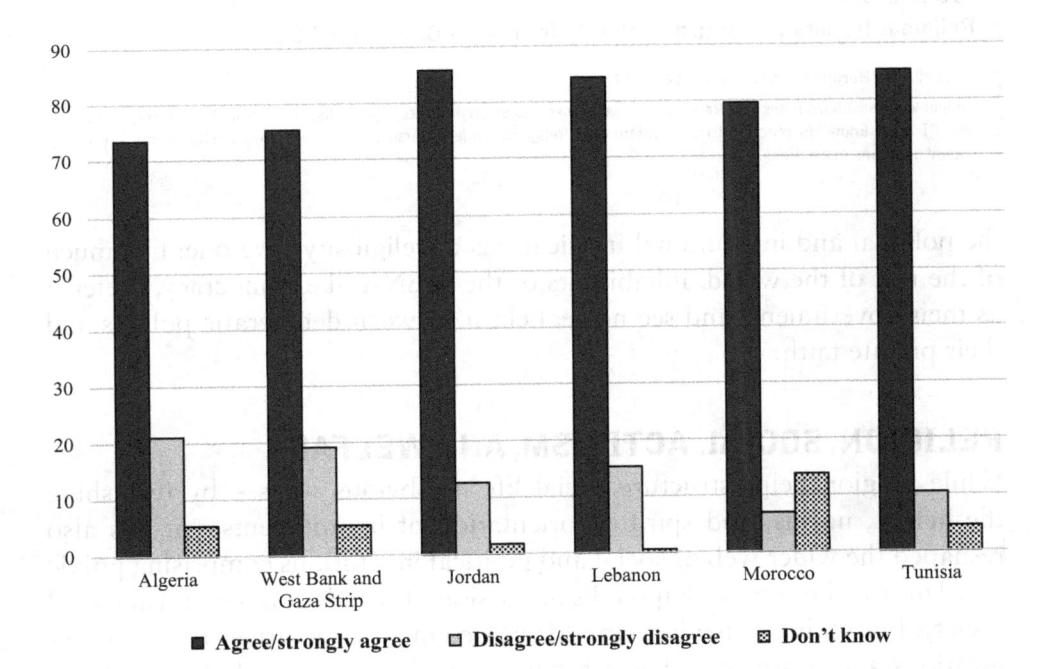

FIGURE 8.2
Preference for democracy from Arab Barometer, 2017.

Source: Arab Barometer, Wave IV (2016–2017).

Online: www.arabbarometer.org. Respondents were asked to strongly agree, agree, disagree, strongly disagree, or respond with "I don't know" in reaction to this statement: "A democratic system may have problems, yet it is better than other systems."

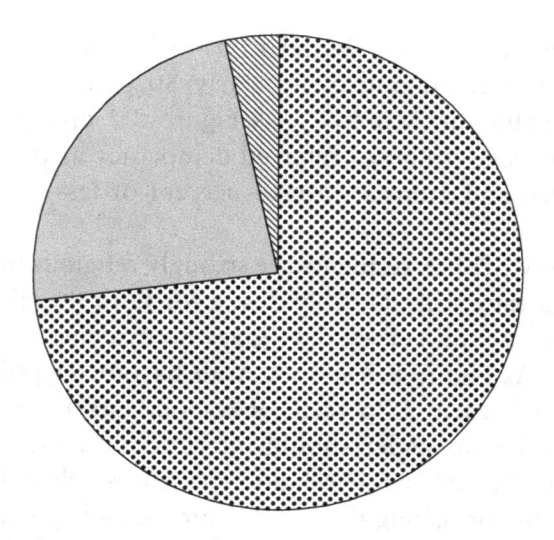

☐ **Agree/strongly agree** ☐ **Disagree/strongly disagree** ▨ **Don't know**

FIGURE 8.3
Religious leaders vs. political authority from Arab Barometer, 2017.

Source: Arab Barometer, Wave IV (2016–2017).

Online: www.arabbarometer.org. Respondents were asked to strongly agree, agree, disagree, strongly disagree, or respond with "I don't know" in reaction to this statement: "Religious leaders (imams, preachers, priests) should not interfere in voters' decisions in elections."

the political and institutional implications of religiosity save one: like much of the rest of the world, inhabitants of the MENA like democracy, prefer it as their government, and see no real clash between democratic politics and their private faith.

RELIGION, SOCIAL ACTIVISM, AND WELFARE

While religion helps structure social life in obvious ways – by furnishing the beliefs, norms, and spiritual orientation of its adherents – it has also reshaped the wider web of social and political institutions comprising public life. This touches upon Chapter 3's discussion of social mobilization and civil society, but with a twist: in many MENA countries, the driver of new organizations and movements has often been religiosity, and a desire to propagate one's creed. More interestingly, the method of attracting members has been to provide social welfare. In many MENA states, stagnant welfarist and social protections by governments suffering from economic burdens – particularly since the 1980s fiscal downturn, as Chapter 5's analysis of the regional economy noted – have led religious movements, particularly Islamists, to play a greater role in furnishing education, health care, and other public goods. In essence, they mobilize to take the place of the state by providing for the social needs of citizens. They adroitly combined three powerful aspects of modern religion: piety, services, and politics.

BOX 8.1 CASE STUDY – MUSLIM BROTHERHOOD OF EGYPT

Consider the Muslim Brotherhood. The Brotherhood was founded in 1928 in Egypt, and gradually expanded to or inspired similar Islamist groups in other Arab countries. Although observers know the organization today primarily as a politically minded organization, its rise to prominence reflects its success as a social provider as well. In Egypt, successive authoritarian regimes starting with Gamal Abdel Nasser in the 1950s began to deliver economic and social goods to the populace, such as universal education and public employment, as part of its political formula. However, financial troubles and the exhaustion of its economic model of state-led development forced the state to retrench these services and pull back from its duties starting in the 1970s. By the time of Hosni Mubarak's tenure from the 1980s onwards, the Egyptian state could no longer fulfill the housing, health care, employment, and educational needs of all citizens. Filling this vacuum was the Muslim Brotherhood, which had been legalized in the 1970s as a social charity. The Brotherhood and other religious organizations began to provide a parallel sector of welfarist services, with their own schools, hospitals, soup kitchens, employment centers, and other institutions. The availability of such public goods helped these Islamists mobilize new supporters to their cause, thereby enabling their growth by the eve of the Arab Spring as social networks with deep roots, especially in urban areas struggling with poverty and deprivation. In doing so, they employed ideas from the theological underpinnings of Islam. For instance, the concept of *waqf* (endowment) played a significant role in delivering charity and public goods. In Islamic law, social foundations managing *waqf* endowments underwrote the provision of new social services by providing common funds and religious assets. Islamists also described their social provisions as a form of *zakat* (almsgiving) and *sadaqa* (benevolence). Zakat is one of the five pillars of Islam, according to which Muslims should give some portion of their wealth to charitable causes. Sadaqa means voluntary giving, which is not enforced but strongly encouraged in religious teachings. The use and deployment of such concepts helped ensconce Egypt's Brotherhood – and later social movements that mimicked it, such as the Gülen movement in Turkey – into public life.

While Islamist movements are the best-known case in the MENA of religious organizations delivering social services and public goods, both for their charitable ends and as a tool of political mobilization, there are important variations. For example, in countries such as Lebanon or Iraq where sectarian divides characterize society, religious organizations do not to distribute benefits on equitable basis. In Lebanon, religious groups anchored in different sectarian communities implement social welfare strategies based on political considerations. The Future Movement, a Sunni Muslim group established and led by former Prime Minister Rafiq al-Hariri until his assassination in 2005, has distributed social services to both Sunnis and non-Sunni Muslims because it competed for state positions and needed to implement an inclusive political strategy to win as many voters and supporters as possible. Christian religious groups, on the other hand, have distributed social services to mostly Christians belonging to their particular communities, resulting in fierce competition amongst them. Hizbullah and Amal, the major Shi'a religious organizations and political parties, stand in the middle. Because they were able to resolve their rivalry after the 1980s, when they coalesced as resistance movements during the Lebanese Civil War, they distributed social services to non-Shi'a groups only when it was politically convenient.

Yet while the increasing role of religious organizations in providing social welfare has diminished the burden placed upon many governments, it also presents a unique threat to the authority and legitimacy of state power. In many cases, once their activities give them credibility and power, religious organizations extend their activities from social activism to political activism and become potential challengers, because they can now offer not simply a political message but an entire framework of well-being that attracts citizens who feel their governments have betrayed them. As a result, MENA governments have often sought to limit their power, as in the case of Islamists. For example, despite that Egypt under Mubarak allowed the Muslim Brotherhood to exist as a welfare provider and social charity, the government also prevented the group from founding a political party, and also regularly monitored and repressed its members. Similarly, the Turkish government took unprecedented measures to dismantle the network of social services institutions run by the Islamist Gülen movement when it became a political rival to the AK Party-led government after 2013. This general pattern is endemic, and sheds insight into the complicated role into religion as a form of social solidarity as well as political affiliation.

Islamism: a closer look
Beyond religiosity, which concerns the expression of faith, rituals, and values concordant with one's religious commitments within private and

public life, lays another question. Religion in the MENA region can also spark social and political mobilization, motivating peoples to congregate, express preferences, and demand change. While there are religiously inspired political parties and resistance movements across the world, nothing embodies this nexus more than the rise of Islamism. Islamism, also known as political Islam, must be differentiated from Islam. While Islam is a religion, Islamism is an ideology based on the premise that a fundamentalist interpretation of Islam should inform how society and politics is organized in modern times. While all Islamists are Muslim, most Muslims are not Islamists. Islamists instrumentalize religion in the pursuit of political objectives, for Islamist ideology requires the capture of political power in order to implement key ideas such as shari'a. Islamists also generally share an anti-Western stance and blame Western imperialism for many of the social, political, and economic ills found in the Middle East, and more widely in the Islamic world.

Islamism is a recent phenomenon. Islam originated in the seventh century, but Islamism emerged in late nineteenth century and only gained wide circulation in the closing decades of the twentieth century. The European colonization of Muslim lands in the nineteenth century, heralding the end of the Ottoman Empire – the last Islamic Caliphate – resulted in a period of theological and social debate among leading Muslim thinkers, such as Muhammad 'Abduh and Jamal al-Din al-Afghani. These progenitors of what would later become Islamist thought questioned why Islamic civilization has entered into a period of material and technological decline, and queried what Muslims could do in order to revitalize their societies. This wellspring of intellectual ferment, often produced through vibrant debate, eventually turned to several conclusions. Among them was that renewal could come from not just turning inwards to embrace greater piety and religious reflection at the personal level, but also an outward struggle against the economic and political structures that seemed to neglect the spiritual needs of Muslims. The pathway to salvation for many Islamists thus combined piety with politics: by winning state power, they could restore Muslims to an era of prosperity – a purer vision of Islamic life as inspired by the first centuries of Islam. The Muslim Brotherhood in Egypt was one of the first organized expressions of this new ideology. Linked to this belief system was the principle that such efforts required not only internal, reflective thought but also outward, external action to transform society at the everyday level. In doing so, they reinterpreted Islamic concepts and legal terms for a modern audience, among them the controversial term *jihad* – a word that generally means struggle on the pathway to God, and can be framed to have both peaceful and violent connotations depending upon its user.

Though initially suppressed, Islamists became increasingly popular in Muslim-majority societies after the 1970s. In the Arab world, their promise of emancipation rang louder than the secular ideology of Arab Nationalism and the promise of economic prosperity through the rentierist social contract. Many leaders of Muslim-majority MENA countries after World War Two fancied themselves as Muslims but also secularists, insofar as they did not believe Islam and Islamic law should structure the institutions of their burgeoning states. These included Mustafa Kemal Ataturk in Turkey, Reza Shah Pahlavi in Iran, Habib Bourguiba in Tunisia, Gamal Abdel Nasser in Egypt, and Houari Boumédiène in Algeria; all suppressed Islamist movements, which they saw as opposition threats to their newly emerging political systems. Islamism, then, was a peripheral ideology and religious movement during the 1940s through 1960s. The monarchies had a slightly more complicated relationship with religion. The Moroccan and Jordanian monarchies were afforded some inherent Islamic standing given these families' genealogical descent from the Prophet Muhammad, as was the Saudi monarchy's control over Mecca and Medina (the latter being the second holiest city in Islam). While these and the other monarchies in the Arabian Gulf never denied the centrality of Islam to their national identities, they also did not tolerate Islamist movements that explicitly challenged monarchical rule in favor of their own version of Islamic order.

In addition to domestic crises, international and geopolitical shocks also catapulted Islamists into the forefront of social and political mobilization after the 1970s. The Cold War era was defined by the competition of two Western ideologies, capitalism and communism. While most MENA governments clearly took sides with either with the US or the Soviet Union, Islamist organizations were critical of both. The establishment of the state of Israel in 1948 and its consequent conflicts with the Arab states also fueled Islamic movements. The question over Palestinian statehood, and widespread sympathy for the Palestinian national movement, gained more relevance after the 1967 Arab-Israeli War, which saw the loss of Jerusalem (Islam's third holiest city) by Jordan to Israel. This conflict signaled the death of Arab Nationalism, and helped rally more anti-Western sentiments among Islamists and their supporters. However, the most significant international event that boosted the rise of Islamism was the Iranian Revolution of 1979. In that episode, an unarmed and peaceful uprising deposed the three decades-long tenure of the Shah, who had grown notorious for both his strong pro-Western orientation and his secularizing tendencies. Though Iran is a largely Shi'a country, the toppling of an absolute monarchist in favor of a popular movement that later installed a theocratic Islamic Republic inspired Islamist activists everywhere. It showed not only that Western-backed dictatorships could be overthrown, but also that the dream of securing state power and then restructuring society, economy, and politics around Islamist ideals was a plausible achievement.

Violent extremism

Today, Islamism describes not a few organizations; it is best explained as an extremely wide spectrum of groups that may subscribe to its basic goals but employ vastly different means to achieve them. Most peaceful Islamists, such as the Brotherhood, rely upon a combination of social mobilization (through the provision of services), religious messaging, and political participation to attain their ideals. Some Islamists, however, reject this gradual pathway of peaceful change. They interpret not simply existing governments in the MENA and elsewhere as illegitimate, but the entire Westphalian order and state boundaries as artificial and un-Islamic, as they are Western impositions that are incompatible with the conception of a timeless and boundless *ummah* (community of believers). For the most radical of these groups, violence is necessary and justified to upend this system and liberate Muslim societies.

Although these groups stand in the minority, they have sowed chaos in the Middle East and beyond. Most Westerners only became acquainted with this violent trend with the terrorist attacks of September 11, 2001, in the US. The al-Qaeda militants who organized and staged those attacks hailed from the MENA. Their leader, Osama bin Laden, founded al-Qaeda as a global network after his experiences fighting as a volunteer in Afghanistan against the occupying Soviet Union in the 1980s. al-Qaeda emerged alongside other radical and extremist variants of Islamism, which each responded to the more unique conditions of their countries; these include al-Gamma' al-Islamiyya of Egypt and the Armed Islamic Group of Algeria, both of which were active during the 1990s in waging armed insurgencies. In recent times, the most infamous example is the Islamic State in Iraq and Syria (ISIS), which arose in 2014 and captured an enormous swathe of territory before being pushed back by 2018 due to the efforts of an international coalition.

As a subset of Islamism, these radical forces are known as Salafi organizations. The term *Salafi* generally refers to the most orthodox and extreme Sunni militant groups that seek not only to capture state power and install an Islamic-inspired order but also to return all of social life back to the ways of the *salaf* (ancestors), meaning the Prophet Muhammad and the first generation of Muslims. The legal, theological, and political innovations made by Islam since are to be discarded in favor of a stricter vision of piety and public life. To be sure, not all Salafis are violent; indeed, most Salafi Islamists in the world today are considered "quietist" insofar as using only peaceful means like education to achieve their aims. The relative handful that are violent, however, are far more visible given their lengthy list of terrorist attacks. Salafis blame not just the West, but fellow Muslims – including the monarchies and republics that govern the MENA today – as equally (if not more so) responsible for corrupting Islamic purity. In fact, while grisly carnage such as the 9/11 attacks are seared into the Western memory, the statistical reality is that the vast majority of all Islamist violence has targeted other Muslims, not Westerners.

Not all violent groups pursue a strategy of *global* violence, which al-Qaeda and to some degree ISIS declared. Hamas and Hizbullah, for example, have combined violent methods to achieve their political goals of liberating their national territories, and those methods coexist alongside other elements of their organizations, such as social service provision and religious activities. Hamas, which was established in 1987, considers Israeli settlements and claims within Palestinian territories as an occupation and aims to end that occupation. The reasons for their rise to prominence are not much different than the rise of Islamism globally. Hamas's success, for instance, is partly due to the failure of its secular counterpart, the Fatah political organization that has dominated the Palestinian Authority, in implementing the Oslo peace process, as well as Hamas's vast network of charities and schools. Similarly, Hizbullah was first formed in 1985 to end the Israeli occupation of southern Lebanon, which is mostly populated by Shi'a. While well known for its large number of militants and fighters, Hizbullah also developed as a social service provider and later on a political party, albeit one squarely aimed at governing Lebanon rather than expanding into other countries. Its deployment of fighters in the Syrian civil war in support of the al-Asad regime reflects Shi'a solidarity, strategic interests, and Iranian involvement; but it does not signal that Hizbullah desires to rule Syria.

There are many reasons why such extremism has arisen in the MENA. Purely religious explanations suggest that these groups are able to manipulate religious texts, such as the Qur'an, to inspire followers. For instance, they not only reinterpret jihad to mean holy war against everyone who stands in their path, Muslim and non-Muslim alike, but also insist that jihad is the sixth pillar of Islam. Indoctrination, brainwashing, and other psychological explanations suggest that the radical (and sometimes, fanatical) emphasis on such religious simplification allows extremists to induce followers to commit violence, including suicide bombings. Economic explanations, however, suggest deprivation and injustice as reasons for extremism. High levels of unemployment, social inequality, and lack of material resources create a suitable environment for these organizations to recruit militants.

Other explanations, however, focus upon politics and institutional factors. Observers note that in places such as Afghanistan, Iraq, and Syria, extremism flourishes only when instability weakens the rule of law and basic security. Iraq became a safe haven for violent extremists after 2003, once the Iraqi state apparatus collapsed with the US-led invasion. Disbanding the Iraqi army before a credible alternative was put in place resulted in a bloody insurgency, some of which was inspired by Islamist ideals. Indeed, the Iraqi insurgency produced the first cell of militants who, in collaboration with former Iraqi army officers, helped found ISIS. Extremist organizations also capitalize on the presence of foreign troops in recruiting militants, since occupation makes for an easy rallying cry.

CASE STUDIES: ISLAM AND SOCIAL FORCES

By focusing upon the dynamics of Islam and Islamism in four MENA countries, we can better understand the complex intersection of religion, society, and politics. These case studies give us a close-range, detailed view about the similarities and contrasts that typify the Islamic experience across the Middle East.

Egypt

The Egyptian Muslim Brotherhood started as a grass-roots movement in 1928, when a high school teacher, Hasan al-Banna, established the organization. One major impetus was social hostilities against the British, who retained significant privileges in the country despite Egypt's formal independence. The Egyptian monarchy worked with British foreign officials in ruling the country, despite the presence of a competitively elected parliament. Al-Banna considered his organization as a religious revivalist movement, intending to preach Islamic precepts and raise religious consciousness among the Egyptian people.

The genesis of the Brotherhood was a microcosm embodying the wider role of colonization and imperialism in spearheading new Islamist movements across the MENA region. Many observers note that it did not take formal occupations to stir feelings of anger and oppression amongst Muslim societies. For instance, Christian missionaries may have inadvertently stoked the rise of groups like the Brotherhood, and well into the twentieth century the weakness of political authority meant that missionary organizations often clashed with local communities in the education of young children in countries like Egypt. Whatever the cause, the rise of the Brotherhood heralded the resistance of local people as they mobilized around a religious, and perhaps, nationalistic goal. A different version of Egyptian nationalism, inflected by the competing and more popular ideology of Arab Nationalism, resulted in the military coup that deposed the monarchy in 1952 – a political revolution that the Brotherhood backed, as it served their interests as well.

However, once the new regime consolidated under Gamal Abdel Nasser years later, its relationship with the Brotherhood became adversarial. As Nasser increased his power and repute through policies such as nationalizing the Suez Canal, Egypt's political system transformed into an a single-party arrangement that gave Nasser and his party apparatus deep control over the economy and civil society. Major institutions of Islamic authority became co-opted and absorbed into the government, thereby depriving the Muslim Brotherhood from capturing these institutions' symbolic discourse. One major example was Al-Azhar University, Egypt's (and indeed, one of the world's) oldest degree-granting educational institutions, having been founded in the tenth century (Photo 8.3). Al-Azhar's faculty and leadership were de facto voices of Sunni Islamic knowledge and authority, and by essentially turning the university into a state-run institution, the Egyptian state was able to control the language of "official" Islam.

As an independent social movement, the Brotherhood was a threat; this resulted in the imprisonment and killings of many of its members, including ideologues like Sayyid Qutb. While in prison, Sayyid Qutb, who once supported Nasser, wrote his most radical political opinions. His writings, as well as the mass suppression that the movement faced, radicalized the Muslim Brotherhood's discourse and turned the organization more militant. Qutb was among the most visible Islamist thinkers in the twentieth century who were willing to reinterpret classical Islamic concepts. He called for the excommunication of other Muslim leaders who worked with Western governments, for instance, and described Egypt and its people as under the veil of *jahiliyya*, an old term meaning ignorance and which refers to the pre-Islamic age. By suggesting that Muslims had reverted back to this stage of

PHOTO 8.3
Inside Al-Azhar University of Cairo, Egypt, 2014.

Source: Public domain.
Online: https://pixabay.com/en/egypt-country-university-al-azhar-3574221/

barbarism, Qutb paved the way for Islamists to see themselves on a path to salvation – to rescue their fellow Muslims, which necessitated jihad.

Despite its repression, the Brotherhood continued to mobilize underground and attracted many new members, including Egyptians from the new middle classes in urban areas who were becoming disenchanted with the authoritarian bargain inherent to political life under Nasser. Their religious message and symbolism struck a moral chord with these adherents, who sought a vision of political order far different than the one offered by the existing system. The turning point came in the 1970s under President Anwar Sadat, who succeeded Nasser following his death in 1970. Sadat adopted a new policy of toleration, allowing the Brothers to openly operate and freeing many Islamist political prisoners. In response, most of the Brotherhood's leaders renounced Qutb's militant vision of jihad and ensured the group maintained a moderate and peaceful path; in return, Sadat allowed them to deepen the Brotherhood's roots in civil society through the creation of charitable organizations, social service providers, and other new functions. However, some fringe groups within the organization separated from the mainstream Brotherhood as they favored the more radical path, and authored violent extremist groups such as Islamic Jihad. One of its members later assassinated Sadat in 1981, partly in response to his groundbreaking peace treaty with Israel several years earlier.

Hosni Mubarak became President afterwards. He continued to maintain a highly centralized regime, with authority concentrated in the presidency and the ruling National Democratic Party. Mubarak was pragmatic; his main concern was to survive without necessarily sticking to an ideology, shifting from the past eras of Arab Nationalism. Mubarak ruled with a combination of repression and toleration; elections were rare, and when held extremely uncompetitive given his party's domination and the suppression of opposition. The Muslim Brotherhood expanded more into politics during the Mubarak era despite obstacles in getting representation in the political field. Mubarak's pragmatic policy of selective accommodation actually helped it organize in society. Most Islamists continued to operate charitable foundations, educational institutions, hospitals and clinics, and other civic entities – but not form political parties, forcing the Brotherhood to field candidates in parliamentary elections as independents. Their popularity grew in professional associations and across many urban neighborhoods, and in 2005 their independent candidates secured 88 out of 454 seats in the legislative elections, thereby becoming the largest opposition bloc in Egypt's highly divided and marginalized parliament.

When the Arab Spring brought revolution to Egypt in January and February 2011, the Muslim Brotherhood remained the strongest and largest opposition movement thanks to its past decades of mobilizing, activating, serving, and preaching within society. It did not, however, openly back the revolution, which was led instead by youth activists and new groups. Still, they reaped the benefits of political change. They not only secured a plurality in the first post-revolutionary parliamentary elections, but also won the Egyptian presidency in the June 2012 presidential elections – the first such democratic contest in the country's modern history. The Brotherhood-led government struggled under the economic and social challenges of an Egyptian society in flux, however, and soon a counter-swell of anti-Islamist opinions coalesced in secularist parts of society that had also distrusted the Brotherhood. The military coup of July 2013 restored authoritarianism in Egypt, but also decapitated the Brotherhood by imprisoning its leaders and banning the organization outright in a return to Nasserist policies.

What can we learn from this historical trajectory? In Egypt, the rise of Islamism through the Brotherhood reflected not just state policies to religion but also social factors, including the need of many people for religiosity as well as a political blueprint to a better system of government. The Egyptian case also suggests that there will always be strong parts of society that do *not* believe that a government issuing religious dictates is appropriate; the July 2013 military coup and subsequent crackdown against the Brotherhood was notably backed by many Egyptians who had protested two years earlier in Tahrir Square against Mubarak. Thus, the presence of Islamism does not in any way foreshadow the *success* of Islamism, even through social service provisions and well-crafted political messages. Like all religious movements, Islamists operate in a social environment filled with competitors, constraints, and sometimes coercion.

Turkey

State institutions largely shaped the mobilization of Islam and religiosity in modern Turkey, which was established in 1923 as the successor republic to the collapsed Ottoman Empire. Shortly after its founding, the new republic created a Directorate of Religious Affairs, which allowed the government to monitor religious discourse (such as the sermons given in mosques) and more broadly define what it meant to be Muslim. Early on, the Turkish government criminalized all non-state religious organizations, including Islamic schools run by independent groups and other Muslim orders, institutions, and movements. Between 1925 and 1928, the state banned traditional religious garments for men, replaced the Arabic script with Latin script, replaced Ottoman-era *shari'a* laws with civil and criminal codes imported from Switzerland, Germany, and Italy, and finally replaced the Islamic calendar with the Western (Gregorian) one. Public displays of Islamic religiosity, such as women wearing the *hijab* (headscarf), were heavily discouraged, although this was not clear whether this empowered or subordinated women: as Chapter 9's treatment of personal dress and gender roles indicates, some pious women see the hijab as empowering whereas others see it as stifling. Regardless, in the pursuit of Western-style secularism which many saw as necessary for modernization and industrialization, the Turkish government aimed to banish Islam into the private lives of the people.

After Turkey's transition to multiparty democracy in 1950, the government relaxed its suppression, and the right-wing parties that came to power implemented more tolerant policies toward Islam. Though political mobilization around Islam was still illegal, authorities allowed for the introduction of religious radio broadcasts, voluntary Islamic courses in primary schools, and new educational institutions to train Muslim prayer leaders (known as *imams*) who led sermons in mosques. In 1970, the first Islamic-oriented political party, the National Order, was established. The 1980 military coup constituted the real turning point for Islamist mobilization, however, as the new government saw Islamists as a useful political tool to balance its primary threat – communism. Subsequently, authorities gradually allowed for more expressions of Islamic piety in the public sphere. The right-wing political parties that ruled the country after the military regime, tolerated, even encouraged, Islamic elements in the public sphere. Liberalizing economic policies allowed peripheral religious forces to be more influential in public debates. Islamist groups became increasingly active, though still cautious given existing political and legal barriers to openly creating religious parties or calling for the Islamization of the Turkish state – a position that was strictly anathema to the secular conception of the Turkish republic.

When an Islamist politician managed to become prime minister in 1997 through a complex coalitional government, the military intervened in politics and again purged Islamists from the ranks of government. This pendulum swing back renewed the impetus for secularism and resulted in strict limitations over religiously inspired social and political organizations. The Council of Higher Education increased its control over universities and strictly banned the wearing of the Islamic headscarf in universities. This led to a divide among Islamists; some reformists desiring more political engagement rather than retreating underground formed the Justice and Development Party (AKP), which declared its allegiance to democracy and pledged to turn away from the Islamist model. The AKP would consistently win elections starting in 2002, and today remains the dominant political party in Turkey. Over time, however, a number of Islamist elements crept into the Turkish mainstream. Under its leader, Recep Tayyip Erdogan, restrictions against Islamic expression and mobilization were relaxed, while the AK Party itself began to expand its powers and nudge Turkey towards a more authoritarian system. Yet many conservatives in Turkish society, including those who had felt alienated under previous years of state-imposed secularism, have continued to staunchly back President Erdogan and the AK Party's unique and still-evolving platform of Islamism.

These historical legacies have resulted in a unique type of Islamic diversity in Turkish society, much of it not so much Islamist (and thus political) as it is purely social or cultural. Apart from Islamism and the Turkish government's own version of official Islam, there are also Sufi movements with particularly charismatic religious leaders. Sufis are widespread across the country but are relatively closed to outsiders and organize as tightly knitted groups. Alevis also constitute about 15–20 percent of the Turkish population, but have suffered much discrimination. In recent years, Alevi foundations have lobbied the government to recognize Alevism as a coherent and official faith, but many – including fellow Alevi groups – see such state intervention into religious identification and faith-based identity as unacceptable. Finally, there are also collectives and communities (in Turkish, *cemaat*) that, as social movements, attempt to provide their own education, welfare, and other services to their religious adherents. One such cemaat that has become well known is the Gülen movement, which emerged in the 1980s. Followers of the Gülen movement (named after its prominent leader) became active in media, education, and politics afterwards; they allied themselves with the AK Party, only to see this collaboration crumble by the early 2010s. The AK Party blames the Gülen movement as the instigator for the July 2016 military coup, for instance, and today the group remains criminalized.

Iran

Iran (traditionally known as Persia) has a different experience of religious mobilization. Iran today resembles a theocracy guided by a Shi'a clergy – not like Turkey, which remains a multiparty democracy with a complex relationship to Sunni Islam. Iran's predominant faith has been Shi'a Islam since 1501, when the Safavid dynasty began ruling Persia; the resulting Safavid Empire formed a unique countering identity to the Sunni Ottoman Empire to its west. The relationship between Islam and society is complex. In the twentieth century, mass mobilizations played a significant role in reshaping social relations starting with the 1906 Constitutional Revolution, which forced the post-Safavid rulership, the Qajar dynasty, to accede to more democracy including an elected parliament. Pro-democracy protests also punctuated Iran's development during World War Two and the early 1950s. Though Persians held their faith close to their personal identity, and religious figures (including Shi'a clerics) participated in these moments of contention, it would be a mistake to call them *religious* uprisings simply because its participants were Muslim – in the same way that any rebellion or protest in a Christian country would be called religious events, simply because its participants were Christian.

The Iranian Revolution tore down the last monarchy of Persia, the House of Pahlavi, in 1979, and with it exposed a fundamental shift in the

Iranian conception of Shi'a Islam and religion in society. For centuries earlier, Shi'a Islam in Persia generally disengaged from politics given the theological notion of the "Greater Occultation" – a concept holding that until the 12th and final successor to the Prophet Muhammad appeared on earth, Muslims should generally not come into political conflicts. Unlike Sunni Islam, Shi'a doctrine also placed importance on the authority of jurists and scholars of religion, who came to command considerable social influence by virtue of their popular standing and sheer knowledge of Shi'a Islam. Yet despite their occasional leanings into politics, Shi'a clerics generally did not conceive of themselves as rulers; nor did they consider conventional doctrine to offer the basis for the creation of a new Islamic state. However, the Iranian Revolution was partly led by well-known Shi'a clerical figures such as the Ayatollah Ruhollah Khomeini, who presented a novel twist on religious doctrine by suggesting that religious figures were actually best positioned to act as political rulers – because only they could ensure that a society abided by the content of Islamic teachings. This interpretation of rulership as filtered through Khomeini represented a Shi'a corollary to the Sunni Islamism of the Brotherhood and other organizations elsewhere in the MENA.

Religion, thus, was inverted: rather than being the target of state control, now sacred inspirations became the source for an entirely new political system, one enshrined in what is now the Islamic Republic of Iran. Such a system does allow for representative institutions through which people elect a president and deputies of the parliament; but it also holds as supreme decision-makers powerful religious councils composed of Shi'a clergy who would act as guardians over the entire political order, and monitor whether legislative and executive decisions conformed with religious demands. Thus, Iran has both an elected president with some policymaking power as well as a Supreme Leader, the latter of whom hails from the Shi'a clerical establishment and theoretically can intervene at any moment to change the course of the country. Post-revolutionary impositions of religion also resulted in dramatic changes in social relations and life – from the status of women and appropriate dress, to the operation of banks and schools, and even to the very nature of private interactions. Whereas the Pahlavi monarchical era from 1925 to 1979 was generally marked by some degree of secular lifestyles in large cities like Tehran, the period after reconfigured public spaces in accordance with a far more orthodox view of Islam. In essence, this meant more restrictions.

Yet Iran shows that, like religion elsewhere, Shi'a doctrine is a matter of contestation and interpretation among its believers. There have been many episodes of political rebellion and social uprising since the 1980s, launched by Iranians who saw no incompatibility between their religious creeds and resistance to authority. One example was the 2009 Green Movement, which protested rigged presidential elections that saw the reelection of very conservative politician Mahmoud Ahmadinejad. Much of this movement was even led, and thus legitimated, by Shi'a religious elites who argued that the most just guardians of an Islamic state would heed the frustrations of its Muslim citizens. Indeed, the depth of Shi'a doctrine has seeded a new generation of jurists and intellectuals willing to criticize Iranian theocracy today by arguing that precisely by entering into the political arena, religious authorities have unwittingly corrupted themselves with material ends.

In terms of public attitudes, opinion polls show that Iranian views on religion and religiosity are likewise becoming more pluralistic and flexible. As Table 8.2 showed, despite living in a theocratic state, Iranians are no more religious than citizens of other MENA countries; 20.3 percent reported attending religious services (e.g., going to mosque) more than once a week – significantly less than Egypt (31 percent) or Morocco (84.5 percent). Likewise, as Table 8.3 illustrated, 78.2 percent of Iranians consider religion as "very important" to their lives; this is a considerable figure, but less than Iraq (95.6 percent), Jordan (94.4 percent), and Egypt (95.4 percent). In sum, then, Iran presents a fascinating case of religion as both the basis of political organization but also a modern framework of social mobilization against the very authority generated by its doctrine.

Saudi Arabia

Religion plays a significant role in Saudi Arabia's social fabric and state institutions. Saudi Arabia is an absolutist monarchy, lacking an elected parliament and other organs of political participation at the national level. This monarchy, the House of Saud, considers Islam as an integral part of its worldview: the kingdom contains Mecca and Medina, making this dynasty the worldwide custodians of these two holy places. Yet unlike Iran, this is no theocracy: political power is wielded and directed by a non-religious entity – a royal family – that regularly consults with Islamic voices, but never needs to subordinate to their derivation of power from social obeisance, oil wealth, and Western support.

The form of Sunni Islam that infuses the social fabric of the country is Wahhabism, a puritan form which can be conceived as a distant branch of today's Islamism and overlaps heavily with contemporary forms of Salafism. Yet it stretches back for centuries. Wahhabism emerged from central Arabia in the mid-eighteenth century by its founder, Muhammad ibn al-Wahhab, whose extremely conservative interpretation of Islam wished to purify Muslim life from virtually all cultural and political innovations that had occurred since the death of the Prophet. This meant profound hostility against the Shi'a, who were seen as straying from Islam given their veneration for Ali and divergent doctrine. It also meant vilification of even small-scale acts – carrying amulets, for instance, to superstitiously ward off evil – which were seen as corrupting the austere and literal message of the Qur'an. Wahhabism demands instead full submission to God and a host of other orthodox social requirements, among them strict gender segregation, female veiling, the banning of music, and mandatory religious performance.

Al-Wahhab formed a pact with the progenitor of the Saudi dynasty, Muhammad ibn Al-Saud, in which the latter pledged to propagate this puritan interpretation in return for the former's legitimation and backing of Al-Saud's political question to establish a new state. That alliance remains intact today, and with it the dissemination of Wahhabi ideals throughout Saudi society. Wahhabi jurists and scholars do not hold the same type of hierocratic power as Shi'a clerics do in Iran, but they nonetheless are sought for consultation and validation by Saudi kings. Public schools both practice Wahhabi norms (such as gender segregation) while expressing religious content and teachings. Until late 2018, the ban against women driving also came from Wahhabi teachings. Social relations in the private realm are somewhat free, but in public they must adapt to purist views: women, for instance, face heavy restrictions regarding interactions with men who are not from their family.

However, the fusion of Wahhabism with Saudi Arabia's national identity has repeatedly run into social challenges given the pluralism inherent in the country's population. Even after the establishment of the modern Saudi kingdom in 1930, many Muslims – including, ironically, those living in the Hijaz, the western region holding Mecca and Medina – struggled to embrace Wahhabism because they practiced more liberal and flexible interpretations of Sunni Islam. Moreover, Saudi Arabia has millions of Shi'a living in the eastern provinces, who face significant social and political marginalization yet have refused to convert to Wahhabism. Third, the state's promotion of religion to justify its own rule has paradoxically engendered opposition from religion, including those whose own interpretations of Islam clashed with the Wahhabi-Saudi alliance. This has occurred periodically throughout the kingdom's history, from the Ikhwan warriors of the 1920s to today's Sahwa movement, which models itself after the Muslim Brotherhood. (Indeed, Wahhabism and the Muslim Brotherhood have long been at odds, revealing a critical division within Islamist ideologies.) Even al-Qaeda falls into this category; it trafficked in Salafist ideology to legitimate its jihad; it targeted first and foremost the Saudi monarchy and state for its perceived transgressions against Islam, including the allowance of US troops to operate inside the kingdom during the 1990–1991 Gulf War.

CONCLUSION

This chapter examined the influence of religion in the social life and political dynamics of the MENA. The religious landscape of the region shows a predominance of Islam, but also startling variety both within Muslim societies as well as outside their boundaries of faith. Christian, Jewish, and other religious minorities express the diversity of the region. It also investigated the nature of religiosity, the social activism of religious groups, the rise of Islamism, and the variegated experiences of four country case studies (Egypt, Turkey, Iran, Saudi Arabia). In doing so, it provides insights about the role of religion. First, it shows that while the Middle East is usually affiliated with Islam, there are other religious groups who call the Middle East home, not to mention that the majority of all Muslims live outside the region; thus, in statistical terms, while the average Middle Easterner is likely to be Muslim, the average Muslim worldwide is not likely to be Middle Eastern. Second, the provision of public goods such as education, welfare, and other protections seems to be central to the spread of religious mobilization and greater religiosity in many countries, if the rise of Islamism is any indication. Whereas Westerners often see religion from the perspective of grounded secularism, in which religious practices and values begin from the private realm and then trickle outwards to the public sphere as a matter of politics or necessity, in other places religion begins from a platform of public articulation, and then penetrates private lives through the leveraging of social activism. Third and finally, while Islam occupies a central place in any discussion of religion and religiosity in the MENA, Islam itself – and for that matter, Islamism – is no monolith. It hosts an astonishing spectrum of differentiated groups and doctrines, some bound by acute commitments to timeless beliefs and truths and others enmeshed in modern debate and contestation.

QUESTIONS FOR DISCUSSION

1 What are the core beliefs of Islam, and what are its primary internal divisions in terms of doctrines and sects?

2 How have non-Muslim minorities fared across the region in historical perspective?
3 Why do nation-states that draw upon religion for their political discourse, from Israel to Saudi Arabia, often struggle dealing with religious pluralism and diversity within their societies?
4 Why would the provision of social services make any religious movement more popular or relevant to society? What kinds of services matter to public audiences?
5 How is Islamism different from Islam? Why is this distinction important in social and political analyses?
6 What accounts for the rise of radical Islamist groups that employ violence in pursuit of their goals?
7 Juxtapose Turkey with its secular heritage with Iran and its post-revolutionary theocratic trajectory. Why does the former feature Islamists aiming to recapture public spaces from secularism, while the latter is the inverse – state-mandated religious spaces losing the commitments of disenchanted citizens?
8 Now, compare Egypt and Saudi Arabia. Both are Sunni Muslim-majority countries, and yet both have very different doctrines of Islamic orientation in their cultural and social life. What accounts for this divergence?

FURTHER READING

There are excellent surveys available on the historical evolution of religion in the Middle East. Two leading books are Marshall G.S. Hodgson's three volume *The Venture of Islam* (Chicago, IL: University of Chicago Press, 1977) and Ira Lapidus's *A History of Islamic Societies*, 3rd ed. (Cambridge: Cambridge University Press, 2014). For studies that focus on religion and politics from a historical perspective, see L. Carl Brown, *Religion and State: The Muslim Approach to Politics* (New York: Colombia University Press, 2000); Michael Cook, *Ancient Religions, Modern Politics: The Islamic Case in Comparative Perspective* (Princeton, NJ: Princeton University Press, 2014); Mansoor Moaddel, *Islamic Modernism, Nationalism, and Fundamentalism: Episode and Discourse* (Chicago: University of Chicago Press, 2005); and John Esposito's *Islam: The Straight Path*, 5th ed. (Oxford: Oxford University Press, 2016). Bruce Lawrence, *Shattering the Myth: Islam beyond Violence* (Princeton, NJ: Princeton University Press, 1998), offers a rigorous investigation of Islam's doctrinal and popular evolution.

Beyond Islam, Bruce Masters' *Christians and Jews in the Ottoman Arab World: The Roots of Sectarianism* (Cambridge: Cambridge University Press, 2004) examines the evolution of Christian and Jewish identities in the Ottoman Empire and in the post-Ottoman world, while Heather Sharkey, *A History of Muslims, Christians, and Jews in the Middle East* (Cambridge: Cambridge University Press, 2017) looks at the cultural syncretism between these three Abrahamic faiths in the pre-Ottoman era. There are also many specialized readers into the various non-Muslim minorities discussed in this chapter; one example focusing on Coptic Christians is Laure Guirguis's *Copts and the Security State: Violence, Coercion, and Sectarianism in Contemporary Egypt* (Stanford, CA: Stanford University Press, 2016).

The following studies provide a rigorous overview of religious mobilization and its relationship to the state. Robert Lee's *Religion and Politics in the Middle East: Identity, Ideology, Institutions, and Attitudes*, 2nd ed. (London: Routledge, 2013) compares Egypt, Israel, Turkey, Iran, and Saudi Arabia in terms of state-religion relations. Mohammad Ayoob's *The Many Faces of Political Islam: Religion and Politics in the Muslim World* (Ann Arbor, MI: University of Michigan Press, 2008) shows different permutations of the state-religion duality in the Middle East and beyond. Furthermore, the following three works are excellent to make sense of the rise of Islamism since the 1950s: R. Hrair Dekmejian, *Islam in Revolution: Fundamentalism in the Arab World*, 2nd ed. (Syracuse: Syracuse University Press, 1994); Olivier Roy, *The Failure of Political Islam*, trans. Carol Volk (Cambridge, MA: Harvard University Press, 1999); John M. Owen IV, *Confronting Political Islam: Six Lessons from the West's Past* (Princeton, NJ: Princeton University Press, 2015); and Quinn Mecham, *Institutional Origins of Islamist Political Mobilization* (New York: Cambridge University Press, 2017). Excellent excerpts from key Islamist thinkers, such as Sayyid Qutb, can be found in Roxanne Euben and Muhammad Qasim Zaman, eds., *Princeton Readings in Islamist Thought: Texts and Contexts from Al-Banna to Bin Laden* (Princeton, NJ: Princeton University Press, 2009). Qutb's life is also explored in John Calvert, in *Sayyid Qutb and the Origins of Radical Islamism* (New York: Columbia University Press, 2010).

Radical Islamism, including jihadism, has elicited a large literature. Among the best overviews of the rise of violent Islamist groups are Michael Doran, "The Pragmatic Fanaticism of al-Qaeda: An Anatomy of Extremism in Middle Eastern Politics," *Political Science Quarterly* 117, no. 2 (2002): 177–90; Jessica Stern, *Terror in the Name of God: Why Religious Militants Kill* (New York: Ecco, 2003); Fawaz Gerges, *The Far Enemy: Why Jihad Went Global* (New York: Cambridge University Press, 2009); Omar Ashour, *The De-Radicalization of Jihadists: Transforming Armed Islamist Movements* (London: Routledge, 2009); and Gilles Kepel, *Terror in France: The Rise of Jihad in the West* (Princeton, NJ: Princeton University Press, 2017). More recent works on ISIS include William McCants, *The ISIS Apocalypse: The History, Strategy, and Doomsday Vision of the Islamic State* (New York: Picador/St. Martin's, 2016); Fawaz Gerges's *ISIS: A History* (Princeton, NJ: Princeton University Press, 2017); and Olivier Roy, *Jihad and Death: The Global Appeal of the Islamic State* (London: Hurst, 2017).

There has been an increase in the books on religion and social welfare in the Middle East and North Africa as of late. Beth Baron's *The Orphan Scandal: Christian Missionaries and the Rise of Muslim Brotherhood* (Palo Alto, CA: Stanford University Press, 2014) demonstrates how the Islamist associations developed social and educational programs for the orphan in reaction to the influx of missionaries under the British influence in the 1930s. Melani Cammett, *Compassionate Communalism: Welfare and Sectarianism in Lebanon* (Ithaca, NY: Cornell University Press, 2014), examines sectarianism and distribution of welfare benefits in Lebanon. Janine A. Clark, in *Islam, Charity, and Activism: Middle-Class Networks and Social Welfare in Egypt, Jordan, and Yemen* (Bloomington, IN: Indiana University Press, 2004), shows the role of Islamic social institutions in strengthening social networks that bind middle-class professionals, volunteers, and clients in Egypt, Jordan, and Yemen. In a recent book, *Generating Generosity in Catholicism and Islam: Beliefs, Institutions, and Public Goods Provision* (New York: Cambridge University Press, 2018), authors Carolyn Warner, Ramazan Kılınç, Christopher Hale, and Adam Cohen compare public goods provision among Catholics and Muslims.

The case studies explored in this chapter also all stand on a large scholarship. Ahmet Kuru and Alfred Stepan's edited volume, *Democracy, Islam, and Secularism in Turkey* (New York: Columbia University Press, 2012) and Jeremy Walton's *Muslim Civil Society and the Politics of Religious Freedom in Turkey* (New York: Oxford University Press, 2017) explore the role of religion in politics and society in Turkey. Carrie Rosefsky Wickham, in *The Muslim Brotherhood: Evolution of an Islamist Movement* (Princeton, NJ: Princeton University Press, 2013) analyzes the evolution of the Muslim Brotherhood in Egypt since the Nasserist era. Naser Ghobadzadeh's *Religious Secularity: A Theological Challenge to the Islamic State* (New York: Oxford University Press, 2017) surveys the religion-based opposition to the Iranian theocracy, challenging the religious-secular bifurcation in the Middle East. Finally, Mohammed Ayoob and Hasan Kosebalaban's *Religion and Politics in Saudi Arabia: Wahhabism and the State* (Boulder, CO: Lynne Rienner, 2008) unpacks Wahhabism's role in shaping Saudi Arabia's culture and societal structures.

Online sources

The US Department of State's annual *International Religious Freedom Reports* provide rich data on state policies toward religions in the Middle East (www.state.gov/j/drl/irf/) as well as it does globally. Likewise, the Pew Forum on Religion and Public Life provides excellent surveys about religion worldwide including the MENA (www.pewforum.org/). The Pew-Templeton Global Religious Futures Project likewise offers systematic information on religious demography and projections in the region (www.globalreligiousfutures.org/regions/middle-east-north-africa).

The two surveys mentioned in this chapter are the World Values Survey, which offers significant information about religious attitudes in MENA countries along with global data (www.worldvaluessurvey.org), and the Arab Barometer (www.arabbarometer.org/), which presents a plethora of interesting data on religious values and preferences in the region since the mid-2000s. Finally, the Brookings Institution's various reports on Islamist movements and groups are extremely insightful (www.brookings.edu/topic/islamist-movements/).

CHAPTER 9

Women and gender

Lindsay J. Benstead

THE RUNDOWN: KEY TOPICS COVERED
- Gender gap
- Private sphere
- Public sphere
- Political representation
- Economic participation
- Patriarchy

INTRODUCTION

Women and gender in the Middle East and North Africa (MENA) are frequently misunderstood. In a region often seen as monolithic, Muslim and Arab women are stereotyped, even by the most educated observers, as absent from education and political life and lacking rights and agency (e.g., the #traditionallysubmissive campaign after British Prime Minister David Cameron referred to Muslim women as traditionally submissive). However, women in the MENA region have diverse experiences across countries, socioeconomic statuses, and the urban-rural divide. Arab and Muslim women act with agency, both individually as they struggle against poverty and insecurity caused by war and occupation, as well as collectively as they oppose patriarchal laws and social norms. So too do individuals and groups for whom conceptions of sexuality run against their cultural grain, challenging not just mainstream values but also the institutional structures of social classification. Israel likewise stands as an exception to regional trends; for a variety of historical and social reasons, the country features more gender-equal political, economic, and cultural structures than other MENA countries.

This chapter interrogates issues of gender in the MENA region. It seeks to explain both the poor performance of the MENA region relative to other world regions, as well as variation across countries. The Arab world will be the primary focal point – not because women, gender, and sexuality are unimportant topics in Israel, Turkey, and Iran, but because we are fortunate to have collected reliable data on the various constraints and opportunities that characterize such topics in Muslim-majority Arab countries. First, the chapter examines gendered cultural practices and women's dress, which is inflected by politics, religion, colonialism, and nationalism in an economically diverse region. Second, it defines patriarchy, with attention to classic and modern approaches, and to its private and public components. Third, it examines negative and positive trends in women's status in the MENA region, highlighting both formidable obstacles, as well as recent successes in the fight for gender equality; women face patriarchal laws and norms, but are increasingly represented in education, the labor force, and government. It also addresses new movements for Lesbian, Gay, Bisexual, Transgender, and Queer/Questioning (LGBTQ) equality, while dispelling the myth that the electoral success of some Islamist movements after the Arab Spring resulted in an Arab winter for women. Fourth, it discusses scholarly approaches to measuring gender inequality. Finally, it explores theoretical approaches to explaining patriarchy within and across countries, returning to the question of how individuals facing challenges find ways to overcome them.

STARTING POINT: THE GLOBAL GENDER GAP INDEX

Before presenting the main sections beginning with women's status, let us set a broad global framework that puts the MENA in comparative perspective. Women's rights movements in the Arab world are neither remnants of colonialism nor the outgrowth of Western influence; they are meaningful expressions of the search for voice and dignity that characterize so many other social forces. Without apologetics, the reality is that women in the MENA region *do* face steep obstacles and harsh inequality, especially when it comes to family law, which, in most Arab countries, is based on conservative interpretations of *shari'a* codified centuries ago. While those conservative laws are contested and have been reformed in several countries, notably in Tunisia and Morocco, traditionalists oppose reform even as secular and Islamic feminists advocate equality, often working together in common cause.

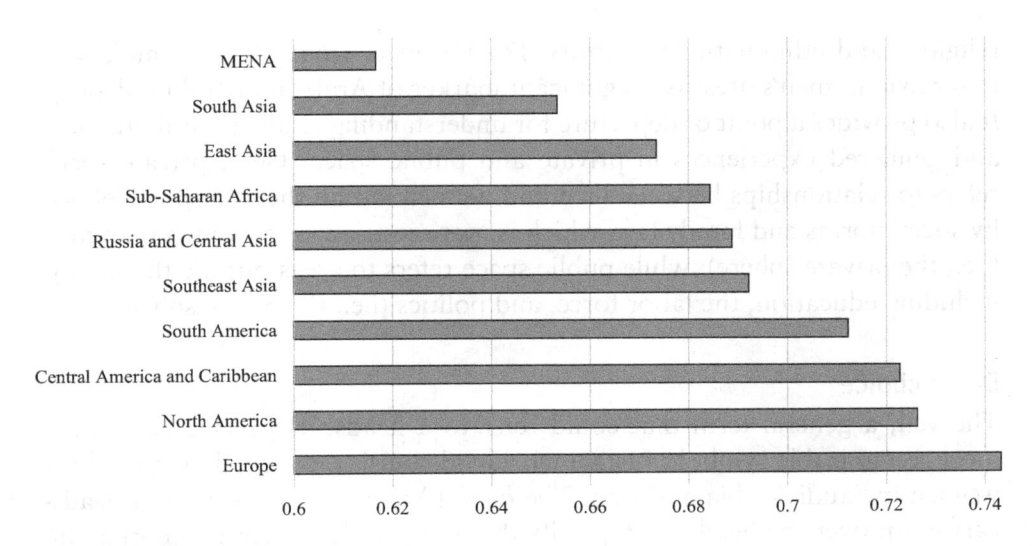

FIGURE 9.1
MENA vs. global regions in Global Gender Gap Index, 2017.

Source: World Economic Forum (2018), *The Global Gender Gap Report 2017*.

Still, women experience more unequal treatment in MENA than in other regions, as shown by the World Economic Forum's Global Gender Gap Index. This is an indicator of gender parity in the economy, education, health, and politics (Figure 9.1), and while theoretically scores run from 0 to 1, most countries cluster between 0.5 and 0.9. Yet within this truncated range, there is remarkable variation across global zones. As the graph shows, the MENA significantly lags behind other regions including South Asia and Sub-Saharan Africa with an average score of 0.62, while Europe, North America, and the Latin American regions achieve the highest gender parity (Europe's regionalized average is 0.74). Both the size of the gender gap in the MENA relative to other regions, as well as the variation in the size of the gender gap across MENA countries, pose a puzzle that scholars and policymakers seek to explain and, importantly, redress.

DRESS AND CULTURE: CONTEXTUALIZING THE PRIVATE AND PUBLIC SPHERE

As Chapter 4's treatment of identity denoted, women constitute not just a constructed category of gender but also a major node of personal and group identity – an identity that is expressed in multiple ways, and intersects with religious and ethnonational identity. For instance, women's dress and, to a lesser extent, men's dress is a significant marker of Arab and Muslim identity. It also provides a point of departure for understanding Arab cultural practices and gendered experiences in private and public space. Here, private space refers to relationships between men and women within the family, as defined by social norms and family law, which is more restrictive of women than men (i.e., the private sphere), while public space refers to areas outside the family, including education, the labor force, and politics (i.e., the public sphere).

Dress choice

The veil, a general term that could refer to a headscarf or face veil, is the most recognizable symbol of Islam worldwide but is only legally required for women in Saudi Arabia and Iran. The *hijab* (Arabic for covering) is a headscarf worn over the head and typically the neck, while the Arabic term *niqab* refers to a veil that specifically covers part of the face. In early Islam, only the Prophet's wives veiled; this was to show their status. Interestingly, the term for headscarf in the Qur'an is *khimar*, which is also used widely in Tunisia; the term *hijab* in the Qur'an refers to a curtain, and only afterwards came to be used as a label for women's dress. Scholars agree that Islam requires modesty for both genders, but disagree about whether and how women should cover.

Many factors, including region and class, affect women's dress choice. In Arab countries, some wear the headscarf as a symbol of Islamic identity. Others wear the hijab to honor their religious convictions and cultural values, or even to be less impeded by sexual harassment, as men are generally reticent with harassing veiled women. In the West, however, the symbol of the hijab is often essentialized as an iconic tool of oppression, despite its complex and contradictory meanings. For instance, women mobilizing in social movements have both veiled and unveiled to resist colonialism and Western consumerism, linking the hijab as much with agency and authenticity as with coercion when it is socially or legally required or repressed. A woman veiling herself in Saudi Arabia or Iran might object to legal requirements to do so, interpreting the headscarf as patriarchal injustice. Yet a woman wearing the hijab in Tunisia under the secularizing rule of its past presidents, whether Habib Bourguiba (1956–1987) or Zine 'Abidine Ben 'Ali (1987–2011), might have interpreted such a dress choice as a defiant act of political resistance against repressive governments to which she never consented. Despite its many social and political meanings, in sum, the hijab is best understood as a symbol of religiosity and adherence to fundamentalist Islam. It projects modesty and chastity – socially important traits needed to ensure one's reputation and improve success in the marriage market – and protects against perceptions of availability or immorality.

Yet, religious dress for women has varied meanings. Typically, Western conceptions of a Muslim woman – and especially an Arab-Muslim woman – conjure images like Photo 9.1, of a black-clad female wearing the full niqab and black robe. While this may be seen more frequently in the Arabian Gulf

PHOTO 9.1
Arab woman wearing abaya and niqab.

Source: Author.

states due to their more conservative nature, as Chapter 6's discussion of rentierism explained, the reality is far more complicated in other Muslim countries like Morocco. Reflective of its pluralistic traditions, European influence, and location in the Arab periphery, Moroccan dress for women and to some degree men has Western, traditional, and religious elements. Some women don the traditional *djellaba* (a loose outer robe) and hijab, whereas others mix a loose-fitting headscarf with Western clothes (Photo 9.2).

PHOTO 9.2
Moroccan woman wearing loose scarf, 2016.

Source: Photo by pcardo is licensed under CC BY 2.0.
Online: www.flickr.com/photos/pcardo/33197647676

In many circles across the MENA, veiled and unveiled women socialize alongside one another without any social distinction, as in this group of female teenagers in Kuwait (Photo 9.3). Western clothing can be common for both genders, although religious styles are generally worn more often by women. Modern, transnational styles of the niqab – seen publicly as a marker of Islamic piety and orthodoxy, and sometimes signaling support for Islamism – can be seen as well.

Besides being a matter of personal choice or familial preference, in purely cultural terms the headscarf may be associated with piety, rural residence, and lower socioeconomic status, in part because religious clothing can be less expensive than Western fashions. In many contexts for women, the hijab projects modesty and chastity – socially important traits – by protecting against perceptions of availability or immorality, especially in public. It furnishes a sense of interiority, allowing women to dress conservatively while accessing public space. The distinction between private and public space is

PHOTO 9.3
Kuwaiti teenage girls with varying dress, 2011.

Source: Photo by q80_outsider is licensed under CC BY 2.0.
Online: www.flickr.com/photos/q80_outsider/5957374501

important in Arab culture and, for better or for worse, a linchpin of patriarchal norms and customs. Although attitudes are changing, for the older generation the home is considered the women's domain, while the public space, including the labor force and politics, that of the men.

With the rise of Islamist political movements in the 1970s and 1980s (see Chapter 8), the hijab has become increasingly politicized. The Maghrib countries offer some revealing contrasts in this regard. Where Islamist parties challenged incumbent regimes, the headscarf was often repressed. For instance, in Tunisia, state secularization and feminism were more complete than in any other Arab country. As a result, before the 2011 Jasmine Revolution, Western-style clothing became associated with support for the authoritarian rule of Ben Ali, secular orientation, and higher socioeconomic class. In Algeria, the veil became more common after the country's civil war in the 1990s, when repressed Islamist groups fought the military following its cancellation of a democratic electoral victory by Islamists. When, in post-revolutionary Tunisia, the Islamist Party *Ennahda* (meaning renaissance) won a plurality in the 2011 Constituent Assembly legislative elections, the hijab and even religious styles among men – such as longer beards and short pant hems – became more common. The hijab has become politicized in Morocco as well, as a consequence of the rise of Islamist movements since the 1970s. In Morocco, pictures of veiled women and girls were removed from school textbooks because some governmental officials feared the hijab overly represented Islamist political opposition. Islamists may also face economic repression, and dress choices make this easier; for instance, women who wear the veil may encounter employment discrimination from businesses or government offices that still abide by secular values, and therefore do not desire their presence.

PATRIARCHY: SOCIAL AND POLITICAL DIMENSIONS

The distinction between the private sphere and public sphere is a key element of the patriarchal social order. The term "patriarchy" refers to a social system in which males have advantages in property, moral authority, and status. In essence, it means the subordination of women to men. Classic versions of patriarchy were characterized by subservience and manipulation, and occurred often in agrarian societies with patrilocally extended households around the world. This is a near-universal trait in human development: there are relatively few cultures in the world where, prior to industrialization, women enjoyed anything approaching equality to men. It was (and in many contexts, remains) a system in which women and girls are expected to obey the authority of the male head of the family, as well as brothers, uncles, and male cousins; fulfill primal roles as wife and mother before all other considerations; and preserve the interests and honor of the family. Under patriarchy, men control women and younger members of the family.

Patriarchy is exercised at all levels and takes the form of structures and norms. Patriarchal structures are formal laws and policies such as personal status (e.g., marriage, divorce, inheritance, mobility) and employment laws (e.g., wage discrimination, gender segregation), giving males more instrumental resources and reproducing stereotypes about women's subordinate abilities and roles in society. Patriarchal norms and attitudes entail traditional views of gender roles which define *public* space as male and *private* space as female, discourage mixing of unrelated males and females, and justify gender discrimination. This distinction is codified within the family codes.

The private sphere: family law (personal status) law

Family or personal status law, often referred to as the Personal Status Code (PSC) in most Muslim-majority MENA countries, dictates roles and relationships between men and women, particularly within the family and private sphere. It is more restrictive of women because of this. It covers areas such as the guardian system (i.e., whether women must have the consent of a male guardian to travel and sign contracts, including marriage), the minimum marital age, rules regarding polygamy, socialized roles, inheritance, and divorce rights.

In Muslim-majority societies in the MENA region, family law derives from Islamic law (*shari'a*), which became increasingly codified under the 'Abbasid dynasty beginning in the tenth century and reflects interpretations of the Qur'an and other Islamic textual sources; customary law, which represents customs and habits derived from everyday practices (*'urf*, in Arabic); and finally, Western legal norms or codes. Many Arab countries have conservative family laws that require women to have male guardians, even if just symbolically; but they also allow men to marry up to four wives. While it is easy to assume the most abusive examples originate from outmoded interpretations of Islamic notions, in reality the evolution of patriarchy is more complex. Many former French colonies, such as Tunisia and Morocco, began their post-colonial statehood in the 1960s with penal codes forgiving to male aggressors. Much of this bias, however, also stemmed from French Napoleonic laws that were impressed during the colonial era, in particular the 1810 Code that allowed men who kidnapped girls to escape prosecution if the female victims married their captors.

Unique in the Arab world, Tunisia enacted a progressive secular family code in 1956, becoming the only Arab country to ban polygamy and giving women the unilateral right to divorce. This led to important social changes which, along with state policies to promote women's dignity and employment, produced a relatively gender-equal society, although women still faced institutionalized violence in some respects (such as the loophole of rapists escaping punishment by marrying their victims). Contrarily, Morocco's 1956 family code established extremely conservative gender roles. Husbands were required to financially support their families and wives were expected to care for children, respect their husband's family, and remain outside public spaces. Reflecting changing social and economic realities, however, including that many Moroccan families came to encompass two wage-earning spouses, in 2004 the Moroccan state reformed its family code in drastic ways; the new version treats spouses as equal partners, banned the guardian system, and restricted polygamy, making Morocco's PSC nearly as progressive as that of Tunisia's. Algeria too has made some reforms in 2005, but still symbolically retains the guardian system; polygamy remains legal.

The public sphere: education, employment, and political life

In contrast to the private sphere, the public sphere consists of spaces that require sustained interaction with other members of society, and typically includes areas like education, the economy, and politics. Much more than in the private sphere, women are increasingly advancing in the public sphere across the Arab world, especially in education and to a lesser extent politics. Yet, it is not without challenges. For instance, women now outnumber men in rates of college and university education in most Arab countries, but they continue to enter the labor market and seek jobs at far lower rates. According to the World Bank, in 2017 the MENA continued to feature the world's lowest rates of female labor force participation, defined as the percentage of women who seek employment – 22.1 percent compared to 53.9 percent worldwide – as well as a gender gap in youth unemployment, which across the region measures 41.1 percent for females versus a far lower 23.2 percent rate for males.

At the same time, important advances have also been made in women's access to political office. In 1997, only 3.3 percent of electable seats in unicameral or lower houses of parliament in the Arab world were held by women. However, as a result of the implementation of parliamentary gender quotas in many Arab countries, which promote women to office through reserved seats or rules about candidate lists, that proportion of women in parliament reached 18.3 percent by 2018. This does not mean that women have equal access to all power structures – as in much of the rest of the world, few women have served as heads of state and have often been unsuccessful in reforming patriarchal family laws – but it illustrates the changing nature of gender relations, as well as the increasing ability of women to shape their circumstances.

The patriarchal bargain: women's agency

These advances in women's status illustrate the usefulness of considering a more modern and expansive conceptualization of patriarchy than described by the classic approaches above. Scholars often refer to gender struggles today not in terms of whether a rigid, fixed set of patriarchal restrictions exists or not, but rather as an open-ended patriarchal *bargain* that refers to how women continually negotiate and expand their autonomy in different areas of life. Women's empowerment is not so much a singular goal as a fluid process that requires different points of engagement, evasion, and contestation.

The strong role of women's movements mentioned earlier are a case in point. Across the Arab world, there has been a strong historical tradition of women's rights organizations to reform discriminatory law, provide social support for women and families, and fight colonialism and occupation. Arab societies are deeply patriarchal, yet war and occupation in Palestine, Algeria, Libya, Iraq, and Syria make women breadwinners and sometimes political leaders. Across the region, including in countries without a history of recurrent civil conflict, such as much of the Arabian Gulf, women are leveraging opportunities to increase their roles in public life through both informal as well as formal political activism.

As a key sector of civil society, women's movements contribute markedly to female advancement across the region. One area of note is honor killings, which describe murders of female members of an extended family or tribe (usually by male kin) under belief that the girl or woman has brought dishonor and shame, such as eloping with an unapproved suitor or engaging in behavior deemed irreligious. Honor killings are hardly unique to Islam or even the Arab world; they can be found in non-Arab Muslim countries like Turkey and Pakistan, but also in non-Muslim countries altogether, particularly India. Within the MENA, civil society activism has helped not only reduce this increasingly rare practice, but also impel many governments to close legal loopholes and prosecute its perpetrators in order to deter future occurrences.

Some caution should be taken, however, in treating any evidence of greater gender equality as examples of patriarchal decline and thus feminist victory. In many cases, female empowerment is the product of male domination, especially when it occurs after political actors instrumentalize women's rights to serve their own authoritarian interests to win domestic or international accolades or to detract attention from other failings of governance. In 2003, for instance, many Moroccans believe that the monarchy commenced the task of reforming the family code in order to secure greater Western support while undermining the main Islamist opposition party, the Party of Justice and Development.

BOX 9.1 CASE STUDY – SAUDI ARABIA AND WOMEN'S RIGHTS

Under sway by the conservative Wahhabi variant of Islam, Saudi Arabia banned women from driving in the 1950s. Women's rights in the kingdom faced many other constraints, among them strict requirements for obtaining permission from male guardians (typically, a father or uncle, if not husband or brother) in order to travel, mandatory gender segregation in schools and workplaces, and an uncodified PSC that gives judges wide discretion for gender bias, especially regarding issues of divorce, children's custody, and property. However, many Western observers saw the ban against women driving as the most onerous. In late 2017, King Salman of Saudi Arabia decreed that women would be granted driving rights, including being able to possess their own licenses – a decision many saw as originating from his young son, Crown Prince Muhammad bin Salman, who promised a more progressive and modernizing kingdom. When the first Saudi women began driving in June 2018, many hailed the move as evidence that Saudi authorities were becoming more open-minded in their views of gender equality. On the other hand, the lifting of the women driving ban was also a political tactic designed to bolster the popularity and legitimacy of the Crown Prince. Saudi women had been campaigning for decades to drive, but to little avail; and more troublingly, more than a dozen women's rights activists were also arrested in a political crackdown on the eve of the reform. As some critics noted, it seemed like this autocratic monarchy was so eager to improve its international reputation and adopt the image of a modernizing regime that it was erasing the social history of women's rights activism, so that any expansion of gender equality would be seen purely as its own contribution – not the indigenous work of grass-roots campaigners and Saudi women. Furthermore, terminating the prohibition on women's driving was an isolated event that seemed calibrated to appease detractors in the international media, not the opening

> **BOX 9.1 (CONTINUED)**
>
> to a long-term dialogue about gender roles and social tradition; today, Saudi women still need the permission of a male guardian to open a bank account or obtain a passport, for instance. The contentious issue of female driving underscores the political hazards of instrumentalizing gendered issues. In plain terms, liberal means can be exploited for illiberal ends.

GENDER GAPS: SOME PATTERNS

Women face considerable obstacles to gender equality, but it would be incorrect to assume that women are disadvantaged relative to men in every respect. Most notably, girls and women enjoy high education and literacy rates in the MENA region. Furthermore, parliamentary gender quotas have been implemented in just less than half of all Arab countries since 2002, leading to growth in women's representation. In addition, important advances in women's rights occurred in Tunisia as a result of the Arab Spring, which also created new openings for activism against sexual violence and in support of LGBTQ rights. Other countries like Morocco have also promulgated new laws cracking down on sexual harassment and forced marriages. Jordan and Lebanon also moved aggressively in 2017 to repeal provisions in their criminal codes that allowed rapists to escape punishment by marrying the victims. Women's rights movements are among the most well-known sectors of civil societies in most MENA countries, including Turkey, and their work in highlighting areas of inequality and pressing both governments and societies for greater pluralism has been vital.

However, obstacles to equality are significant. Large gender gaps and negative trends include discriminatory personal status laws in all countries. The Arab world also has very low rates of female labor force participation (that is, the number of women who enter the job market and seek employment) and high wage inequality, as well as low female political participation and discriminatory social attitudes. In addition, violence and instability place a significant burden on women and greatly increase the prevalence of rape and child marriage (i.e., marriage of persons under 18 years).

Positive trends

The increase in women's educational enrollment is an important and often overlooked positive trend in the MENA region in recent years. In 1970, the MENA region had much lower enrollment rates at all levels of education – for both boys and girls – than today. For instance, in 1970, only 3 percent of Omani children were enrolled in primary school, and none were in secondary school. In that same year, Saudi Arabia, had 45 percent enrolled in primary education for both genders, 19 percent in secondary, and 3 percent in post-secondary (also known as tertiary, or college-level) education, while Bahrain had 98 percent enrollment in primary school, 51 percent in secondary, and 1 percent in post-secondary (see Table 9.1). Primary education refers

TABLE 9.1

Rates of enrollment for primary, secondary, and tertiary (college) education, 1970

	Primary			Secondary			Tertiary		
	Female	Male	Total	Female	Male	Total	Female	Male	Total
Algeria	58	93	76	6	16	11	1	3	2
Bahrain	84	113	98	43	60	51	2	1	1
Egypt	53	81	68	19	38	28	4	10	7
Iran	52	93	73	18	36	27	2	4	3
Iraq	**	**	**	**	**	**	**	**	**
Israel	95	97	96	60	54	57	17	20	18
Jordan	65	79	72	23	41	33	1	3	2
Kuwait	76	100	88	57	70	63	4	4	4
Lebanon	112	131	121	33	49	41	10	31	21
Libya	84	136	111	8	33	21	1	5	3
Morocco	36	66	51	7	17	13	0	2	1
Oman	1	5	3	0	0	0	**	**	**
Qatar	88	104	96	30	41	36	**	**	**
Saudi Arabia	29	61	45	5	19	12	0	3	2
Syria	59	95	78	21	54	38	3	13	8
Tunisia	80	121	100	13	33	23	1	4	3
Turkey	93	122	107	15	37	26	2	8	5
UAE	72	115	95	10	30	22	**	**	**
West Bank and Gaza Strip	**	**	**	**	**	**	**	**	**
Yemen	**	**	**	**	**	**	**	**	**

Source: World Bank (2018), *World Development Indicators*. ** denotes no available data.

generally to grades one through five; secondary education entails grades six through twelve; and post-secondary, also known as *tertiary*, education refers to college and university-level learning.

Enrollment rates rose dramatically by 2005 (Table 9.2). This year is important because it marked a tipping point in terms of the gender imbalance within educational enrollments leveling off or reversing in favor of girls – a regional trend that has only increased today. In 1970, boys outnumbered

TABLE 9.2

Rates of enrollment for primary, secondary, and tertiary (college) education, 2005

	Primary			Secondary			Tertiary		
	Female	*Male*	*Total*	*Female*	*Male*	*Total*	*Female*	*Male*	*Total*
Algeria	107	116	112	86	80	83	24	19	21
Bahrain	106	107	106	100	94	97	46	19	31
Egypt	93	99	96	77	82	79	**	**	31
Iran	138	112	125	7	78	77	23	22	23
Iraq	89	106	98	37	56	47	12	20	16
Israel	110	109	110	92	93	93	67	50	58
Jordan	99	98	99	85	83	84	39	36	37
Kuwait	97	99	98	98	93	95	29	10	19
Lebanon	97	100	99	87	79	83	49	42	46
Libya	105	107	106	112	94	103	58	53	56
Morocco	101	113	107	45	53	49	10	13	11
Oman	82	82	82	85	89	87	19	18	19
Qatar	119	122	120	113	85	97	33	6	13
Saudi Arabia	95	98	97	86	94	90	35	24	29
Syria	124	130	127	65	69	67	**	**	**
Tunisia	110	114	112	89	81	85	36	26	31
Turkey	93	99	96	69	84	76	27	36	32
UAE	104	105	104	86	84	85	37	13	23
West Bank and Gaza Strip	87	87	87	96	91	93	42	40	41
Yemen	74	100	87	30	61	46	5	14	9

Source: World Bank (2018), *World Development Indicators.* ** denotes no available data.

girls in primary school in every MENA country, and the gender gap exceeded 30 percent in Syria, where 21 percent of girls and 54 percent of boys were enrolled. However, by 2005, while total enrollment greatly increased, the gains for women were especially felt at the collegiate level. At the primary and secondary levels, most MENA countries still enrolled more boys than girls in 2005; but the gaps are relatively small and sometimes reversed. In 2005, we also began to see higher enrollment rates for girls than boys across various levels for many countries – including the fact that more women than men enrolled at colleges and universities. In Saudi Arabia, for example, 35 percent of women were enrolled at a college or university, compared to 24 percent of men.

Since 2005, the MENA region has seen a "reverse" gender gap. By 2016, girls and women had made gains in even *more* countries. At the primary level, girls are as enrolled or more enrolled in school than boys in seven countries; at the secondary level, they were equally or more enrolled in 11 countries; and at the tertiary level, women match or exceed men's enrollment in every country except just three – Yemen, Morocco, and Turkey. The particularly high increase in women's education at the collegiate and university level has elicited several explanations from researchers, among them increasing returns to female education which attract more women to apply in the first place; the perception that a college degree is an important credential not just in the job market, but in the "marriage market" and hence makes women more suitable for suitors; and finally, the persistence of workplace inequality, which often necessitates women to become more educated than men in order to obtain the type of position and salary.

In 2009, the World Bank notably found that girls were almost as likely to be enrolled in school and become as literate as boys in the MENA region, with 96 girls enrolled in primary and secondary school for every 100 boys; there were also 93 literate young girls for every 100 literate boys. Today, the ratio has not only equalized but reversed in some countries. For instance, Sweden-based Gothenburg University's Program on Governance and Local Development (GLD) estimates that in Tunisia, more boys than girls now drop out of school; indeed, more Tunisia boys (11.9 percent, or 107,674) than girls (8.9 percent, or 70,667) under 17 years of age do not attend school. In other countries, it is primarily rural areas where girls face the greatest constraints. For example, in rural Morocco, the lack of jobs, legality of child marriage, social pressures, and overall lack of resources results in many women not reaping high returns on their education despite outperforming men in their younger years of schooling. The same pattern holds for other countries with

TABLE 9.3

Rates of enrollment for primary, secondary, and tertiary (college) education, 2011–2016

	Primary			Secondary			Tertiary		
	Female	Male	Total	Female	Male	Total	Female	Male	Total
Algeria	111	117	114	102[a]	98[a]	100[a]	54	32	43
Bahrain	102	100	101	104	103	104	63	34	47
Egypt	104	104	104	85	87	86	35	34	34
Iran	112[e]	106[e]	109[e]	89[e]	89[e]	89[e]	66	72	69
Iraq	**	**	**	**	**	**	**	**	**
Israel	104	103	104	105	103	104	75	54	64
Jordan	**	**	**	71[d]	69[d]	70[d]	38	35	36
Kuwait	103	99	101	98[e]	94[e]	101[e]	43[c]	23[c]	33[c]
Lebanon	85	93	89	60	60	60	46[d]	40[d]	43[d]
Libya	**	**	**	**	**	**	**	**	**
Morocco	107	113	110	64[b]	75[b]	70[b]	31	33	32
Oman	110	107	108	104	110	107	60	33	45
Qatar	103	104	104	101	86	93	47	6	15
Saudi Arabia	115	117	116	102[d]	131[d]	117[d]	67	67	67
Syria	75[c]	77[c]	76[c]	49[c]	49[c]	49[c]	43	36	39
Tunisia	113	116	115	98	88	93	41	24	33
Turkey	103	104	103	102	104	103	89	102	95
UAE	109	113	111	93	99	96	53	27	37
West Bank and Gaza Strip	94	94	94	88	80	84	53	33	43
Yemen	86	99	92	43	59	51	6[b]	14[b]	10[b]

Source: World Bank (2016), *EdStats Database*. ** denotes no data between 2011–2016. [a]2011. [b]2012. [c]2013. [d]2014. [e]2015.

large rural areas, such as Turkey, Iran, Yemen, Sudan, and Egypt: in the most underdeveloped provinces, villages, and towns, the gender gap has proven more difficult to close than in major urban areas.

A second positive trend is the expansion of female representation in elected legislatures across the region – particularly in Arab countries, where gender quotas have produced a six-fold increase in female legislators in national parliaments since the 1990s. The MENA region lagged behind other world regions in 1997, when only 3.3 percent of seats in unicameral or lower houses of parliament were held by women. As a result of parliamentary gender quotas diffusing across the region (that is, spreading and becoming a popular policy mechanism), the proportion of women in Arab-elected parliaments reached nearly 18.3 percent by 2018. By comparison, the global average in 2018 was 23.7 percent. While not as high as European countries, the Arab figure ranks as a sizable improvement that puts Arab countries on par with many other states and regions. In the US, for instance, the 115th Congress (2017–2019) featured just 19.4 percent female representation. Outside the Arab world, other MENA countries vary. Israel outpaces other countries in terms of female representation in politics; in 2018, women comprised 28 percent of its Knesset. On the opposite end of the spectrum, women constituted just 6 percent of Iran's parliament. In Turkey, the figure hovers in between the two extremes; in the June 2018 elections, 103 women won office in the 600-person legislative assembly.

In the Arab world, this increase of women in parliaments has been fostered in large part by electoral gender quotas, which currently exist for seven Arab countries. There are three types of quotas. First, *voluntary party* candidate quotas are measures by parties to increase the number of female candidates, or to improve their placement on party lists. Second, *legislated quotas* are system-wide requirements that make each competing political party have a certain percentage of women on its elections list. Third, *reserved seat* quotas sequester a fixed number of parliamentary seats only for women (and often minority groups); men cannot compete for such quota seats. Since 2002, Algeria, Iraq, Jordan, Sudan, and Saudi Arabia have implemented reserved seat quotas, while Libya, the Palestinian territories, and Tunisia have instituted legislated candidate quotas. While all three types of quotas have been implemented in the Arab world, reserved seat quotas are most common, not least because they are compatible with authoritarian governance. In countries like Jordan, nonelected leaders (such as kings) can simply increase the size of parliament by adding on extra seats specifically for women; this does not take away seats from existing parties, while also bolstering the image of leaders as progressive. Table 9.4 lists the Arab countries, plus Israel, Iran, and Turkey, to highlight variations in female quotas.

Egypt was the first country in the Arab region to implement a parliamentary gender quota – a reserved seat quota in place from 1979–1986. In Tunisia, under President Ben Ali's state-manipulated version of feminism, the dominant Constitutional Rally for Democracy (RCD) party instituted

TABLE 9.4

Female quotas in legislative bodies by type, 2018

	Voluntary party candidate quotas?	Quotas in legislative bodies (legislated versus reserved seats)
Algeria	No	Reserved seats
Bahrain	No	No
Egypt	No	No
Iran	No	No
Iraq	No	Reserved seats
Israel	Yes	No
Jordan	No	Reserved seats
Kuwait	No	No
Lebanon	No	No
Libya	No	No
Morocco	No	Reserved seats
Oman	No	No
Qatar	No	No
Saudi Arabia	No	Reserved seats (legislative body is unelected)
Sudan	No	Legislated
Syria	No	No
Tunisia	No	Legislated
Turkey	Yes	No
United Arab Emirates	No	No
West Bank and Gaza Strip	No	Legislated
Yemen	No	No

Source: International IDEA (2018), *Gender Quotas Database*.

an internal 20 percent party quota in 1999, which it increased to 30 percent in 2009. This had a major impact on the proportion of women in office: on the eve of the Arab Spring, 28 percent of Tunisia's Chamber of Deputies and local councils was made up of women, but only because the RCD was also the dominant ruling party that faced little real opposition. Meanwhile, Morocco became a regional model when in 2002 it implemented a "gentlemen's agreement" (typically considered a legislated quota) among political parties to field all-female party lists for 30 reserved parliamentary seats. Following the 2011–2012 Arab Spring, this was increased to 60 seats. In 2012, Algeria also implemented a legislative quota which called for the proportion of women on parties' electoral lists to include 20 to 50 percent women, depending on the district, and providing financial incentives to parties for compliance. Finally, thought often forgotten, Sudan has instituted some of the highest female quotas in the world over the past decade; as of 2018, 30.5 percent of its elected parliament comprises women – by far the highest in the Arab world, and the MENA region as well.

These gains must be contextualized. Overall, political leadership in the MENA is still overwhelmingly male, even in countries with parliamentary gender quotas. The rise in women's representation in the lower or single house parliament is not typical of all structures of government and the judiciary. Instead, parliament is the high-water mark, in that women's representation there is much higher in lower houses and unicameral parliaments than in upper houses (i.e., senates), the executive branch (i.e., heads of state and cabinets), the judiciary, political party leadership, and the military. While women have served as political leaders in the highest offices, such as prime ministers (e.g., Turkey, Israel), and in monarchies some figures such as Queen Rania of Jordan have become prominent advocates for gender equality, these examples are still infrequent. In global context, we can see such scarcity is not reflective of religion alone: the three most populous Muslim countries in the world – Indonesia, Pakistan, and Bangladesh – have all had female Prime Ministers elected to office, while a number of OECD countries like Spain, Japan, and the US have never had a woman hold the top executive leadership.

In addition, most Arab countries have authoritarian regimes that make elected bodies like parliaments and municipal councils deliberately weak. Thus, even if these elections are competitive and fair (they are often not), and even if women do win office, they – alongside their male counterparts – cannot do much against far more powerful kings and presidents. An interesting paradox lies in that some women elected to parliament run with Islamist parties, whose core constituencies do not demand secularly progressive laws. This may limit the impact of quotas on promotion of gender equality.

A third positive trend is the continuation of demands for and, in some cases, gains in women's status following the Arab Spring. The 2011–2012 protests and uprisings in the region may not have created democracies overnight, but they emboldened many women to continue mobilizing against injustices. For instance, new activist campaigns against sexual harassment and assault have taken root in Egypt, Jordan, Lebanon, and Morocco. The #MeToo movement may have rocked Western countries by starting with celebrities and politicians, but in the Arab world the effect reverberated at the grass-roots level, as many women – even in the Arabian Gulf kingdoms, which are generally more conservative than the Maghrib and Mashriq – disseminated their own stories of abuse and mistreatment through social media.

Furthermore, despite the expectations of pundits who predicted that the Arab Spring would produce Islamist electoral success that would roll back women's rights, nothing of the sort happened. For one, Islamist parties have been unable to hold power for a sustained period in the MENA region, either before or after the Arab Spring. In countries like Jordan, Algeria, and Libya, Islamist parties have enjoyed only limited electoral success in recent elections, which some women's activists in civil society greeted with relief. Even in Tunisia, Ennahda only gained a plurality rather than absolute majority in post-revolutionary elections for parliament, and thus had to compromise with secularist political parties to govern. Morocco's Party of Justice and Development also won a plurality (27 percent) in 2011, but always governed under the monarchy's tutelage and control. In Egypt, the Muslim Brotherhood's Freedom and Justice Party won the presidency as well as majorities in parliament in the country's first truly democratic contests in 2012, but was overthrown in a coup in July 2013.

For another, Islamists have needed to compromise or liberalize themselves under public scrutiny. In Tunisia, there were fears that the gender-equal PSC would be abolished by the ascendant Islamist Ennahda party after the Arab Spring and during the country's transition to democracy. During the constitution drafting process (2011–2014) and in response to popular pressures, Ennahda agreed to preserve the PSC and even remove a clause in the proposed constitution describing men and women as complementary. To describe the sexes as complementary, women's rights activists argued, might open a door in the future for the repeal of the PSC. Moreover, Ennahda was among the parties at the forefront of promoting women in their ranks, with women representing 41 percent of its deputies in the first post-revolutionary parliament. Indeed, the party had 240 women's committees campaign in all of Tunisia's 24 governorates to ensure its popularity among female voters across all parts of Tunisian society.

Negative trends

Inversely, though, some negative trends and large gender inequities stubbornly persist. At the basic level of political rights, most studies find that women consistently vote less than men in countries that hold some type of election (however flawed or open) for local or parliamentary offices, such as Egypt, Tunisia, Libya, and Jordan. These are substantial gender gaps which suggest that politicians do not need to cater to female constituents' needs, since women are less likely to vote than male constituents.

Moreover, despite their high levels of education – which match or exceed their male counterparts – women also face substantial barriers in the economy. While most countries in the world exhibit variance in their labor force participation rates for women versus men (that is, the proportion of working-age women versus men who choose to enter the job market and look for employment), the divergence is particularly pronounced in several MENA countries (Figure 9.2). In Yemen, Jordan, and Iran, just 6, 14, and 17 percent of all women participate in the labor force respectively. On the other hand, wealthier MENA countries like Kuwait, Qatar, and Israel sport rates of female labor force participation of 47, 58, and 59 percent respectively – figures that compare favorably to the average of the OECD countries. The

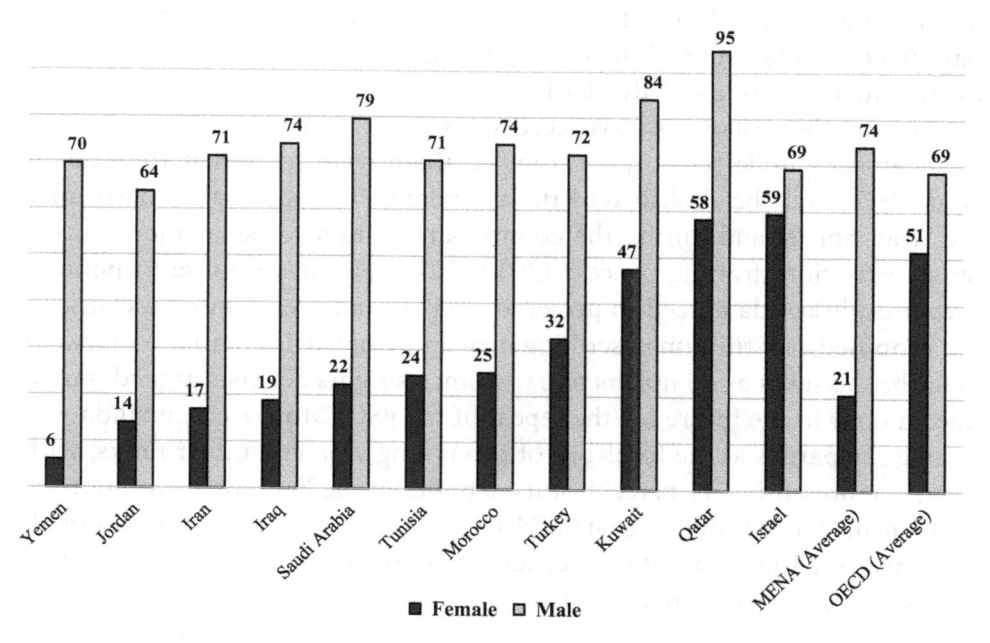

FIGURE 9.2
Labor force participation rates by gender, 2017.

Source: World Bank (2018), *World Development Indicators*.

regional average, however, lags behind the OECD, with just 21 percent of women across the MENA seeking employment, as opposed to 74 percent of all men.

Beyond participation in the economy, there is also wage discrimination perpetuated by government policies. In most MENA countries, public-sector salaries for men are higher than women on average; furthermore, women typically need more qualifications to obtain comparable work. Although data are spotty, we know from some research that inequality in salaries and wages can also be substantial between genders. The gender wage gap, in terms of the amount that women make compared to a man doing identical work, is 21 percent in Tunisia, the region's most gender-equal society, 35 percent in Turkey, and a staggering 56 percent in Saudi Arabia. Indeed, in Saudi Arabia, some estimates suggest there are up to 160 poor women for every 100 poor men.

What underlies female underrepresentation in politics and the economy are social attitudes, which still reflect broad patriarchal bias in the MENA. Data from the World Values Survey from the past decade, for instance, indicate that many people (including women themselves, as respondents in these polls were not segregated by gender) did not see women as politically capable as men. When asked for their views about the statement, "Men make better political leaders," just 14 percent of Egyptians, 18 percent of Jordanians, 21 percent of Kuwaitis, 24 percent of Tunisians, 30 percent of Moroccans, and 41 percent of Lebanese either disagreed or strongly disagreed. While there is considerable variation here, such figures rank less than many other diverse countries outside the MENA region, such as South Africa (49 percent), Romania (56 percent), Brazil (69 percent), Mexico (77 percent), and Ethiopia (77 percent). When asked the same statement about men making better business executives, 19 percent of Egyptians, 29 percent of Jordanians, 29 percent of Libyans, and 36 percent of Tunisians disagreed or strongly disagreed.

Moreover, unequal personal status codes, which give women unequal rights in marriage, divorce, mobility, and inheritance, still persist in most Arab countries with Tunisia being a rare exception. Although there is some variation, on average women have a more difficult time starting businesses, claiming inheritance, and obtaining jobs than men do. What exacerbates these vulnerabilities in the recurrence of conflict? Civil and international wars in Syria, Libya, Iraq, and Yemen exact high costs on innocent victims, many of them women and girls who are subject to sexual assault, human trafficking, and forced and child marriage.

The LGBTQ community

Other developments show a positive trajectory in gender-based activism. Over the past decade, lesbian, gay, bisexual, transgender, and queer/questioning (LGBTQ) communities in the MENA region have slowly become more vocal in their demands for recognition. To be sure, homosexuality is illegal in most MENA countries, either due to religious interpretations of sexual preferences or traditional cultural biases that see deviations from rigid expectations as sinful. LGBTQ citizens thus suffer severe restrictions. For instance, male homosexuality is illegal and punishable by imprisonment in Kuwait, Egypt, Oman, Qatar, and Syria and punishable by death in Iran, Saudi Arabia, Qatar, and the UAE. Female homosexuality is legal in a few countries, but still suffers broad recrimination by disapproving societal censors. Israel is the exception in the region, as discrimination on grounds of sexual orientation is illegal; and despite criticism from ultra-Orthodox Jewish groups whose views on homosexuality are little different than their Muslim and Christian fundamentalist counterparts, LGBT Jewish citizens can also openly serve in the armed forces and fulfill other state offices.

In most MENA countries, the effect of such bias and illegality targeting LGBTQ individuals and groups has been predictable. Most LGBTQ equality and activist movements themselves are not legal organizations, and so must be careful in not outing public members or pushing too hard against political authorities. Still, in many countries, LGBTQ communities flourish – just on the margins of visibility for fear of arrest and punishment. For instance, despite periodic crackdowns by some governments seeking support from conservatives, there are thriving underground gay scenes in large Arab metropolises, such as Casablanca, Morocco; Beirut, Lebanon; and Amman, Jordan. Indeed, travel sites online make it easy for LGBTQ travelers to find friendly hotels, bars, and restaurants in most countries. In essence, the situation resembles many other places in the world where a combination of societal norms and governmental institutions seek to eliminate unapproved norms, identities, and practices: those under duress and prosecution still exist, but must do so in creative ways to avoid sanction.

MEASURING EGALITARIANISM: PUBLIC AND PRIVATE PATRIARCHY

Considering these trends, several approaches to measuring patriarchy across countries have been proposed. One approach uses public opinion research, which allows scholars to tap into social norms. According to the Arab

Barometer's ongoing surveys, attitudes in the Arab world are mixed toward gender issues, and it often depends on the *type* of right being discussed. As Figure 9.3 shows, women's mobility (i.e., a private right) is much less supported than work and pay items (i.e., public rights). Further, the gender gap in attitudes is slightly larger, just as the theoretical distinction between private and public rights might suggest. On average, though, females hold significantly more egalitarian views than males – not a surprising result.

However, as surveys expand into the Arab world and include many more questions about women and gender – covering both public as well as private rights – there is a danger of lumping indicators of multiple dimensions into a single, unreliable scale. For example, as shown in Table 9.5, correlations between the seven gender-related items included in the very first wave of the Arab Barometer, undertaken during 2006 to 2008 in seven countries, never exceed 0.58 and in many cases are substantially lower. This means that it is possible for someone to support women in the public space, for instance,

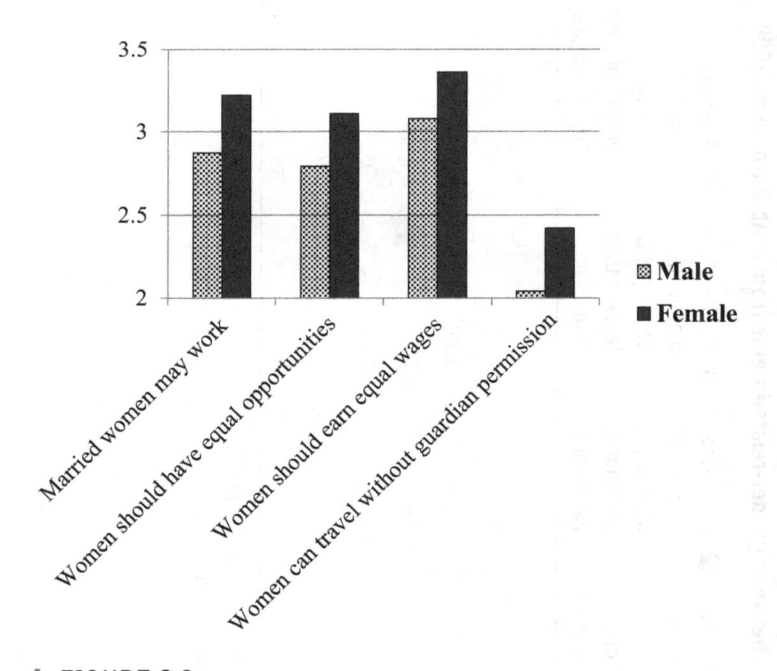

FIGURE 9.3
Support for different areas of gender equality from Arab Barometer, 2008.

Source: Arab Barometer, Wave I (2006–2008).

Online: www.arabbarometer.org. Higher values indicate greater support for issue area (i.e., women's rights in work, opportunity, wages, and travel).

TABLE 9.5

Correlations between gender-related items from Arab Barometer, 2008

	1. A woman can be a president or prime minister of a Muslim country.	2. A married woman can work outside the home if she wishes.	3. On the whole, men make better political leaders than women do.	4. A university education is more important for a boy than a girl.	5. Men and women should have equal job opportunities and wages.	6. Men and women should receive equal wages and salaries.	7. A woman can travel abroad by herself if she wishes.
1.	1.00						
2.	0.46	1.00					
3.	−0.32	−0.17	1.00				
4.	−0.18	−0.28	0.25	1.00			
5.	0.43	0.48	−0.22	−0.21	1.00		
6.	0.29	0.43	−0.12	−0.27	0.58	1.00	
7.	0.47	0.43	−0.33	−0.20	0.41	0.31	1.00

Source: Arab Barometer, Wave I (2006–2008).
Online: www.arabbarometer.org

while opposing reform of family law/PSC (i.e., a private right). It is therefore important to separate these dimensions in order to understand what truly causes support for equality.

The same is true of aggregate measures of gender equality, which often are not highly correlated. For instance, not all the countries with the most conservative family laws – for instance, Jordan, Libya, the Palestinian territories, and Yemen – do not always have the lowest women's labor force participation or formal political representation. Countries with poor social acceptance of women in government sometimes have high numbers of women in parliament (e.g., Algeria). According to the United Nations Development Programme's Gender Inequality Index (GII), which combines indicators of health, labor force participation, and politics, Libya is actually the most gender equal among Arab countries, despite its conservative family law and public image of being anything but. Conversely, Jordan does not measure high on any standard measure of gender equality, such as labor force participation, but women there not only enjoy a healthy seat quota in parliament but are also commonly found as ministers and other elites due to their intersecting resources they may draw upon as members of a powerful tribe or community.

To cut through the confusion, many researchers simply utilize a single measure of gender inequality to measure patriarchy and women's rights. This may lead to misleading results, however, since patriarchy is a complex, multidimensional concept with different causes and consequences, depending on the dimension under study. For example, some believe that oil wealth perpetuates patriarchy because the oil-rentier kingdoms of the Arabian Gulf seem to have the most conservative family laws; but this does not explain variations *among* these wealthy kingdoms, such as why Kuwaiti women are radically less constrained than Saudi women in terms of economic mobility. Likewise, some researchers simply point to parliamentary quotas as evidence of female advancement. However, quotas are easily manipulated or implemented to artificially boost female representation in the short term, and not affect the entirety of gender politics in a country. For instance, as of 2018, Algeria and Tunisia feature women comprising 32 percent and 31 percent of their elected parliamentary houses, respectively, which is higher than the US; but by all other measures, women do not enjoy more rights in these countries than in America.

EXPLAINING PATRIARCHY AND EGALITARIANISM

Thus far, this chapter has discussed ways that patriarchy manifests, as well as wrinkles in how we conceptualize and measure women's rights. Now comes the thorniest question: what *explains* male dominance in the private or public spheres, and why do some MENA countries outperform others when it comes to gender equality?

As Table 9.6 shows, scholars typically leverage three types of theories to explain gendered outcomes in developmental contexts. The first and oldest category encompasses cultural and classical theories, which suggest something *inherent* to the MENA countries (such as Islam or economic backwardness) stymies women's dignity and freedom. The second suggests that not anything cultural or essentialist, but rather structural – that is, the institutions and patterns that come to shape the region's historical development over time – is operating here. The third category is the broadest, and indicates

TABLE 9.6

Theories of patriarchy in the MENA region

Type of theory	Core explanatory variable	Main outcomes: how do we measure?
Cultural or conventional theories that see MENA region as *inherently* monolithic and systemically different from the West	*Islam and Muslim traditions* *Economic backwardness and modernization*	Individual-level attitudes about gender issues (e.g., support for gender equality/ patriarchal attitudes)
Structural theories about political and economic institutions that appear over course of historical development in MENA, and may or may not be inherent to region	*Oil* *Institutions* *Regime type and patrilineal tribal norms*	Aggregate, country-level outcomes such as women in government Aggregate, country-level outcomes such as parliamentary gender quotas Aggregate, country-level outcomes such as family law
Psychological and social theories that see gender inequality as explained by something endemic to human thinking and thus found worldwide well outside MENA countries	*Psychology of stereotyping and bias* *Networks and homo-sociality*	Individual-level attitudes such as candidate stereotypes and voter preferences Individual-level behaviors such as propensity of male parliamentarians to affiliate with other men versus women

Source: Author

that psychological and social mechanisms innate not to the region but simply to the human experience explain gender biases and patriarchal hegemony.

Cultural and conventional theories

One type of cultural theory views attitudes as determined by a set of constant attributes, ideas, and linguistic notions that are assumed simplistically to exist due to some deep and unchanging foundation, such as Islam, tribalism, or Arab identity. For many observers, the Islamic faith is the main culprit; thus, Muslims will hold less egalitarian views than non-Muslims, while higher religiosity among Muslims will preserve patriarchal views. The rise of Islamism, a broader regional trend discussed in Chapter 8's analysis on religion, does not help matters, since fundamentalists across all major faiths – including, for instance, Judaism, Christianity, and Hinduism – tend to be more tolerant of male domination more than gender equality in line with orthodox, conservative interpretations of religious doctrine.

Conventional theories argue that social attitudes are shaped by economic development. Modernization theorists contend that education, urbanization, and mobilization create more complex interactions among citizens and lead them to demand participation and democracy, eventually leading to personal freedoms and gender equality. Yet for various ingrained reasons, most MENA countries never purportedly modernized or developed fully. Thus, like culturalism, conventional views take an extremely deterministic and static approach to the MENA region: once patriarchal, always patriarchal, and women in most of these countries unfortunately have little real chance for true empowerment given the weight of cultural and economic impediments.

Yet the evidence here is mixed, to say the least. Most studies examining individual-level attitudes do find that respondents' Muslim identity is related to higher support for patriarchy, and that in general wealthier and more urbanized citizens tend to be more tolerant. Yet we know that outside the MENA region, plenty of Muslim-majority countries have outperformed on many indicators of gender equality, and that within and across the MENA itself there is dramatic variation in terms of female integration into society, economy, and politics – the geographic zone is not one monolithic crescent. We also know that these attitudes change over time, which at least suggests there is nothing static about them. We also know, perhaps most of all, that social attitudes are *malleable*. Sociological studies, for example, show that when women and men experience the economic benefits of women's employment (such as their households having increased financial security or their children attending better schools), their interests change and expressed support for gender equality actually rises. Likewise, positionality matters: men are more likely to hold egalitarian views if they are married to a woman who works, versus if they are single or married to a nonworking spouse. That having a wife who is employed can predict one's attitudes about women suggests that rather than being intrinsic, beliefs and values are at least partly the product of one's environment, and thus do evolve.

Relatedly, exposure-based theories of attitude change argue social beliefs and economic change go hand in hand: as women enter the labor force, they, their husbands, and others in society develop more egalitarian attitudes. Exposure to women's employment has this equalizing effect through five mechanisms. First, when women are employed, they are more likely to be exposed to discrimination, which increases the salience of gender-based inequality and fosters a feminist identity. Second, exposure to the workforce dispels myths about women's capabilities, reducing psychological incongruities between perceived traits of women and the qualities expected of a leader or occupant of a traditionally male role. Third, workforce participation supports the development of networks of women in the labor force, mobilizes movements for women's rights, and fosters feminist identity. Fourth, women's employment dispels myths that women cannot manage work and family. Finally, cross-generational effects of women's employment occur as a result of socialization, as children are raised in a home with two breadwinners.

Political economic and sociological theories

Cultural and conventional theories squarely target the MENA: they suggest there is something peculiar, exotic, and altogether exacting about this region's religious or traditional essence that holds women back. By contrast, structural theories focus upon institutions, and argue that certain political forms of organization and economic patterns of interaction that arose in the modern MENA over the past century have worked to escalate gender inequality and amplify male authority. This may or may not be inherent to the region.

For instance, many argue that abundant oil reduces women's opportunities to enter the labor force by increasing household incomes and moving jobs from the tradable to the non-tradable sector, such as construction, which is less welcoming to female employment. As a result of exclusion from the paid labor force, women fail to develop skills to gain representation in parliament and other bodies. Moreover, in many rentier states, men earn higher wages because the pay structure is based on years of service, and men can enter government employment at a younger age and with fewer educational credentials than women. Men also receive generous family subsidies, further widening pay gaps. Authoritarian regimes and nondemocratic politics, generally, also reinforce patriarchy; while citizens across the board suffer under dictatorships, political systems that do not offer civil liberties and political freedoms make activism for women's rights even more difficult, since they must climb a steeper slope simply to have a voice at the policymaking table.

Tribes, too, can be thought of as a type of social institution, as Chapter 4's discussion on identity and tribalism explained. While there are a large number of matrilineal societies in Africa and Asia, Arab and some Amazigh tribal communities (i.e., the indigenous population of North Africa that makes up more than 30 percent of Morocco and Algeria's population) are patrilineal. The notable exception is the Tuareg, nomadic peoples who live in the Saharan region of Morocco, Algeria, and Niger. In patrilineal settings, kinship is traced through father's lineage and inheritance of property, rights, names, or titles by persons related through male kin. In contrast, in matrilineal systems, women have a more prominent role than in patrilineal systems. Women do not move away from their mother's family when they marry but stay in their communities; descent is traced through the female line. Patrilineality reduces women's bargaining power in society, and strong tribes in countries like Jordan and Saudi Arabia are thus both served by, and supportive of, conservative family codes.

Such theories are measured by aggregate, country-level indicators such as the presence or absence of parliamentary gender quotas and the representation of women in offices of political authority. To some degree, researchers find these structural explanations for gendered inequities more convincing than cultural and conventional theories, but with a caveat – there is still the possibility of dramatic change over time, suggesting the institutional landscape of women's rights is shaped not just by historical legacies but by the autonomy and agency of activists today. For instance, many breakthroughs in women's rights have occurred due to sustained mobilization by civil society organizations that sought to pressure rulers into realizing the absurdity of excluding an entire gender from certain arenas, such as politics. Thus, while structural theorists may explain gendered inequalities in Kuwait by virtue of its political system and rentier attributes, they struggle to account for why, in 2005, the Emir granted women the right to vote in parliamentary elections. Civic advocates have an answer: it was because thousands of

Kuwaiti women peacefully protested, petitioned, and advocated for their fair voice, even in the face of ridicule, until they convinced the ruling monarch to relent on the issue.

> **BOX 9.2 CASE STUDY – NORTH AFRICA AND PSC**
>
> While there are many variables that can influence the development of patriarchal PSC (that is, family laws), patrilineal tribes may be one of them. For instance, consider the Maghrib countries of Algeria, Morocco, and Tunisia. All three neighboring states became independent in the same general time period, from 1956 to 1962, after prolonged episodes of French colonialism or occupation. All three are Muslim-majority. Yet the type of personal status code enacted following each state's post-colonial independence was extremely different: Tunisia's was extremely progressive, Morocco's was extremely conservative, while Algeria's was modestly in between. Further, these countries did not promulgate their laws at the same time; Tunisia did so shortly after independence, Morocco took nearly two years to finish its family laws, while Algeria took 22 years to fully articulate a personal status code to regulate personal and female behavior. Why these differences? One answer, from scholars like Mounira Charrad, could be the presence of patrilineal tribes: the stronger the level of tribalism and the more that new post-colonial regimes needed their support to rule the country, the more likely the resulting family laws would be very patriarchal and therefore reflect the gendered biases and social preferences of tribal communities. Therefore, the most progressive PSC resulted in Tunisia, where tribalism was extremely weak and the new government did not need rural support. The most conservative PSC resulted in Morocco, where the monarchy desperately needed tribal and rural backing to stabilize the country; the family laws were in part a tool to appease their social orthodoxy and gendered biases. In Algeria, patrilineal tribes existed but the militarized regime was even stronger, and so only needed to engage some of this traditional community while undergoing its own internal political spasms before finally releasing its PSC after two decades. In essence, the cause of divergent gender equality within PSC laws in the North African states was not religion or culture (as cultural and conventional theorizing would hold), but rather how a social formation (i.e., patrilineal tribes) interacted with political institutions over time.

Psychological and social theories

Psychological and social theories are the most universal, and perhaps the most sobering. Whereas cultural and conventional theories make the MENA look exceptionally backward, and structural theorizing at least concedes the possibility of change but nonetheless casts the region as a prisoner of history, psychological and social theories remind us that patriarchy may well be endemic to all human civilizations. Far from being an Arab, Islamic, or Middle Eastern phenomenon, gender inequality results from generic thinking processes and cognitive mechanisms that can be found in any regional or national context.

For instance, some argue that personal biases against females holding leadership roles stems from a mismatch between stereotyped gender roles and the traits associated with a "good leader." Gender role congruity theory posits that while women are stereotyped as extremely capable in domestic arenas, and in fact are often viewed as superior to men with regards to traits such as honesty and kindness, they were not seen as having psychological traits associated with effective leadership. Men are seen as more ambitious, forceful, and independent – qualities that are famously associated with leaders of the past. Meanwhile, focusing on networks, theories of homo-sociality argue that gender inequality is perpetuated by men's numerical dominance in politics and the tendency for individuals to have denser networks with people of the same gender, which generates a self-perpetuating cycle of patriarchy: men in power make friends with other men in power. Males are able to enjoy close trusting relationships while accessing the resources they need through these networks with other males, while women must often jump through more hoops and work harder simply for the same level of benefit.

CONCLUSION

Explaining differences in outcomes for women within and across countries is a major focus of scholarly inquiry, but there is no easy answer: women's status and the norms and laws that shape it are complex. As this chapter discussed, the notion of women's rights and female empowerment is hardly a Western concept. Though the MENA region struggles with gender inequality, girls and women have made major progress in certain arenas (such as educational achievement and parliamentary representation) while facing stifling challenges in others (such as family laws and participation in the economy). There is also impressive variation across the region; in their own ways, Israel, Tunisia, and some Arabian Gulf kingdoms stand out. The propensity of authoritarian regimes to instrumentalize women's rights issues makes the issue carry moral and political complexity, as debates about feminism and female breakthroughs can be driven at the grass-roots level by courageous activists but also be appropriated from above by political elites seeking to appropriate these issues for their own campaigns.

Still, positive trends in women's rights are too frequently overlooked by observers, who at times hold unhelpful biases and stereotypes about Arab or Muslim women. It is vital to remember that patriarchy is universal; that excepting a handful of small European countries, women around the world continue to lag behind men in their respective country regarding labor force participation, wages and salaries, political representation, and other indicators of gender equity. Perhaps the key takeaway is that women are diverse. The experiences of a wealthy woman in Qatar differs substantially from those of a poor woman in Morocco; each may relate to the general idea that men have unfair advantages, but they may do so from very different social and personal perspectives.

QUESTIONS FOR DISCUSSION

1 Why do Arab and Muslim women wear different styles of clothing, and what misunderstandings do people outside the region have about women's dress, including *hijab*?
2 What is the gender gap as it manifests in different areas of social, cultural, and economic life?
3 What is the private sphere as it relates to female autonomy, and how do we measure it?
4 What is the public sphere as it pertains to women's rights, and is it more or less important than the private sphere?
5 How can we devise a good measurement of gender equality, one that can treat all countries equally and objectively?
6 What is patriarchy? Discuss some examples from the MENA and other regions.
7 What are the main theoretical explanations for the lagging status of women in terms of economic and social opportunities in the MENA region? Which do you find compelling, and why?
8 Do you believe that the MENA region will improve its record on women's rights? What are the obstacles, whether internal or external to the region, that perpetuate or even widen gender gaps?

FURTHER READING

In empirical terms, the gender gap in the MENA region has been comprehensively charted out by social scientists. See, for instance, Valentine Moghadam, *Modernizing Women: Gender and Social Change in the Middle East*, 3rd ed. (Boulder, CO: Lynne Rienner, 2013), and Elhum Haghighat-Sordellini, *Women in the Middle East and North Africa: Change and Continuity* (London: Palgrave Macmillan, 2010) for excellent overviews. The Maghrib case study invoked in this chapter comes from Mounira Charrad, *States and Women's Rights: The Making of Postcolonial Tunisia, Algeria, and Morocco* (Berkeley, CA: University of California Press, 2001). Other interventions that are worthy of reading include Fariba Solati, *Women, Work,* and *Patriarchy in the Middle East and North Africa* (London: Palgrave Macmillan, 2017); Nikkie Keddie, *Women in the Middle East: Past and Present* (Princeton, NJ: Princeton University Press, 2008); Eleanor Doumato and Marsha Pripstein Posusney, eds., *Women and Globalization in the Arab Middle East: Gender, Economy, Society* (Boulder: Lynne Rienner, 2003); and Laurie Brand, *Women, the State, and Political Liberalization: Middle Eastern and North African Experiences* (New York: Columbia University Press, 1998). Rigorous article-length studies about the gender gap and public attitudes towards it include Helen Rizzo, Abdel-Hamid Abdel-Latif, and Katherine Meyer, "The Relationship between Gender Equality and Democracy: A Comparison of Arab versus Non-Arab Muslim Societies," *Sociology* 41, no. 6 (2007): 1151–70; Amy C. Alexander and Christian Welzel, "Islam and Patriarchy: How Robust Is Muslim Support for Patriarchal Values?" *International Review of Sociology* 21, no. 2 (2011): 249–76; and Lindsay J. Benstead, "Explaining Egalitarian Attitudes: The Role of Interests and Exposure," in *Empowering Women after the Arab Spring*, eds. Marwa Shalaby and Valentine Moghadam (London: Palgrave Macmillan, 2016). An excellent overview of LGBT status in Israel can be found in Aeyal Gross, "The Politics of LGBT Rights in Israel and Beyond: Nationality, Normativity, and Queer Politics," *Columbia Human Rights Law Review* 46, no. 2 (2015): 81–152.

The patriarchal "bargain" mentioned in this chapter is a concept pioneered by Deniz Kandiyoti in her article, "Bargaining with Patriarchy," *Gender and Society* 2, no. 3 (1988): 274–90. There have been, since then, many excellent overviews of patriarchy, gender, and women within the Muslim world and MENA region that draw upon philosophical, cultural, sociological, theological, and historical approaches. Among them are the essays: Mounira Charrad, "Gender in the Middle East: Islam, State, Agency," *Annual Review of Sociology* 37 (2011): 417–37; and Nawar Al-Hassan Golley, "Is Feminism Relevant to Arab Women?" *Third World Quarterly* 25, no. 3 (2004): 521–36. The following books are considered canonical in the study of patriarchy within Islam and the Middle East: Leila Ahmed, *Women and Gender in Islam: Historical Roots of a Modern Debate* (New Haven: Yale University Press, 1993); Lila Abu-Lughod, ed., *Remaking Women: Feminism and Modernity in the Middle East* (Princeton, NJ: Princeton University Press, 1998); Amina Wadud, *Qur'an and Woman: Rereading the Sacred Text from a Woman's Perspective* (Oxford: Oxford University Press, 1999); and Saba Mahmood, *Politics of Piety: The Islamic Revival and the Feminist Subject* (Princeton, NJ: Princeton University Press, 2005).

The 2011–2012 Arab Spring cast new light onto gender roles given the important role that many female activists played in national uprisings, as argued in Maha El Said, Lena Meari, and Nicola Pratt, eds., *Rethinking Gender in Revolutions and Resistance: Lessons from the Arab World* (London: Zed Books, 2015), as well as Nermin Allam, *Women and the Egyptian Revolution: Engagement and Activism during the 2011 Arab Uprisings* (Cambridge: Cambridge University Press, 2018). An excellent LGBTQ perspective is furnished by Scott Kugle, *Homosexuality in Islam: Critical Reflection on Gay, Lesbian, and Transgender Muslims* (Oxford: OneWorld, 2010).

Women's dress has also elicited a heated and lively literature. For different views on how preferences, such as the hijab, shapes social and personal relations, see Lindsay J. Benstead, "Does Interviewer Religious Dress Affect Survey Responses? Evidence from Morocco," *Politics and Religion* 7, no. 4 (2014): 734–60; Megan MacDonald, "SUR/VEIL: The Veil as a Blank(et) Signifier," in *Muslim Women, Transnational Feminism and the Ethics of Pedagogy: Contested Imaginaries in Post-9/11*

Cultural Practice, eds. Lisa K. Taylor and Jasmin Zine (London: Routledge, 2014); and well-acclaimed scholarly volumes like Fatima Mernissi, *The Veil and the Male Elite: A Feminist Interpretation of Women's Rights in Islam* (New York: Basic Books, 1992); Joan W. Scott, *The Politics of the Veil* (Princeton, NJ: Princeton University Press, 2010); and Leila Ahmed, *A Quiet Revolution: The Veil's Resurgence, from the Middle East to America* (New Haven, CT: Yale University Press, 2011).

The causes of patriarchy remain contested. While cultural and conventional theories are disputed by most authors, political-economic explanations are popular; see, for instance, Michael Ross, "Oil, Islam and Women," *American Political Science Review* 102, no. 1 (2008): 107–23. Sources on psychological and social structural theories include: Lindsay J. Benstead, Amaney Jamal, and Ellen Lust, "Is It Gender, Religion or Both? A Role Congruity Theory of Candidate Electability in Transitional Tunisia," *Perspectives on Politics* 13, no. 2 (2015): 74–94; and Elin Bjarnegård, *Gender, Informal Institutions and Political Recruitment: Explaining Dominance in Parliamentary Representation* (London: Palgrave Macmillan, 2013); and finally, Alice H. Eagly and Steven J. Karau, "Role Congruity Theory of Prejudice toward Female Leaders," *Psychological Review* 109, no. 3 (2002): 573–98.

There are also enlightening films on women's status in the MENA worth watching. For instance, consider Julie Meltzer and Laura Nix's 2012 film, *The Light in Her Eyes*, which focuses upon a Syrian Muslim woman who is a preacher; Lut Vandekeybus's 2005 film, *Linda & Ali: Two Worlds within Four Walls*, which chronicles an American woman who converts to Islam and moves to Qatar; Gini Reticker's 2015 film, *The Trials of Springs*, which shows the struggle of an Egyptian woman to voice her political demands during and after the Arab Spring; and Loubna El Younssi's 2015 program, *Marriage and Divorce in Morocco* for Al-Jazeera, which explores the family code and PSC in Morocco before and after its 2003 reform.

Online sources

Numerous organizations maintain programs and clearinghouses for data related to women's rights and gender equality, including many mentioned in this chapter. These include the World Economic Forum's Global Gender Gap Index in its latest report (www.weforum.org/reports/the-global-gender-gap-report-2018). See also the Women, Peace, and Security Index, produced by Georgetown Institute for Women, Peace and Security (https://giwps.georgetown.edu/the-index/); the Harvard Kennedy School Women and Public Policy Program's Gender Action Portal (http://gap.hks.harvard.edu/); and UN Women's digital library on gender equality issues (www.unwomen.org/en). The UN Development Programme likewise maintains a gender inequality index as part of its rankings for human development around the world (http://hdr.undp.org/en/composite/GII). A gathering place for scaled maps and visualized data regarding gender inequality across the globe, including the MENA, is WomanStats and its Maps section (www.womanstats.org/maps.html). The World Bank also maintains a useful portal for gender-related data (www.worldbank.org/en/topic/gender), while the ILGA provides a global map highlighting the status of LGBT rights and status laws in all regions, including the MENA (https://ilga.org/maps-sexual-orientation-laws). Finally, the raw data for surveys often used to gauge public attitudes for women are also online. See, for instance, the World Values Survey (www.worldvaluessurvey.org/) and the Arab Barometer (www.arabbarometer.org/).

CHAPTER 10

The youth generation
Education and transition

Sean Yom

THE RUNDOWN: KEY TOPICS COVERED
- Demography
- Education
- Jobs
- Resistance
- Cultural innovation
- Technological savvy

INTRODUCTION

The social churning of young people has always resulted in political roars in the MENA. Young citizens helped lead transformative periods of unrest over the past century, such as Iran's 1906 Constitutional Revolution, Turkey's Kemalist triumph after World War One, and the zenith of pan-Arabist ideology in the Arab world after World War Two. Today, however, the generational situation of MENA youths is unprecedented. In this chapter, "youth" refers to those aged 15 to 29, a definition used by major organizations like the World Bank and which currently encompasses over 150 million people – nearly a third of the region's total population. As a result, this youth cohort today is the single largest, best educated, and yet most unemployed generation in history. This cohort is also responsible for the Arab Spring. Young citizens led most new opposition movements that mobilized during the tumult of 2011–2012, including the social justice protests of Israel, the Gezi Park demonstrations of Turkey, and the resurgence of Iran's Green Movement. Splashed across its cover in February 2011, *Time Magazine* proclaimed the

MENA's youth generation as "changing the world," taking its place in history alongside the epic personalities and global leaders that have graced *Time* covers over the past century.

What do youths in the MENA represent today? Undeniably, many have suffered a delayed transition to adulthood due to failing educational standards and poor employment prospects. Yet culturally, youths also express marked divergence from their elders. They have a collective repertoire of shared experiences, technological awareness, and modern values. They are rewriting the rules of social and political engagement, questioning authority in dynamic and creative ways. This chapter explores how and why through four topics: *demography*, *education*, *economics*, and *cultural experience*. Each provides a different but important dimension about what youth, and youthfulness, means in the modern MENA.

DEMOGRAPHY

For decades, demographers spoke of the MENA's youth "bulge" – the disproportionately large pool of young people that outnumbered older generations. In 1960, for instance, over 40 percent of the regional population of over 100 million people were children – that is, 14 years of age or younger. Today, however, what was once a dry statistical topic has become a very real political quandary. As the Arab Spring showed, youth bulges can generate revolutionary explosions. For that reason, it is necessary to demographically unpack how and why young people dominate the face of most MENA societies. The underlying problem is not that the region's population is exploding at a breakneck pace; far from it, the overall populational growth rate has slowed down from its peak of 3.4 percent in the mid-1980s to under 2 percent today. Rather, it is that the proportion of youths in most societies has remained extremely high relative to other generations, underscoring the inability of governments to meet their aspirations and needs.

The MENA's youth bulge today has two components. First, many MENA societies have large generations of children, or those aged 14 years and under. Apropos the number of children, Figure 10.1 ranks global developing regions as well as the countries of the Organization of Economic Cooperation and Development (OECD) in terms of percentage of people aged 14 and under. The OECD includes the nearly three dozen wealthiest countries in the world, such as the United States and Canada, the European Union states, and prosperous Asia-Pacific countries like Japan, Korea, Taiwan, Australia, and New Zealand. The figure illustrates that in contrast to the OECD and

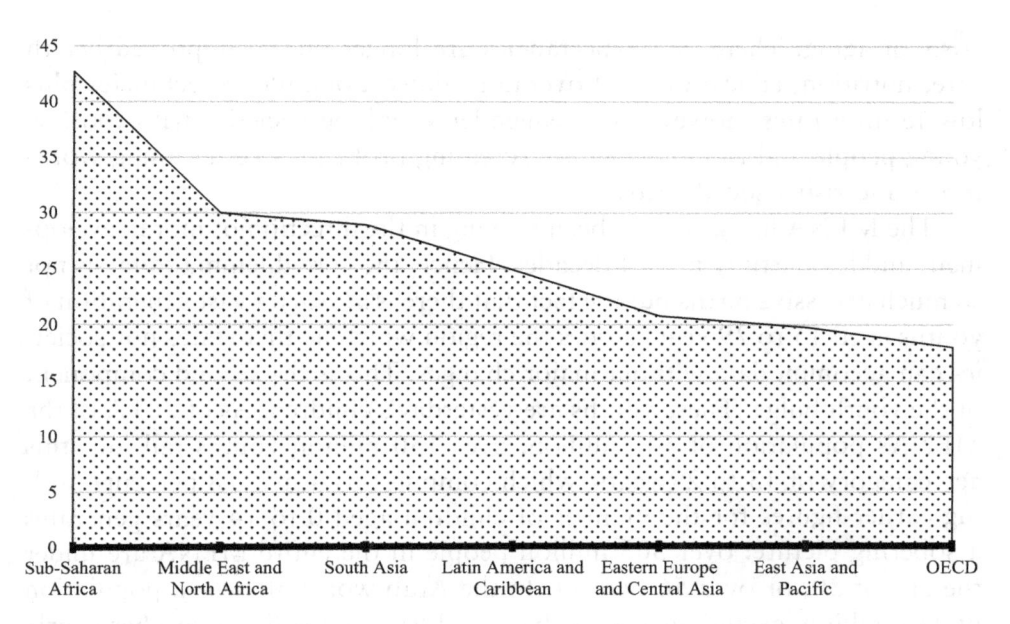

FIGURE 10.1
MENA vs. global regions – proportion of regional population aged 0–14 years, 2017.

Source: World Bank (2018), *World Development Indicators*.

less-developed regions, about 30 percent of the MENA's population falls in this category of the extremely young, second only to sub-Saharan Africa. According to the World Bank, as of 2017, over 153 million of the 541 million people living in the region (that is, the Arab world plus Israel, Turkey, and Iran) are 14 years of age or under, or over 28 percent.

Over the next decade, children as a proportion of the MENA population will shrink for a simple reason. It is a general principle that fertility rates (that is, how many births the average child-bearing woman has) are inversely correlated with social and economic development. Thus, in plain terms, mothers in richer countries bear fewer children than mothers in poor countries. For instance, 42.7 percent of the sub-Saharan African population is aged 14 or under, the highest regional proportion in the world. That less-developed societies are younger by virtue of higher fertility rates stems from several explanations – more traditional cultural views, stricter laws against contraception, and the perceived necessity of families needing to have more children due to shorter life expectancies and high infant mortality. By contrast, the world's richest countries like Japan often suffer from the opposite crisis of aging. There, life expectancies are longer due to improved health care, nutrition, education, and overall stability. Long life expectancies plus low fertility rates, however, can engender shrinking societies with too few young people and too many elderly, creating problems like declining workforces and rising social costs.

The MENA has generally been moving in the direction of more development and less fertility in past decades. Hence, the core dilemma today is not so much excessive births but the fact that there is *already* a vast generation of youths aged 15 to 29 years across the region which neither states nor societies can accommodate without major changes. This is the second component of the youth bulge. These youths are yesterday's children. As of 2017, of the MENA's population of 541 million, over 150 million youths fall into this age category of 15 to 29 years, which computes to nearly 28 percent. Adding earlier figures for the number of children aged 0 to 14 years generates a sobering picture: over 303 million people in the entire MENA are under the age of 30, or over 56 percent. In the Arab world alone – a population of 415 million, excluding Turkey, Iran, and Israel – the figure reaches nearly 60 percent; the Arab countries contain over 137 million children aged 0 to 14, and over 110 million youths aged 15 to 29.

The enormity of this bulge makes the median age of somebody living in the MENA at around 25 years. This makes the region unique in comparative perspective, matched only by some parts of Latin America, South Asia, and Southeast Asia. The poorest countries in the world are dominated by its youngest inhabitants, in that children comprise the largest single cohort of people; this is the case with sub-Saharan Africa. The wealthiest countries have graying societies, with its residents living longer and having fewer children; this is the case with the OECD and some East Asian countries like Japan. The MENA and some other middle-income regions, however, lay in between. These societies feature fairly long lifespans combined with large numbers of teenagers and young adults.

This demographic challenge is something of a double whammy. Currently, governments across the MENA are struggling to cope with the aspirations and demands of its youth – but tomorrow, they will need to deal with the *next* generation of youth, as today's children come of age and become young adults. To be sure, the category of youth brushes over major cross-national differences, for each country carries a particular cultural and historical legacy that informs its societal values. It also obscures issues of gender, class, and geography: women suffer far greater constraints than men, the poor struggle to survive far more than the wealthy, and rural inhabitants often face far worse conditions than many urbanites. However, one can still make generalizations that capture the majority of youth experiences across these important categories, and which underscore the fundamental problem about the stalled transition to adulthood.

In broad terms, becoming an adult entails several stages of growth: first obtaining literacy and education, next gaining employment and livelihood, and finally securing personal happiness by establishing new relationships and families. Over the course of life, individuals become increasingly independent, as much aware of their choices and opportunities as the constraints and obstacles holding them back. They constantly interact with the rules and routines set forth by their governments, such as laws and institutions, as well as the expectations established by their societies, such as religion and authority. For this reason, the values and skills gained through education are vital. They shape not just the beliefs of transitioning adults, but also prepare them to enter the economy and earn jobs. However, as the next section illustrates, educational systems across most of the MENA are lacking.

EDUCATION

In the MENA, the problem with education has shifted in recent decades. Today, it is less about *access* for the youngest and more about *quality* for those graduating. Especially in the Arab world, citizens across the region have attained more educational achievement as measured by degrees and diplomas with each passing generation. However, the skills provided by such schooling achievement are not necessarily guaranteeing meaningful and secure jobs in an economic marketplace defined by bloated public sectors and intense competition.

Universalizing access

Over the past several decades, the MENA has made impressive progress in broadening access to education to its youngest citizens. By the 2000s, free primary education had become accessible to most citizens; hence for the average child growing up by the age of 5 or 6, there was likely to be some accessible public school nearby teaching elementary skills in reading, writing, math, and other compulsory subjects. In 2013, the World Bank reported that in the MENA, 94 percent of all children eligible for primary education were enrolled in school, with the figure well balanced across boys and girls. This also exceeded the global average primary enrollment ratio of 89 percent.

Two additional statistics bear out the universalization of basic education. First, the MENA ranks favorably compared to other regions in terms of public spending for education. Across the region, governments spend on average nearly 15 percent of their budgets on schooling – more, in fact, than the OECD, as well as most former Communist countries. While expenditures on items like teachers, classrooms, books, technology, and other components can always be higher, these figures suggest that most MENA governments are not necessarily worse than those from other regions when it comes to financially allocating resources to the educational sector. In some countries, education is the single largest item on the national budget. This has been the case for Turkey for some time; in 2014, for instance, the IMF reported that the Turkish government spent $31.4 billion on education compared to $13.2 billion on the armed forces, the latter of which remains the second largest military in NATO after the US.

Second, the MENA also ranks well compared to the rest of the world in terms of youth literacy, which the World Bank defines as basic literacy among those aged 15–24 years. As of 2017, the region has a 90.8 percent youth literacy rate and a 79.6 percent adult literacy rate. The latter is a major improvement from the 59 percent adult literacy rate seen in 1990. Still, the statistics reveal that, in general, *young people are more educated and literate than adults*. There is significant variation within the region, however, especially when compared to the rest of the world. Figure 10.2 breaks down the MENA into the Arab countries, Iran, Turkey, and Israel, and juxtaposes them alongside other major global zones. The Arab world lags behind non-Arab countries in youth and adult literacy, but places higher than the poorer regions of sub-Saharan Africa and South Asia. Inversely, Turkey and Israel more closely resemble the rates seen in developed countries like those of East Asia and the OECD.

These numbers about educational access are positive but hardly perfect. For one, access can diminish. Education is often the first public service disrupted during civil conflicts; by the mid-2000s, for instance, in many areas of Libya, Syria, Iraq, and Yemen, schools and universities had become inoperative due to violence and warfare. For another, even discounting these wars, some children still do not have access to schooling due to poverty and geography. The 2014 Arab Learning Barometer estimated that in the Arab countries, 8.6 million children (of which 5 million were girls) were not enrolled in school. In addition, gender gaps persist in some countries beyond the primary level, with boys advancing at a greater pace than girls. The issue is especially pronounced in rural areas and urban slums, where

☐ Adult literacy rate   ■ Youth literacy rate (ages 15–24 years)

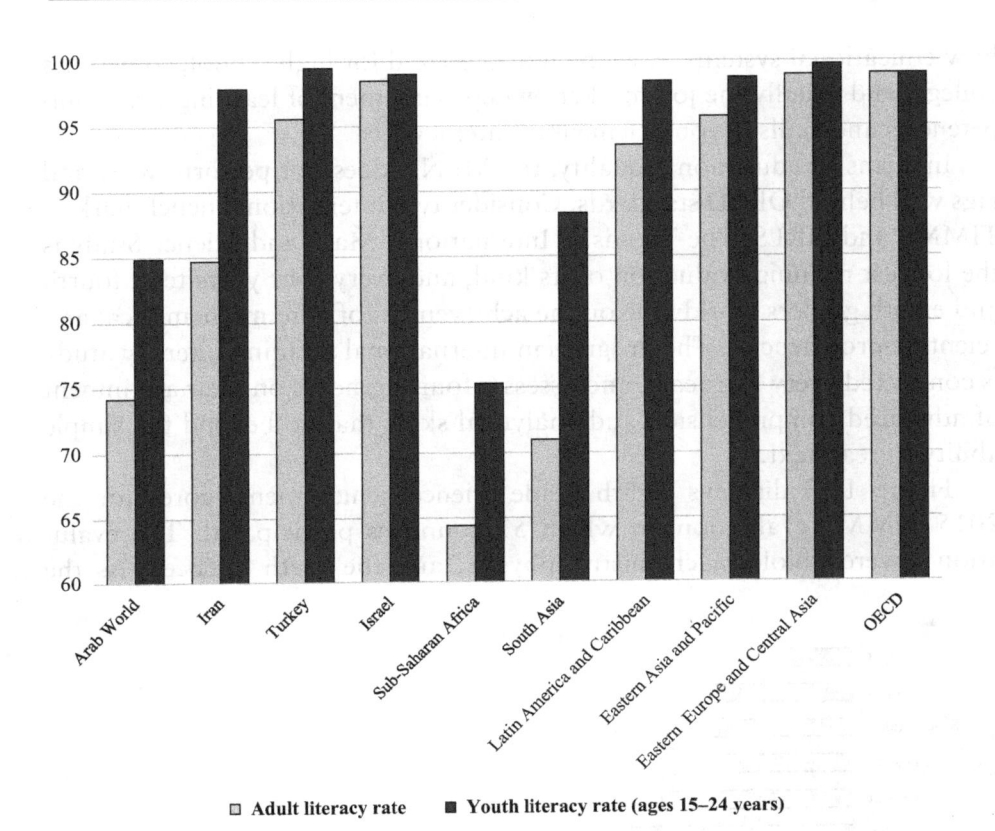

FIGURE 10.2
MENA vs. global regions – youth literacy vs. adult literacy, 2017.

Source: World Bank (2018), *World Development Indicators*.

female educational achievement is lowest. These are no small problems, and serve as an austere reminder about the difficulties of fully universalizing educational access across populations.

Still, advancements in overall enrollment and literacy rates across the region underscore an undeniable historical trend: over time, this has become an increasingly educated region. All else being equal, the MENA's average level of schooling has quadrupled since the 1960s and illiteracy has been halved since the 1980s.

Problems in underperformance and skills

A major crisis of education is not that youths do not have a school available for attendance; many do. Rather, it is what they absorb *inside* school, and how educational systems leave them ill-prepared for high school, sometimes college, and usually the job market by depriving them of learning vital competencies and skills beyond elementary literacy.

In terms of educational quality, the MENA does not perform well, and lags well behind OECD standards. Consider two international benchmarks – TIMMS and PIRLS. The Trends in International Math and Science Study is the longest running evaluation of its kind, and every four years tests fourth and eighth graders worldwide on the achievement of core mathematical and scientific proficiencies. The Progress in International Reading Literacy Study is conducted every five years, and assesses fourth graders on their attainment of advanced comprehension and analytical skills that go beyond the simple ability to read text.

Figure 10.3 displays eighth grade science achievement scores for the 2015 TIMMS evaluation, in which 57 countries participated. The evaluation covered biology, chemistry, physics, and the earth sciences. As the

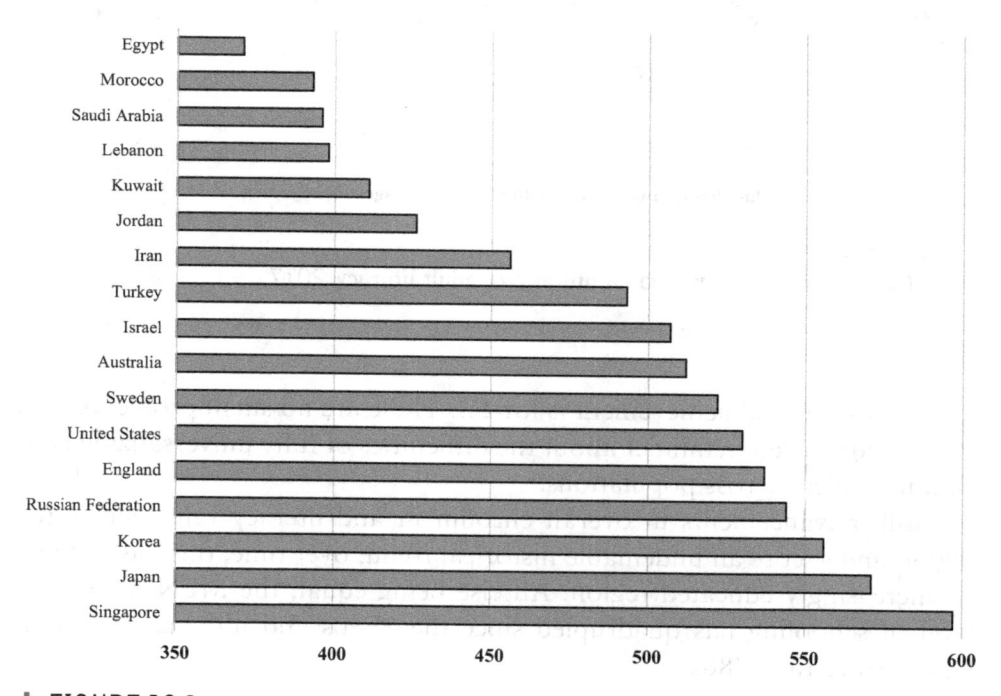

FIGURE 10.3

Select global countries – scores for eighth grade TIMMS science achievement evaluation, 2015.

Source: TIMSS (2016), *2015 International Results in Science*.

representative sample shows, the MENA countries scored far lower than leading Western and Asian countries, with the scoring scale set at 500 as the average. Figure 10.4, likewise, displays fourth grade achievement scores for the 2016 PIRLS evaluation, in which 61 countries participated. The test covered inferential skills such as drawing conclusions, retrieving information, and evaluating passages, and like TIMMS was designed with a 500 score as the central reference point. Again, the figure's selected sample (with some TIMMS countries missing as they did not participate in PIRLS) illustrates the MENA trailing badly, with only Israel approaching levels of wealthier and more industrialized countries.

What accounts for such poor levels of skill acquisition among MENA youths despite their high rates of attendance at the primary level? One major problem lies in the public educational systems that absorb students. First, physical resources at the primary and secondary levels are frequently

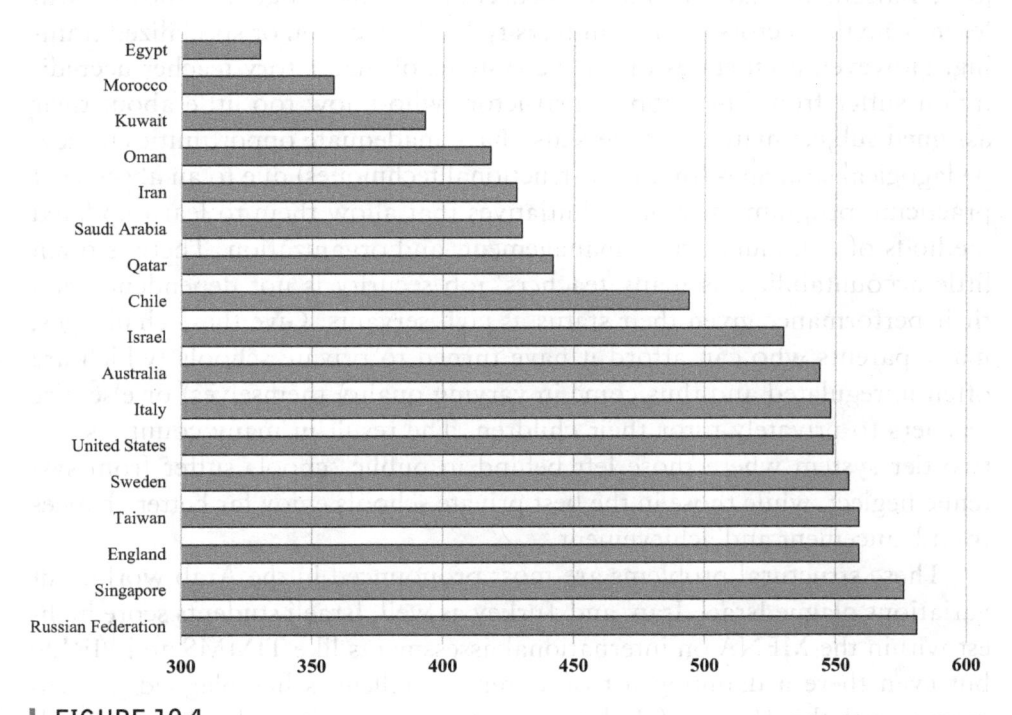

FIGURE 10.4
Select global countries – scores for fourth grade PIRLS reading achievement evaluation, 2016.

Source: PIRLS (2017), 2016 International Results in Reading.

inadequate. Educational facilities have been victimized by civil conflicts over the past two decades in places like Iraq, Syria, Libya, and Yemen. However, even in relatively stable countries like Egypt, Morocco, Algeria, and Sudan, public school buildings are too often dilapidated and insecure. Instructional spaces such as classrooms and study halls can be overcrowded, as infrastructure built a generation ago toils to accommodate the youth bulge. Curricula may be outdated and textbooks provide too limited viewpoints, especially when controlled by religious institutions. In addition, too many school libraries are small or even non-existent, and are poorly wired for new technologies. Refugee influxes amplify these obstacles to learning. After 2011–2012, for instance, many schools in Jordan, Lebanon, and Turkey experienced difficulty in accommodating many thousands of Syrian refugee children, whose own schools back home were decimated by war.

Second, too many primary and secondary level teachers are underprepared. Not all teachers in the MENA are qualified and certified for their jobs. Indeed, in many less-developed countries like Algeria, students will learn from instructors with no university-level education or specialized training. However, even states that have systems of mandatory teacher accreditation suffer from ill-equipped instructors who know too little about their assigned subject matter. Teachers also have inadequate opportunities to new pedagogical strategies (that is, instructional techniques) due to an absence of practicum programs and other initiatives that allow them to learn updated methods of communication, management, and organization. There is often little accountability, as many teachers' job security is not dependent upon their performance given their status as civil servants. Give these challenges, many parents who can afford it have turned to private schools (which are often unregulated and thus come in varying quality themselves) or else hire teachers to privately tutor their children. The result in many countries is a two-tier system where those left behind in public schools suffer from systemic neglect, while those in the best private schools enjoy far better chances for advancement and achievement.

These structural problems are most pronounced in the Arab world, but variations plague Israel, Iran, and Turkey as well. Israeli students score highest within the MENA on international assessments like TIMMS and PIRLS, but even there a daunting list of systemic challenges has plagued governments since the 1990s, including poor teacher quality, school overcrowding, and unequal access between native-born Jewish students on the one hand and Arab and new Jewish immigrants on the other, both of which are less integrated into society. In Turkey, the quality of public schooling varies considerably between urban and rural areas, and low teacher quality remains worrisome for many parents. Further, legal changes made in 2012 have also helped drive a wave of new enrollments in Islamic institutions that operate separately from older secularist public schools, and thus are not as regulated. In Iran, inequities in educational access persist across the regional divide, with schooling in central urbanized areas like Tehran and Isfahan better resourced than in outlying provinces. Education is also highly segregated along gender lines, an outgrowth of the country's Islamic transformation after the 1979 revolution, and instruction in many subjects must abide by strict religious and governmental censorship.

The third problem is pedagogy, which afflicts most of the region. Learning methods in primary and secondary schools, as well as many universities, remain teacher-oriented rather than student-focused. Innumerable classrooms still abide by the restrictive atmosphere of didactic lecturing by teachers, which emphasizes rote memorization and is geared towards high-stakes examinations that determine students' future advancement. In Palestine, for instance, high school learning is heavily tethered to the goal of scoring well on the seminal *tawjihi* (post-secondary graduation exam), which dictates which university programs they may attend. However, as the TIMMS and PIRLS results reveal, the ability to recall information in high-stakes tests does not necessarily signal real absorption of underlying skills, or the ability to apply them.

This predicament applies even at the college level. Most MENA countries feature large public university and college systems that furnish low-cost or free education to citizens. However, classroom environments at the undergraduate and graduate levels leave too little room for students to engage in critical thinking, creative empowerment, and analytical questioning – the type of activities that encourage adaptation and entrepreneurship later on in knowledge-based economies. Certain educational pathways perceived by students as ironclad guarantees for prestigious white-collar jobs, such as those in medicine, business, and government, attract disproportionate attention, leaving other fields underpopulated. For instance, in Jordan, overcrowding in these "prestige" trajectories since the 1990s has generated a dire shortage of learners entering vocational and technical occupations that are also important for the economy to function, such as hospitality, tradecraft, electronics, mechanics, and agriculture.

While international assessments like TIMMS and PIRLS indicate that younger students across the MENA have failed to keep pace with the best Western and Asian performers, higher educational evaluations also expose regional universities and colleges as similarly deficient. Almost no institution from the region regularly places within the top 150 universities in the QS World University Rankings and other global ranking tables. Problems at the primary and secondary level of education replicate at this tertiary (that is, college) level of schooling: too often, instructors are underqualified, facilities inferior, and curricula too restrictive, which severely depresses innovation, research, and productivity. Digital learning and technological usage at most universities lags behind the OECD. While there are islands of excellence, such as Israel's Hebrew University, Lebanon's American University of Beirut, Turkey's Bilkent University, and a handful of new Gulf institutions, in an overall sense most MENA universities and colleges have struggled to adapt and grow alongside evolving global standards.

There are two implications of this struggling educational ecology. First, youths are not obtaining the competencies and opportunities necessary for their lifelong development, from critical thinking and scientific aptitude to intellectual awareness and civic responsibility. As we know in Western countries like the US, high-quality education is central to active citizenship: it prepares learners for social futures, political engagement, and of course economic mobility – that is, to obtain work that provides dignity, purpose, and satisfaction. Unsurprisingly, in the Arab world, students recognize the failings of their educational systems. The Arab Youth Survey, which regularly polls young men and women from the Arab states, reported in 2017 that outside the hydrocarbon-rich Gulf countries, only about 33 percent of Arab youths believed their education adequately prepared them for the future.

This relates to the second ramification of underperforming education. Young citizens are expected to enter the job market after they finish schooling, and after obtaining financial security establish new lives and families. The problem is that many youths across the MENA cannot find viable employment. For many, education provides a very low return on investment because the skills furnished by classroom learning prove insufficient or even irrelevant to compete in increasingly globalized and competitive economies. This education-employment mismatch places additional stress on economies that already cannot generate enough jobs for everyone.

FINDING WORK

Economically, youth bulges can be framed in a constructive sense. When young citizens in great numbers become productive workers, they can quickly outweigh dependents and the old, thereby driving the national economy forward. Indeed, economists and demographers agree that there is always untapped potential in young adults to catalyze innovation, creativity, and industry.

For this to happen, however, youths need to find jobs, and it is here that the MENA faces another crisis. *Work* is the life stage that comes after schooling. Every year, hundreds of thousands of youths leave their respective schools and enter the job market – but instead of work, they must wait often years until they obtain their first full-time job. Since the mid-2000s, in fact, 25–30 percent of all young men and women across the MENA have annually suffered from unemployment. In 2012, the United Nations Development Programme warned that the MENA would need to generate 60 million new jobs over the next decade to fully accommodate its maturing youth generation; more than six years later, the region has not yet matched this ambitious scale. Figure 10.5 puts the MENA's problem in global perspective. The data illustrate two insights. First, the MENA has the world's highest youth unemployment rate by far, at 27 percent. To add additional depth to this number,

■ **Youth unemployment rate (ages 15–24)**   □ **Total unemployment rate**

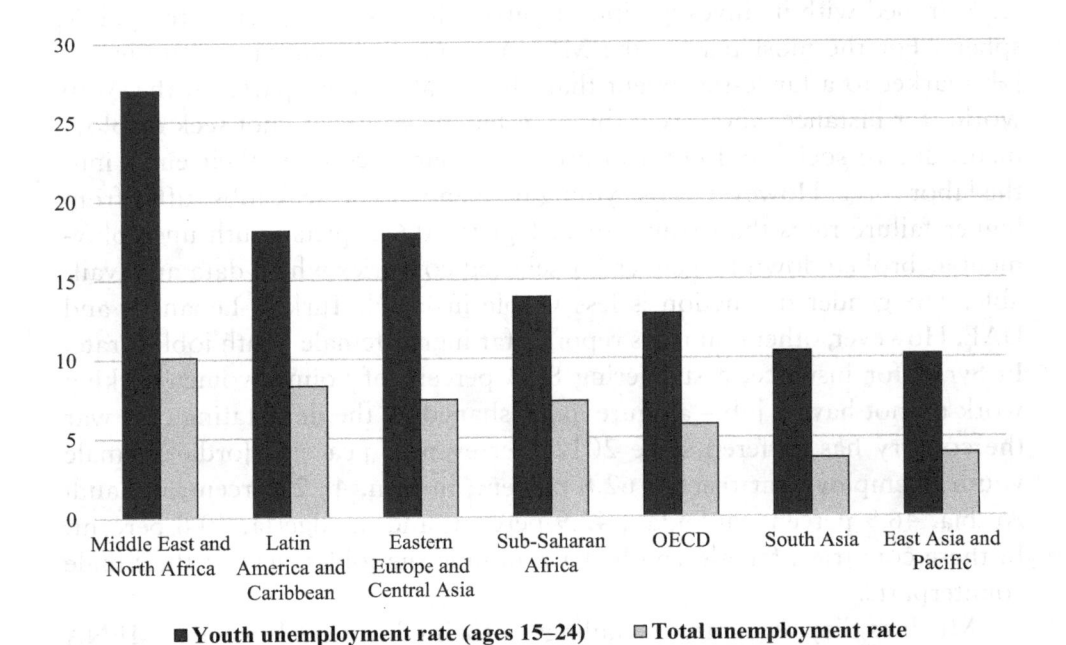

FIGURE 10.5
MENA vs. global regions – youth unemployment, 2017.

Source: World Bank (2018), *World Development Indicators*.

youths in the region comprise more than 40 percent of all the unemployed. Second, the MENA's youth unemployment rate dwarfs its overall joblessness rate of 10.1 percent (also the highest among global regions). This is especially worrisome given that nearly a third of the region's overall population falls under the age of 14, meaning that the demand for more jobs is staggered – it will only continue to rise over the next decade as these youths exit their education and enter the economy.

While all regions show difficulty in placing youths in the labor market, this problem is most pronounced in the resource-poor countries of the Arab world, and to a lesser extent Turkey and Iran. It holds less urgency for the wealthiest and smallest hydrocarbon-rich countries – essentially Kuwait, Qatar, and the UAE – because oil and gas wealth have allowed these governments to provide near-universal employment for all citizens of working age. However, this strategy is clearly not replicable across the MENA; it works only when there are just a few hundred thousand citizens and profuse hydrocarbon revenues flowing into government coffers.

Youth unemployment has a gender gap as well, validating what Chapter 9 argued with its investigation of patriarchy and its legacy in the public sphere. For the most part in the MENA, young women participate in the job market to a far lesser extent than their male counterparts. In the Arab world, for instance, about two-thirds of female youths do not seek employment, due to social and political pressures that discourage their entry into the labor force. However, those young women who do seek jobs suffer from higher failure rates than young men. Figure 10.6 depicts youth unemployment as broken down by gender for selected countries where data are available. The gender distinction is less visible in Israel, Turkey, Lebanon, and UAE. However, other countries report a far higher female youth jobless rate. In Syria, for instance, a staggering 80.3 percent of young women seeking work do not have a job – a figure likely shaped by the devastating civil war the country has suffered since 2012. Yet even in peaceful Jordan, female youth unemployment reaches 62.8 percent; in Iran, 48.2 percent; in Saudi Arabia, 46.9 percent; in Sudan, 42.9 percent; and in Algeria, 40.8 percent. In these countries, female youths have double the joblessness of their male counterparts.

Much as they recognize the failings of their educational systems, MENA youths also understand the dire straits of the job market. The 2017 Arab Youth Survey showed that 35 percent believed that unemployment was the single biggest obstacle facing the region – equal to the threat of violent extremism in the form of the Islamic State, and far more than the Palestinian-Israeli

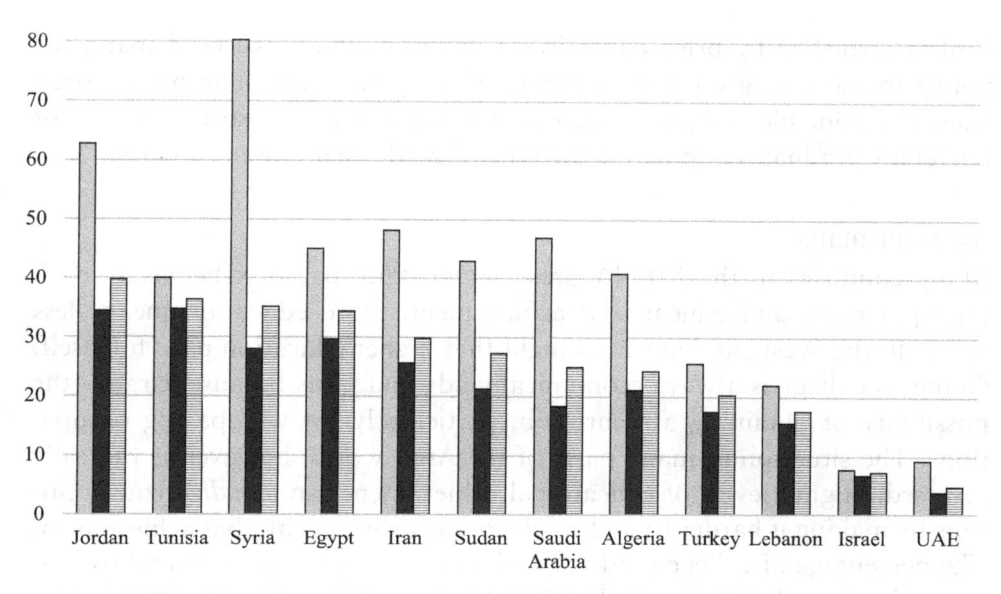

☐ Female youth unemployment rate ■ Male youth unemployment rate
☐ Total youth unemployment rate

FIGURE 10.6
Female vs. male youth unemployment rates, 2017.

Source: World Bank (2018), *World Development Indicators*.

conflict (16 percent) or loss of traditional values (12 percent). This runs consonant from results from other opinion polls. The Al-Jazeera Center for Studies, a think tank based in Qatar, conducted a more focused survey in 2013 about how the Arab Spring erupted. For many youths, the stagnant economy constituted a primary reason why it was necessary to mobilize on the streets and demand change: in Tunisia, 57 percent believed so; in Egypt, 60 percent; and in Yemen, 70 percent. The Pew Research Center's 2015 global survey of economic conditions likewise revealed sobering attitudes in the MENA, where about 44 percent of parents believed the next generation would be worse off, including nearly half of all Israelis and 52 percent of Turks.

What accounts for this bleak outlook? Excepting the smallest hydrocarbon-rich countries, the reasons for why MENA economies do not provide enough employment for job-seekers are complex. Here, however, they can be boiled down into supply and demand – that is, the *supply* of youths seeking jobs and the *demand* for youths by job providers. A major problem affecting the supply of youths in the labor market is the underwhelming quality and skillset furnished by prior education. Conversely, there is low demand for young job-seekers given the weakness of the private sector in many countries, alongside bloated public sectors that can no longer absorb long lines of university graduates hoping for the type of work their parents secured.

Skills mismatch

Many countries in the MENA present a striking paradox between youth unemployment and educational achievement: more education means less work. In the West, students are taught that higher education pays for itself. Going to college is always economically advantageous because it raises the possibility of obtaining a secure job, particularly for well-paying occupations. The situation in many parts of the Arab world, however, is radically reversed. Higher levels of educational achievement can *penalize* young citizens by making it harder to find work commensurate with that achievement. The percentage of college graduates who are unemployed compared to, say, high school graduates reveal the dismal situation in some countries, as Figure 10.7 charts out. In the OECD countries, rising up the educational ladder means less unemployment, because greater schooling means more skills, knowledge, and viability in the economy: only 7 percent of college degree holders in the workforce are jobless, whereas the figure for those with just primary schooling is 14 percent. The picture in many MENA countries is the inverse. There is an educational *penalty*, in that college degree holders have a higher unemployment rate than those with less educational achievement in places like Saudi Arabia, Iran, and Tunisia. In Turkey and Egypt, the figure is only marginally above the unemployment rate for workers with only a high school education.

With a few exceptions, such as Israel and the smallest rentier states in the Arabian Gulf (like Qatar) that can sidestep problems by offering virtually unconditional employment in the public sector, what accounts for the mismatch between educational output and job market needs? First, too many high schools and universities have become credential factories, in that they produce students who have diplomas but not enough innovative skills like multilingual fluency, scientific literacy, and analytical proficiency. Further, few countries have job-related internship and training programs that would give students practical experience that go beyond their classroom lessons. In past generations, credentials alone were often enough for many citizens to obtain positions in the public sector, such as the civil service and other government jobs. Yet today, the same graduates do not possess relevant skills

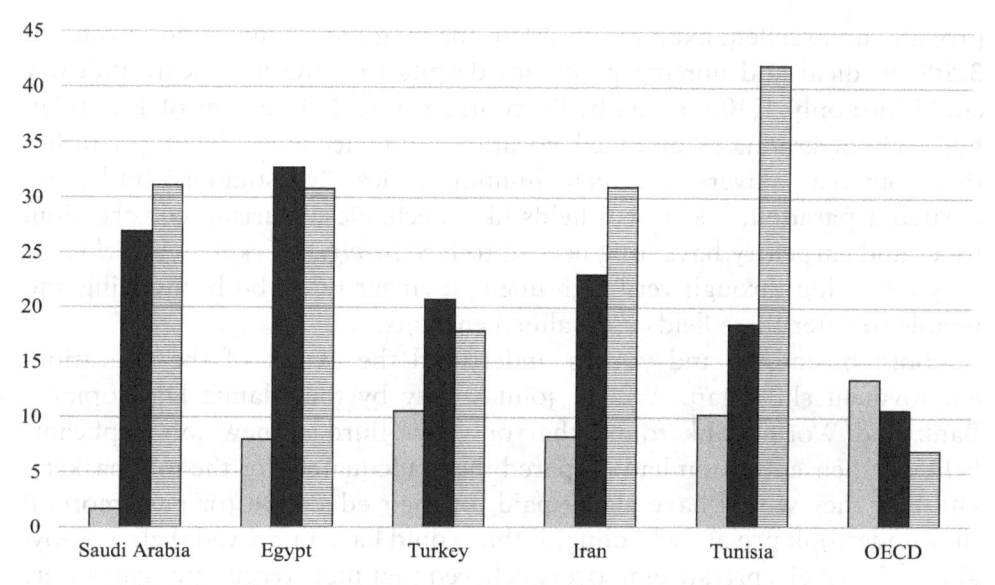

[Bar chart showing unemployment percentages by educational level across Saudi Arabia, Egypt, Turkey, Iran, Tunisia, and OECD]

- Percent workers with only primary education who are unemployed
- Percent workers with secondary education who are unemployed
- Percent workers with tertiary (i.e., college) education who are unemployed

FIGURE 10.7
MENA countries vs. OECD – unemployment by educational level, 2017.

Source: World Bank (2018), *World Development Indicators*.

when applying for a broad range of occupations in the private sector. They lack what human resource specialists call "work readiness" in booming industries driven by technology like telecommunications, media, and consumer services; sectors fueled by innovation like entrepreneurship, logistics, and pharmaceuticals; and even traditional fields that demand practical and relevant skills, such as finance and engineering.

Second, especially in the Arab world, too many students gravitate to highly theoretical specializations such as engineering, medicine, and finance under the belief that this will guarantee them a high-status job, while conversely too few enter vocational training that would lead to positions in technical crafts and physical trades. This "culture of shame," as discussed in Chapter 5, is a peculiar by-product of social and economic expectations. One implication in some countries is that certain professional fields are overcrowded while occupational pathways are starved of workers. Jordan provides an excellent example: in 2014, the kingdom's universities produced 3,500 medical and nursing graduates despite that the healthcare industry could hire only 1,300 annually. By contrast, just 2–3 percent of Jordanian high school graduates attended vocational and technical institutes rather than four-year universities. Such shunning of less "prestigious" trades has created a paradox; vocational fields like mechanics, tourism, construction, food, and carpentry have long needed to hire *foreign* workers while *domestic* youths slug through very high unemployment rates, both unwilling and unable to enter these fields as qualified entrants.

Both businesses and youths understand the extent of the education-employment skills gap. A 2011 joint survey by the Islamic Development Bank and World Bank found that only one-third of new job applicants believed their education had prepared them adequately for the job market – and that they would have gladly paid for their education (or paid more, if they undertook private schooling) if this would have improved their employability. Inversely, private employers believed that most recent graduates were not ready for the workplace, meaning they had to invest expensive resources for on-site training and work readiness. In some countries, such as Egypt and Morocco, less than a third of human resources managers believed that freshly minted graduates had appropriate skills due to their having undertaken imprudent specialization-filled outdated curricula. Companies and firms often complained that even in highly specialized fields like engineering, job applicants lacked technical knowledge and technological understanding. They also noted that would-be employees struggled to communicate clearly, solve problems, lead teams, and work independently – deficiencies that begin at the primary level of schooling. Excepting Israel, MENA businesses also desired more job applicants to understand multiple languages beyond their native one (e.g., Arabic, Turkish, Persian).

Weak job creation

In addition to the mismatch between educational output and job market needs, most MENA countries also suffer from undersized private sectors – that is, for-profit businesses and companies – that simply cannot generate enough jobs for new school graduates every year. There is significant regional variation in this problem, however. For instance, while not without their own economic challenges, Turkey and Israel have each developed competitive and diversified private sectors that have produced globally competitive firms. Turkish banks and manufacturers, along with Israeli high-tech and pharmaceutical companies, are examples. Furthermore, the tiny but prosperous Gulf kingdoms of Kuwait, Bahrain, Qatar, and the UAE can afford to have relatively small private sectors because in these compact societies, governments can still afford to provide college graduates ready-made jobs in the public sector so long as their oil and gas exports sell abroad. Elsewhere in the Arab world, however, there is another trend in that most private-sector economies are not adequate job creators. To be sure, this comes with a caveat: even in less-developed countries like Jordan and Lebanon, there exist many non-government jobs that educated youths shun because they lack prestige and reputation, from serving food to working in factories, and which instead go to foreign workers.

More broadly, however, there are several reasons why the job supply to young citizens has been lacking, which implicates the institutional framework of business development. If businesses cannot flourish, they cannot hire more people. First, many economies have not attracted private investment by domestic and foreign financiers, which for decades has reflected fears on part of many potential investors that dilapidated infrastructure, financial volatility, and regional conflicts could distort growth and returns. Yet without infusions of capital from sources other than the government, industries and sectors cannot grow. Second, new companies in these countries frequently run into obstacles in obtaining credit – i.e., financial loans to purchase assets, underwrite operations, and expand business. Banking systems are underdeveloped, and generally favor large established firms over start-ups and entrepreneurial ventures. Many small companies sidestep this by working informally, cutting costs by operating outside existing legal regulations. However, this also means employees cannot benefit from the protections afforded by labor laws such as social security, workplace safety, and wage protection.

Third, excessive government regulations have stifled growth. Bureaucratic red tape makes simple tasks extremely daunting like obtaining export licenses, enforcing legal contracts, registering new property, approving construction permits, and hiring new employees. In some cases, first-time business owners are also stymied by recurrent corruption, which systematically advantages those with superior financial resources who can bribe their way into success. Indeed, the World Bank's 2017 Ease of Doing Business Index, which assesses the difficulties faced by private firms given their regulatory environment, ranks only two MENA countries in the top third of all national economies worldwide – Israel and the UAE. That youths are worried about corruption is an understatement; in almost every single protest wave during the 2011–2012 Arab Spring, demonstrators chanted and marched against the perceived spread of corruption in both politics and business. However, the 2010 Silatech Index, a comprehensive regional survey undertaken in partnership with Gallup, exposed this resentment before the Arab Spring. In that poll, the majorities of youth in most countries, including 89 percent in Lebanon, 87 percent in Algeria, and 85 percent in Morocco, believed corruption was widespread in business.

In addition to these challenges within the private sector, many MENA economies are also burdened with very large public sectors that cannot furnish enough jobs to youth applicants, despite the perceived desirability of working within this area. Public sector refers to government-related jobs such as the civil service, bureaucratic administration, armed forces, and state-owned enterprises like oil firms, national airlines, and other government-run companies. Chapters 5 and 6 aptly analyzed the problem of state-led development, which even when fueled by hydrocarbon rents relies upon public employment to soak up workers. The resulting social contract, swapping economic security for political freedom, became unsustainable by the 1980s for all the factors those two chapters discussed – oil price shocks, fiscal burdens, demography, and external pressures. Despite this, the public sector remains the single largest employer in most MENA countries, and continues to provide salaries and pensions that equal or exceed the private sector. According to the World Bank, government wages across the MENA as percentage of GDP measures nearly 10 percent – far higher than sub-Saharan Africa (6.7 percent), Latin America (4.9 percent), and the OECD (4.5 percent). Put another way, simply paying public-sector workers requires governments to set aside more previous money than almost anything else. In Jordan, the Department of Statistics estimated in 2015 that there were about 400,000 public-sector employees to 800,000 private-sector workers – one of the most lopsided ratios in the region. In Israel, as of 2016 more than 16 percent of the national workforce remains on the government payroll, a proportion roughly equivalent to Iran; further, wages in the Israeli public sector increased nearly 10 percent in the 2000s, compared to just 2 percent in the private sector.

What's the upshot? Financially inefficient yet driven by political imperatives, public sectors continue to be seen by youths as the most attractive places to work: that is, *they are preparing for economic lives that became obsolete a generation ago*. In most countries, university graduates continue to prefer government-related work over other options despite the obvious financial inability of most governments to hire them. Figure 10.8 furnishes the work preferences of Arab youth as taken from the 2010 Silatech Index,

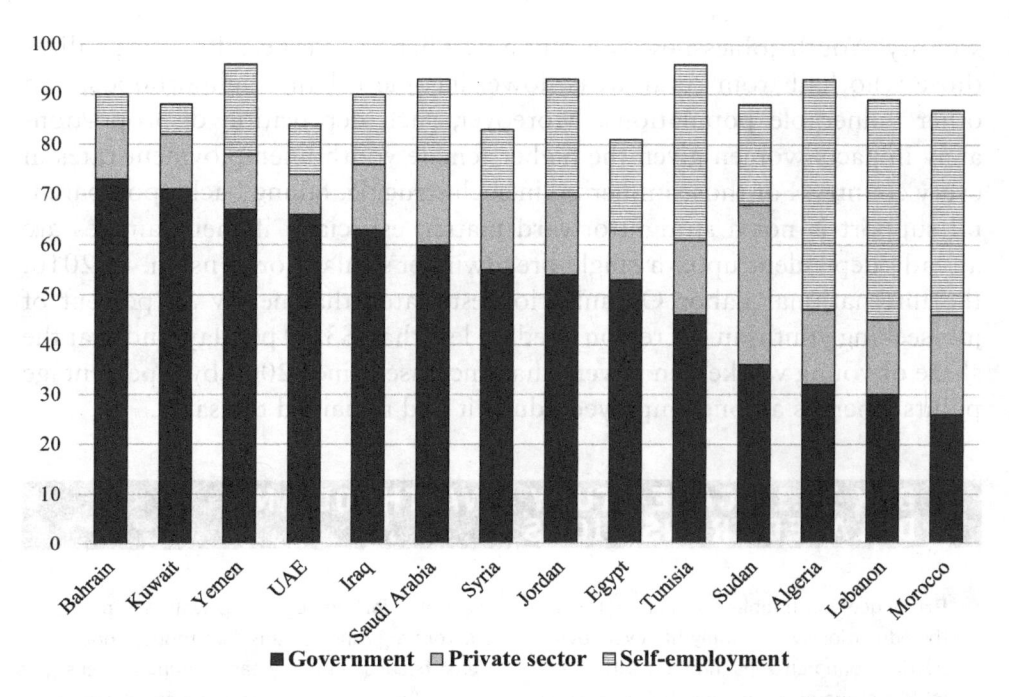

FIGURE 10.8
Work preferences among Arab youth, 2010.

Source: Silatech (2010), *Silatech Index: Voices of Young Arabs.*

a groundbreaking study. The data show that in most Arab states, a majority of youths prefer to work in the public sector even assuming similar pay and work conditions. Pointedly, in no country do youths prefer private-sector jobs over government-related work. In a few places, such as Algeria, Lebanon, and Morocco, they see self-employment (e.g., entrepreneurship) as more viable than work in either the public or private sectors. The inability to translate these desires into concrete outcomes exposes the suffocating regulations and obstacles aforementioned that discourage new businesses.

THE CONSEQUENCES OF CRISIS

The enormous demand for, and underwhelming supply of, jobs across most of the MENA for aspiring youths has devastating consequences. Most obviously, it has impoverishing effects, amplifying all the physical and mental harms that can afflict human communities as discussed in Chapter 2's engagement of over-urbanization and Chapter 7's concern about environmental security. Youth joblessness – essentially, idleness – especially marginalizes those who hail from rural areas, lower-income urban neighborhoods, and other vulnerable populations. Moreover, such deprivation disproportionately impacts women given the higher female youth unemployment rates in every country. For those immersed in such struggle, falling back upon parental support is not a straightforward matter, especially if their families are already dependent upon a single breadwinner's salary or pension. In 2016, the International Labor Organization estimated that nearly 39 percent of job-seeking youths in the region lived on less than $3.10 per day, and that the share of young workers in poverty had increased since 2007 by 3 percentage points whereas among employed adults it had remained the same.

BOX 10.1 CASE STUDY – WAITHOOD AND DELAYED TRANSITIONS

Prolonged youth joblessness disrupts the education-work-family life cycle by putting young citizens in limbo with the middle stage of finding employment, stuck in the netherworld between adolescence and adulthood. Such "waithood," as psychologists term it, delays the transition to marriage, starting a family, and becoming involved in their communities, because in most MENA countries buying a house is the prerequisite for marriage – and a steady job is the prerequisite for buying a house. The 2016 Arab Human Development Report indicated that in Jordan, Palestine, and Tunisia, the majority of young job-seekers reported waiting more than one year before finding a single sustainable job; in Egypt, the figure was 72 percent. Such long-term joblessness not only diminishes skills and knowledge, it also induces frustration, anxiety, hopelessness, and anger on part of many young citizens who feel they have ticked every checkbox but were never told what the job market would be like in real life. The shortage of perceived desirable jobs in both the private and public sectors aggrandizes this "waithood," not least because in many cases young citizens will voluntarily queue for a job perceived as more prestigious rather than opting to work immediately at a less attractive but income-bearing occupation. For instance, in 2014 Jordanian authorities reported that over 200,000 job applicants had passed their Civil Service exam and were awaiting their turn for a job opening in the government – an enormous number given that the entire public sector only employs 400,000 people. This situation of deliberative joblessness paradoxically coexists with a private-sector economy that must hire hundreds of thousands of foreign workers to fill unskilled positions, such as retail, construction, and other basic service jobs in a frustrating duality. Not surprisingly, the 2010 Silatech Index reported that within the Arab world, most young job-seekers would prefer an increase in higher quality jobs over affordable housing available and reducing the cost of marriage.

Second, the job crisis severely erodes the confidence of young citizens to become active members of their communities. Indeed, especially in the lesser developed MENA countries, it prompts many youths to emigrate – to leave their societies altogether in hopes of seek new lives in foreign countries. The 2016 Sahwa Youth Survey, jointly carried out between MENA and the European Union, found that more than a fifth of the Arab youths polled wished to move abroad, with job-related reasons frequently cited as the justification. The 2010 Silatech Index uncovered a similar finding: in its surveys, 30 percent of those aged 15–29 would migrate permanently to another country if given the opportunity. Indeed, it is well known that the vast majority of emigrants who leave the MENA voluntarily (that is, excluding refugees, who are forced to leave their homes due to conflict and violence) fall under 35 years of age.

Another outcome of such social and economic disempowerment is political transformation. One externality has been the stream of youths towards radical Islamist organizations, including Salafi-jihadist groups like the Islamic State. Key to understanding why so many young citizens would gravitate to such extremist violence is not just the alluring ideological message of these forces, but also the emptiness and despair of the lives they leave behind. Most youths from the Arab world who have joined the Islamic State, for instance, suffer from relative deprivation. They are neither elite nor peasant: they are educated enough to understand that their inability to get a job and start a family has less to do with their own dreams, and more to do with the myriad obstacles placed in front of them by their states and societies.

The second manifestation hits closer to home: especially in crowded urban areas, disenchanted but determined youths desiring lives of dignity and meaning are more likely to collectively mobilize and express their grievances in order to demand political reforms and, in some cases, revolution. As Chapter 3's analysis of social mobilization pointed out, this dynamic characterized the Arab Spring, in which youths ceased to be a faceless demographic figure and instead became agents of change in their societies. They authored the evocative events and images of that memorable period, fleshing out large demonstrations which paralyzed entire cities and playing an elusive cat-and-mouse game with older authorities – governments, police officers, tribal leaders, religious figures – who sought to quell their voice. Photo 10.1 shows this scene in one of the iconic nighttime marches of revolutionary Egypt.

PHOTO 10.1
Youth march to retake Tahrir Square, Egypt, 2011.

Source: Photo by elhamalawy is licensed under CC BY-SA 2.0.
Online: www.flickr.com/photos/elhamalawy/6297245605

That many youths are disappointed with the performance of their governments, and in a wider sense the moral and political weight of authority figures, is self-evident. The 2017 Arab Youth Survey, for instance, revealed that across the Arab states, between 71 and 85 percent of youths did not believe their countries were doing enough to address the needs of their young generation. The problem is not isolated to the Arab world, either. The 2017 Youth Study of Israeli youths, undertaken by the German research organization Friedrich-Ebert-Stiftung, found that nearly 41 percent of Jewish youths were not sure about whether they could achieve their personal goals in Israel – a sharp drop from the less than 20 percent recorded in 1998 – and that, likewise, the same proportion was pessimistic about their social and economic futures. The 2015 IRIS Millennial Survey's work on Turkey divulged similarly disconcerting results. Only 9 percent of Turkish millennials were satisfied with the economy and less than half felt optimistic about the future.

CULTURAL EXPERIENCE

However, MENA youths are more than demographic statistics, educational figures, and unemployment outcomes. It would be a mistake to characterize this generation as nothing more than revolutionaries-in-waiting. To be certain, politics is everywhere, and once-a-generation events like the Arab Spring cannot be ignored. However, what is also happening is that MENA youths are undergoing new cultural experiences that are refashioning the fabrics of their societies. They are asserting their identities, articulating new values, utilizing technology, and creating synergies that have astonished older generations, as well as Western observers. The expression of such youthfulness, and how it affects socialization and empowerment, occupies this chapter's last section.

Consumption and identity

To be sure, it is difficult to impose one coherent identity upon this generation. While Chapter 4's discussion of identity categories correctly notes that being young *is* a marker of self-conception, to employ the term "youth" to encompass the nearly 150 million people who range from their mid-teens to late twenties in age across the MENA can be problematic. In reality, this is a sprawling social category, encompassing people in two dozen countries who speak multiple languages and practice different faiths. Most are Arabs, who are more similar to their Turkish, Iranian, and Israeli counterparts than they might believe, but also exhibit considerable diversity. They have all grown and matured while living under distinctive types of regimes – democracies and autocracies, republics and monarchies, secular and theocratic – and are inheriting unique historical legacies and national burdens. Given this, it is vital to characterize this generation not in terms of what it may *lack* but rather by its dynamism and orientation, especially in terms of culture. The MENA's youth cultures today, like those elsewhere around the world, flourish in their synergistic creativity. Young people have fused indigenous identities and forms with Western and globalized elements, resulting in innovative new styles and routines that amplify the generational gap between themselves and their parents.

Of course, to some extent every new generation distinguishes itself by casting off the seemingly tired values of their parents in favor of newer fashions and rule-breaking behavior. More than one CNN news special has roamed the streets of Muslim-majority countries, exposing Western viewers to apparent contradictions – of young Muslim women in Cairo or Tehran who veil themselves but shop for expensive European cosmetics and jewelry, or of Arab men in Beirut or Casablanca quaffing tequila at Irish pubs on Thursday before sleeping it off and attending mosque on Friday. Visitors to Tel Aviv, being told of its relative Westernization, may not be surprised to find loud nightclubs filled with dancers swigging Heineken. If they traveled to neighboring Jordan, though, they would find an Amstel factory (the first ever opened outside the Netherlands, back in 1958), as well as new craft breweries whose beers adorn Amman's many bars and lounges. Likewise, 20-somethings pack into globally branded stores across the MENA – American Eagle Outfitters in Saudi Arabia, Banana Republic in Qatar – and form a hungry audience for the latest sushi offerings in Rabat or Abu Dhabi. Indeed, fast food neatly frames the intersection between youth tastes and globalized consumption. Witness crowds of teenagers, eyes glued to iPhone screens glowing with the latest Instagram posts or Facebook feeds, that jam into Johnny Rockets in Bahrain, Dairy Queen in Saudi Arabia, Burger King in Turkey, Papa John's in Kuwait, Fatburger in Tunisia, Hardee's in Egypt, KFC in Palestine, Shake Shack in Oman – and of course, McDonald's in more countries than not.

These visual observations are biased: they illuminate the everyday social routines of MENA youths who predominantly live in urban areas and come from middle class or wealthier backgrounds. Still, they are useful images insofar as they capture elements of lived experiences that are too frequently ignored by Western observers. Beyond consumption, moreover, youth identity has also expressed itself through artistic form. Take, for example, the visual arts. Over the past decade, the Arab world has given rise to a new wave of contemporary male and female artists. Their varied products, ranging from traditional paintings and sculptures to photo collages, video installations, and documentaries, began gracing modern galleries around the world in the mid-2000s, often circulating amongst collectors based in Dubai, New York, and London. In some cities, like Beirut, grass-roots initiatives such as art collectives have helped propel new local artists forward by providing gallery spaces, sponsoring competitions, and financing travel abroad. Within the cinematic industry, new filmmakers have pushed back against social expectations to create groundbreaking movies. Since the late 2000s, these efforts have borne fruit, with both short and long productions made by bold new directors, such as Jordanian Naji Abu Nowar's drama

Theeb, featuring prominently in international film festivals and global award competitions.

The aesthetic spectrum of artistic expression also encompasses street art, which during the Arab Spring emerged as a powerful medium to convey the joys, rage, and humor of young activists. In countries that witnessed the largest protests, like Tunisia, Egypt, Libya, and Syria, paint-wielding artists appropriated public spaces and city buildings to leave behind elaborate murals, drawings, and graffiti that garnered international attention. Rebelling against not only police restrictions but also the perceived constrictions of aesthetic norms, street artists depicted a dizzying array of defiant images: impish cartoons of dictators stumbling over themselves; memorials to protesters and martyrs; path-breaking Arab women, such as Olympic athletes, running through local streets; and innumerable abstract motifs and images. Iran also owns a vibrant independent street art and graffiti scene, one whose young participants collaborate frequently and organize online in order to preserve works that authorities target for destruction.

Music provides another powerful example of the creative reformulation of youth identity. Today, satellite television watchers recognize the high popularity of shows like *Star Academy*, *Super Star*, *Arab Idol*. Modeled after Western hits like the British *Pop Idol* and US-based *American Idol*, these telecasts enable young singers and musicians from various Arab countries to compete in front of a regional audience that votes weekly on their favorite contestants. The origins of this musical diffusion, however, go back decades. Many MENA countries by the late twentieth century had developed unique genres of localized music that became popular amongst teenagers and young adults. In Algeria, for instance, the eclectic musical aesthetic known as Rai, which drew upon not just folk and Arab but also French, Spanish, and African elements, became popular by the 1980s amongst younger citizens chafing against military rule and economic decay. By the 2000s, however, global fashions had brought new Western genres into national musical scenes but heavily filtered through the experiences of national youths. Intrepid music tourists could listen to everything from bubblegum pop singers to death metal bands in countries like Morocco, Lebanon, Egypt, and Kuwait, singing in a mish-mash of French, Arabic, or English. Photo 10.2, for instance, depicts several Kuwaiti teens belonging to a heavy metal and rock enthusiast group, whose dress appears nothing like the traditional Gulf attire described in Chapter 6.

PHOTO 10.2
Fans from the Kuwait Rock Army, 2011.

Source: Photo by q80_outsider is licensed under CC BY 2.0.
Online: www.flickr.com/photos/q80_outsider/5957948136

BOX 10.2 CASE STUDY – HIP-HOP MUSIC

Youth music often intersects with politics everywhere, as in the example of hip-hop. Across the region, rap music (much like its Western counterpart) has been led over the past two decades by young lyricists articulating often-controversial lyrics about the difficulties of everyday life – from being misunderstood by parents and elders, to grittier topics of corruption, poverty, and decay. In North Africa, especially Morocco and Algeria, French hip-hop became popular by the 1990s, with new local rappers quickly attracting not just devoted underground crowds but also commercial interests from record labels.

In Lebanon, Palestine, and other Arab countries, both European and American rap music began shaping youth tastes at around the same time period, but with different themes. Many Palestinian MCs by the 2000s were lyricizing both historical topics, such as the Arab-Israeli conflict and the refugee diaspora, and contemporary issues like drug use and corruption inside Palestine. The 2007 hit show on MTV Arabia, *Hip Hop-Na* (which means, in Arabic, our hip-hop), cemented the genre as a mainstay among Arab youths. More recently, outwardly revolutionary rap songs became popularized during the

> **BOX 10.2 (CONTINUED)**
>
> Arab Spring. Throughout 2011–2012, activists and artists could pen catchy anthems that quickly became regional hits not because of marketing deals and concert tours, but because so many youths could easily download and replay their songs at will across borders. Among them were the Tunisian artist El General's "Rayes Le Bled," the Libyan rapper Ibn Thabit's "Benghazi II," and the Egyptian group Arabian Knightz's "Rebel" (which featured a sampled hook from Lauryn Hill). Crucially, the hip-hop trend has not been limited to Arab-speaking countries. In Israel, Hebrew rap amassed great popularity by the 1990s and sprouted multiple subgenres, from the patriotic and religious to subversive and critical. Ethiopian-Israeli artists, for instance, took inspiration from American artists like Tupac Shakur to loudly criticize other Israelis for exuding racism and prejudice at newly arrived Jewish immigrants from Africa. In Turkey, transnational connections were on full display with the rise of the hip-hop scene in the 1990s. Early MCs were influenced by the musical tastes of young Turkish emigrants in Germany, whose underground cassette recordings and battle tapes helped catalyze the new genre when brought back to the homeland and played among young urban crews. All these songs and artists are easily watchable today on YouTube, or listenable on Spotify, iTunes, and other music streaming services.

History and memory

The globalized tastes and consumptive fashions of MENA youths distinguish this generation from their elders. Yet they also point to a more fundamental historical reality, one that helps situate the values and orientation of young people in context. Youths today share the collective experience of living in a twenty-first century defined by rapid change. Most lack the memories and events that punctuated the lives of their parents and grandparents, which forged the identities of their nations and laid the foundations of political order. In Israel, for instance, it has been decades since the military has deployed its young conscripts for battle on a national basis. In Turkey, unlike past generations, today's youth have come of age under an elected government that has resisted temptations of military coup d'état. In Iran, young citizens are not the revolutionaries who overturned the monarchy in 1979 and installed the Islamic Republic; they are their descendants. Yet nowhere is the generational divide strongest than in the Arab world. Arab youths came of age during the Arab Spring, a period of extraordinary uncertainty and unrest that saw seemingly invulnerable dictatorships in countries like Tunisia, Egypt, Libya, Syria, and Yemen buckle to uprisings led not by intellectuals and elites, but by everyday people.

However, even before this historic tumult, it was clear that young Arabs were being raised in a very different political environment than their parents. For one, many had little recollection of long-serving presidents and kings who ruled their countries from the 1960s through 1990s, whose legendary reputations for survival and craftiness made them almost mythical figures – but who also inevitably passed away. In 1999 alone, the deaths of three kings enabled their much younger and seemingly Western-oriented sons to take power: in Jordan, King Hussein gave way to Abdullah II; in Morocco, King Hassan II to Mohammad VI; and in Bahrain, Emir Isa bin Salman to Hamad bin Isa. A year later in 2000, Hafez Al-Assad's passing in Syria gave rise to his son, Bashar Al-Assad. Young faces continue to pop up around regional leadership, such as when 33-year-old Tamim bin Hamad ascended to become new Emir of Qatar in 2013, and four years later 31-year-old Muhammad bin Salman became the Crown Prince in Saudi Arabia.

Second, many Arab youths also matured long after the traumatic national crises that defined the social and political lives of their elders had ended, and so have been more willing to believe in the possibility of rapid and positive change. For instance, many Algerian young adults do not remember the horrific civil war of the 1990s, which left a lasting cultural imprint. Lebanese youths learn about their own civil war, which lasted from 1975 to 1990, from relatives and schoolbooks rather than their own memories. Even in Palestine, teenagers today were barely born (if at all) when the Second Intifada and Israel's military occupation exploded at the turn of the century.

Sociologists familiar with public attitudes, religious trends, and social mores in the MENA have noted that given this new historical pathway, many youths in the region are moving away from traditional values. While the term "traditional" has many connotations, in the regional context such values can refer to the organizing principles and internal conventions that have long influenced social structures – ideals like male-dominated leadership, unquestioned familial obedience, and deference to authority, which are being replaced by what theorists call "self-expression" values, or those associated with greater individualism, pluralism, and subjectivity. For instance, today's youths are far more liberal than their parents in terms of issues like gender equality. The 2017 Arab Youth Survey revealed that two-thirds expected their leaders to do more to advance the rights of women, a high proportion reflected equally amongst the men and women surveyed. Perhaps more indicative of this social change is the fact that the majority of university graduates across the MENA, including Israel, Turkey, and Iran, are now women.

Critically, in most MENA countries, this does not mean declining religiosity and religious identity. A 2016 survey of Arab-Muslim millennials by the UAE-based Tabah Foundation, in concert with the US-based Zogby polling firm, found that a consistent majority believed Islam played an important role in their countries' futures as well as in their personal identities, but also rejected extremist groups like the Islamic State and al-Qaeda as perversions of Islam. To be sure, many Muslim youths in the Arab world have also registered their concern that religion may play too big of a role; but the overall conclusion is that the new generation is not one that has wholeheartedly embraced secularism. More than a few Islamist political parties, such as the Muslim Brotherhood, have maintained large and active cadres of young activists drawn to their religious ideology. They are as much a part of the youth generation as are equally vocal and perhaps more rebellious teenagers declaring themselves atheists.

That youth does not equate to secularization is made plain also in non-Arab countries. In Israel, the fastest growing youth cohort has been those of the ultra-Orthodox Jewish community, whose birthrate is three times as high as non-Orthodox and secular Jewish communities. In Turkey, governance by the ruling Justice and Development Party since the early 2000s – an Islamic party that has consistently won contested elections – has energized a new generation of young conservatives bucking their country's long tradition of political secularism. And while survey data in Iran is scarce, all evidence suggests that Iran's youths are not so much secularizing as combining their religious beliefs with modern pursuits. Young Iranians are far more likely than their parents to listen to Western pop music, or have unmarried yet romantic relationships in a continual testing of government-imposed boundaries of social permissiveness.

Technology and instantaneity

These social and cultural experiences are inseparable from the absorption of communicative and media technology unimaginable a generation ago. This is the most globalized and interlinked cohort in history, connected to the outside world and new ideas through the Internet – and, in turn, connected to each other through mobile phones capable of sharing texts, images, videos, and social media instantly. One easily overlooked sign of this is the rapid ascent of English, which internationally has become the most indispensable language for commerce, science, and Internet content. Since the 1990s, British or American English has become the most popular second language in almost every MENA country, taught in secondary schools as either a mandate or else the most popular second language. Generationally, today's youths know English far better than their parents: the 2017 Arab Youth Survey found that most Arab youths maintain Arabic as central to their identity, but that over half used English more than Arabic in their everyday lives at school, work, or play. The high popularity of Hollywood dramas, Billboard-charting music, or American television series across the region is another indicator.

More concretely, the MENA has rapidly developed in terms of its online technologies and digital media over the past decade, empowering youths with the ability to access information and communicate with one another like never before. Table 10.1 lists trends in Internet usage by region. Much of the developing world saw skyrocketing Internet usage in the ten-year period from 2008 to 2017; the MENA was no exception, with its rate nearly tripling from 18.8 to 58.6 percent.

Second, the same rise in connectivity can be seen in mobile cellular subscriptions, which Table 10.2 displays. The MENA currently possesses one of the highest such rates in the world, at 112.1 per 100 people, a large increase from the prevailing rate in 2008 of about 67.6 percent. While other regions like South Asia and sub-Saharan Africa experienced faster growth rates, they started with far less mobile phone penetration.

The dizzying tempo of instant interconnectedness means that especially for youth, technology has permeated the fabric of social interaction. For one, it has transformed how information is obtained and shared by democratizing access to anyone with a mobile device capable of getting online. The 2017 Arab Youth Survey revealed that 35 percent of youths get their news from Facebook and almost as many read their news online; only 30 percent watched television and 9 percent read print newspapers to receive their news.

TABLE 10.1

MENA vs. global regions – percent population using Internet, 2008–2017

	2008	2012	2017	Percent increase, 2008–2017
South Asia	4.4	11.5	26.5	502.3
Sub-Saharan Africa	3.9	10.3	19.9	410.3
East Asia and Pacific	25.3	40.7	55.6	119.8
Middle East and North Africa	18.8	31.6	58.6	211.7
Latin America and Caribbean	26.5	43.2	57.4	116.6
Europe and Central Asia	47.3	63.6	76.6	61.9
OECD	63.9	71	78.7	23.2

Source: World Bank (2018), *World Development Indicators*.

TABLE 10.2

MENA vs. global regions – mobile phone subscriptions (per 100 people), 2008–2017

	2008	2012	2017	Percent increase, 2008–2017
South Asia	31.8	67.7	86.6	172.3
Sub-Saharan Africa	31.8	58.7	74.7	134.9
East Asia and Pacific	57	91.6	118.8	108.4
Middle East and North Africa	*67.6*	*102.6*	*112.1*	*45.3*
Latin America and Caribbean	79.2	109.1	107.4	35.6
Europe and Central Asia	115.1	122.7	125	8.6
OECD	98.6	107.8	117.8	19.5

Source: World Bank (2018), *World Development Indicators*.

In January 2017, the World Map of Social Networks, an independent website that ranks the most popular social media for all countries, verified that Facebook was the most popular social network for all MENA countries excepting Iran, for which Instagram ranked number one. Instagram and Twitter were frequently the second most popular social networks. This has created an enormous imaginary space – a regional public sphere, as often called – in which the attitudes, opinions, and beliefs of everyday youths can be easily discerned by a casual observer clicking through public blogs, Tweets, Facebook feeds, and Instagram posts. Twitter hashtags linked to major happenings, from social events to political protests, have become a critical reference point among teenagers and young adults, much like in the US and other Western countries. And much as MENA youths are connected to each other and the outside world as never before, inversely outsiders can peer into the region and witness, in real-time, the kinds of information, images, and discussions occurring among young people.

The proliferation of this informational space became undeniable in the Arab Spring, but it was building for some time. Before the 1990s, most governments could control their national media sectors (i.e., newspapers, magazines, radio stations, television broadcasts, and the like) through simple force of law. And control these authoritarian regimes did through censorship and other regulations, which squelched any reporting of sensitive issues like national security, royal corruption, and dissident opposition. Even relatively democratic Israel invoked emergency statutes and security laws to prohibit the publication of information that could embarrass its international standing or damage relations with key external allies. In the 1990s, however, technological advancements corroded such mechanisms of control. Satellite television gave rise to new stations like Al-Jazeera, which to the Arab world provided a radically alternative stream of information separate from government-vetted sources. During the 2000s, urban youths became the vanguard of this wave of change by pioneering online innovations like Arabic and English Internet blogs. These exposed to both national and regional audiences a host of novel commentaries on diverse issues not found in print formats, ranging from the pedantic (such as traffic laments, musical criticisms, and food comedies) to the serious (like political repression, religious conservatism, or in the Iraqi case life under occupation).

During the Arab Spring, social media networks took the limelight by helping the first revolts in Tunisia spread contagiously across borders, including into Israel, Iran, and Turkey which sprouted their own youth protests. By 2011, websites like Facebook had become sufficiently popular in the region: in January of that year, one study estimated that Tunisia – a nation of ten million people – had about two million Facebook users. Over the course of the 2011–2012 revolutionary protests across the MENA, endless hours of YouTube videos, millions of Tweets, and many thousands of blog posts and Facebook updates enabled young people to communicate with one another like never before. Some activists were inspired to action; others emulated and learned new strategies. Musicians like Emel Mathlouthi (Photo 10.3) became regional phenomena, as songs such as her "Kelmti Horra" became something of revolutionary anthems.

In addition, Facebook groups proliferated, enabling opposition groups to produce new content and disseminate messages. In addition, social media helped create virtual networks of solidarity within each country, enabling activists and protest leaders to coordinate events while sidestepping government monitors. Youth oppositionists thousands of miles apart, between Morocco and Bahrain, held identical slogans and chanted the same Arabic refrains as signs of collective defiance against repression and governments.

Of course, the role of social media in these contentious politics should not be overstated. The Arab Spring did not occur because of trending Twitter hashtags, but because of a visceral offline act: masses of citizens poured onto streets to withstand repression and demand dignity and voice from their governments. Many countries that saw tech-savvy youths lead marches for democratic reform and economic justice did not witness real change. Facebook alone could not compel monarchies in Jordan, Kuwait, or Morocco to capitulate to surging opposition forces. And even in countries that did see

PHOTO 10.3
Tunisian singer Emel Mathlouthi, 2014.

Source: Photo by mikecogh is licensed under CC BY-SA 2.0.
Online: www.flickr.com/photos/mikecogh/13281350325

deposals of autocrats, like Egypt, Libya, and Yemen, the majority of citizens were not regular Internet users. It was a vocal youth minority, not an online majority, that spread information, circulated images, and coordinated events through the Internet and SMS texting. More perversely, years later, the same technological connectedness that typified the Arab Spring protests has also come to define new civil wars as in Syria during the apex of that conflict, when MENA youths and global observers alike could watch battles unfold and people perish in real time.

It is also difficult to deny that when all was said and done the combination of youth activity and technological networking, made for a historic development, is still transforming societal trends. In the week before Egyptian President Hosni Mubarak's downfall in early February 2011, the rate of Egyptian Tweets about politics mushroomed from 2,300 to 230,000 per day, while the top 23 YouTube videos (many taken from mobile phones) about the unfolding revolution received nearly 5.5 million views. For many, the events of the Arab Spring encapsulated the frustrations but also hope of living as young people. Many in number, overeducated, underemployed, and wielding new cultural and technological weapons, youths became agents of transformative change. It was not the first time in regional history, and it will likely not be the last. Technology provides a way for observers to continue monitoring, and tracking, the aspirations and struggles of these citizens.

CONCLUSION

This chapter analyzed the circumstances of the youth generation in the Middle East and North Africa. It presented four major topics, which each highlighted both the challenge and the promise of the region's youth bulge. To repeat a seminal point tying together demography, education, and economics, this youth cohort today is the single largest, best educated, and most unemployed generation in MENA history. Most MENA countries struggle to deal with the demands of not just teenagers and young adults, and in a little over a decade's time will need to confront the next youth generation – today's children, who are more numerous and whose march towards maturity cannot be stopped. Those demands include the call for higher-quality education that teaches lifelong skills and competencies, not simply basic literacy, which requires comprehensively revamping all levels of schooling – from primary and elementary institutions to colleges and universities, which could become incubators of talent and ambition.

Improving the regulation and maintenance of educational systems in turn can help youths transition easily into tight job markets, which have today made the MENA the world's leading region in terms of youth unemployment. In most economies, government work is no longer the panacea; but private-sector firms, when flourishing, require work-ready citizens capable of adapting to the increasingly competitive and globalized marketplace. These educational shortcomings and the joblessness epidemic accentuate the disconnect many youths feel from political authorities, as evidenced by cultural transformations wrought by young entrepreneurs who do not share the historical memories and values of their elders. We see the results of youth-driven innovation in both mass consumption patterns – e.g., art, music, fashion – and technology, especially social media. The technological underpinnings of the Arab Spring and its youth activists are testament to this fiery cocktail for change.

QUESTIONS FOR DISCUSSION

1. The MENA's youth bulge includes not just current teenagers and young adults, but today's children. What will happen when they come of age?
2. Can belonging to the same generation alone, regardless of religious, national, linguistic, or ethnic differences, provide the basis for enduring social and political identity?
3. What concrete policies can help improve the quality of MENA education in ways that will make school graduates more skillful and knowledgeable?
4. How can today's youths, too often the products of deficient schooling systems, be trained or retaught to better match what their national and regional job markets demand?
5. What steps can be taken to dissuade many youths from treating the public sector, including government work, as the most attractive work option after college?
6. What major cultural trends, historical understandings, and consumptive factors make today's youths different from their parents and elders?
7. Are there similarities in the artistic, musical, culinary, and other aesthetic tastes we see among young people in the MENA today?
8. If social media and instant connectivity enable young people to mobilize and communicate without constraint, does this mean revolution is inevitable?

FURTHER READING

A modest but expanding literature has engaged the implications of the MENA's youth generation, building upon the ideas of this chapter and pointing to new directions for additional research and learning. General overviews include Haggai Erlich, *Youth and Revolution in the Changing Middle East, 1908–2014* (Boulder, CO: Lynne Rienner, 2015), which historically explains why young people have always led political change in the region. More contemporary surveys of Arab youths have appeared since the 2011–2012 Arab Spring, with most noting the role they played in driving forward these national uprisings. Appropriate works include Bessma Momani, *Arab Dawn: Arab Youth and the Demographic Dividend They Will Bring* (Toronto: University of Toronto Press, 2015); Juan Cole, *The New Arabs: How the Millennial Generation Is Changing the Middle East* (New York: Simon and Schuster, 2015); and Samir Khalaf and Roseanne Saad Khalaf, eds., *Arab Youth: Social Mobilisation in Times of Risk* (London: Saqi Books, 2012). These are fairly optimistic and emphasize the creativity, innovation, and freshness that young faces bring to both economics and politics when given adequate voice. Another is the policy-oriented OECD report, *Youth in the MENA Region: How to Bring Them In* (Paris: OECD, 2016), which focuses upon the dividends of mainstreaming youth demands into governance and society. Linda Herrera and

Abdelrahman Mansour's "Arab Youth: Disruptive Generation of the Twenty-First Century?" in *The Oxford Handbook of Contemporary Middle-Eastern and North African History*, eds. Amal Ghazal and Jens Hanssen (Oxford: Oxford University Press, 2015), is also an excellent and accessible primer.

Other works take the less emotive approach, presenting instead the hard facts and real challenges facing the young. The latest is Elhum Haghighat, *Demography and Democracy: Transitions in the Middle East and North Africa* (Cambridge: Cambridge University Press, 2018), which advances the earlier findings of Onn Winckler, *Arab Political Demography: Population Growth, Labor Migration, and Natalist Policies* (Eastbourne, UK: Sussex Academic Press, 2009). Both are unmatched in their discussion of populational trends, migration patterns, and socioeconomic implications of the youth bulge. Another is Navtej Dhillon and Tarik Yousef's, eds., *Generation in Waiting: The Unfulfilled Promise of Young People in the Middle East* (Washington, DC: Brookings Institution, 2009), which explores how economic difficulties and social restrictions are suffocating today's youths as they enter school, find jobs, and start families. An old but useful anthology remains *Alienation or Integration of Arab Youth: Between Family, State, and Street* (London: Routledge, 2000), which charted out even two decades ago the coming generational conflicts that would play out in culture and politics.

More studies have unpacked the educational dilemma facing most MENA states. Liesbet Steer, Hafez Ghanem, and Maysa Jalbout, *Arab Youth: Missing Educational Foundations for a Productive Life?* (Washington, DC: Brookings Institution, 2014), presents the most readable and generalized overview of how public schooling institutions have fallen behind global standards across the Arab world. A sweeping catalog of most Arab countries' national educational systems, including their origins and development since the early twentieth century, is Serra Kirdar's, ed., *Education in the Arab World* (New York: Bloomsbury, 2017). A more scholarly overview is Osama Abi-Mershed's, ed., *Trajectories of Education in the Arab World: Legacies and Challenges* (London: Routledge, 2011), which provides an historical overview of these problems across various countries. For a modern Turkish perspective, an excellent interrogation lies in Sam Kaplan, *The Pedagogical State: Education and the Politics of National Culture in Post-1980 Turkey* (Stanford, CA: Stanford University Press, 2006).

Excellent reports and studies have been published about the youth unemployment crunch in the MENA. The World Bank has published many of them; two examples are *Jobs for Shared Prosperity: Time for Action in the Middle East and North Africa* (Washington, DC: World Bank, 2013) and *Jobs or Privileges: Unleashing the Employment Potential of the Middle East and North Africa* (Washington, DC: World Bank, 2015). Both highlight the trends abutting youth job demands, including the shortage of public-sector employment and the need for sustainable long-term job creation in the private sector. A more recent one is *Education for Employment: Realizing Arab Youth Potential* (Washington, DC: IFC, 2011), which explores joblessness from the perspective of inadequate education. The International Labour Organization's *Global Employment Trends for Youth* (Washington, DC: ILO, 2015) has an especially sobering section on the MENA countries. The UNDP's *Arab Human Development Report 2016* (New York: UNDP, 2016) focuses on youth as a vector of change and aspiration, as well as the constraints against this. All is not doom and gloom, however. Christopher Schroeder, *Startup Rising: The Entrepreneurial Revolution Remaking the Middle East*

(New York: St. Martin's Press, 2013), is one example of how many young people are turning to entrepreneurship and innovation, thereby providing an inspiring alternative to job-seekers.

Works on youth culture, technology, and identity in the MENA are fewer in number. An aging but enlightening volume is the edited *Youth and Youth Culture in the Contemporary Middle East* (Aarhus, DK: Aarhus University Press, 2005), which captures well the expressions of youthfulness and social engagement in the Arab world, Turkey, and Iran. One of the best newer works about social media and youth activism, as in the Arab Spring, is Marwan Kraidy, *The Naked Blogger of Cairo: Creative Insurgency in the Arab World* (Cambridge, MA: Harvard University Press, 2016), which deeply explores the intersection between culture, politics, and technology at the heart of that unrest. Mahmood Monshipouri, *Democratic Uprisings in the New Middle East: Youth, Technology, Human Rights, and US Foreign Policy* (London: Routledge, 2014), is an excellent regional survey of the same period. The edited volume by Linda Herrera and Rehab Sakr, *Wired Citizenship: Youth Learning and Activism in the Middle East* (London: Routledge, 2014), also captures the dynamic practices and boundary-pushing efforts of youth activists in the region, including Turkey and Iran.

Online sources

The online world is a paradoxical domain for those looking for information about youth views, politics, and emotions in the MENA. Youths are connected more than ever, especially through social media, and yet there are relatively few aggregators and directories that can fully capture the regional scope of this. On Instagram or Twitter, for instance, simply following a hashtag (e.g., #amman or #jordan for those interested in the Hashemite Kingdom) can uncover a labyrinthian trove of people, images, posts, and activities from young people. Still, there are some formal online resources. One start is Al-Bawaba, which rounds up relevant news stories and insights aimed at young citizens (www.albawaba.com/mena-voices). There are also many blog rankings with traffic reports; among the ones that lists the region's most popular blogs is Feedspot's listing (https://blog.feedspot.com/middle_east_blogs). Youth Policy maintains not only a global youth well-being index but also MENA-specific essays and commentaries (www.youthpolicy.org). There are also many youth polls undertaken by regional monitors and civil society organizations, which are extremely important in understanding generational attitudes. The best include Asda'a Burson-Masteller's annual Arab Youth Survey, as referenced in this chapter (www.arabyouthsurvey.com); the Silatech Index, also used in this chapter (www.silatech.org); the Sahwa Youth Survey (http://sahwa.eu/Media/Sahwa/Youth-Survey); the Tabah-Zogby Arab-Muslim Millennial survey (www.tabahfoundation.org/en/); and the referenced poll by Al-Jazeera Center for Studies (http://studies.aljazeera.net/en/reports/2013/07/20137296337455953.html).

INDEX

Note: Page numbers in *italic* indicate a figure, map, or photo and page numbers in **bold** indicate a table or box on the corresponding page.

'Abbasid Empire 18
access 39, 49, 55–56, 61, 64; and economic development 148, 149, 156; education and 311–313, *313*; and environmental change 210, 213; and identity 138; and rentierism 188, 191–192; to services and infrastructure 65–66, **65–66**; and social mobilization 98–100, 106; and women and gender 280–281; and the youth generation 316–317, 338
activism 21, 24, 160, 224, 290, 294; anti-colonial 88; environmental 39, 102, 108, 225–226; and independence 92; post-Arab Spring 79, 81, 106–108, 110; post-Cold War 102–106, 111; in the post-colonial era 96–100; religious 238, 250–257, 260, 267; social 111, 250–257, 267; and the youth generation 333, 335, 337, 340, 342; *see also* women's rights
'Aden 84, 94, **211**
age 13, 25, 192, *309*; *see also* youth
agrarian societies 22, 34, 37–40, 187; change in 33–35, 48–57; production in 59, 228; *see also* agriculture
agriculture 17, 22, 55; abandoned cultivation *229*; and economic development 145, 147, 149, 151, 163, 170; employment in **51**, *52*; and environmental change 209, 214–215, 219, 222–223, 228, 230–231; and land distribution **54**; and rentierism 187, 190; and social life 33–35, 37–39, 48–49, 51–60, 66–67, 74–75; and water scarcity **224**; and the youth generation 317
al-'Alim al-'Arabi 10–13
'Alaouite 127, 129
'Alawite 89, 132, 242
Al-Azhar University 18, **87**, 258–259, *259*
Al-Bu Nasir tribe 129

Algeria 5, 13, 19, 52; and economic development 148, 151, 154, 168, 171; and environmental change 218, 220, 225, 230; and identity 120, 122, 134, 139; and religion and faith 244, 254–255; and rentierism 179, 182, 185, 193, 195; and social mobilization 82–85, 94–95, 98–101, 105, 108; and women and gender 278, 280–281, 288, 290–291, 297, 301–302; and the youth generation 316, 320–321, 326–327, 333–334, 336
'Ali, Muhammad 83, 94
Aliye, Fatime 91
al-Mukhtar, Umar 86–87
al-Khattabi, 'Abd al-Krim 89–90
al-Mu'askar 83
al-Sharif, 'Abd al-Qadir Ibn 82, 84–85
al-Tijani, Ahmad 82
Amin, Qasim 91
Arab Barometer: and economic development 172; and identity 118, *119*; and religion and faith 248–249, **248–249**; and rentierism **193–194**; and social mobilization 108–109, *109–110*; and women and gender 295, **295**, **296**
Arab Spring 1–2, 17, 21, 23, 25–26; and economic development 146, 169, 172; economic factors of 159–161; and environmental change 215, 224–225; hip-hop music and **335**; and identity 130, 138–139; membership in civil society organizations before and after *109*; and refugees in Jordan **72**; and religion and faith 242, 260; and rentierism 182, 195, 204; and social life 58, 67, 75; and social mobilization 79–81, 97, 102, 107–109, 111; water scarcity and **224**; and women and gender 272, 283, 289–291; and the youth generation 307–308, 321, 325–326, 329, 333, 339–342

347

armed conflicts 20, 24, 83, 210, **211**, 255
artifact 17, 196
Ataturk, Mustafa Kemal 37, 125, 254
authoritarianism 6, 20, 26, 160, 182, 245, 260

Bahn, Rachel 22
Bahrain 13, 18–19; and environmental change 220; and identity 131–132, 138; and religion and faith 241, 242; and rentierism 179–180, 182–184, 186, 188–189, 192, 195–196; and social life 43, 45, 46, 66; and social mobilization 98, 101, 106, 108; and women and gender 284; and the youth generation 325, 332, 336, 340
Ba'th 38, 95
bay'a (allegiance) 129
Bedouin 35, 38, 49–50, *50*, 57; and environmental change 218; and identity 125, 128
Behnassi, Mohamed 24
Ben 'Ali, Zine 'Abidine 1, 102, 108, 125, 274
Benstead, Lindsay J. 25
bread riots 58, 99, 154, **155**, 215, 224
Bouazizi, Mohamed 1–2
Boumédiène, Houari 98, 254
Bourguiba, Habib 95, 98, 125, 254, 274

caliphates 4, 219, 238; 'Umayyad Caliphate 18; *see also* Ottoman Empire
Christianity 120, 237–240, **239**, 242–244; Coptic 116, 131, 134, 242; and the *dhimmi* paradigm **126**; and homogenizing tendencies 122, 125, 127–128; and identity categories and claims 130–131, 134–135, 137, 139; and Islam 258, 263, 267; Maronite 83–84, 92, 131, 243; missionaries 258; and social activism 252; and society 17, 24; and women and gender 294, 299
citizenship 17, 24, 116, 131, 138; and foreign residents *199*; and identification with country *193*; and refugees in Jordan **72**, **136**; and rentierism 178, 183, 192–201, **193**, 203–204; and the youth generation 318; *see also* citizens
civil society 5, 22, 80–81, 95–96, 110–111, 194; after the Arab Spring 106–110; the post-Cold War renaissance of 100–106; and environmental change 225; and religion and faith 250, 258–259; and women and gender 281, 291; *see also* civic society freedom; civil society organizations
civil society freedom 109–110, *110*
civil society organizations 81, 101–102, 105–107; membership in *109*; and the MEPI foreign aid program **105**
clients 181, 193, **193**, 204
climate change 24, 49, 56, 74–75, 207–208; and conflict 210, 212, 214–216; and environmental security 219, 223; managing environmental impacts 224–227, 231; march at UN Conference 227
Cold War 21, 36, 80, 95, 208, 254; post-Cold War 100–106
colonialism 25, 36–39, 57, 61, 210; and agricultural distribution 51–53; and economic development 147; and identity 122–124, 134, 140; resistance to 80, 84–91, **87–88**, 93, 95, 99, 107, 274; and social mobilization 86, 88, 90–92, 94, 107; and women and gender 272, 274, 279, 281, **302**
conflict 18–20, 23–24, 26–27, 38–39, 67–68, 74–75; criticisms of the environment-conflict thesis 216–217; and economic development 168–169; environmental change and 207–208, 210–216, **211–212**; and identity 116–117, 120–121, 123–124, **126**, 136–137, 139–140; internal displacement due to 70, 73; natural resources and 213–214, **213–214**; and refugees in Jordan 72; regional 72, 180, 325; and religion and faith 241–242; and social mobilization 83–84; *see also* armed conflicts
consumption 40, 60, 154, 179, 185, 188; and environmental change 209, 216; and identity 331–333; and the youth generation 342
cultural experience 308, 331; and consumption 331–335; and memory 335–337; and technology 337–342
cultural innovation 318–319, 322, 323, 331, 340, 342

Darqawiyya Sufi brotherhood 82
democracy 6, 16–17; and identity 138; Islam and 248; and the MEPI foreign aid

program **105**–106; preference for *249*;
and religion and faith 248–250, 261–263;
and rentierism 182, 193, 203; and social
mobilization 81, 97, 100, 105, 107, 109,
111; and women and gender 291, 299
demography 5, 138, 224, 308–311,
326, 342
deprivation 63–64, 146, **251**, 257, 328;
relative 23, 49, 159–161, 182, 184, 329
desertification 219, 228–229, *229*
development *see* divergent development;
industrialization, state-led
developmental assistance 183–184; MEPI
foreign aid program **105**; top recipients
of **184**
dhimmi paradigm **125**–**126**, 131, 140
dimuqratiyyat al-khubz (democracy of
bread) 95
displacement *see* internal displacement
divergent development 165–169
dress: abaya *275*; Gulf traditional female
198; Gulf traditional male *197*; of Kuwaiti
teenage girls *277*; niqub *275*; scarf *276*
drinking water 65–66, *65*, 222
Durac, Vincent 22

ecological contexts 34–40
education 102–103, 105–106, 192–193,
195–196, 201–204, 262–263; rates
of enrollment **284**–**285**, 287; and
unemployment *323*; and women and
gender 271–274, 283–287; and the youth
generation 307–308, 310–311, 315–318,
322–324, 342–344
egalitarianism 294–297, 299–301
Egypt 4–5, 10, 13, 18–19, 24; anti-British
resistance in 87; boom years in **148**; bust
years in **154**; and economic development
148–149, 151, 153–156, 159–160,
164–168, 173; and environmental change
215, 218, 223–224, 226, 233; handicraft
workshop in *104*; Human Rights Watch
in *103*; and identity 116, 122, 126,
131, 134, 141; Muslim Brotherhood of
251; projected urbanization in *190*; and
religion and faith 241–242, 244–248,
252–255, 257–261, 265, 267–270; and
rentierism 179, 183–193, 195, 202; and
social life 36, 41, 44–45, 49, 52–59, *55*;
and social mobilization 82–91, 93–99,
101–104, 107–109; street march in
82; Tahrir Square *330*; and women and
gender 287–288, 291–294, 305–306;
and the youth generation 316, 322, 324,
328–330, 332–333, 335; youth march
in *330*
employment 59–60, 75–77; in agriculture
48–49, 51, *52*; and economic development
145–146, 148–149, 156–158, 160–161,
167–171; and rentierism 186–188; and
women and gender 278–280, 292–293,
300–301; and the youth generation 326–328
energy *see* hydrocarbon energy; oil
environmental conflict *see under* conflict
environmental migration *see under*
migration
environmental security 209, **213**, 217–224
environment-conflict thesis 216–217
Erdogan, Tayyip Recep 125, 262
ethnonationalism 23, 128, 133–136, 140
expatriates 136–138, 167–168, 199–200
extremism 20, 24, 237, 255–257, 260; and
the youth generation 329, 337

Facebook 8, 109–110, *110*, 332, 338, 340
family law 272, 274, 297–298: Personal
Status Code 100, 279–280, 282, 291,
297, **302**
fellahin 35, 38, 52, 57, 128
food: food insecurity **58**; food production
39, 56, 60, 223; food security 56–58,
77–78; *see also* agriculture
foreign aid *see* developmental assistance
freedom *see* civic society freedom
Front de Liberation Nationale (FLN) 94–95

gas 11, 177–180, 203–205, 225–227,
229–230
gender **296**; female quotas in legislative
bodies **289**; gender gap 273, 280,
286–287, 295, 304–306, 320; labor
force participation rates by *292*; youth
unemployment and *321*; *see also* Global
Gender Gap Index; women; women's
rights
Gérôme, Jean-Léon: *Bonaparte before the
Sphinx* 7
Global Gender Gap Index 272–273; MENA
vs. global regions in *273*; support for
gender equality *295*

Government Wage Bill *170*
Gülen movement **251**, 252, 263
Gulf states 94, 158–159, 196; *see also* specific countries

Hananu, Ibrahim 89
hip-hop music **334–335**
historical trends 116, 313
history: and memory 335–337; *see also* historical trends
Hizbullah 3, **211–212**, 252, 256
homogeneity 117, 123, 129, 196
homogenization 116, 121–127, 131, 134, 140
human capital 24, 178, 186, 201–203
Human Rights Watch 102–103, *103*
human security 24, 207–209, **223**, 228, 231
hydrocarbon energy 178–179, 184–187

identity 115–116, 140; and ethnonationalism 133–136; and expatriates 137–138; explaining 120–121; and gender 138–139; and homogenizing tendencies 121–127; Jordan and **136**; measuring and observing 117–120; multiplicity and 116–117; and refugees 136–137; and religiosity 130–133; revealed identity choices *119*; and tribalism 128–130; and youth 138; *see also under* conflict
industrialization, state-led 20, 23, 145–147, 150–152, 154
infitah (Open Door) policy 39, **155**
infrastructure 55–56, 60–61
innovation *see* cultural innovation
instantaneity 337–342
internal displacement 70–75, **73**
Iran 6, 9–10, 16, 18–21, 23–25; and cultural experience 331, 333, 335–337, 339–340; and demography 308, 309–310; and economic development 148, 156, 164, *165*, 168, 171; and education 312, *314–315*, 316–317; and employment 320, 322, *323*, 326; and environmental change **211–212**, 218, 220, **221**, 225–226; and identity 122–123, 127, 131–135, 140; and religion and faith 238, 241–242, 244–247, 254–256, 263–267; and rentierism 177, 179, *180*, 182, 196;

and social life 35, 41, 53, 70; and social mobilization 84, 88, 91; and women and gender 272, 274, 288, 292, 294; *see also* Iraq-Iran War
Iraq 13, 18–19, 21; and social life 35–36, 38–39, 68–70, **72**, 74; and economic development 148, 151, 168; and environmental change 218, 220, 222, 230; and identity 122–124, 126, 129–132, 134, 137; and religion and faith 237, 241–247, 255, 257, 264; and rentierism 177, 179, 185, 196; and social mobilization 86, 88–89, 91–92, 95–97, 99, **105**; and women and gender 281, 288, 293; and the youth generation 312, 316, 340; *see also* Kurdistan Region
Iraq-Iran War 36, 39, **211**
Iraq War 21, 36, **72**, 97
Islam 3–8, 17–18, 237–238, 240–242, 244–247, 267–270; and democracy *248*; and diversity of identity 127–135; and homogenizing tendencies 124–127; and identity 121–122, 137–138; importance of religion to individuals in Muslim-majority countries **247**; religious service attendance in Muslim-majority countries **246**; and social activism 251–257; and social forces 257–267; and social life 35–36; and social mobilization 88–89, 100–102; and women and gender 277–278, 281–282, 290–291, 298–299, 305–306; *see also* Mecca; Muslim Brotherhood
Ismaʻil 85
Israel 5, 10, 13, 16, 19–21, 24–25, 27; and cultural experience 331, 334–337, 339–340; and demography 309–310; and economic development 153, 157, 165, 174; and education 312, 315–316; and employment 318, 320, 322, 324–326, 330; and environmental change 212, 220, 223, 225, 230–231, 233; and identity 120, 123, 127, 131, 133–134, 138–139; and religion and faith 237, 244–245, 254, 256, 260, 268; and rentierism 178, 180, 189, 195–196; and social life 38–39, 44, 61, 72, 74; and women and gender 271–272, 288, 290, 292, 294, 303

Jeong, Hae Won 23
Jordan 13, 19; and economic development 153–154, 156, 159, 168–171, 173, 175; and environmental change 219, 222–224, 230–231; and identity 118–119, 123–124, 127, 130, **136**, 137; refugees in **72**; and religion and faith 249, 254, 265, 269–270; and rentierism 179–180, 184–186, 188–189, 191, 193–195, 202; and social life 37–38, 43–44, 50, 53, 58–59, 67–70; and social mobilization 86, 89, 92, 95, 99, 101, 108; and women and gender 283, 288–294, 297, 301; and the youth generation 316–317, 320, 324–326, 328, 332, 336
Jordan River 38, **136**, 222
Judaism 238–240, 244–245, 267–268; and identity 126–127, 130–131, 137–138, 141–142

Khalifa, 'Ali Ibn 85
Kılınç, Ramazan 24
Kumaraswamy, P.R. 23
Kurdish people 122, 135, 139–140
Kurdistan Region 135, *135*
Kuwait 5, 13–14, 18; dress in *277*; and economic development 153, 158, 166, 169, 171; and environmental change 213, 220, 225; Gulf traditional male garb in *197*; and identity 129, 132, 134, 138; migrant workers in *200*; and rentierism 179–183, 186–190, 192, 196–199, 200, 204–205; and social life 36, 38, 43, 61, 66, 68; and social mobilization 94, 101, 106, 108; and women and gender 277, 292–294, 297, 301–302; and the youth generation 320, 325, 332–333, 340
Kuwait Rock Army *334*

Lebanon 13, 19; and economic development 153–154, 159, 164, 168; and environmental change 218; and identity 118–119, 123, 131–132, 136–137; and religion and faith 237, 242–244, 248–249, 252, 256, 269; and rentierism 180, 184–187, 189, 191, 193–195; and social life 37–39, 41–43, 53, 58, 61, 66; and social mobilization 83, 86, 92–93, 95, 101, 108–109; and women and gender 283, 291, 294; and the youth generation 316, 318, 320, 325–327, 333–334
legislative bodies: female quotas in **289**
Libya 13, 19; and economic development 159, 166, 169; and environmental change 212, 230; and identity 123, 127, 134, 139; and religion and faith 237; and rentierism 179–180, 182, 185, 189; and social life 43, 65–66, 84–87, 106–107; and women and gender 281, 288, 291–293, 297; and the youth generation 312, 316, 333, 335, 341
literacy 311–314, *313*

MacInnes, Morgan 23
Mashriq, the 13, 19, 37–40, 49, 76; and environmental change 222; and identity 118, 123–125, 128, 131; and rentierism 178, 188; and social mobilization 83, 86–87, 89, 92, 99; and women and gender 291
Mathlouthi, Emel 1, 340–341, *341*
Mecca 8, 17, 240, 254, 265–266; and identity 122, 124, 126–127, 139
MENA countries: age of regional population *309*; demographics and government in **14**; and environmental preservation *226*; and exported goods *180*; farms and agricultural land distribution in **54**; GDP growth *150*; in Global Gender Gap Index *273*; importance of religion to individuals in **247**; informal economic sectors in *150*; Internet use in **338**; literacy in *313*; major armed conflicts in **211**; mobile phone subscriptions in **339**; public sector in *170*; religious landscape in **239**; religious service attendance in **246**; renewable water resources in **221**; rural population *41*; theories of patriarchy in **298**; unemployment in *323*; urban population *43–44*; youth unemployment in *319*; *see also specific countries*
MEPI: foreign aid program **105–106**
migrants 67–69, **69**; *see also* migrant workers; refugees
migrant workers 70, 137, 167–168, 188, 200, 203

migration 33–34, 67–68, 72–73, 76–77, 130–131; environmental 74–75; and rentierism 188–189, 199–200, 205–206; *see also* internal displacement; migrants; migrant workers; refugees
Momani, Bessma 23
Morocco 5, 10, 13, 18–19; desertified and abandoned cultivation in *229*; dress in *276*; and economic development 152, 154, 156, 159, 164, 168; and environmental change 218, 222, 226, 228–230; and identity 118, 120–121, 127, 129, 131, 134; projected urbanization in *190*; and religion and faith 241, 244–246, 249, 254, 265; and rentierism 179–180, 184, 187–188, 191, 193–195; and social life 51, 56, 58–59, 61, 66–67; and social mobilization 84–85, 89, 93, 95, 99–101, 105; and women and gender 278–280, 282–283, 291, 293–294, 301–302, 304–305; and the youth generation 314–316, 324, 326–327, 333–334, 336, 340
Muhammad (Prophet) 17, 238, 240–241, 254, 256, 264; and identity 122, 127, 131
Muhammad V 93
multiplicity 23, 116–117, 132, 140
Muslim Brotherhood **251**, 257–258, 260, 266

Nawfal, Maryam Nahhas 91
neoliberalism 155–159

OECD 150–151, 157–158, 292–293, 308–310, 318, *323*
oil 3–5, 19–20, 23–24, 38–39; and economic development 152–153, 158–159, 166–171; and environmental change 213–214; exported from MENA countries *11*; and rentierism 177–186, 190–191, 196–197, 203–205; and the youth generation 325–326
Orientalism 6–9, 25–26, 35–36, 245
Ottoman Empire 18–19, 37; and identity 123–125; and religion and faith 253, 261, 263; and social mobilization 79, 82, 86, 90, 110

Palestinian Territories 5, 13, 19; and economic development 168; and environmental change 210–212, 231; and identity 120, 134, 136–137, 139; and religion and faith 237, 244–245, 254, 256; and rentierism 184, 193, 195, 202; and social life 37–39, 45, 61, 63, 65–66, 68, 72; and social mobilization 86, 97, 105, 108; and women and gender 281, 288, 297; and the youth generation 317, 320, 328, 332, 334
patriarchy 271–272, 278–279, 294–295, 297–299, 301–304
Personal Status Code (PSC) *see under* family law
personal status law *see* family law
PIRLS reading achievement evaluation 314–317, *315*
political authority 79, 107, 247, 258, 301; religious leaders vs. *250*
post-colonial, the 20–22, 39, 61; and economic development 147, 173; and identity 123, 125, 128, 133; and religion and faith 242; and rentierism 193, 196; and social mobilization 79, 92, 94–100, 111; and women and gender 279, **302**
poverty 63–64, 77–78

Qadiriyya Sufi brotherhood 84
Qatar 3–4, 13, 19; Climate Change March 227; and economic development 153, 159, 164, 166–167, 171–172; and environmental change 226–227, 230; and identity 129, 137–138; migrant workers in **200**; and rentierism 179–182, 184, 188–189, 192, 196–199, 202–204; and social life 36, 43, 46, 53, 61; and social mobilization 94, 101; and women and gender 292, 294, 304, 306; and the youth generation 320–322, 325, 332, 336

refugees 3–4, 22–23, 33–34, 37–38, 67–68, 70–75; and environmental change 215–216; flows of **71**; and identity 136–137; in Jordan 72; and rentierism 193–194
religion 23–24, 246–258, 260–262, 264–270; and identity 118–119, 126–127, 133–134; importance of **247**; misunderstandings of 246–250; religiosity 130–133; religious landscape **239**; religious service attendance **246**;

and social activism 250–257; *see also* Christianity; Islam; Judaism; *see also under* activism
religious leaders *250*, 263
rentierism 177–178, 203–204; and human capital 201–203; material impacts of 182–187; rentier citizenship 192–201, **193**; rentier state theory (RST) 178–182; and urbanization 187–192
riots *see* bread riots
rural-urban population 40–48

sanitation 33, 58, 61, 65–66, *66*
Saudi Arabia 3, 13, 16, 19, 24; and economic development 153, 158, 166–169; and environmental change 219–220, 230; and identity 116, 120–121, 127, 129–134, 137–138; and religion and faith 237–242, 248, 254, 265–268, 270; and rentierism 179–180, 182–184, 186–187, 189–192, 196–199, 202–203; and social life 37–38, 43, 68, 72; and social mobilization 92, 94; and women and gender 274, **282**, 283–288, 293–294, 297, 301; and the youth generation 320, 322, 332, 336; *see also* Mecca
security *see* environmental security; human security; *see under* food
Shahin, Tanyus 84
shari'a **125–126**, 241, 253, 261, 272, 279
slums 62, **62**, 75, 312
social adaptation 208, 231
South Asia 67, 213, 217, 310, 312, 338; construction workers from *201*
Southeast Asia 67, 137, 168, 310
stagnation 150–152, 158, 224
Sudan 4, 13, 20; and environmental change 212, 218; projected urbanization in *190*; and rentierism 189, 192; and social life 44, 49, 57, 61, 63–66, 70; and social mobilization 106; and women and gender 287–290; and the youth generation 316, 320
Syria 13, 19; and economic development 148, 151, 156, 159–160, 164, 168–169; and environmental change 220; and identity 122–124, 127, 132, 134, 136–137, 139; and religion and faith 241–242, 244, 255–257; and rentierism 184, 188, 194–195; and social life 36–38, 44, 49, 52, 68–70, 74–75; and social mobilization 83, 86, 89, 93, 95, 106–107; and women and gender 281, 293–294; and the youth generation 312, 316, 320, 333, 335–336, 341; *see also* Hizbullah

technology 157–158, 337–338, 342, 345
Tell, Tariq 22
TIMMS science achievement evaluation 314–317, *314*
tribalism 115, 128–130, 140, 301–302
Tunisia 1, 13, 16, 19; and economic development 152, 154, 156, 159, 168, 171–173; and environmental change 215, 224; and identity 125, 138; and religion and faith 244, 249, 254; and rentierism 186, 188, 193, 195; and social life 58, 64, 67; and social mobilization 84–85, 93, 95, 98–99, 101–102, 105–107; and women and gender 272, 274, 278–280, 288–289, 291–293, 302–306; and the youth generation 321–322, 328, 332–333, 335, 340–341; *see also* Mathlouthi, Emel
Turkey 3, 10, 13, 20, 23–25; and cultural experience 332, 335–337, 340, 344–345; and demography 309–310; and economic development 148, 154, 156, 174; and education 312, 316; and employment 318, 320–324; and environmental change 219–220, 230, 234; and identity 123–125, 131, 133–134, 137, 140–142; and job crisis 330; and religion and faith 238, 241–242, 244–246, 251, 261–263, 267–268; and rentierism 178, 180, 184, 196, 205; and social life 37, 44, 65, 70; and social mobilization 90–91, 113; and women and gender 272, 281, 283, 286–290, 293

unemployment 150, 160, 167, 169, 171, 319–324; by educational level *323*; of youth *319*, *321*
Union Nationale des Femmes Algériennes (National Union of Algerian Women) 100
United Arab Emirates (UAE) 13, 94, 153, 179, 222; Gulf traditional female garb in *198*; power and desalination station in *222*; and social life 41–43, 51, 65, 68
'Urabi, Ahmad 85–86

urban bias 66–67
urbanization 33–34, 43–45, 47–49, 75–77; projected *190*; and rentierism 177–178, 187–191, 202–204

water: renewable water resources **221**; water scarcity 219–220, 222, **223**, 231, 233–234; *see also* drinking water
women 271–280, 284, 288–296, 298–299, 302, 304–306; and identity 128–130, 138–139; and social mobilization 79–80, 99–101; and society 3–4, 9–10, 23–25; and the youth generation 318–320, 332–333; *see also* women's rights
women's rights 272, 281–283, 291, 295, 297, 300–301, 303; and identity 139; Saudi Arabia and **282**; and social mobilization 91, 94, 99–100, 105; and society 3, 7, 16; and the youth generation 336

Yemen 10, 13, 19–20; and economic development 153, 159–160, 164, 169; and environmental change 212, 215, 220, 224, 230; and identity 121, 130–131, 133, 139; projected urbanization in *190*; and religion and faith 237, 242, 269–270; and rentierism 180, 184, 191–192, 195, 197; and social life 41, 51, 53, 57, 61, 63–70, 74; and social mobilization 84, 94–95, 101, 105, 107; water scarcity in **223**; and women and gender 286–287, 293, 297; and the youth generation 312, 316, 321, 335, 341
youth 307–308, 342; and consumption and identity 331–335; and demography 308–311; and education 311–318; in Egypt *104*; and finding work 318–327; and history and memory 335–337; and job crises 331–331; and technology and instantaneity 337–342; unemployment of *319*, *321*; work preference among *327*

Zaghloul, Sa'd **87**, 91, 93
Zurayk, Rami 22

NEW 9TH EDITION COMING IN 2019!

THE GOVERNMENT AND POLITICS OF THE MIDDLE EAST AND NORTH AFRICA

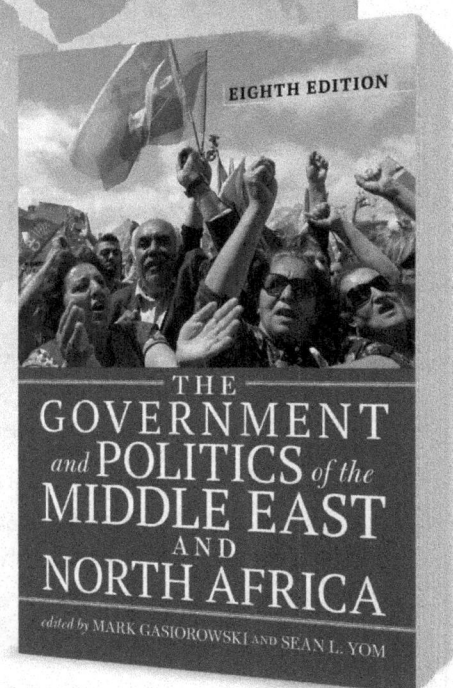

8TH EDITION

Edited by **Mark Gasiorowski** and **Sean L. Yom**

With recent upheavals in the Middle East and North Africa, the eighth edition of *The Government and Politics of the Middle East and North Africa* has been thoroughly revised to provide a necessary, comprehensive and current examination of the domestic politics and foreign policies of this crucial region.

Pb: 9780813349947
Hb: 9781138380653
eBook: 9780429494482

Routledge
Taylor & Francis Group